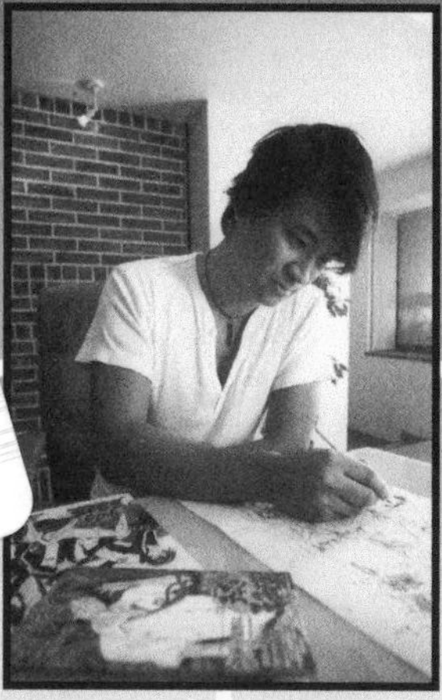

I was interviewed by *Tokai*, the magazine of my alma mater Tokai University. My hat goes off to the photographer's skills. He showed me some of his techniques and equipment. This is a photo from that session.

— Takeshi Konomi, 2007

About Takeshi Konomi

Takeshi Konomi exploded onto the manga scene with the incredible **THE PRINCE OF TENNIS**. His refined art style and sleek character designs proved popular with **Weekly Shonen Jump** readers, and **THE PRINCE OF TENNIS** became the number one sports manga in Japan almost overnight. Its cast of fascinating male tennis players attracted legions of female readers even though it was originally intended to be a boys' comic. The manga continues to be a success in Japan and has inspired a hit anime series, as well as several video games and mountains of merchandise.

THE PRINCE OF TENNIS
VOL. 37
SHONEN JUMP Manga Edition

STORY AND ART BY
TAKESHI KONOMI

Translation/Joe Yamazaki
Touch-up Art & Lettering/Vanessa Satone
Design/Sam Elzway
Editor/Daniel Gillespie

VP, Production/Alvin Lu
VP, Sales & Product Marketing/Gonzalo Ferreyra
VP, Creative/Linda Espinosa
Publisher/Hyoe Narita

Printed in Canada

Published by VIZ Media, LLC
P.O. Box 77010
San Francisco, CA 94107

10 9 8 7 6 5 4 3 2 1
First printing, May 2010

www.viz.com

THE WORLD'S
MOST POPULAR MANGA

www.shonenjump.com

テニスの王子様

THE PRINCE OF TENNIS

VOL. 37
The Terror of Comic Tennis

Story & Art by
Takeshi Konomi

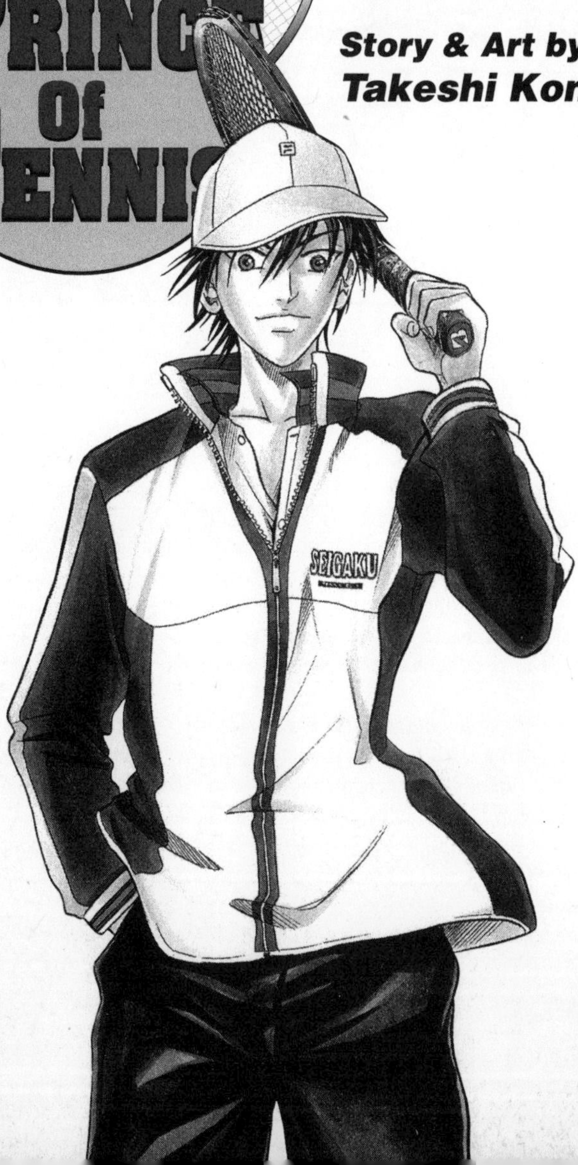
SEIGAKU

ENNIS CLUB

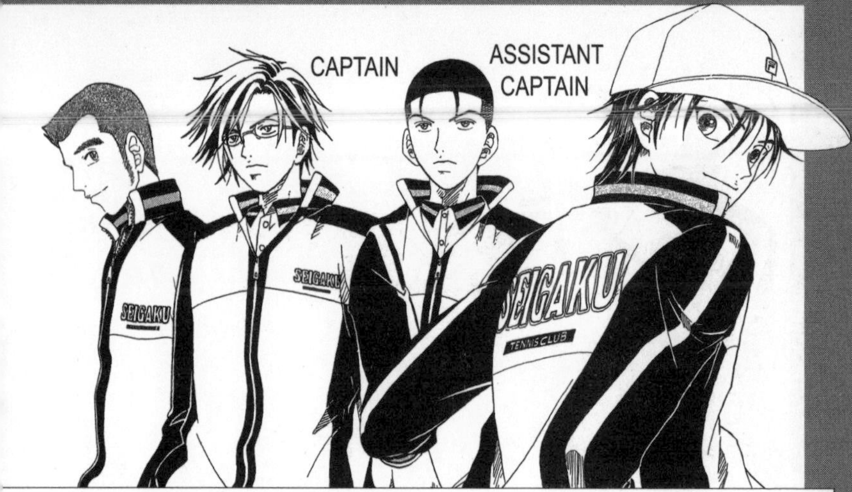
CAPTAIN
ASSISTANT CAPTAIN

• TAKASHI KAWAMURA • KUNIMITSU TEZUKA • SHUICHIRO OISHI • RYOMA ECHIZEN •

Seishun Academy student Ryoma Echizen is a tennis prodigy, with wins in four consecutive U.S. Junior Tennis Tournaments under his belt. He became a starter as a 7th grader and led his team to the District Preliminaries! Despite a few mishaps, Seishun won the District Prelims and the City Tournament and earned a ticket to the Kanto Tournament. Despite losing team captain Kunimitsu and assitant captain Shuichiro to injury, Seishun pulled together as a team to defeat national champion Rikkai, winning the Kanto Tournament and earning a slot at the Nationals!

With Kunimitsu recovered and back on the team, Seishun enter the Nationals with their strongest lineup and defeat Okinawa's Higa Junior High in the opening round and Hyotei in the quarterfinals, advancing to the semifinals against Osaka's Shitenhoji, last year's top-four team. Shusuke loses a tightly played Singles 3 match. Momo and Kaoru take to the court for Doubles 2! Their opponents are Yuji Hitoji and Koharu Konjiki. This pair stands out prominently, even among the stacked Shitenhoji line-up!

STORY &

HARACTERS

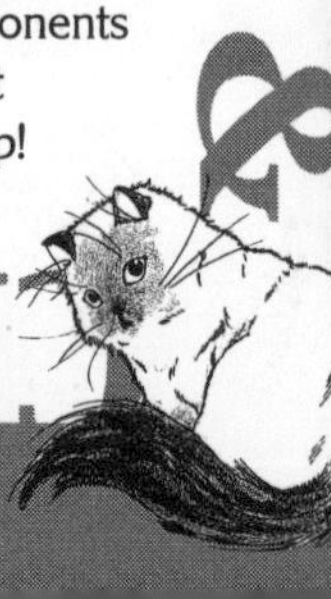

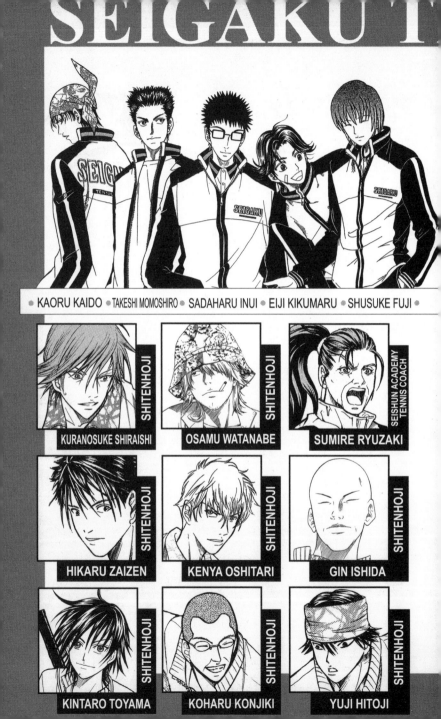

SEIGAKU T

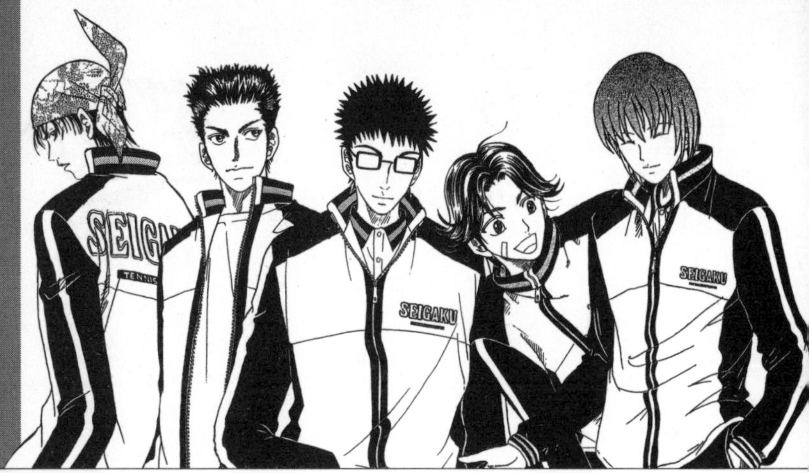
SEIGAKU
TENNIS
SEIGAKU
SEIGAKU

• KAORU KAIDO • TAKESHI MOMOSHIRO • SADAHARU INUI • EIJI KIKUMARU • SHUSUKE FUJI •

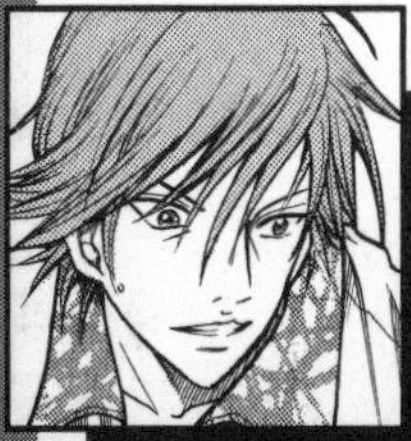

SHITENHOJI
KURANOSUKE SHIRAISHI

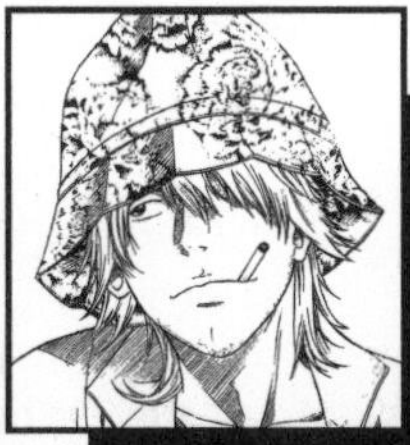

SHITENHOJI
OSAMU WATANABE

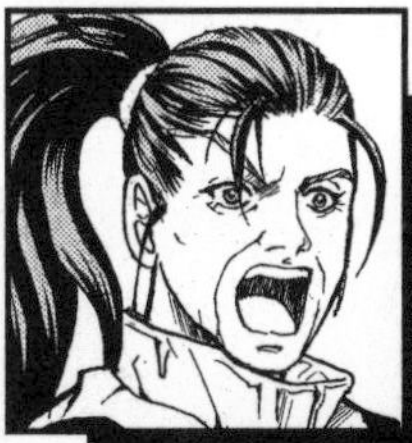

SEISHUN ACADEMY TENNIS COACH
SUMIRE RYUZAKI

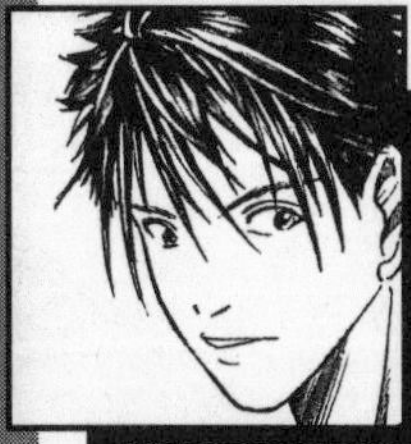

SHITENHOJI
HIKARU ZAIZEN

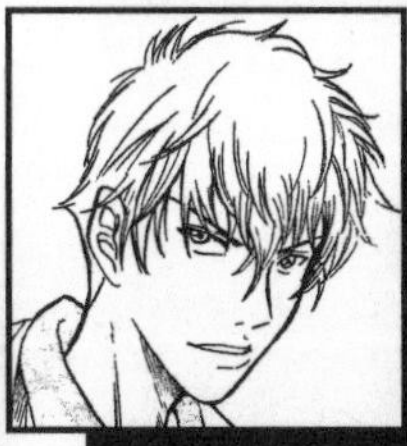

SHITENHOJI
KENYA OSHITARI

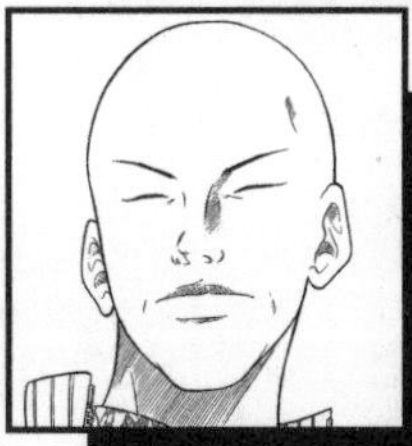

SHITENHOJI
GIN ISHIDA

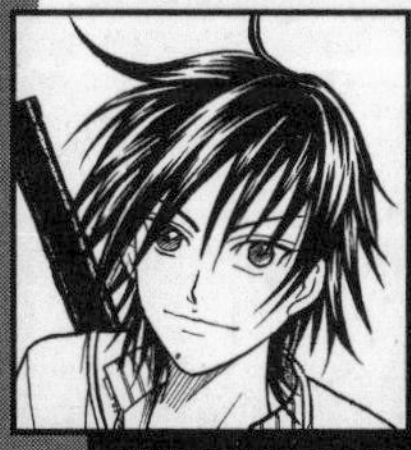

SHITENHOJI
KINTARO TOYAMA

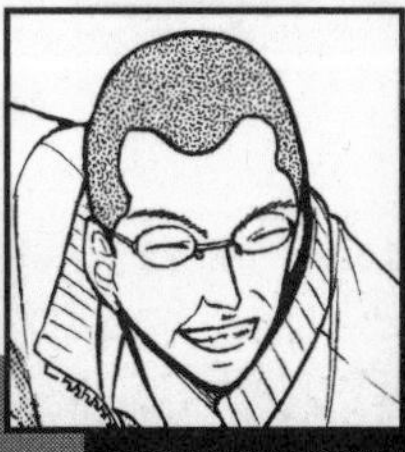

SHITENHOJI
KOHARU KONJIKI

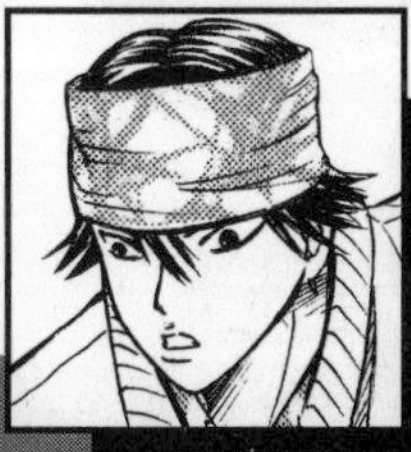

SHITENHOJI
YUJI HITOJI

CONTENTS

Vol. 37
The Terror of Comic Tennis

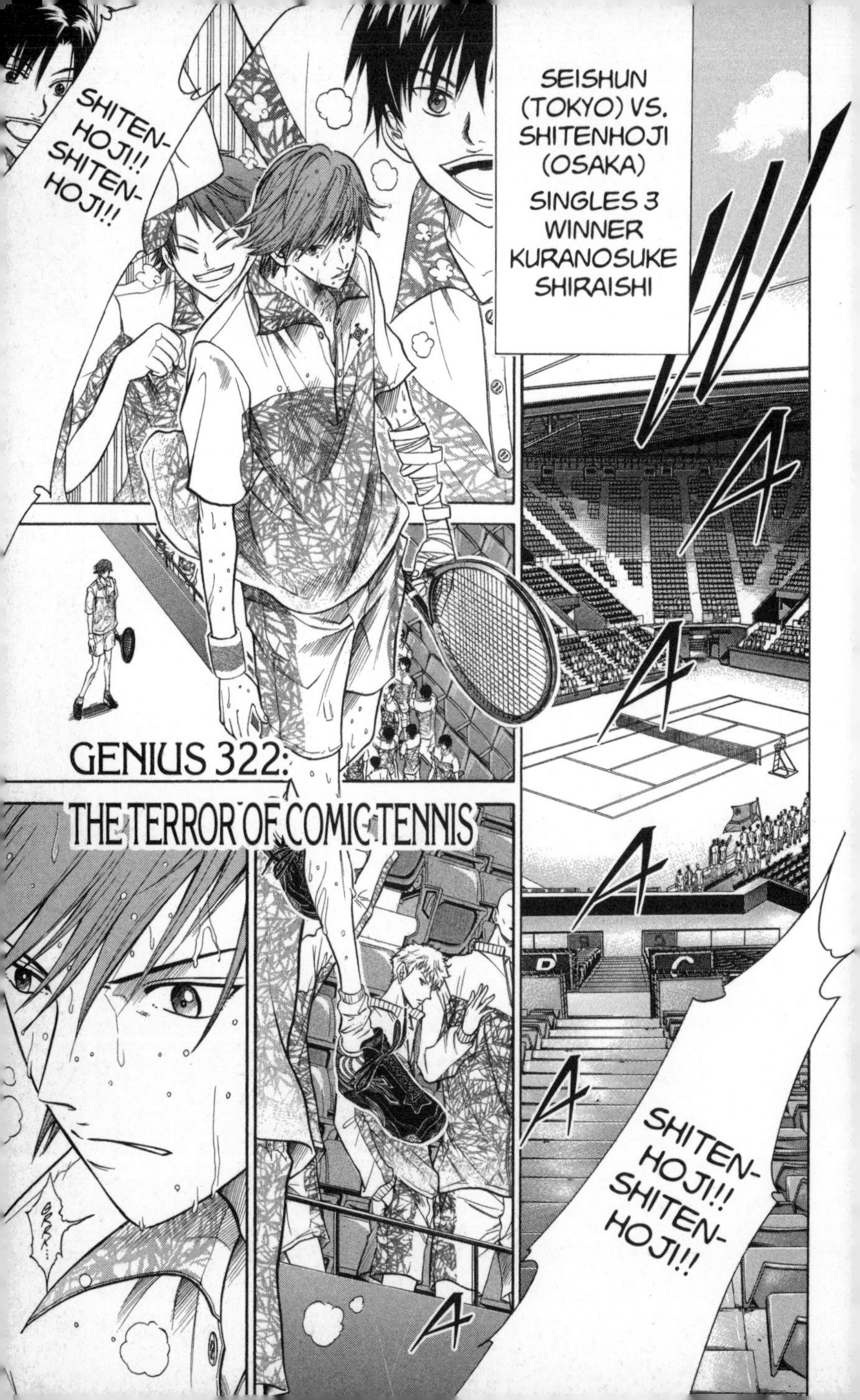
SEISHUN (TOKYO) VS. SHITENHOJI (OSAKA)
SINGLES 3 WINNER KURANOSUKE SHIRAISHI
WAAAAA
SHITEN-HOJI!! SHITEN-HOJI!!
SHITEN-HOJI!! SHITEN-HOJI!!
GENIUS 322: THE TERROR OF COMIC TENNIS
GRRR...

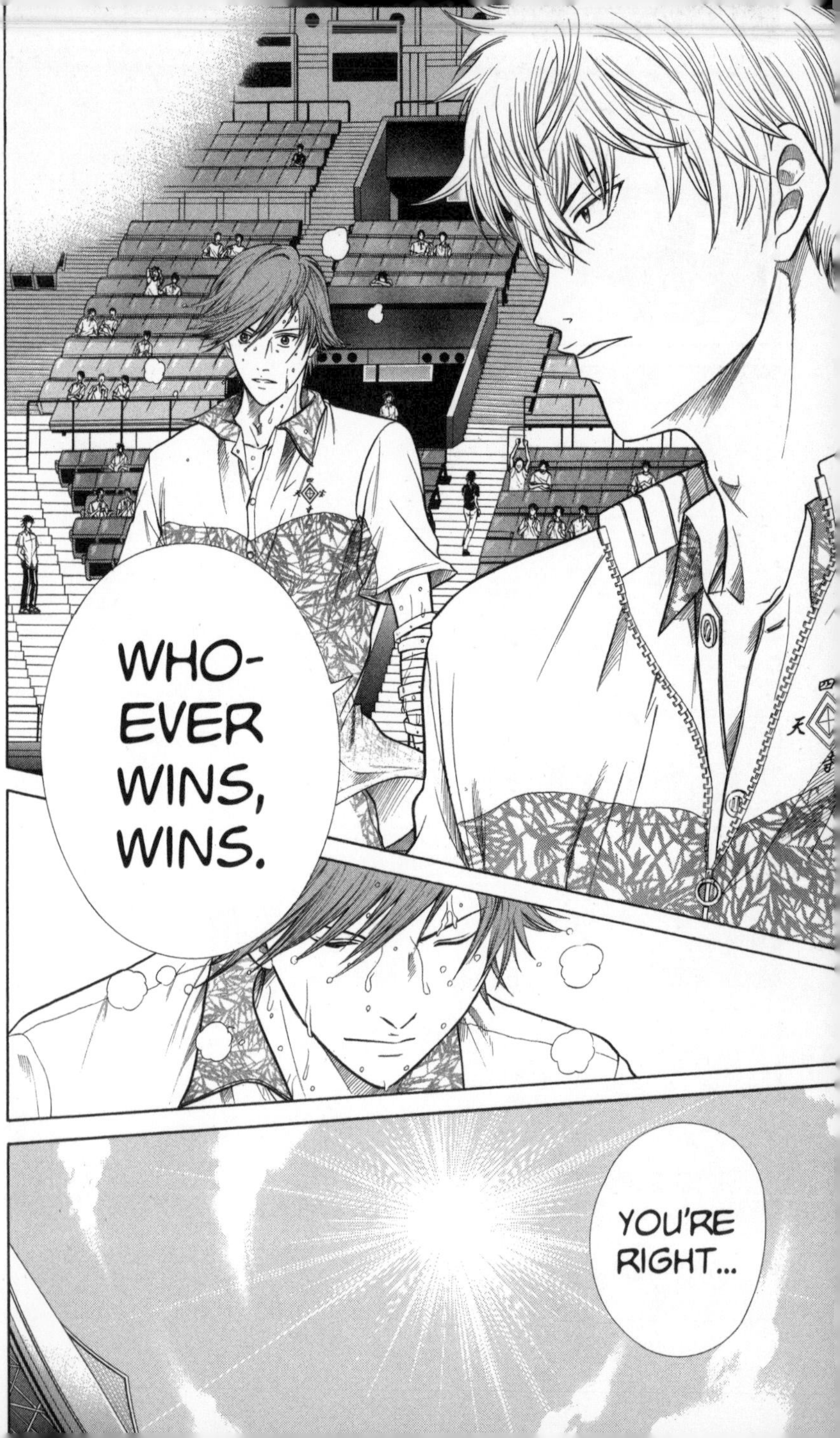
WHO-EVER WINS, WINS.
YOU'RE RIGHT...

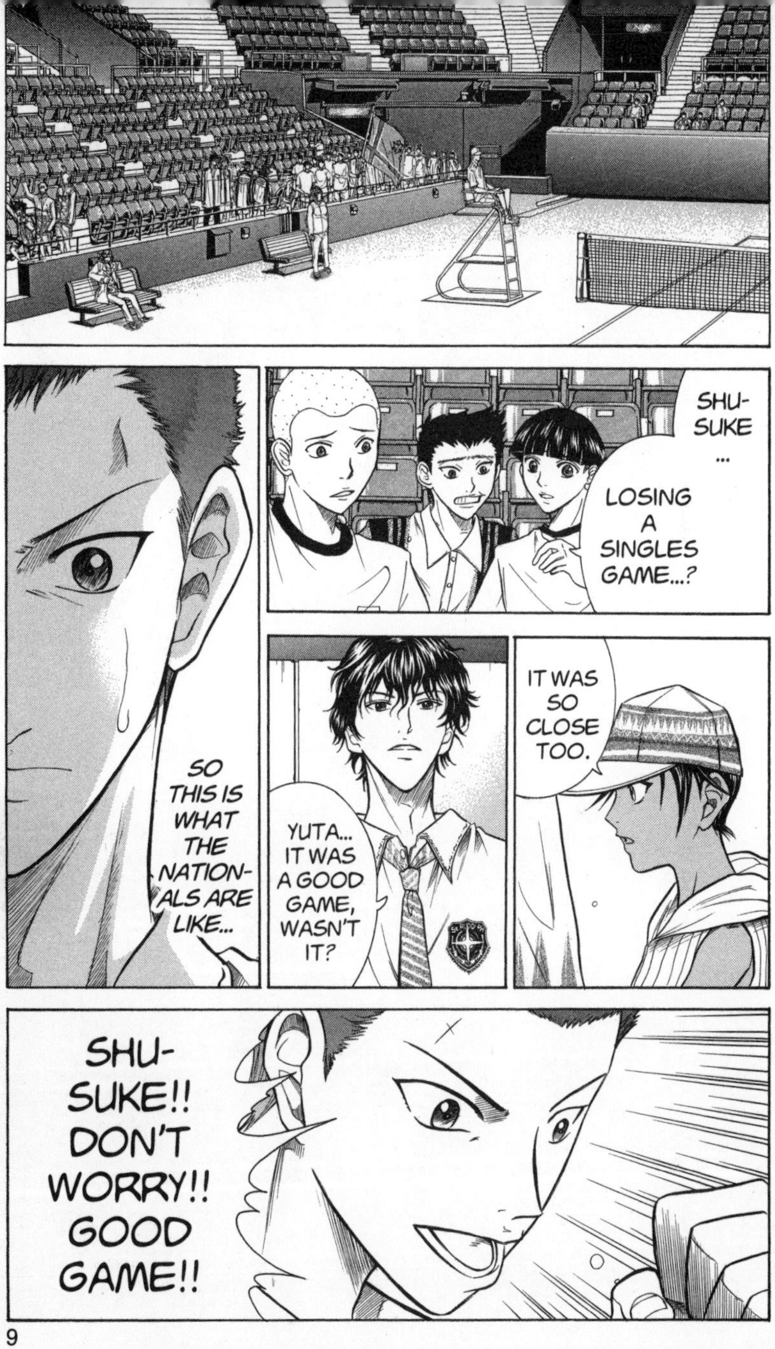
SHU-SUKE ... LOSING A SINGLES GAME...?
IT WAS SO CLOSE TOO.
YUTA... IT WAS A GOOD GAME, WASN'T IT?
SO THIS IS WHAT THE NATION-ALS ARE LIKE...
SHU-SUKE!! DON'T WORRY!! GOOD GAME!!

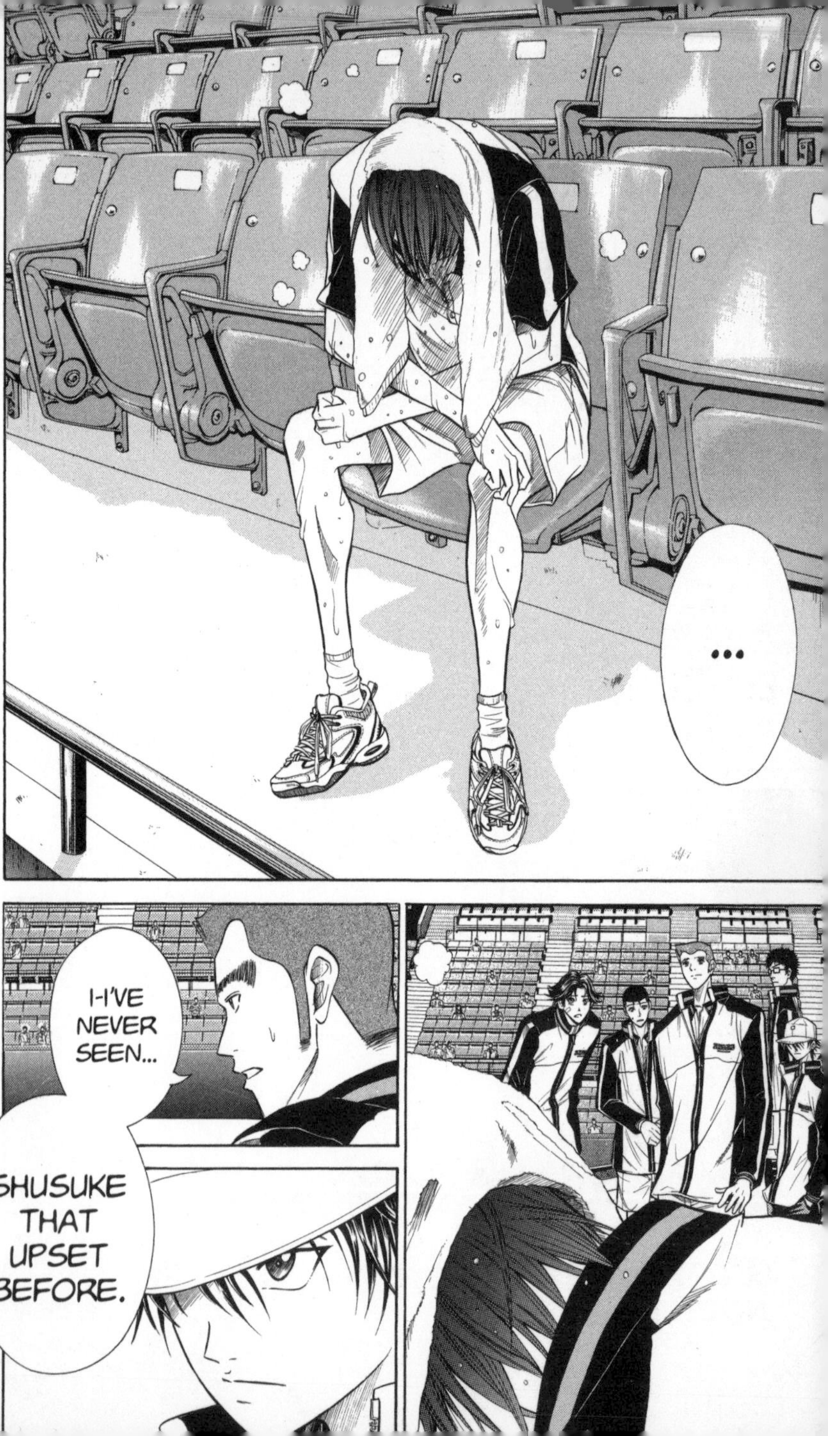
...
I-I'VE NEVER SEEN...
SHUSUKE THAT UPSET BEFORE.

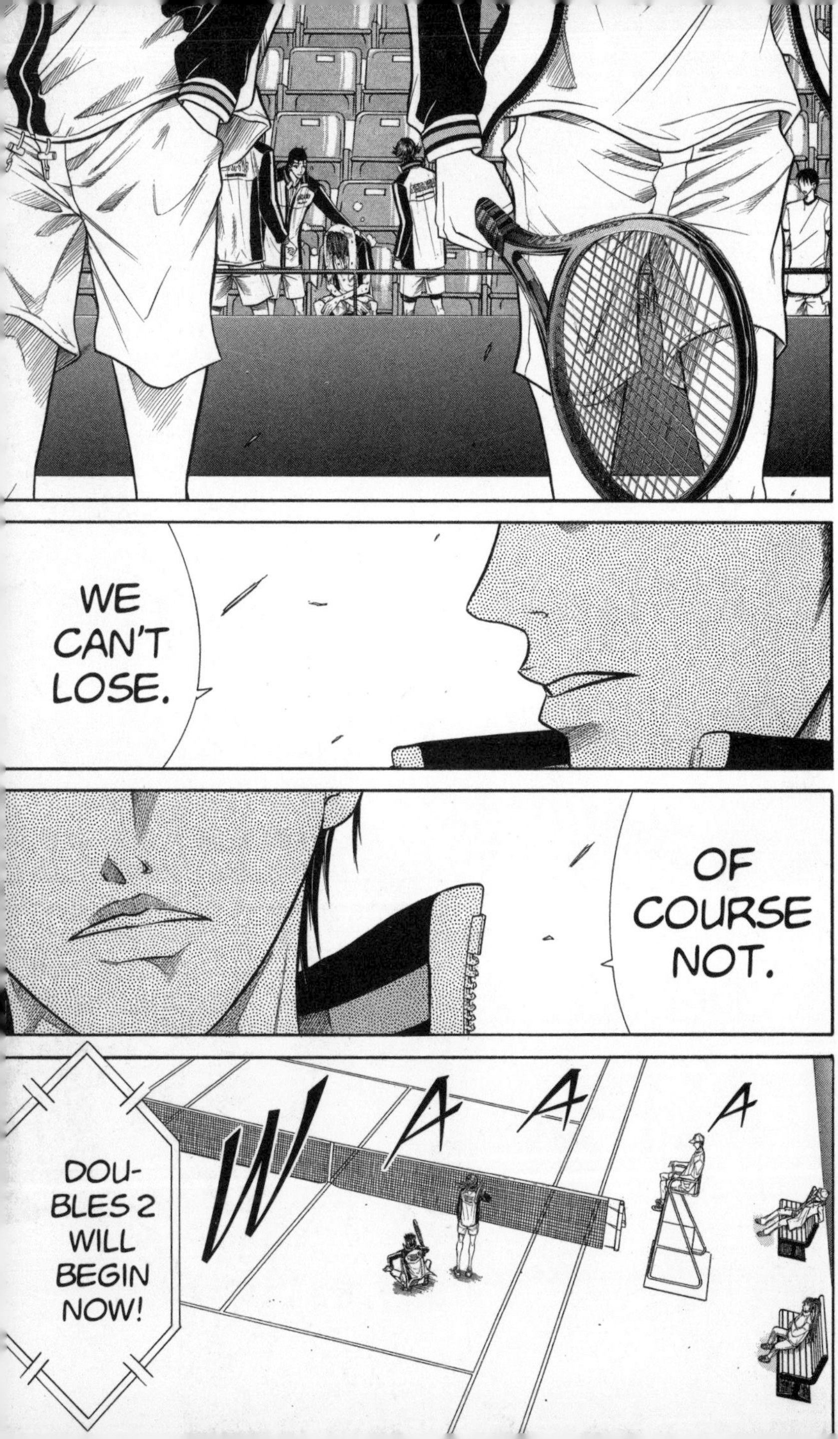
WE CAN'T LOSE.
OF COURSE NOT.
WAAA
DOUBLES 2 WILL BEGIN NOW!

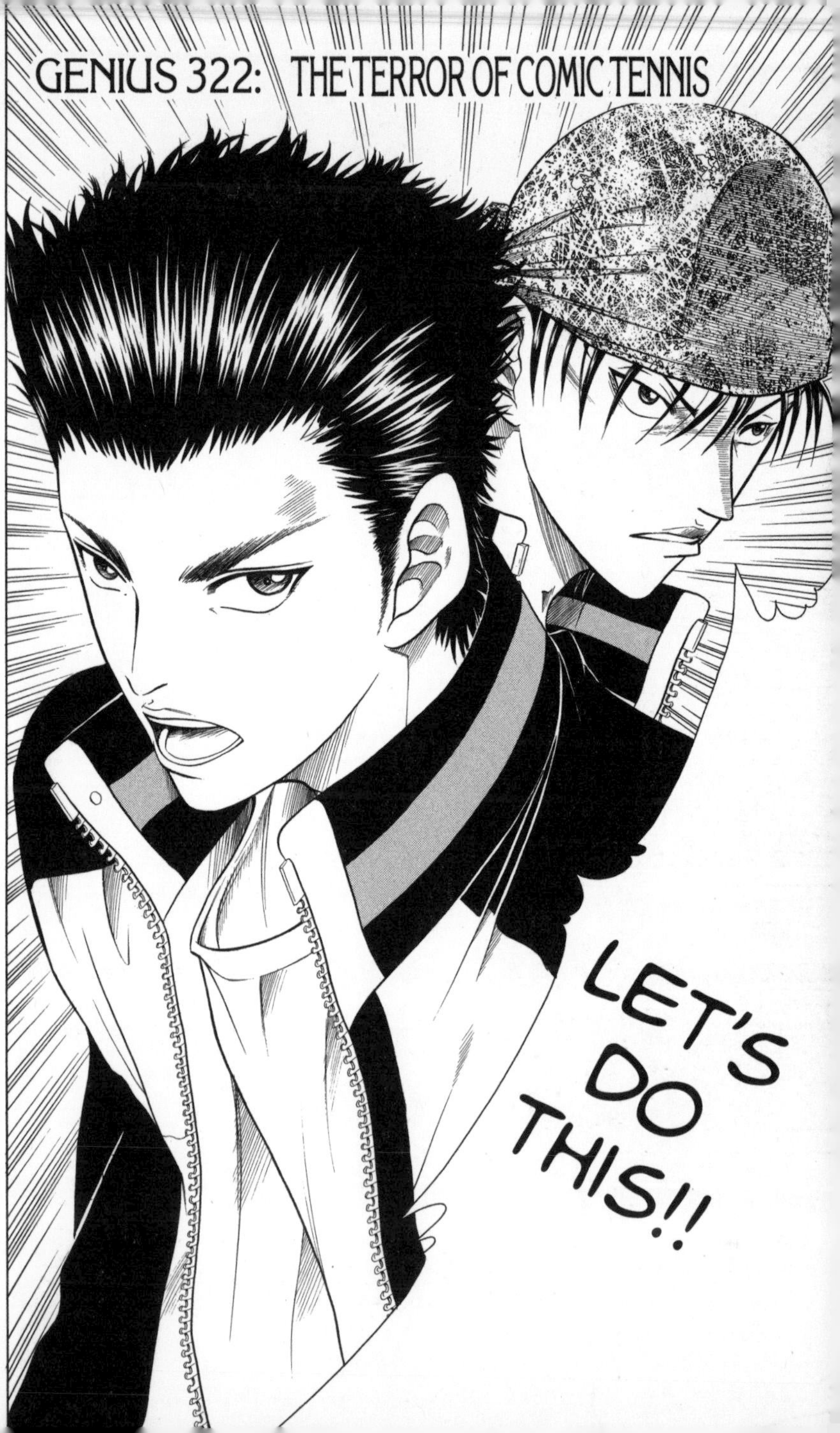
GENIUS 322: THE TERROR OF COMIC TENNIS
LET'S DO THIS!!

READ THIS WAY

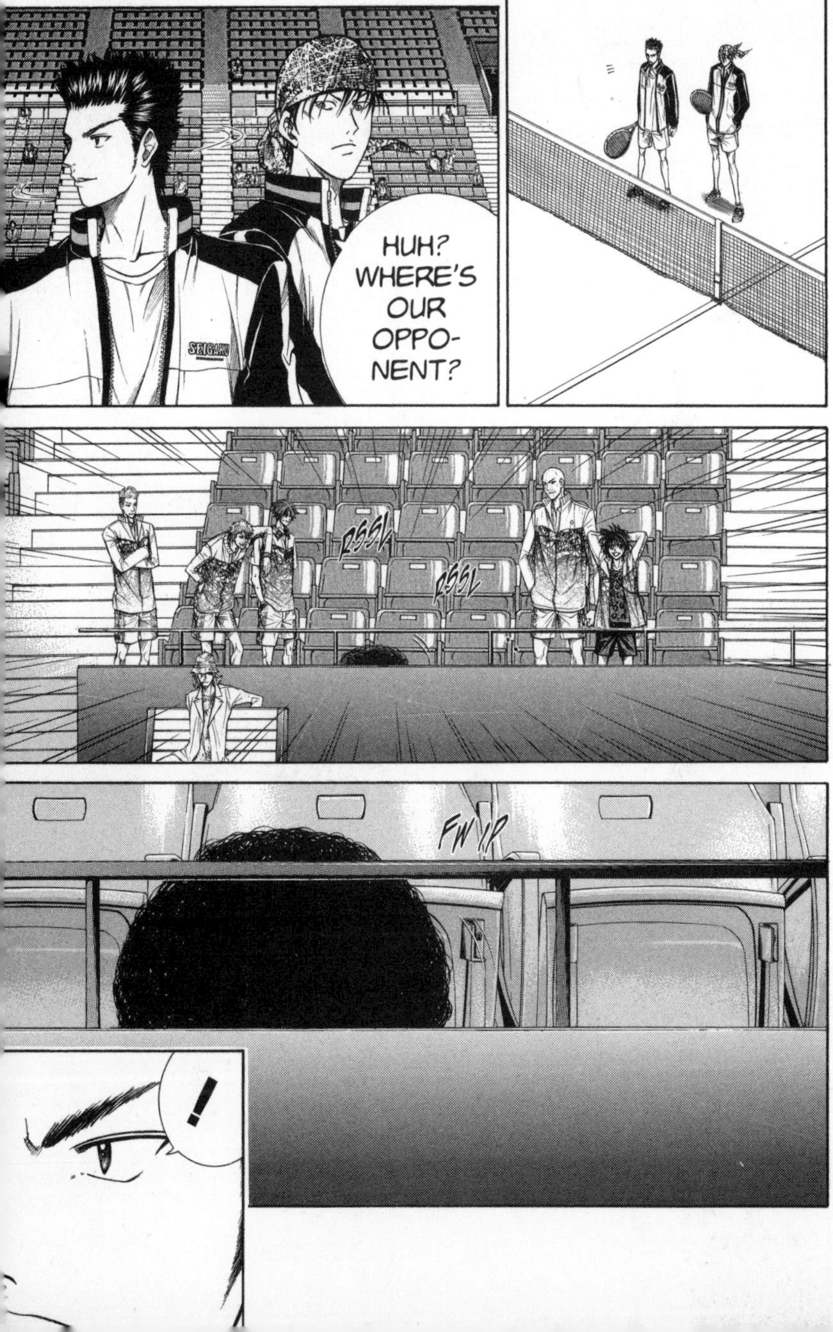
HUH? WHERE'S OUR OPPO-NENT?
RSSL
RSSL
FWIP
!

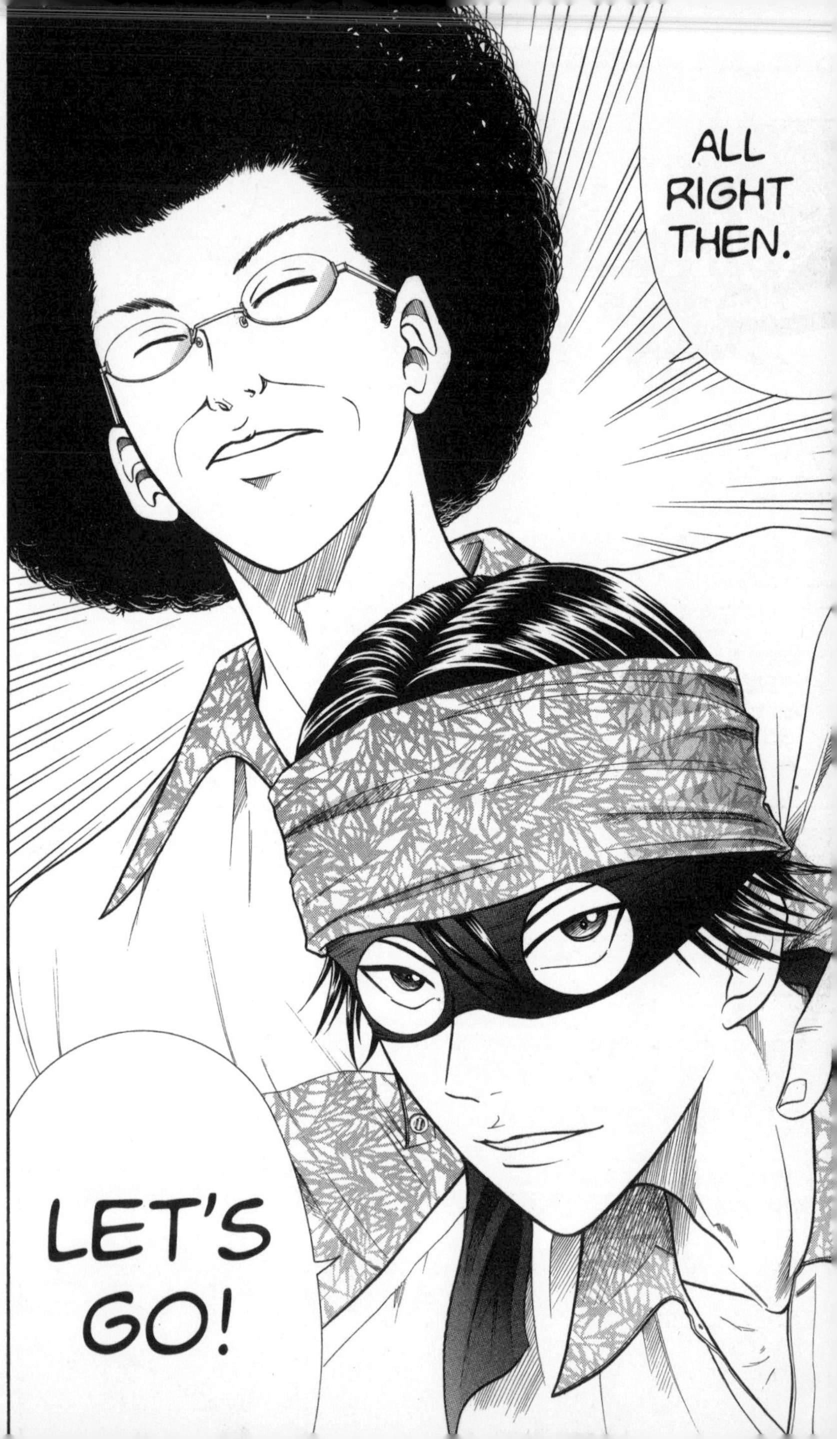
ALL RIGHT THEN.
LET'S GO!

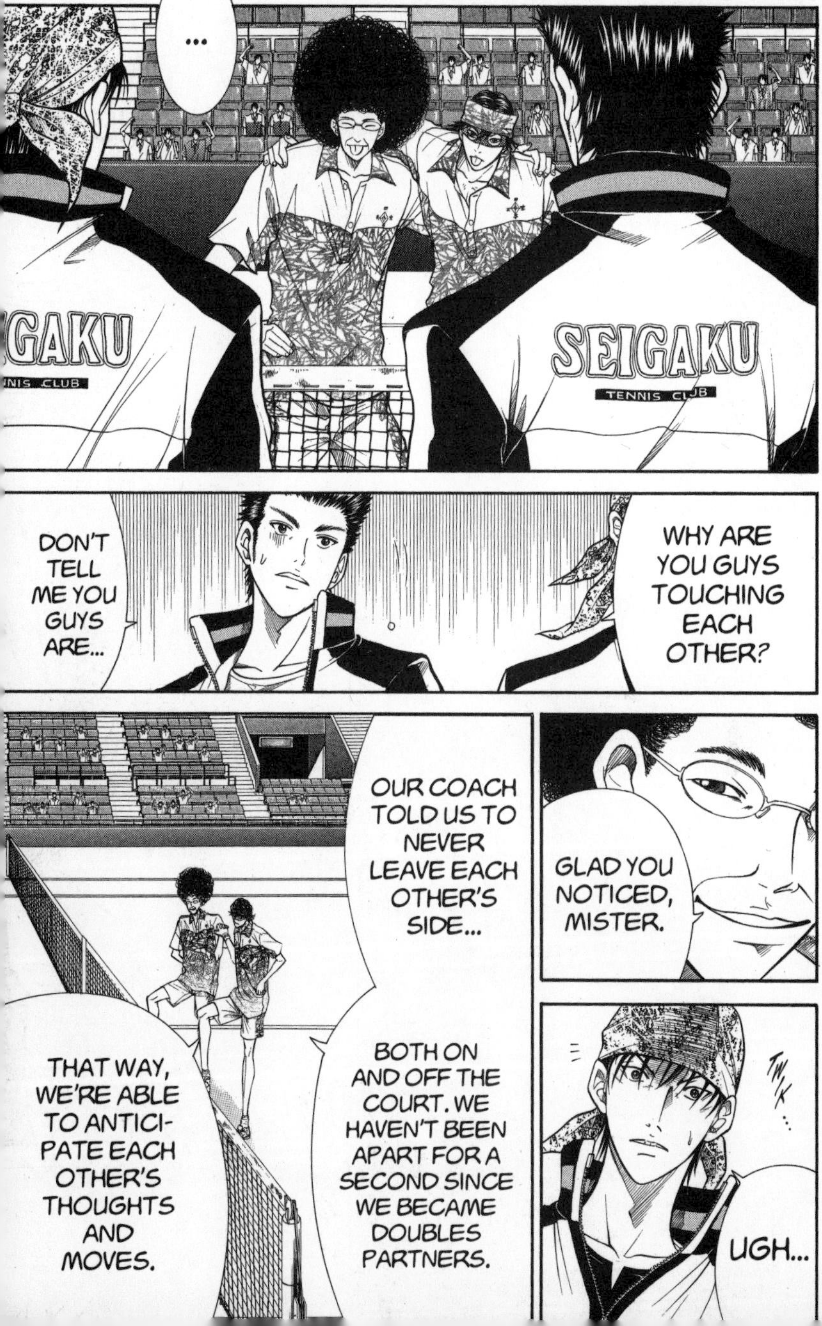
...
SEIGAKU
TENNIS CLUB
WHY ARE YOU GUYS TOUCHING EACH OTHER?
DON'T TELL ME YOU GUYS ARE...
GLAD YOU NOTICED, MISTER.
TWIK...
UGH...
OUR COACH TOLD US TO NEVER LEAVE EACH OTHER'S SIDE...
BOTH ON AND OFF THE COURT. WE HAVEN'T BEEN APART FOR A SECOND SINCE WE BECAME DOUBLES PARTNERS.
THAT WAY, WE'RE ABLE TO ANTICI-PATE EACH OTHER'S THOUGHTS AND MOVES.

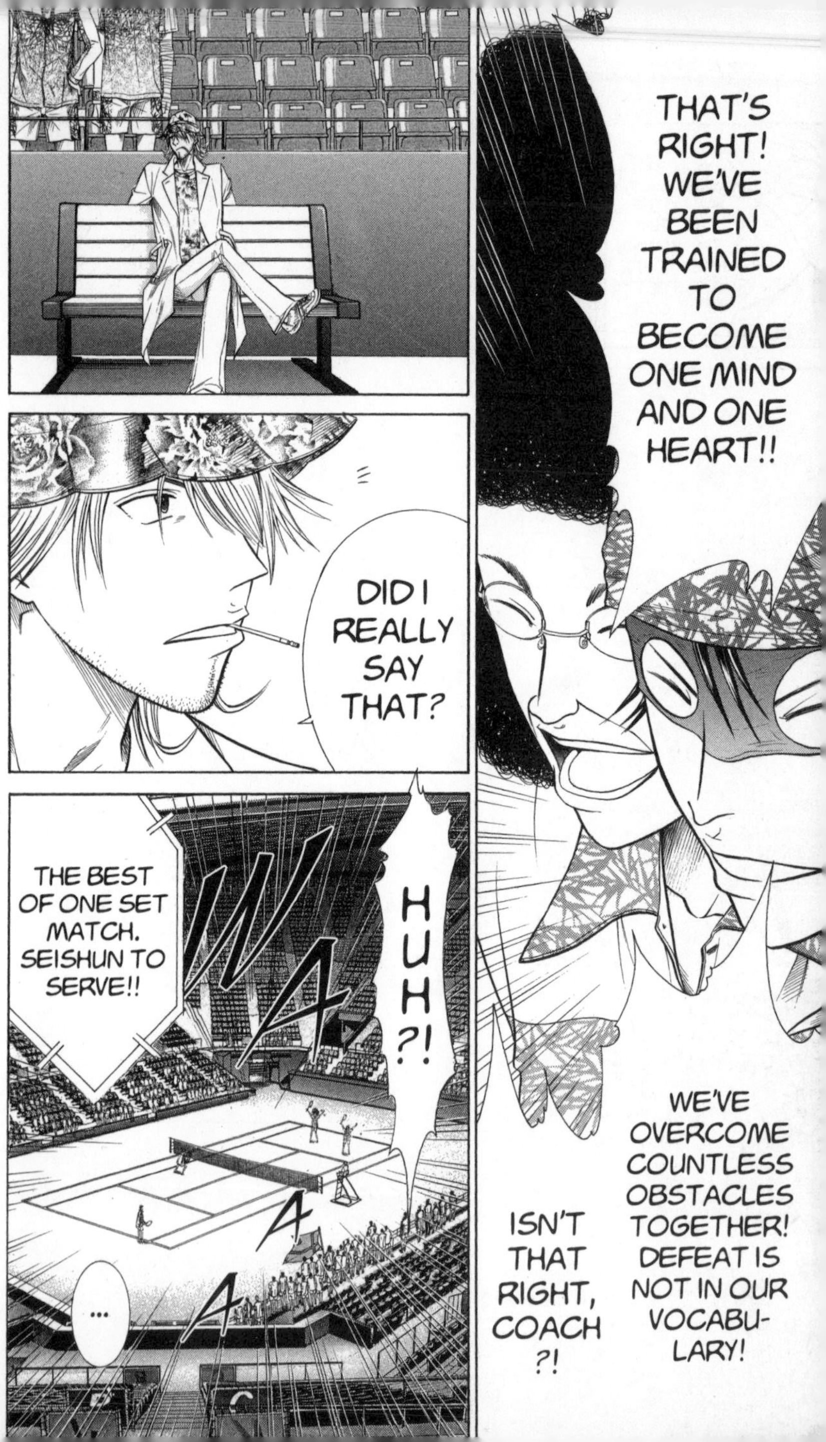
THAT'S RIGHT! WE'VE BEEN TRAINED TO BECOME ONE MIND AND ONE HEART!!
WE'VE OVERCOME COUNTLESS OBSTACLES TOGETHER! DEFEAT IS NOT IN OUR VOCABU-LARY!
ISN'T THAT RIGHT, COACH?!
DID I REALLY SAY THAT?
HUH?!
THE BEST OF ONE SET MATCH. SEISHUN TO SERVE!!
WAAA
...

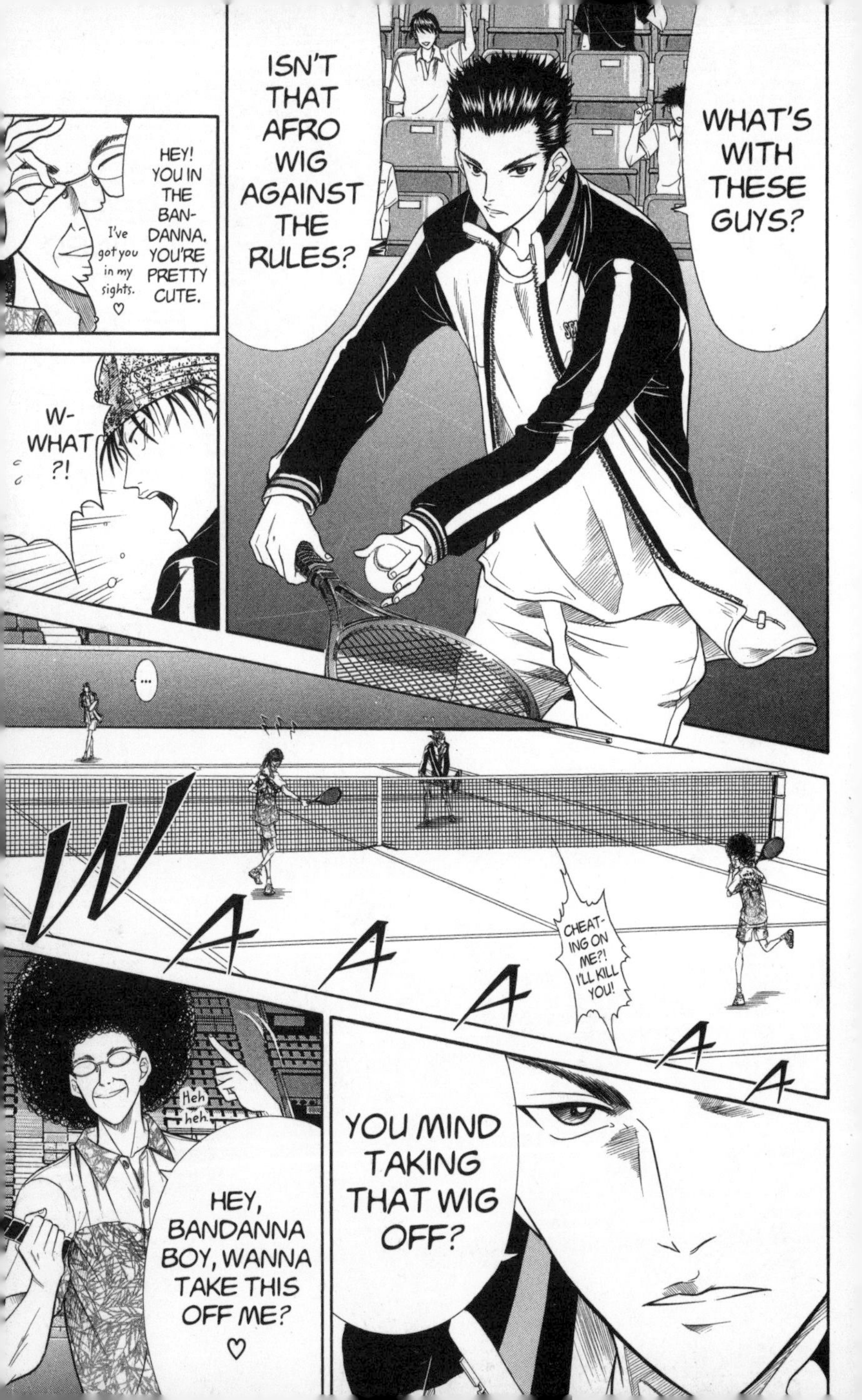
WHAT'S WITH THESE GUYS?
ISN'T THAT AFRO WIG AGAINST THE RULES?
HEY! YOU IN THE BANDANNA. YOU'RE PRETTY CUTE.
I've got you in my sights. ♡
W-WHAT?!
CHEATING ON ME?! I'LL KILL YOU!
...
WAAAAAA
YOU MIND TAKING THAT WIG OFF?
Heh heh.
HEY, BANDANNA BOY, WANNA TAKE THIS OFF ME? ♡

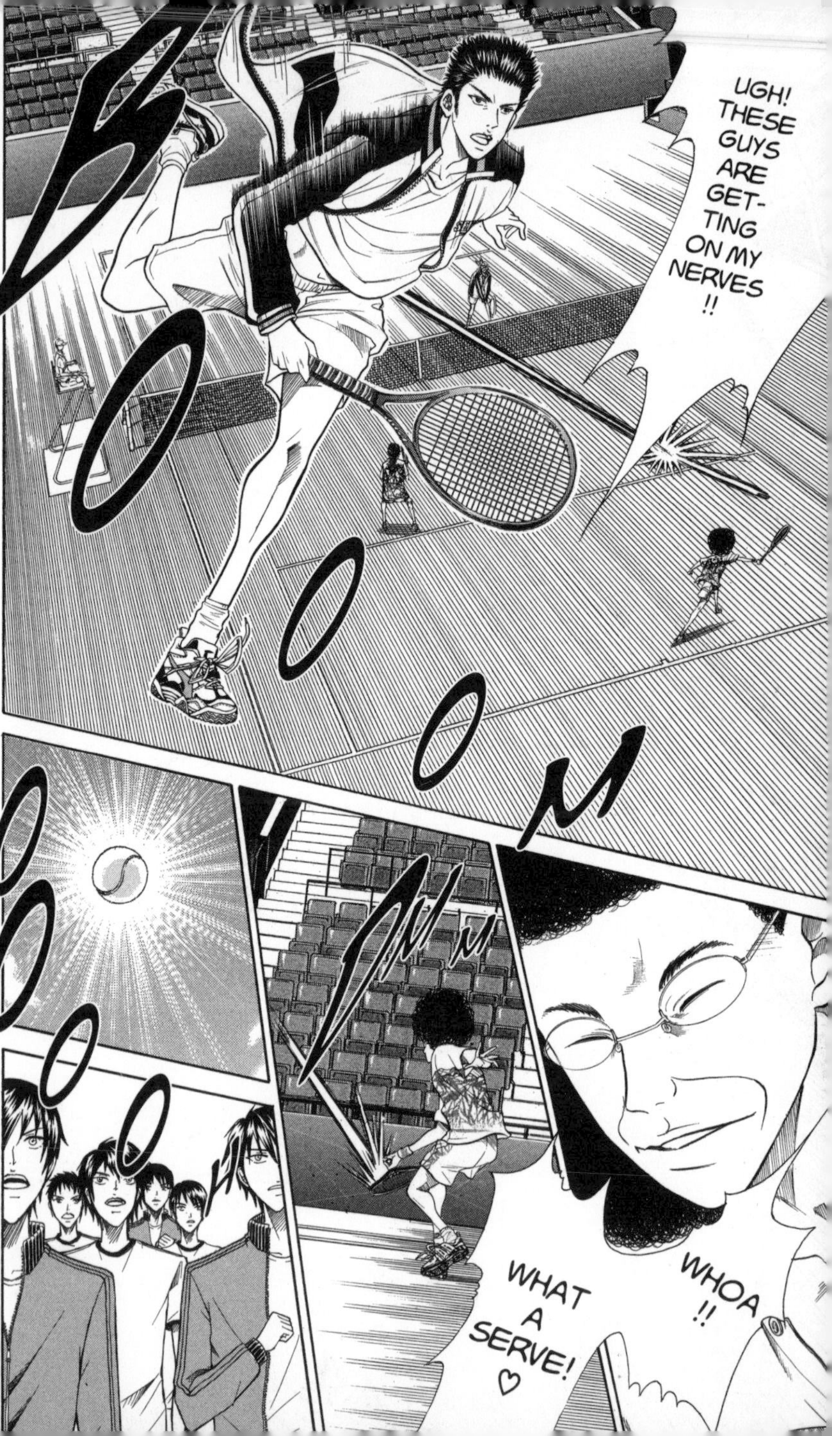
UGH! THESE GUYS ARE GET-TING ON MY NERVES!!
BOOOOM
WHOA!!
WHAT A SERVE! ♡

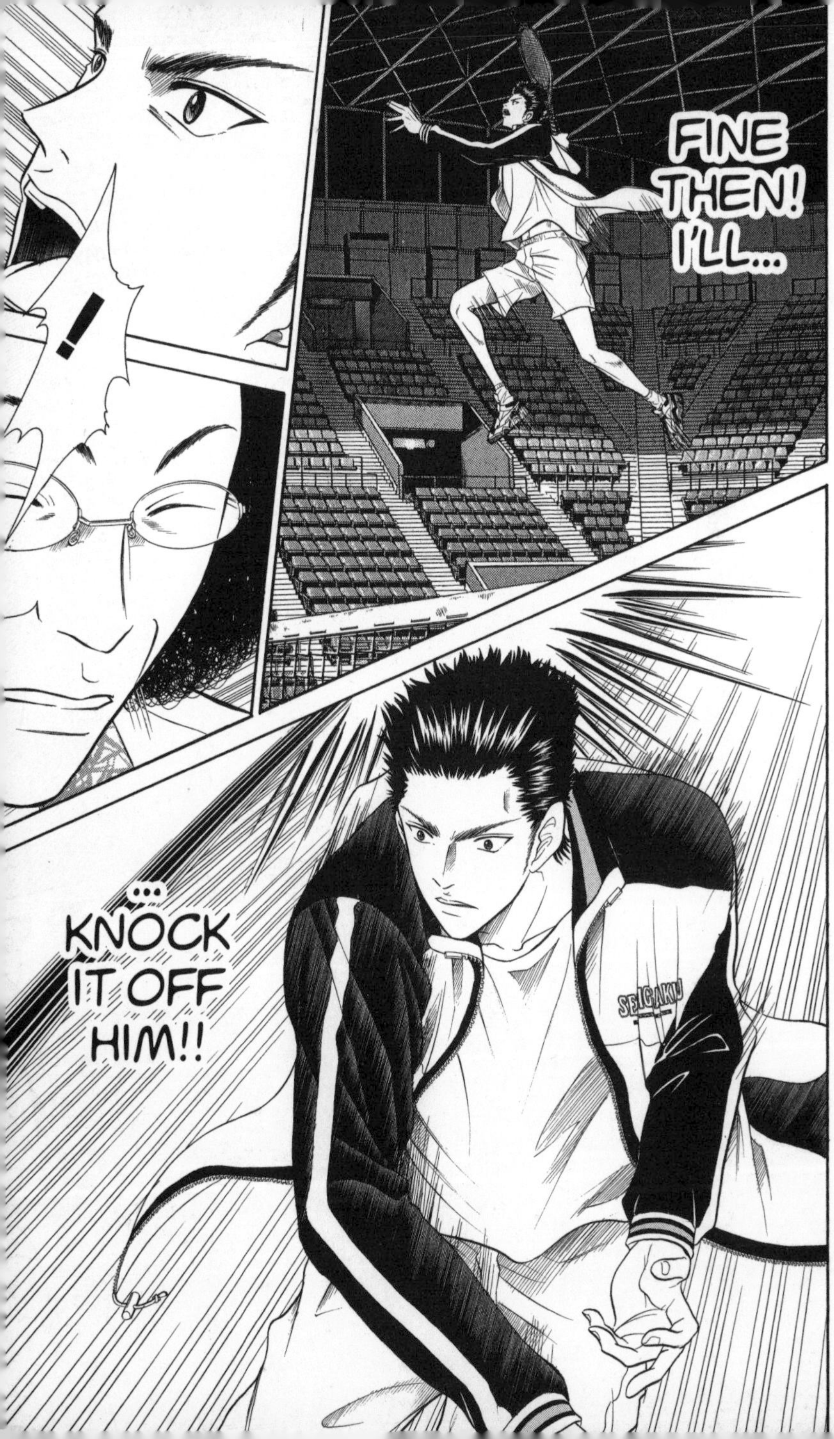
FINE THEN! I'LL...
!
...KNOCK IT OFF HIM!!
SEIGAKU

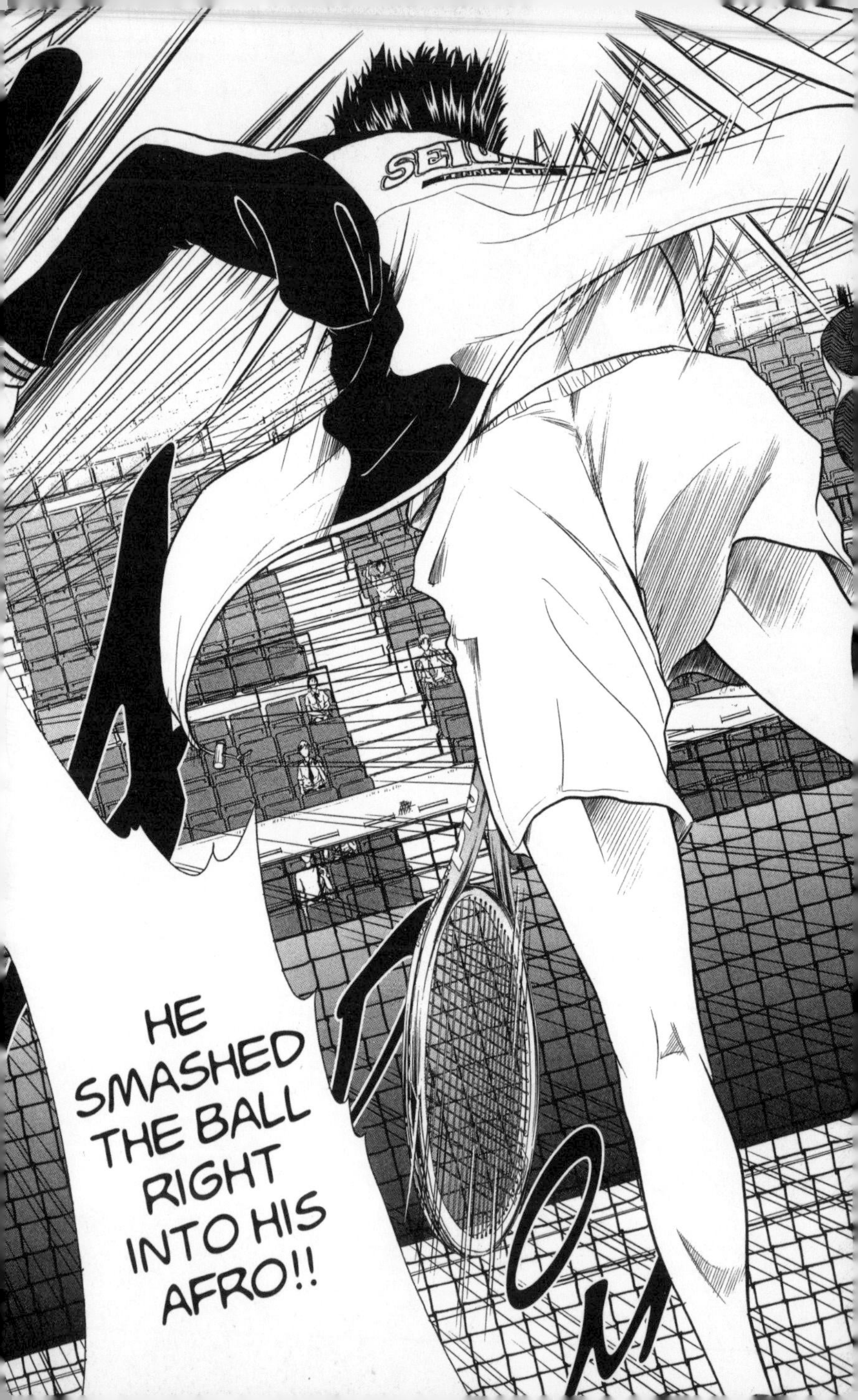
HE SMASHED THE BALL RIGHT INTO HIS AFRO!!
OM

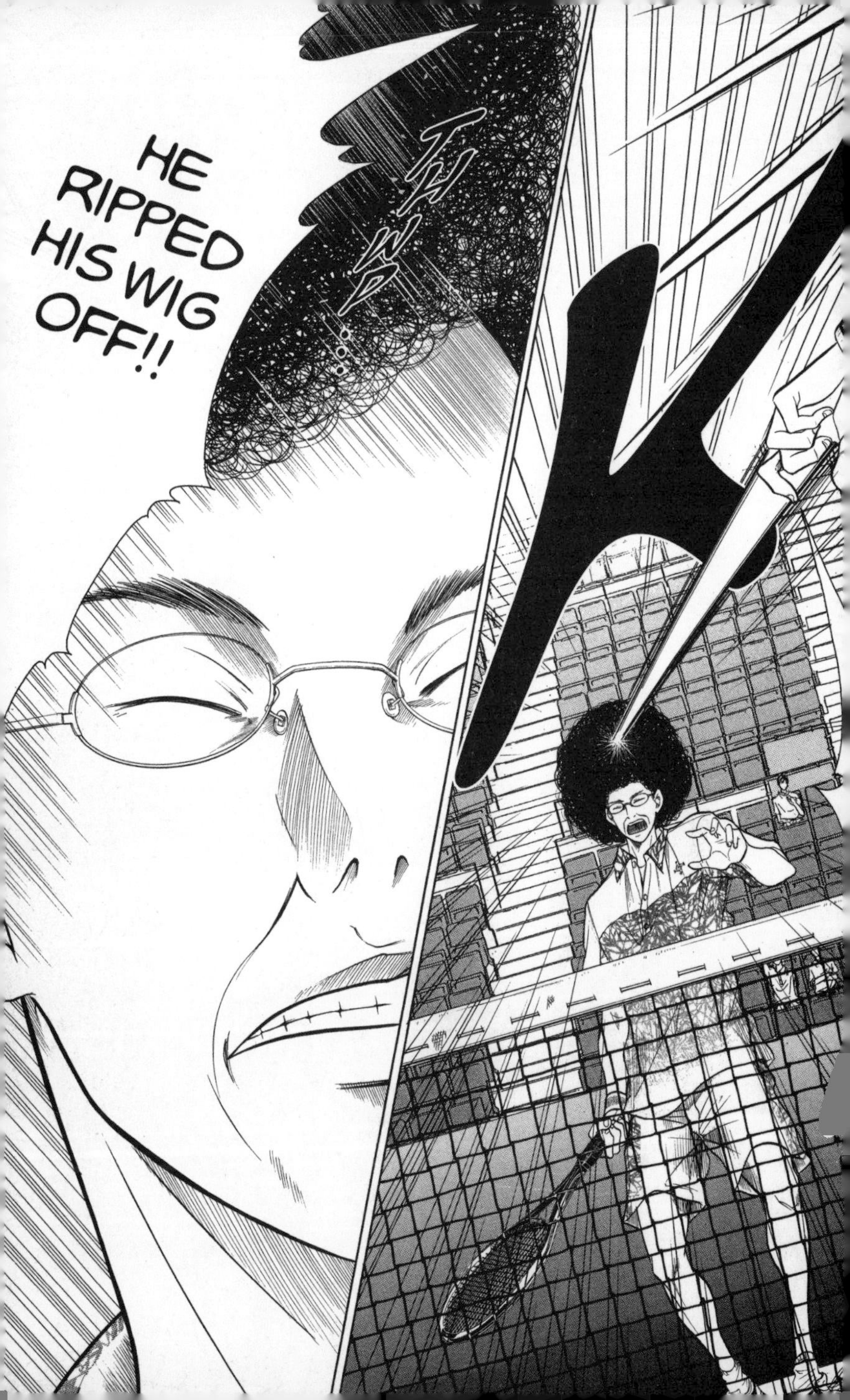
HE RIPPED HIS WIG OFF!!
THWD...

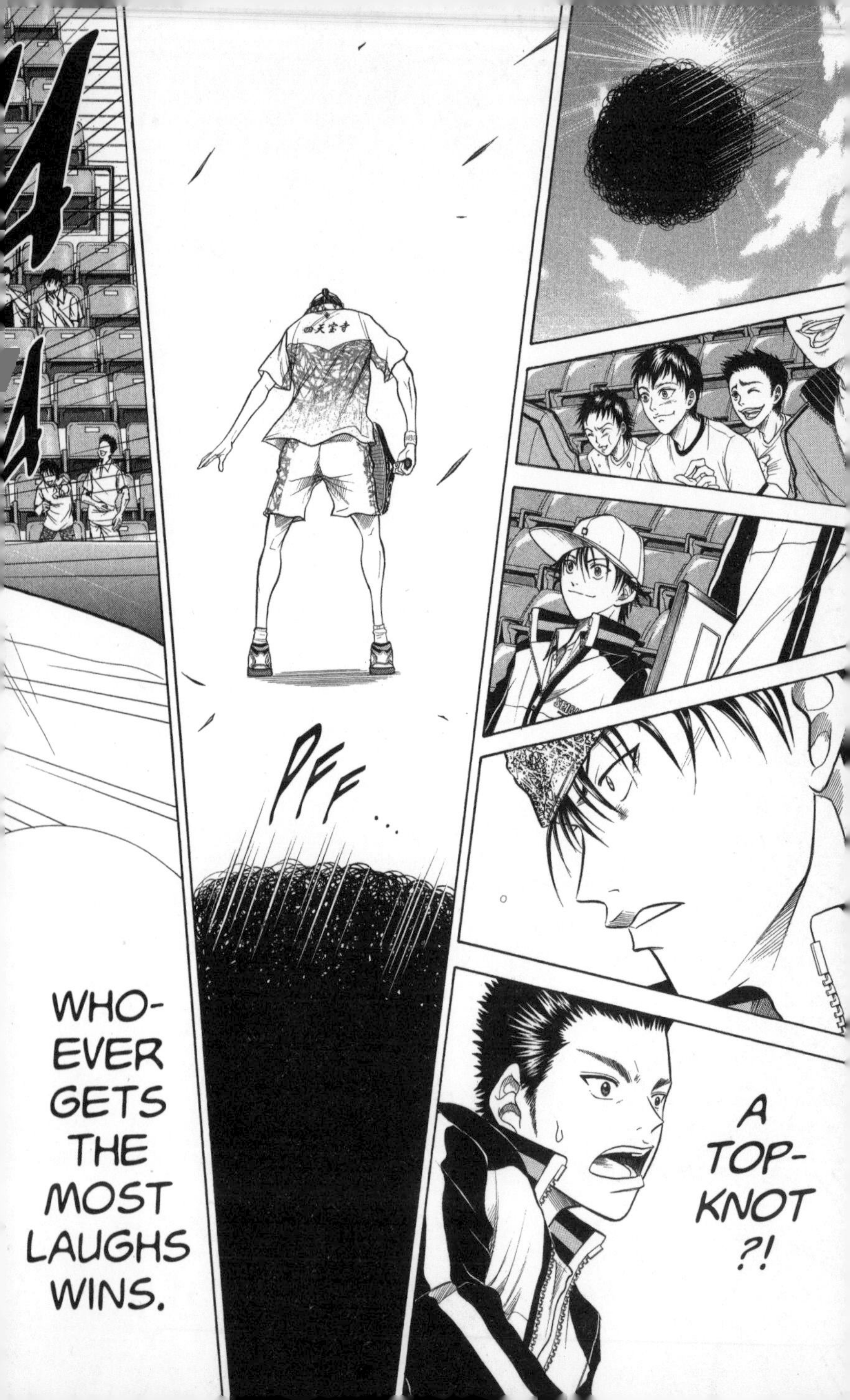
A TOP-KNOT ?!
PFF...
WHO-EVER GETS THE MOST LAUGHS WINS.

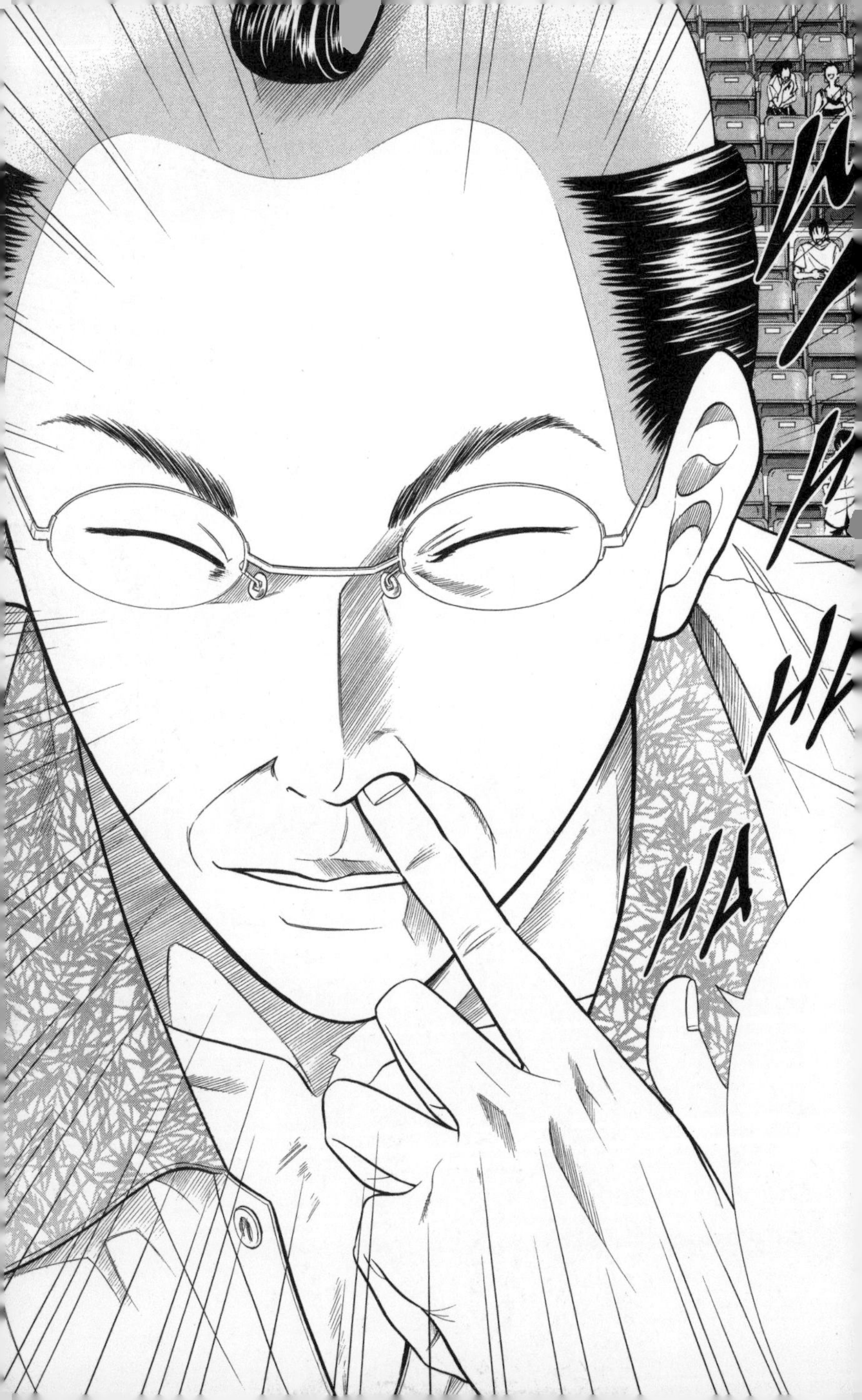
HA

テニスの王子様

THE PRINCE OF TENNIS

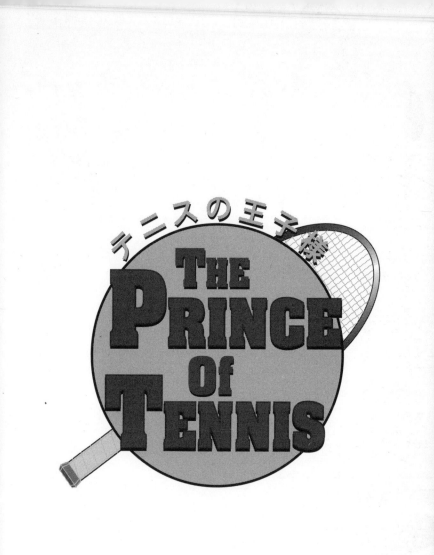

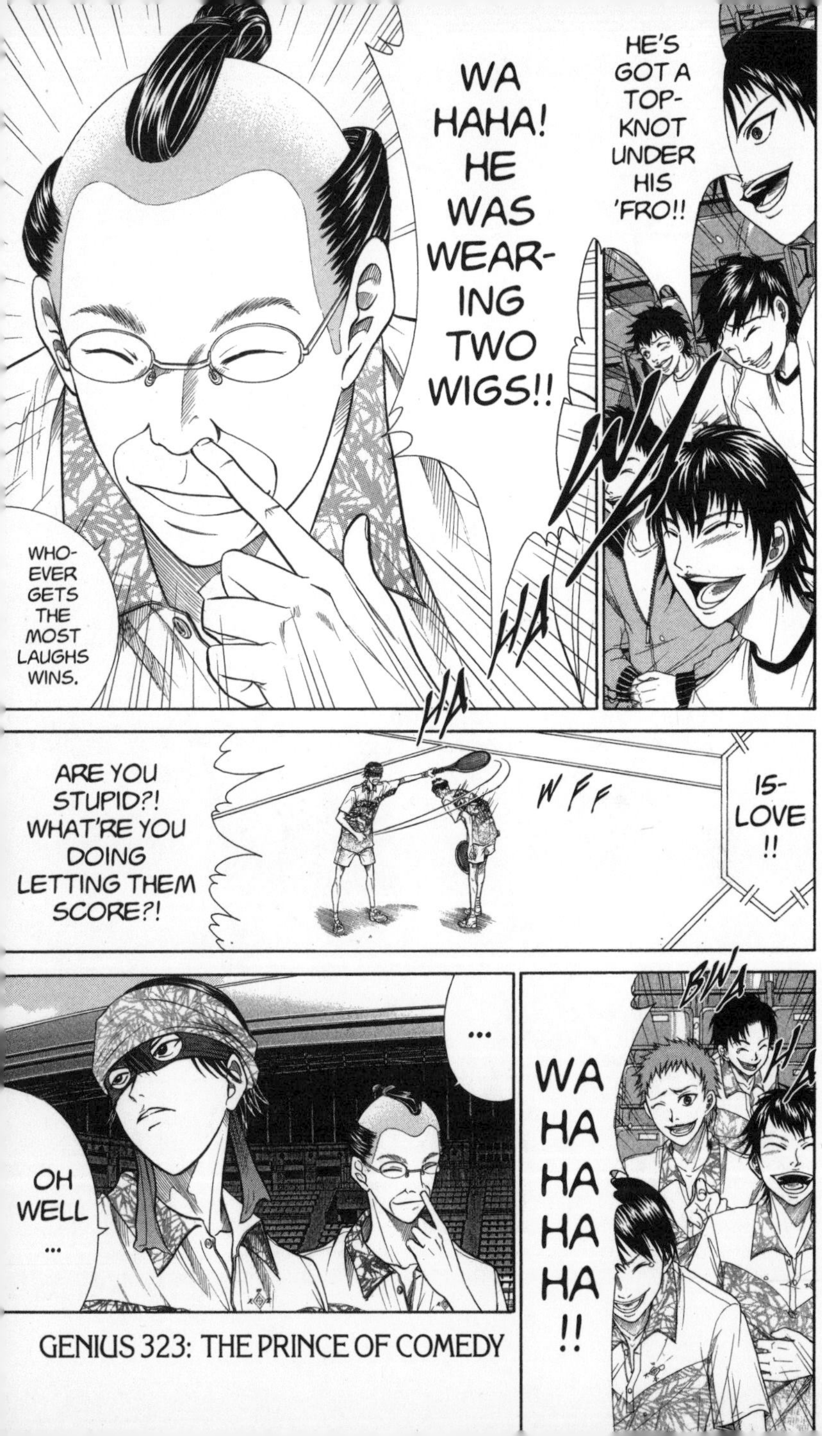
HE'S GOT A TOP-KNOT UNDER HIS 'FRO!!
WA HAHA! HE WAS WEARING TWO WIGS!!
WA HA HA
WHO-EVER GETS THE MOST LAUGHS WINS.
15-LOVE!!
WFF
ARE YOU STUPID?! WHAT'RE YOU DOING LETTING THEM SCORE?!
WA HA HA HA HA HA!!
...
OH WELL ...

GENIUS 323: THE PRINCE OF COMEDY

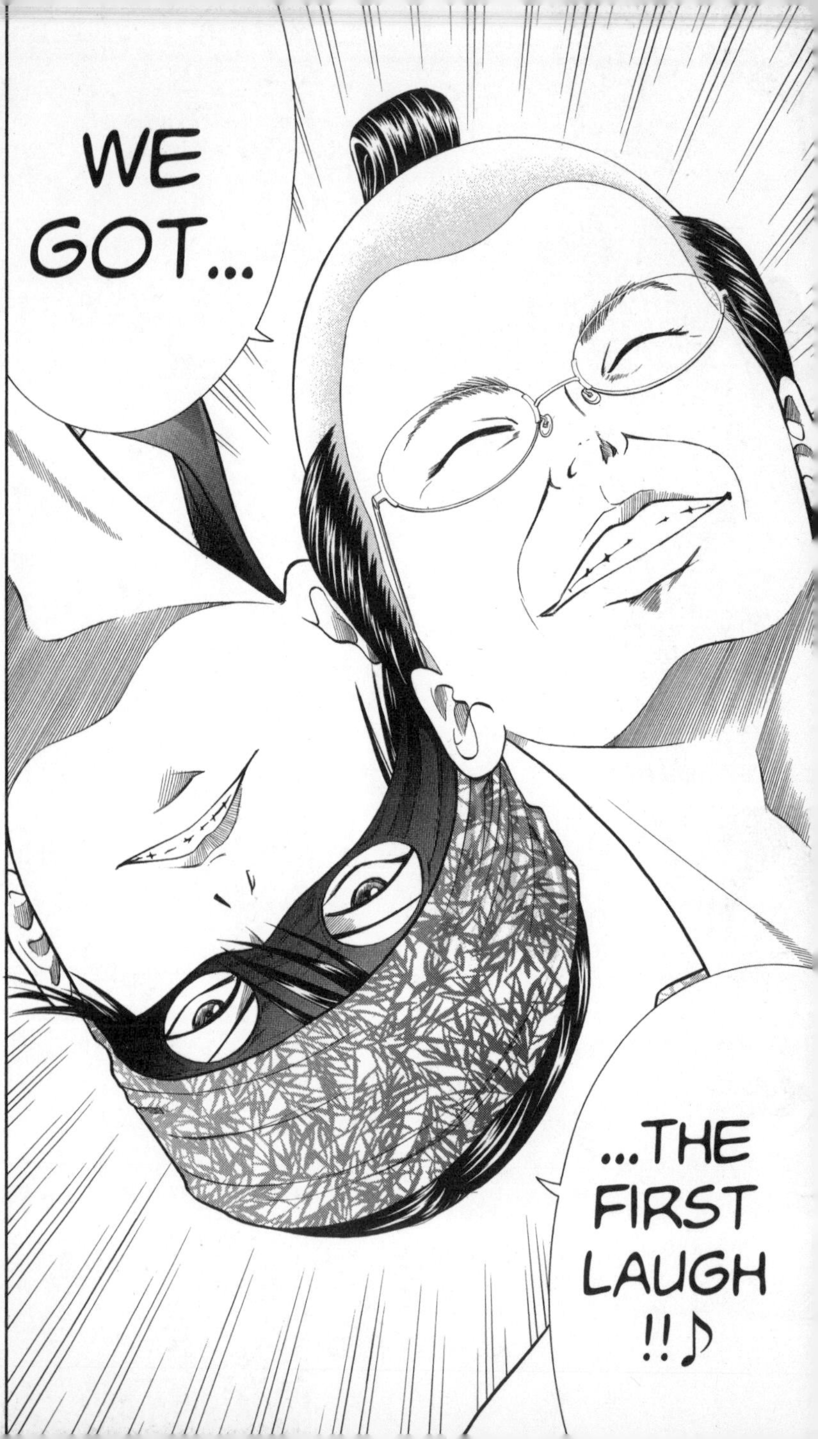
WE GOT...
...THE FIRST LAUGH !!♪

GENIUS 323: THE PRINCE OF COMEDY

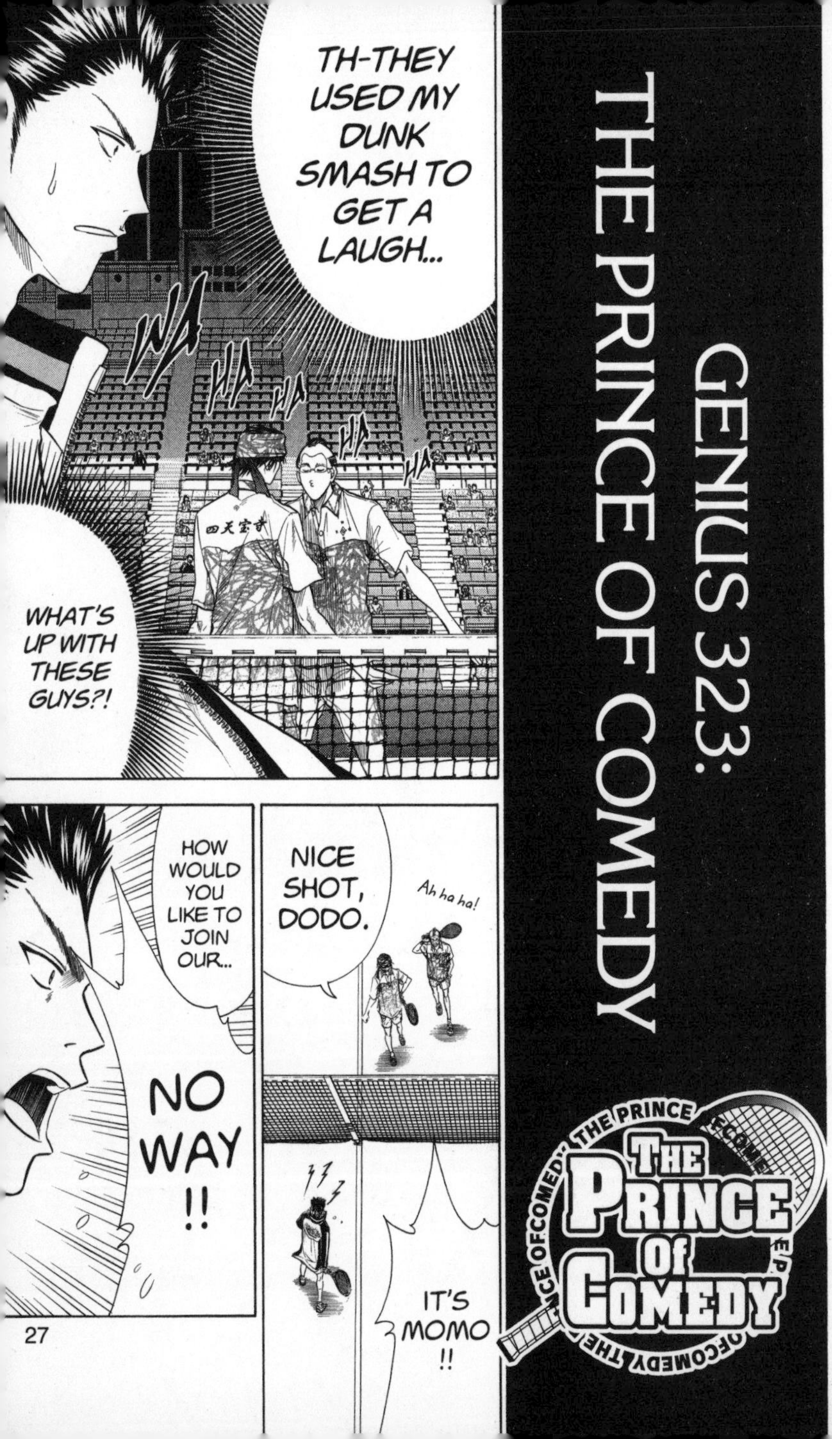
TH-THEY USED MY DUNK SMASH TO GET A LAUGH...
WA HA HA HA HA
WHAT'S UP WITH THESE GUYS?!
NICE SHOT, DODO.
Ah ha ha!
IT'S MOMO!!
HOW WOULD YOU LIKE TO JOIN OUR...
NO WAY!!

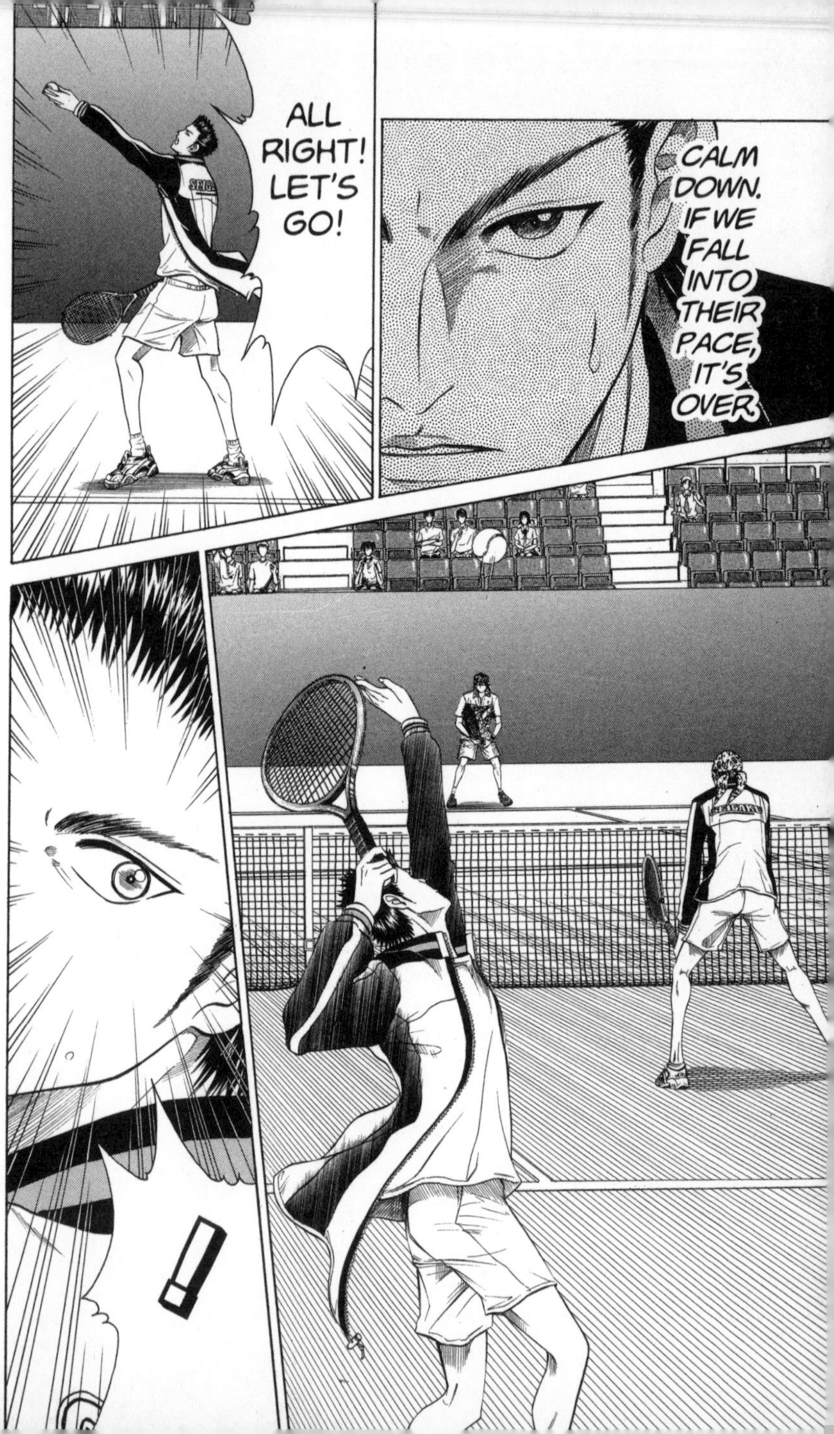
CALM DOWN. IF WE FALL INTO THEIR PACE, IT'S OVER.
ALL RIGHT! LET'S GO!
SEIGAKU
!

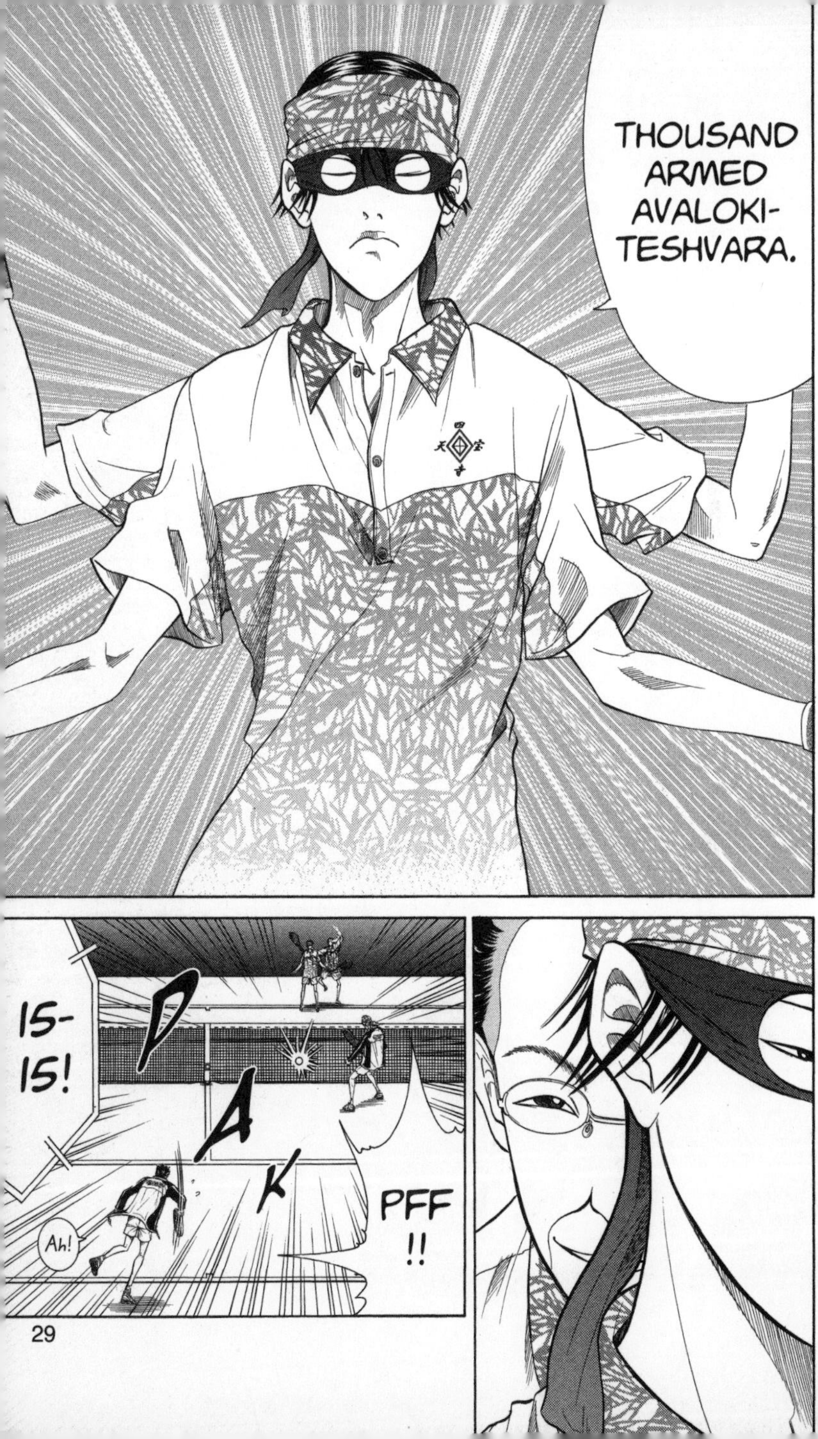
THOUSAND ARMED AVALOKI-TESHVARA.
DAK
15-15!
PFF !!
Ah!

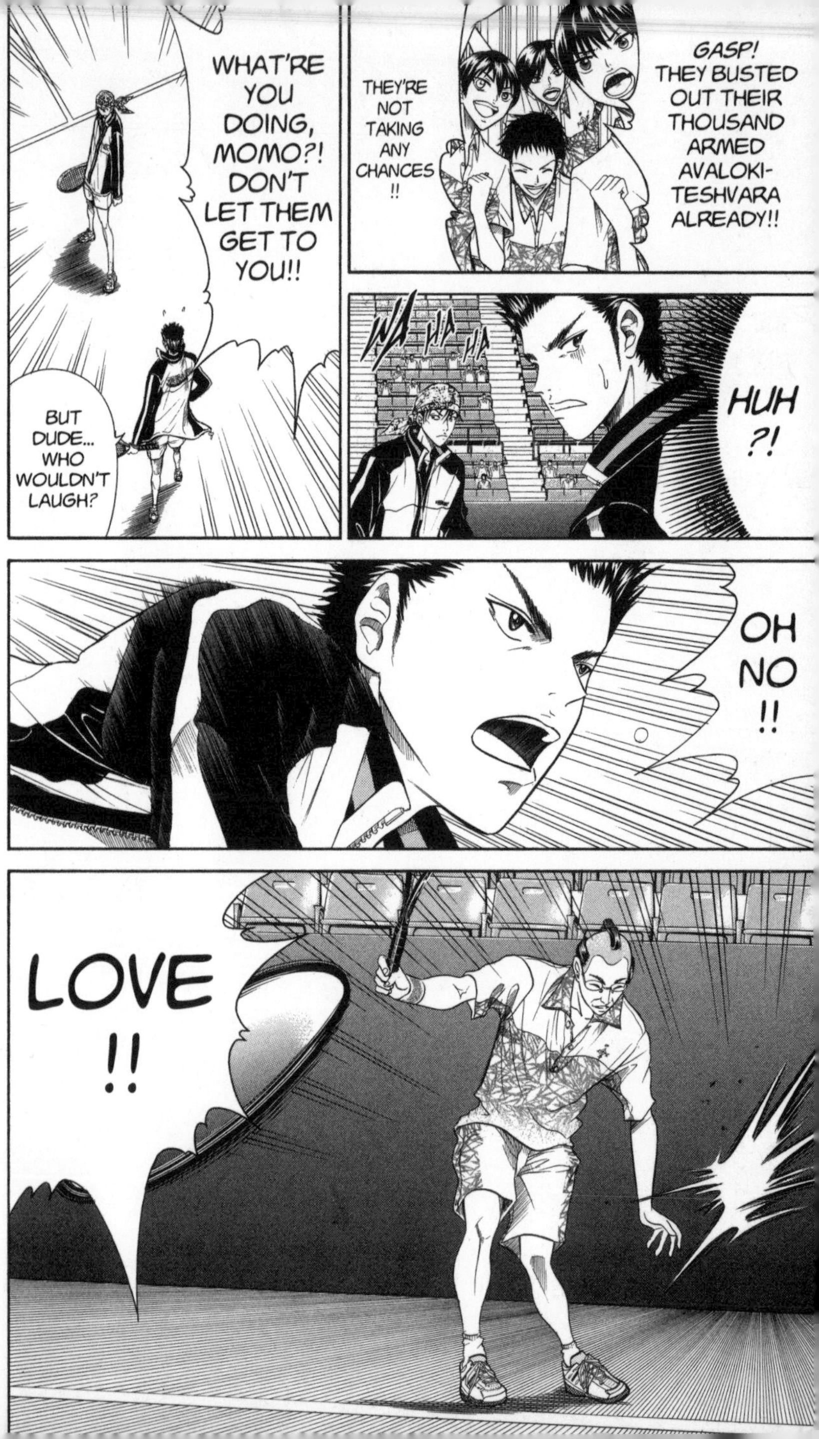
GASP! THEY BUSTED OUT THEIR THOUSAND ARMED AVALOKI-TESHVARA ALREADY!!
THEY'RE NOT TAKING ANY CHANCES !!
WA HA HA
HUH ?!
WHAT'RE YOU DOING, MOMO?! DON'T LET THEM GET TO YOU!!
BUT DUDE... WHO WOULDN'T LAUGH?
OH NO !!
LOVE !!

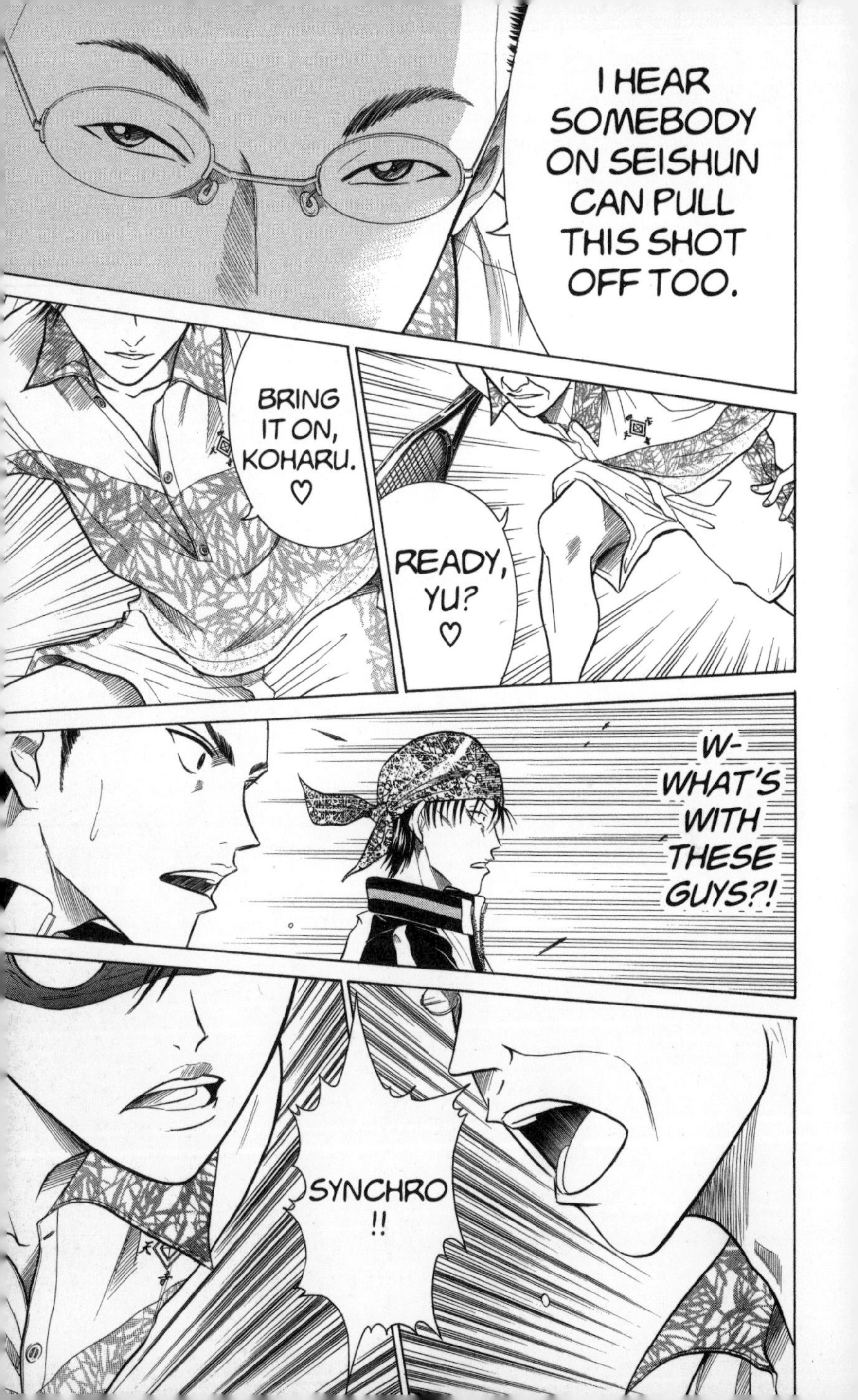
I HEAR SOMEBODY ON SEISHUN CAN PULL THIS SHOT OFF TOO.
READY, YU? ♡
BRING IT ON, KOHARU. ♡
W- WHAT'S WITH THESE GUYS?!
SYNCHRO !!

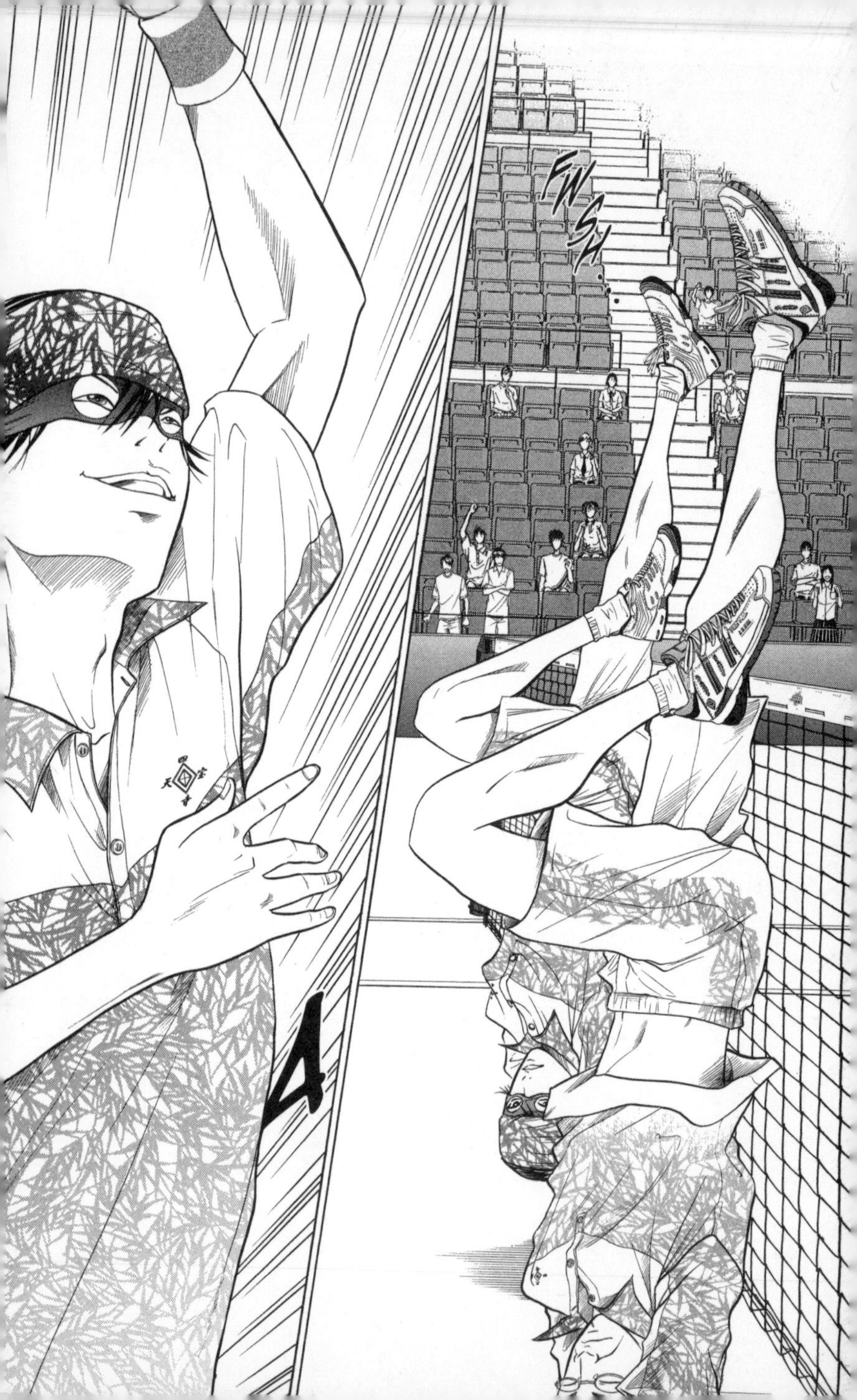
FWSH...

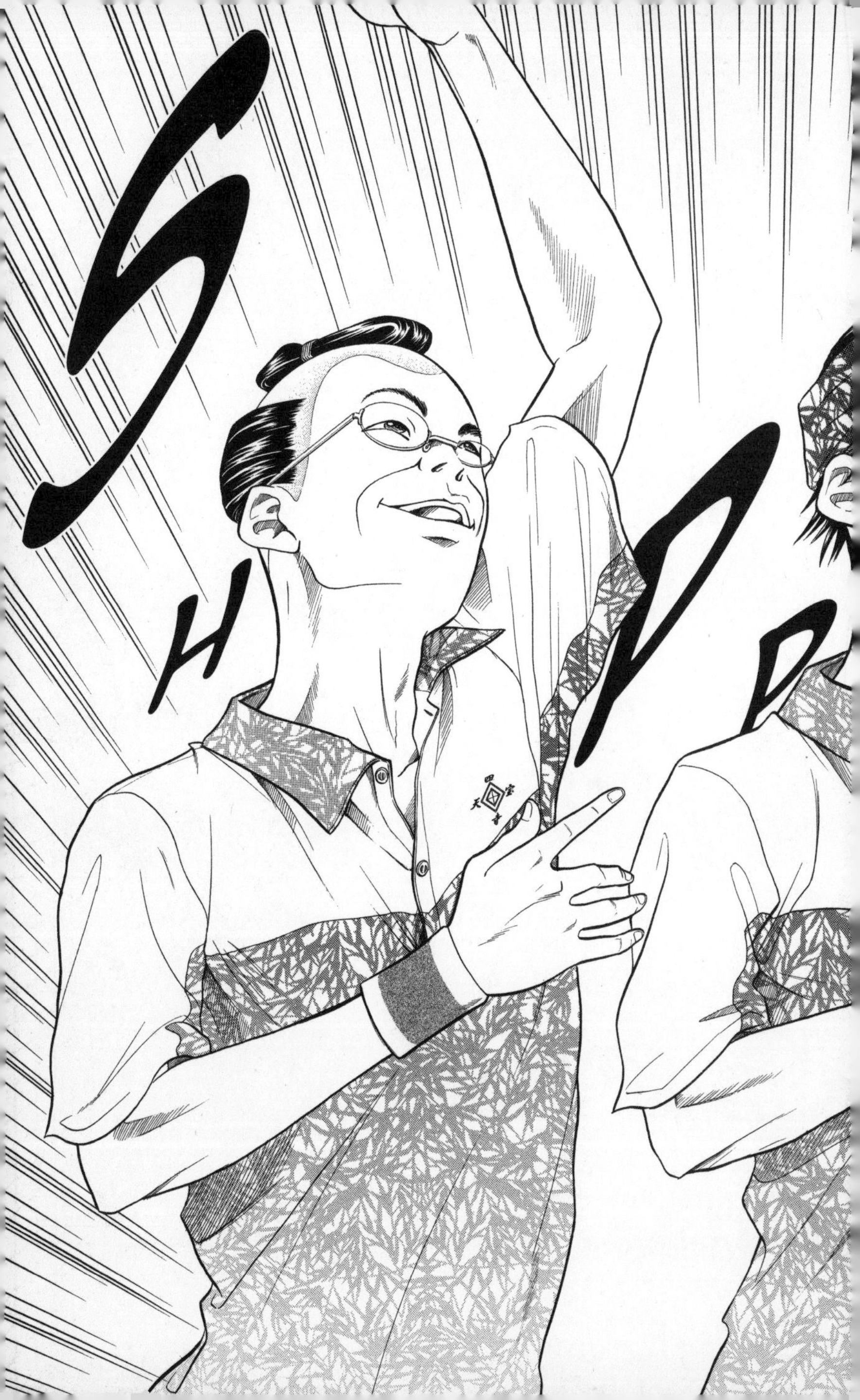

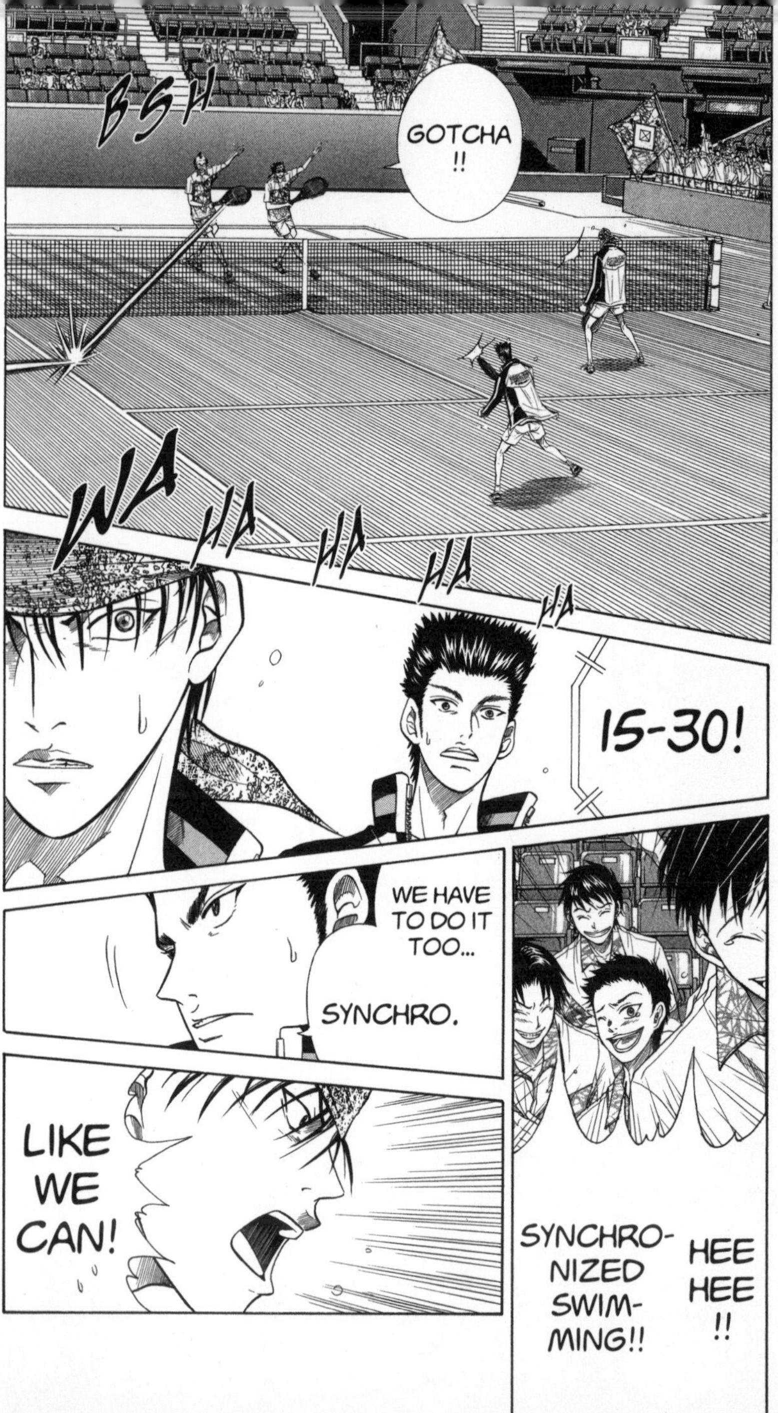
GOTCHA!!
BSH
WA HA HA HA HA
15-30!
HEE HEE!!
SYNCHRO-NIZED SWIM-MING!!
WE HAVE TO DO IT TOO...
SYNCHRO.
LIKE WE CAN!

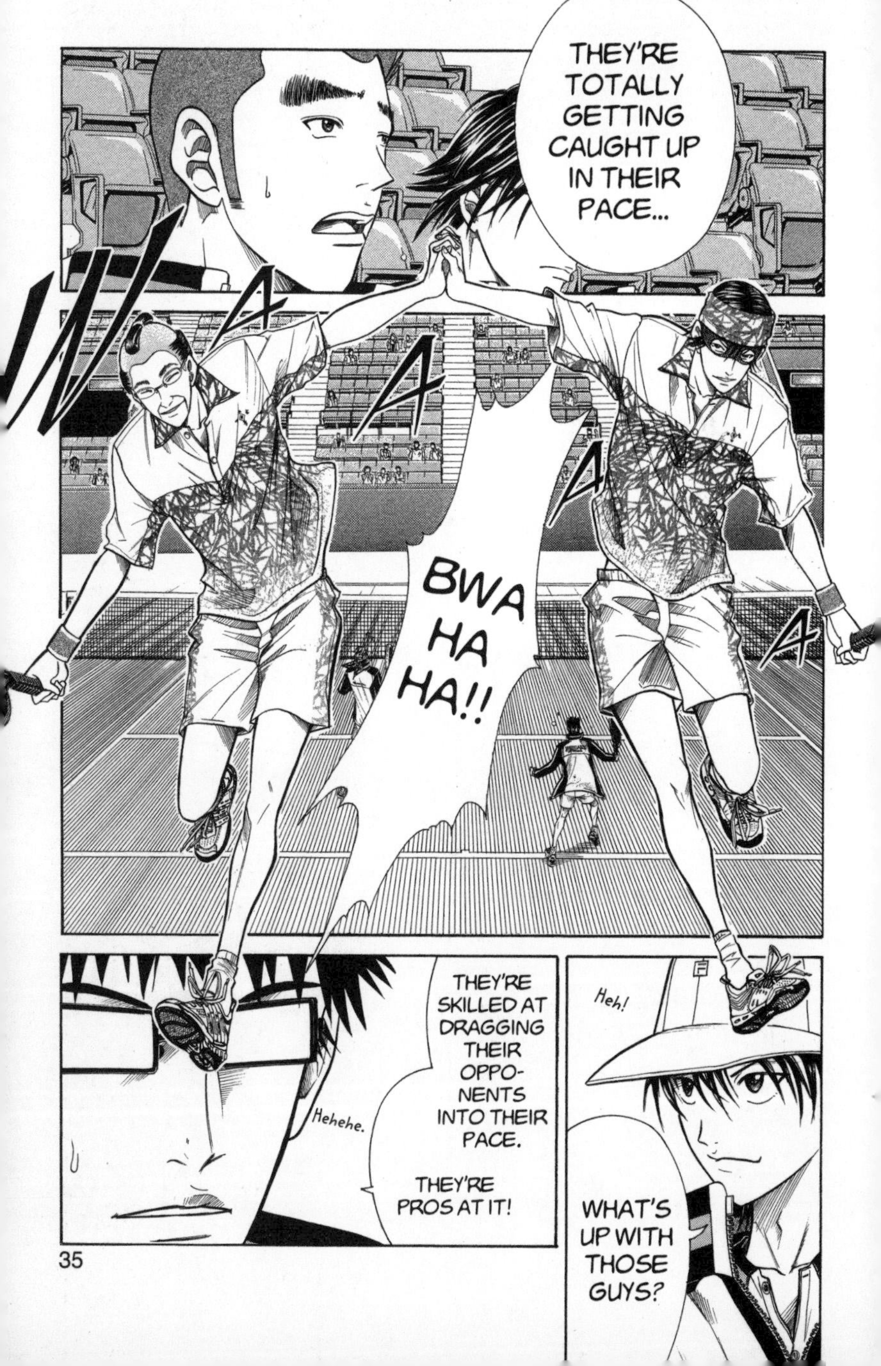
THEY'RE TOTALLY GETTING CAUGHT UP IN THEIR PACE...
WAAAAA
BWA HA HA!!
Heh!
WHAT'S UP WITH THOSE GUYS?
THEY'RE SKILLED AT DRAGGING THEIR OPPO-NENTS INTO THEIR PACE.
THEY'RE PROS AT IT!
Hehehe.

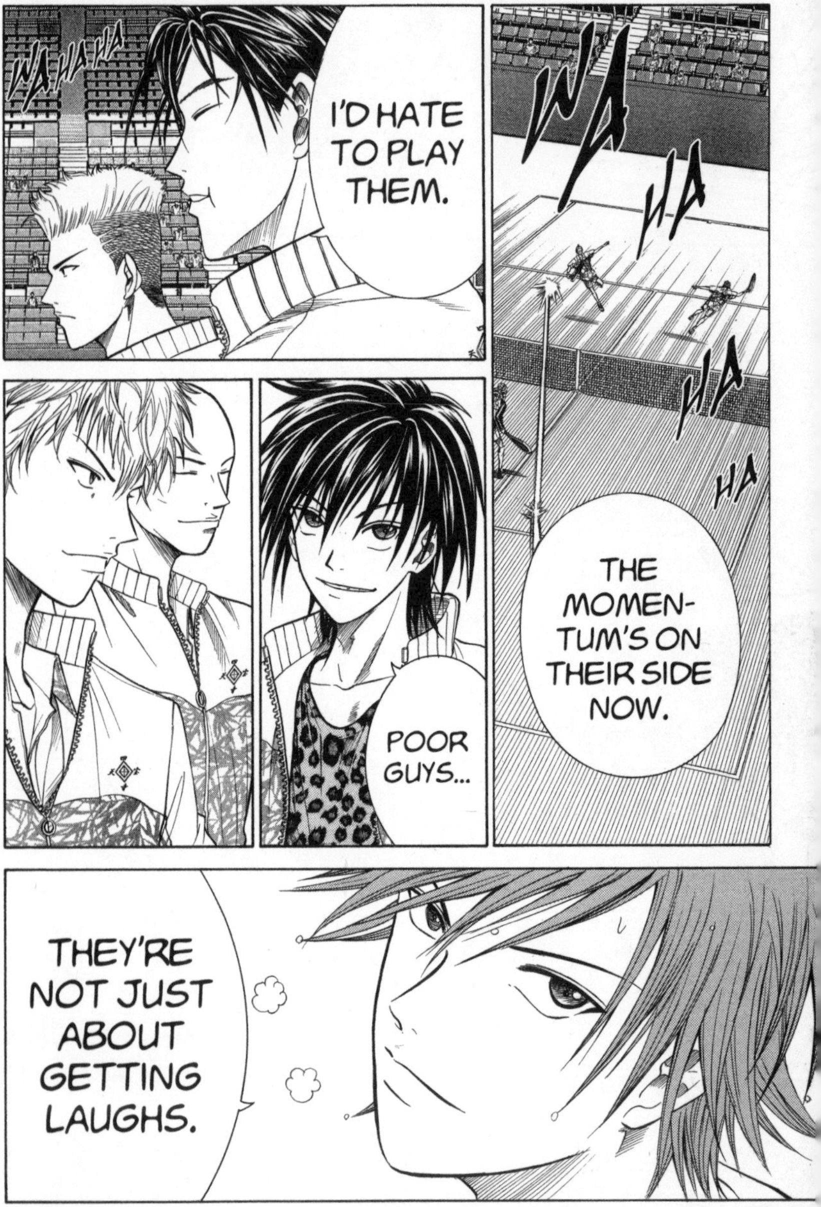
WA
HA
HA
HA
THE MOMEN-TUM'S ON THEIR SIDE NOW.
I'D HATE TO PLAY THEM.
WA HA HA HA
POOR GUYS...
THEY'RE NOT JUST ABOUT GETTING LAUGHS.

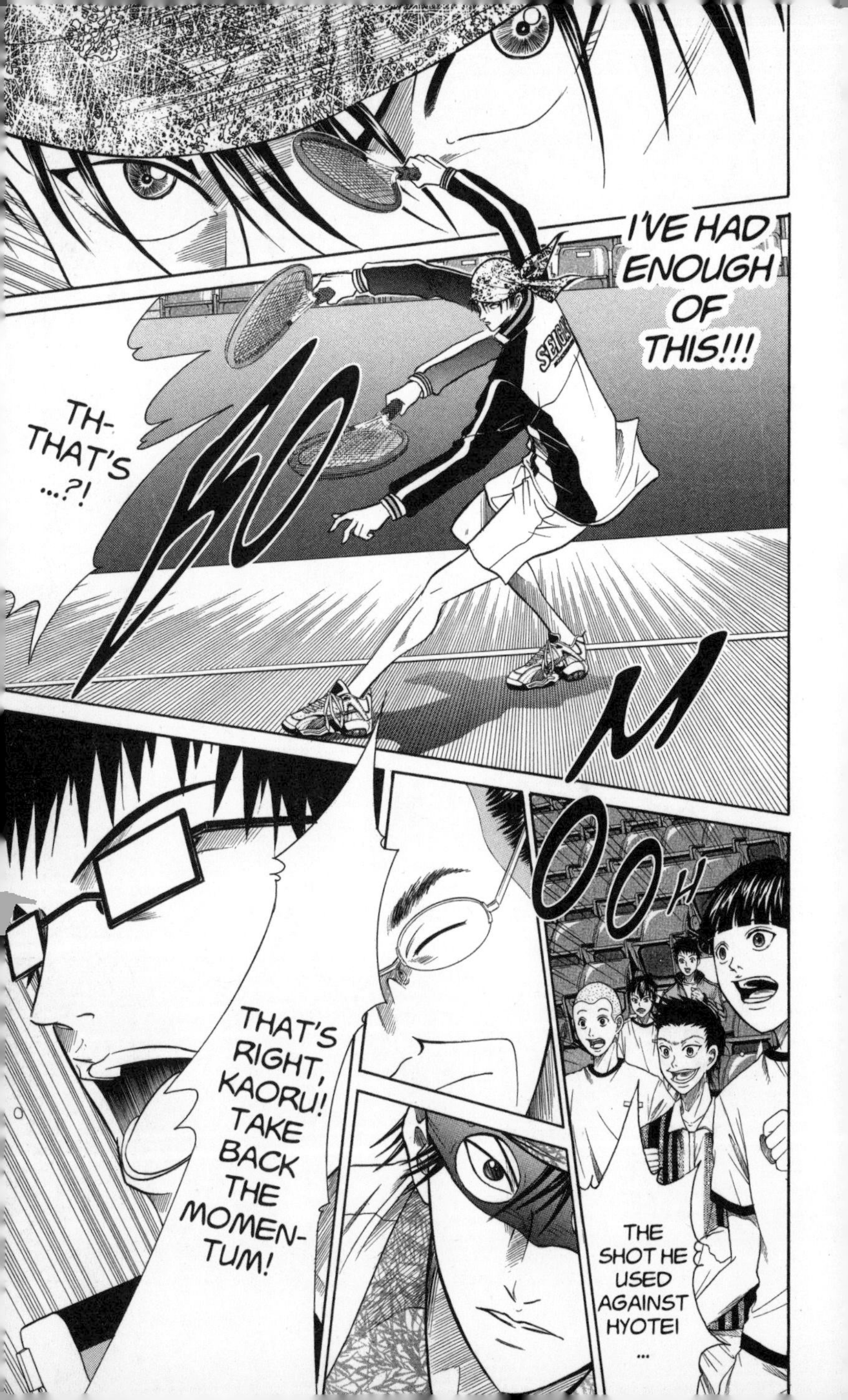
I'VE HAD ENOUGH OF THIS!!!
TH- THAT'S ...?!
ZO
M
OOH
THE SHOT HE USED AGAINST HYOTEI ...
THAT'S RIGHT, KAORU! TAKE BACK THE MOMENTUM!

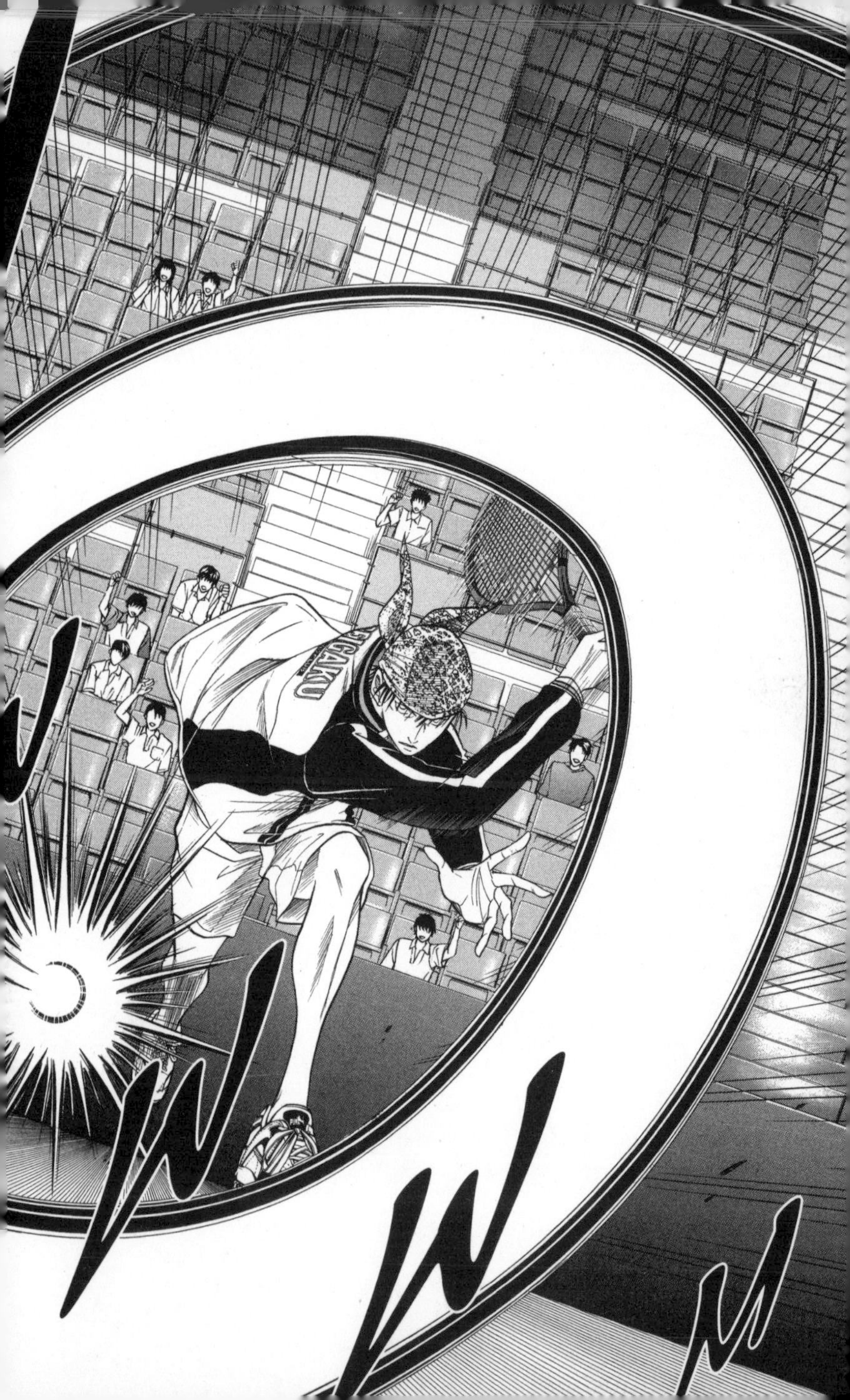

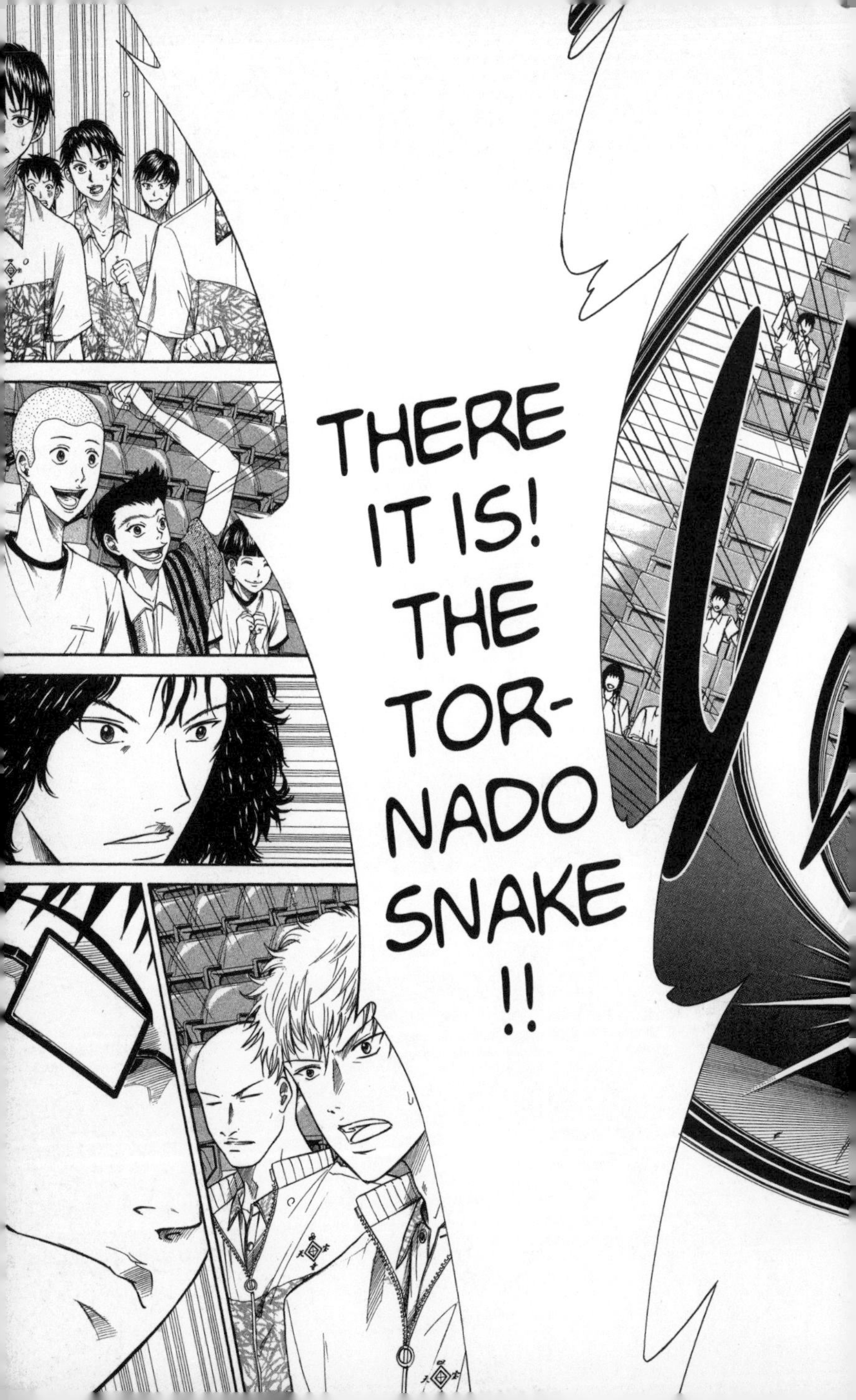
THERE IT IS! THE TOR-NADO SNAKE !!

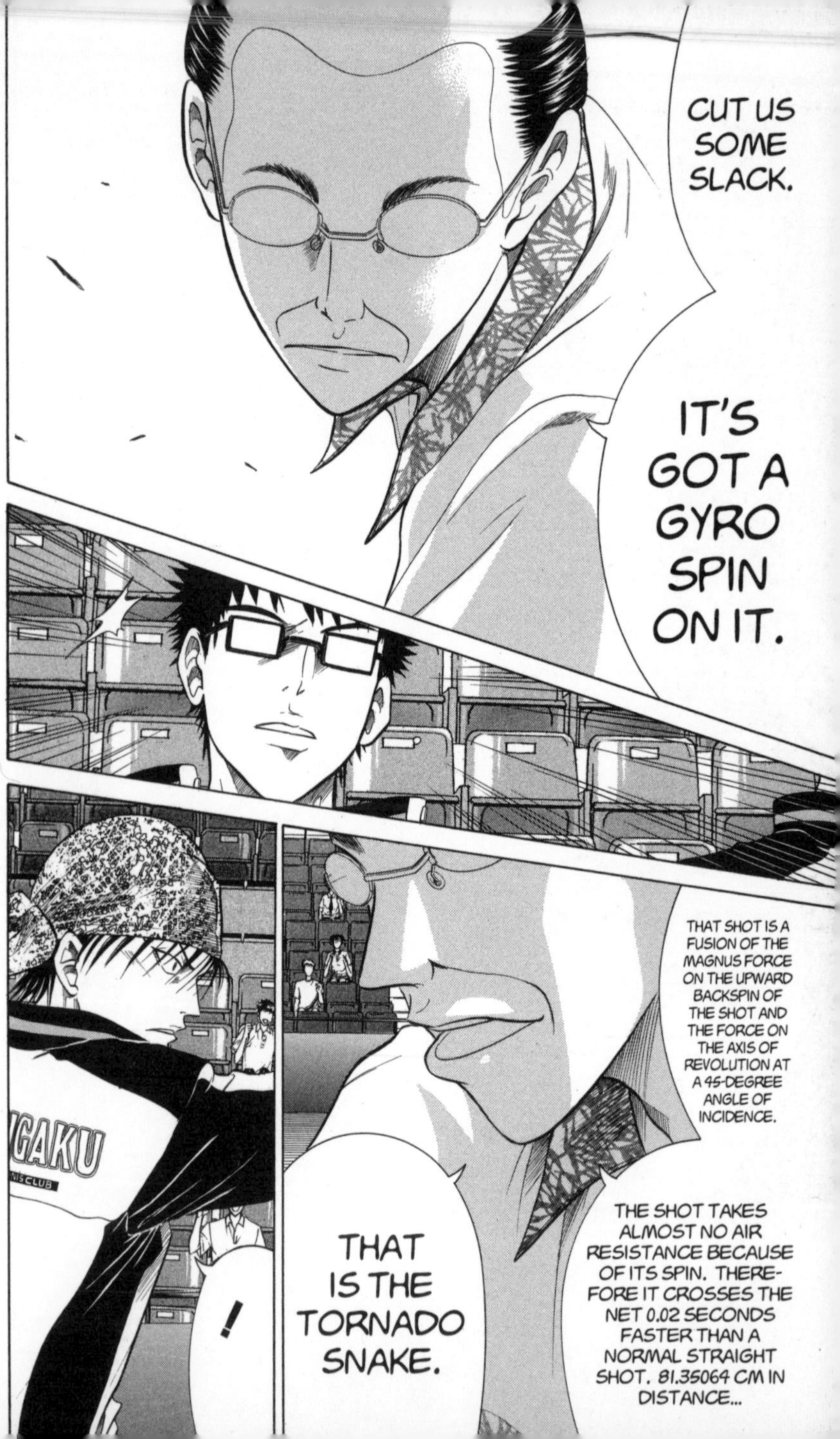
CUT US SOME SLACK.
IT'S GOT A GYRO SPIN ON IT.
THAT SHOT IS A FUSION OF THE MAGNUS FORCE ON THE UPWARD BACKSPIN OF THE SHOT AND THE FORCE ON THE AXIS OF REVOLUTION AT A 45-DEGREE ANGLE OF INCIDENCE.
THE SHOT TAKES ALMOST NO AIR RESISTANCE BECAUSE OF ITS SPIN. THERE-FORE IT CROSSES THE NET 0.02 SECONDS FASTER THAN A NORMAL STRAIGHT SHOT. 81.35064 CM IN DISTANCE...
THAT IS THE TORNADO SNAKE.
!

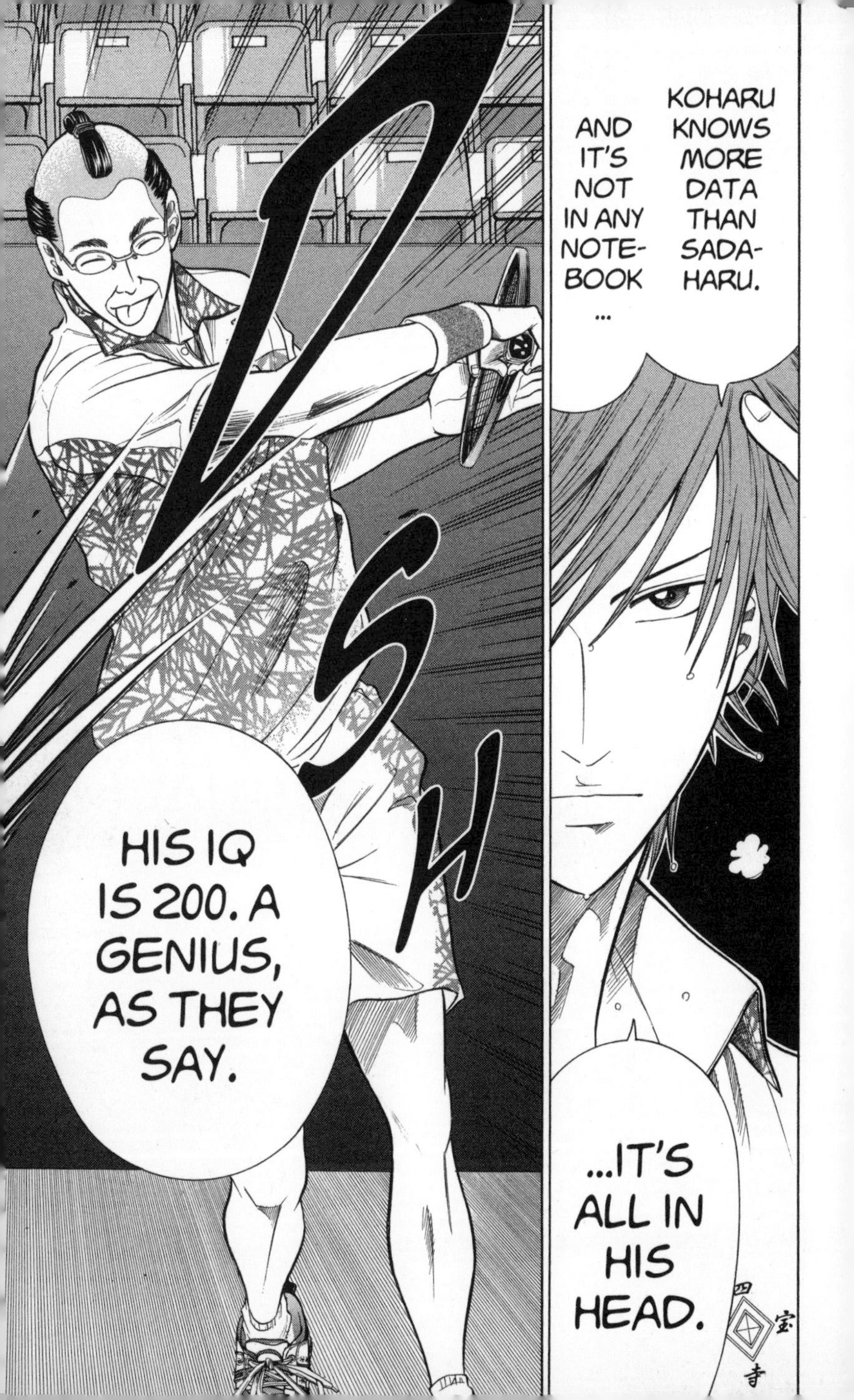
KOHARU KNOWS MORE DATA THAN SADAHARU.
AND IT'S NOT IN ANY NOTEBOOK ...
...IT'S ALL IN HIS HEAD.
HIS IQ IS 200. A GENIUS, AS THEY SAY.

テニスの王子様

THE PRINCE OF TENNIS

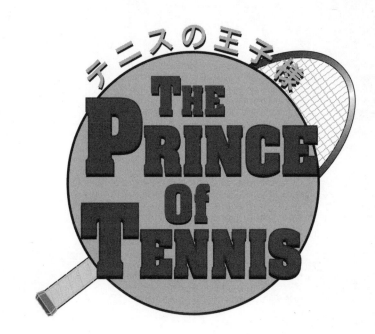

5th Match No. 1 Singles	4th Match No. 1 Doubles		3rd Match No. 2 Singles	2nd Match No. 2 Doubles		1st Match No. 3 Singles
Kintaro Toyama (7th Grade) Blood Type: B	Kenya Oshitari (9th Grade) Blood Type: B	Hikaru Zaizen (8th Grade) Blood Type: A	Gin Ishida (9th Grade) Blood Type: O	Yuji Hitoji (9th Grade) Blood Type: B	Koharu Konjiki (9th Grade) Blood Type: B	Kuranosuke Shiraishi (9th Grade) Blood Type: B

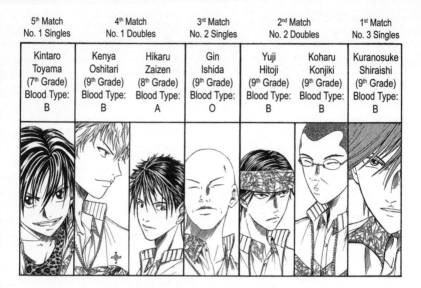

GENIUS 324: POKER FACE!

Ryoma Echizen (7th Grade) Blood Type: O	Kunimitsu Tezuka (9th Grade) Blood Type: O	Sadaharu Inui (9th Grade) Blood Type: AB	Takashi Kawamura (9th Grade) Blood Type: A	Kaoru Kaido (8th Grade) Blood Type: B	Takeshi Momoshiro (8th Grade) Blood Type: O	Shusuke Fuji (9th Grade) Blood Type: B

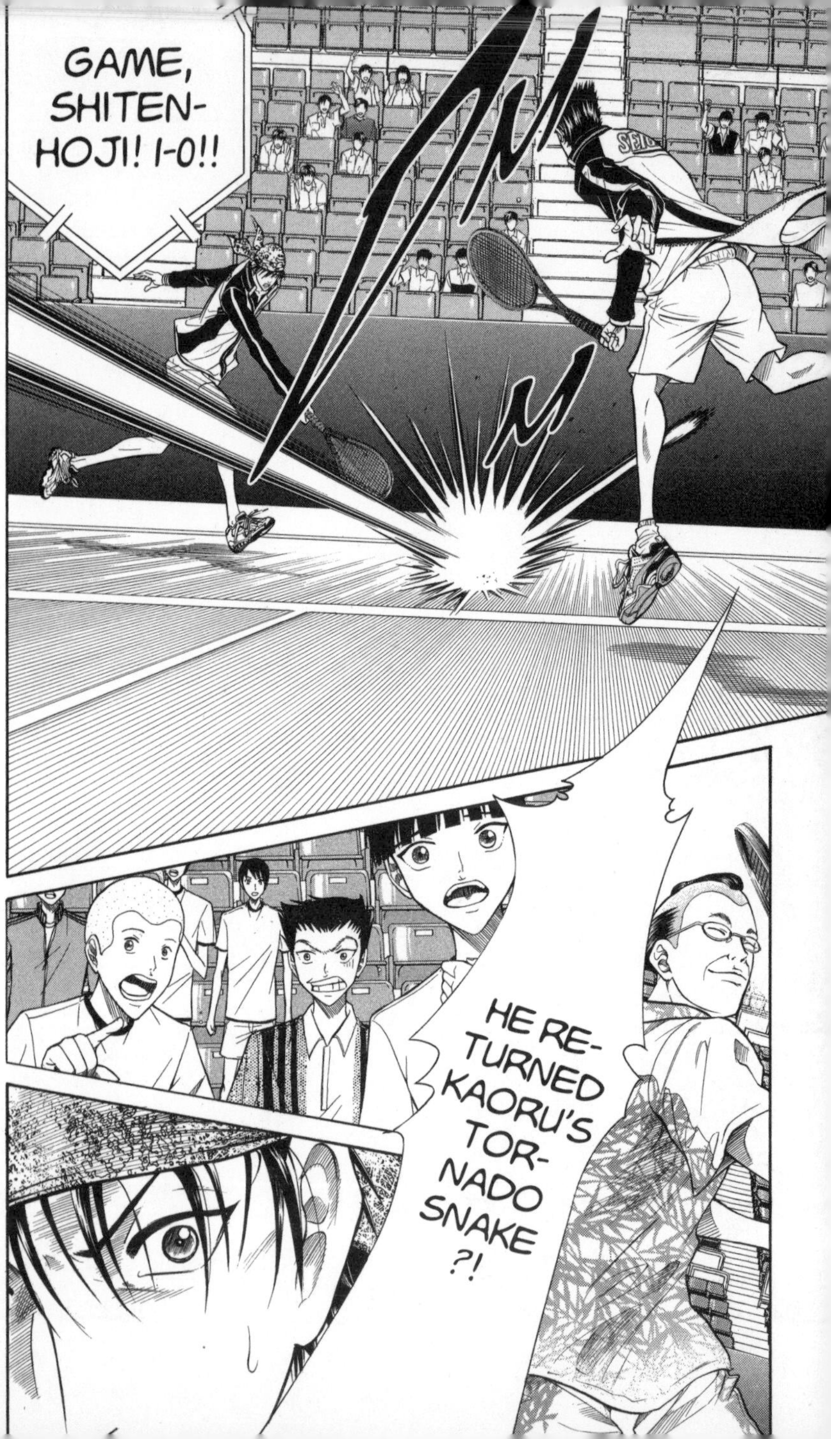
GAME, SHITEN-HOJI! 1-0!!
HE RE-TURNED KAORU'S TOR-NADO SNAKE ?!

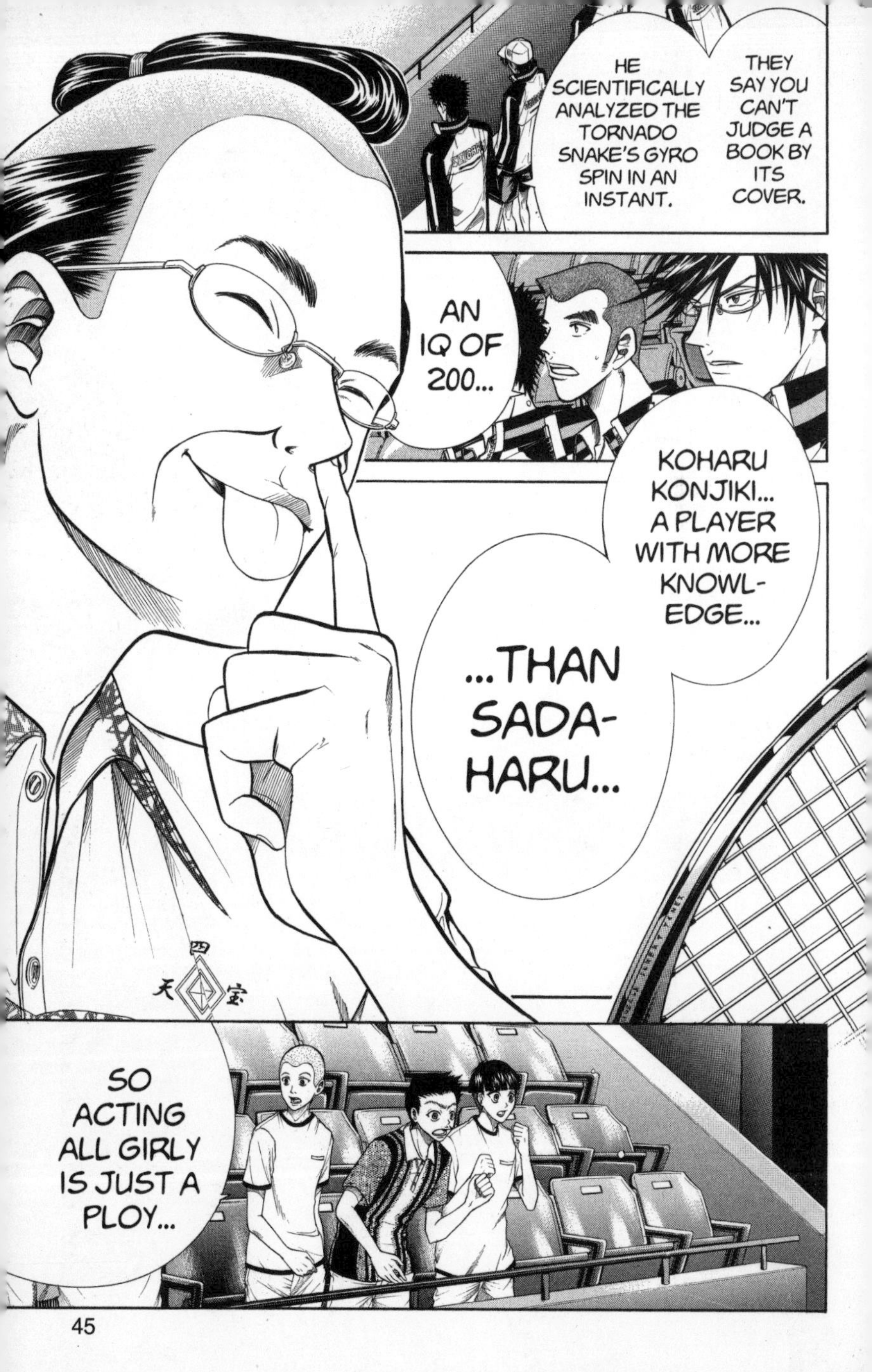
THEY SAY YOU CAN'T JUDGE A BOOK BY ITS COVER.
HE SCIENTIFICALLY ANALYZED THE TORNADO SNAKE'S GYRO SPIN IN AN INSTANT.
AN IQ OF 200...
KOHARU KONJIKI... A PLAYER WITH MORE KNOWL-EDGE...
...THAN SADA-HARU...
SO ACTING ALL GIRLY IS JUST A PLOY...

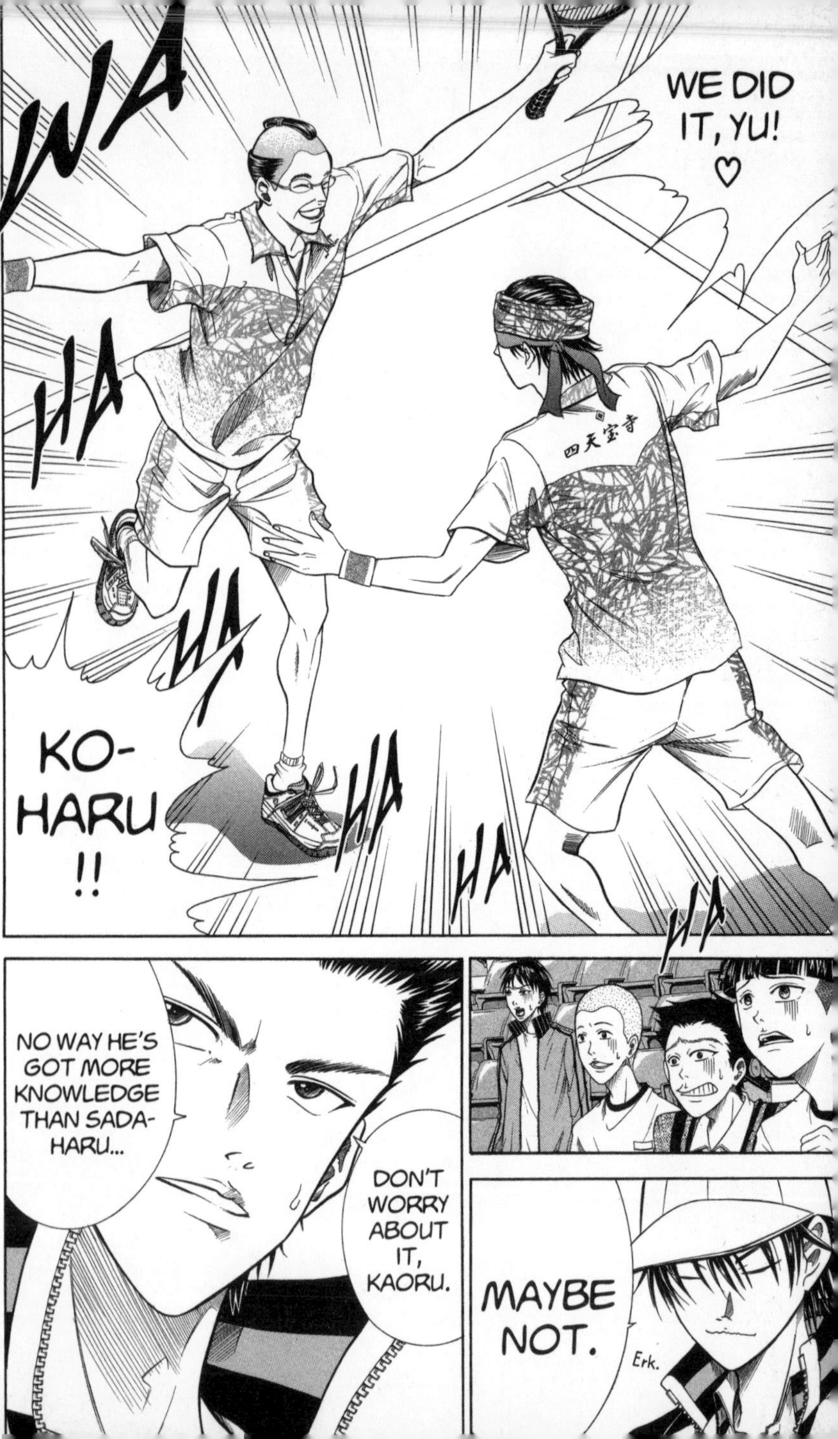
WE DID IT, YU! ♡
WA HA HA HA HA HA
四天宝寺
KO-HARU!!
MAYBE NOT.
Erk.
NO WAY HE'S GOT MORE KNOWLEDGE THAN SADA-HARU...
DON'T WORRY ABOUT IT, KAORU.

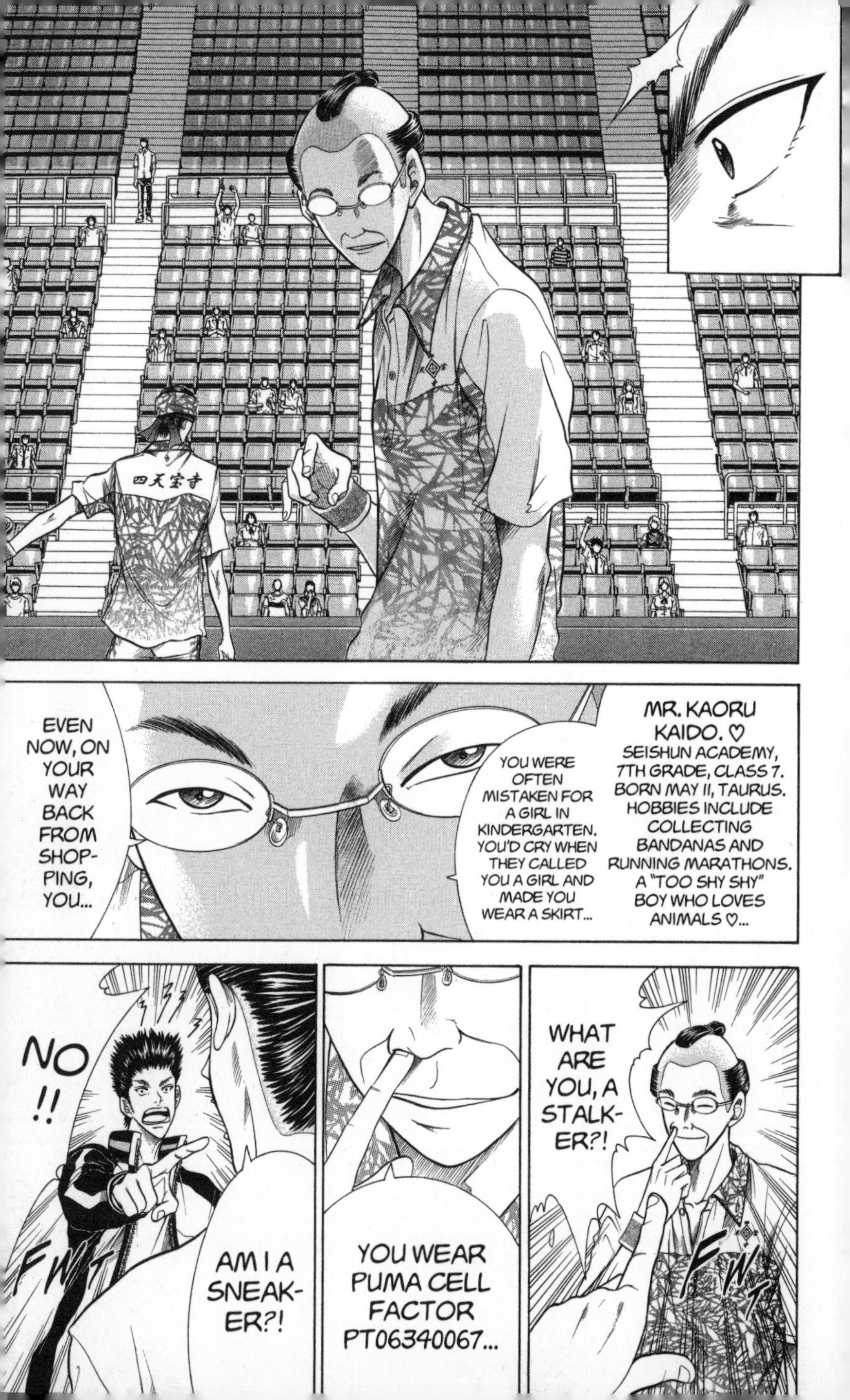
四天宝寺
MR. KAORU KAIDO. ♡ SEISHUN ACADEMY, 7TH GRADE, CLASS 7. BORN MAY 11, TAURUS. HOBBIES INCLUDE COLLECTING BANDANAS AND RUNNING MARATHONS. A "TOO SHY SHY" BOY WHO LOVES ANIMALS ♡...
YOU WERE OFTEN MISTAKEN FOR A GIRL IN KINDERGARTEN. YOU'D CRY WHEN THEY CALLED YOU A GIRL AND MADE YOU WEAR A SKIRT...
EVEN NOW, ON YOUR WAY BACK FROM SHOP-PING, YOU...
WHAT ARE YOU, A STALK-ER?!
FWT
YOU WEAR PUMA CELL FACTOR PT06340067...
NO!!
AM I A SNEAK-ER?!
FWT

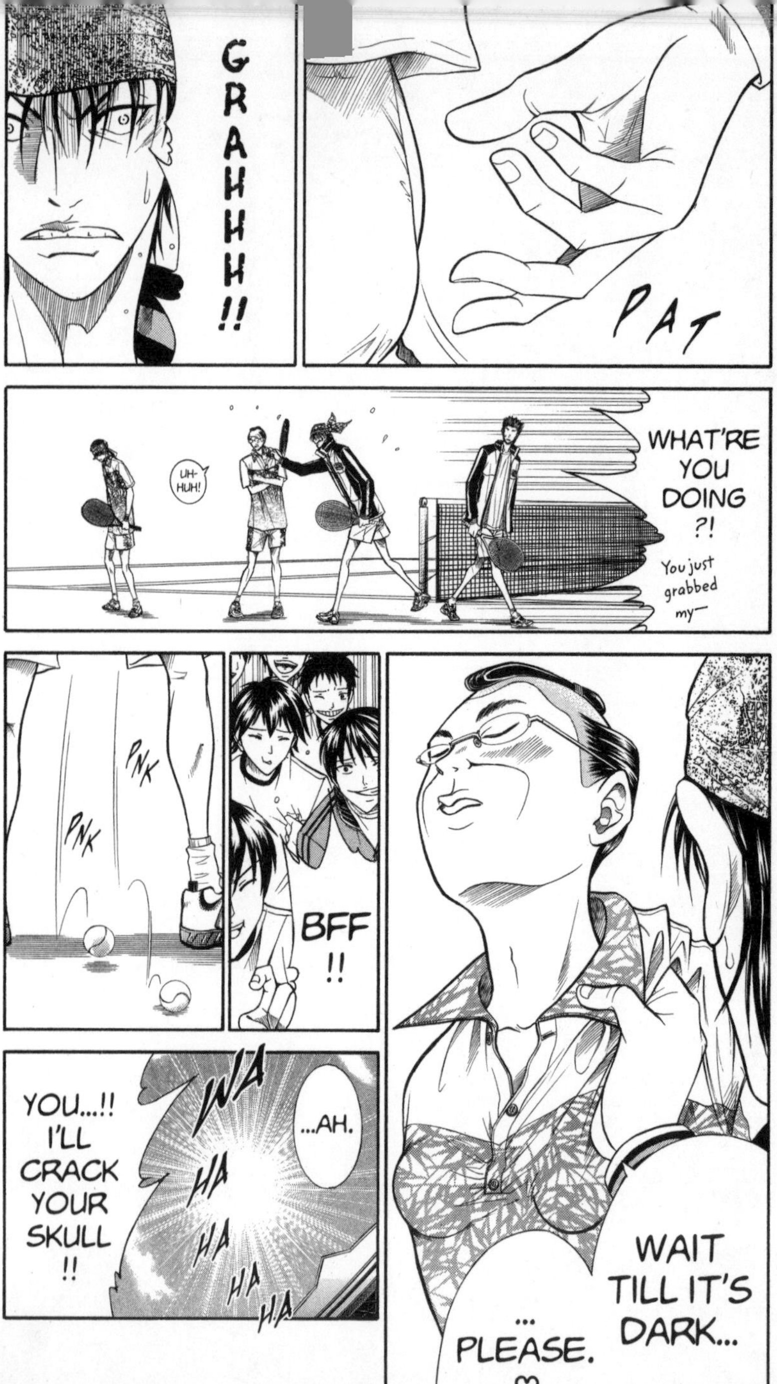
PAT
GRAHHHH!!
WHAT'RE YOU DOING?!
You just grabbed my—
UH-HUH!
WAIT TILL IT'S DARK...
... PLEASE. ♡
BFF!!
PNK
PNK
...AH.
WA HA HA HA HA
YOU...!! I'LL CRACK YOUR SKULL!!

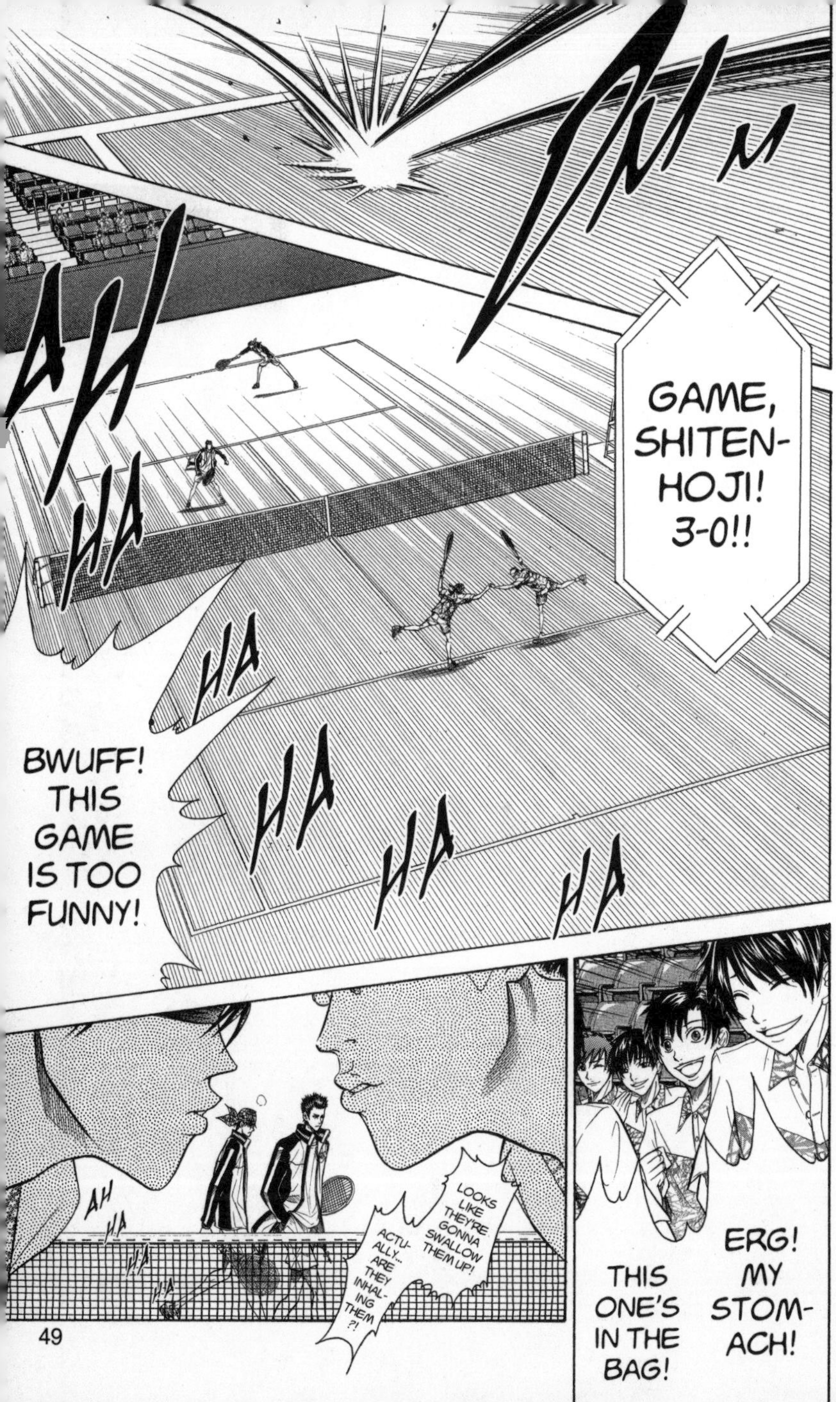
GAME, SHITEN-HOJI! 3-0!!
HA
HA
HA
HA
HA
BWUFF! THIS GAME IS TOO FUNNY!
ERG! MY STOMACH!
THIS ONE'S IN THE BAG!
LOOKS LIKE THEY'RE GONNA SWALLOW THEM UP!
ACTUALLY... ARE THEY INHALING THEM?!
AH HA HA HA

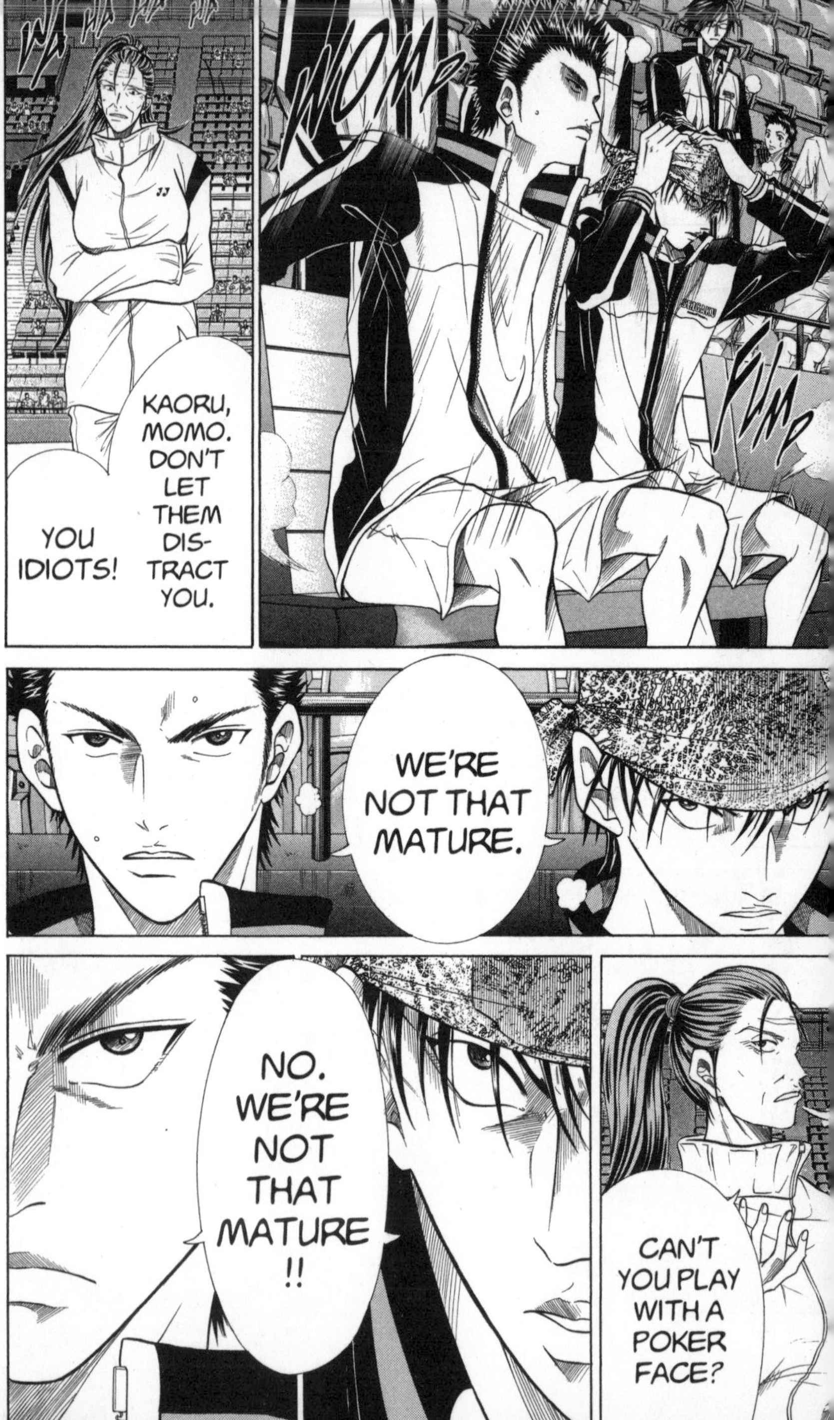
WOMP
FUMP
KAORU, MOMO. DON'T LET THEM DIS-TRACT YOU.
YOU IDIOTS!
WE'RE NOT THAT MATURE.
CAN'T YOU PLAY WITH A POKER FACE?
NO. WE'RE NOT THAT MATURE !!

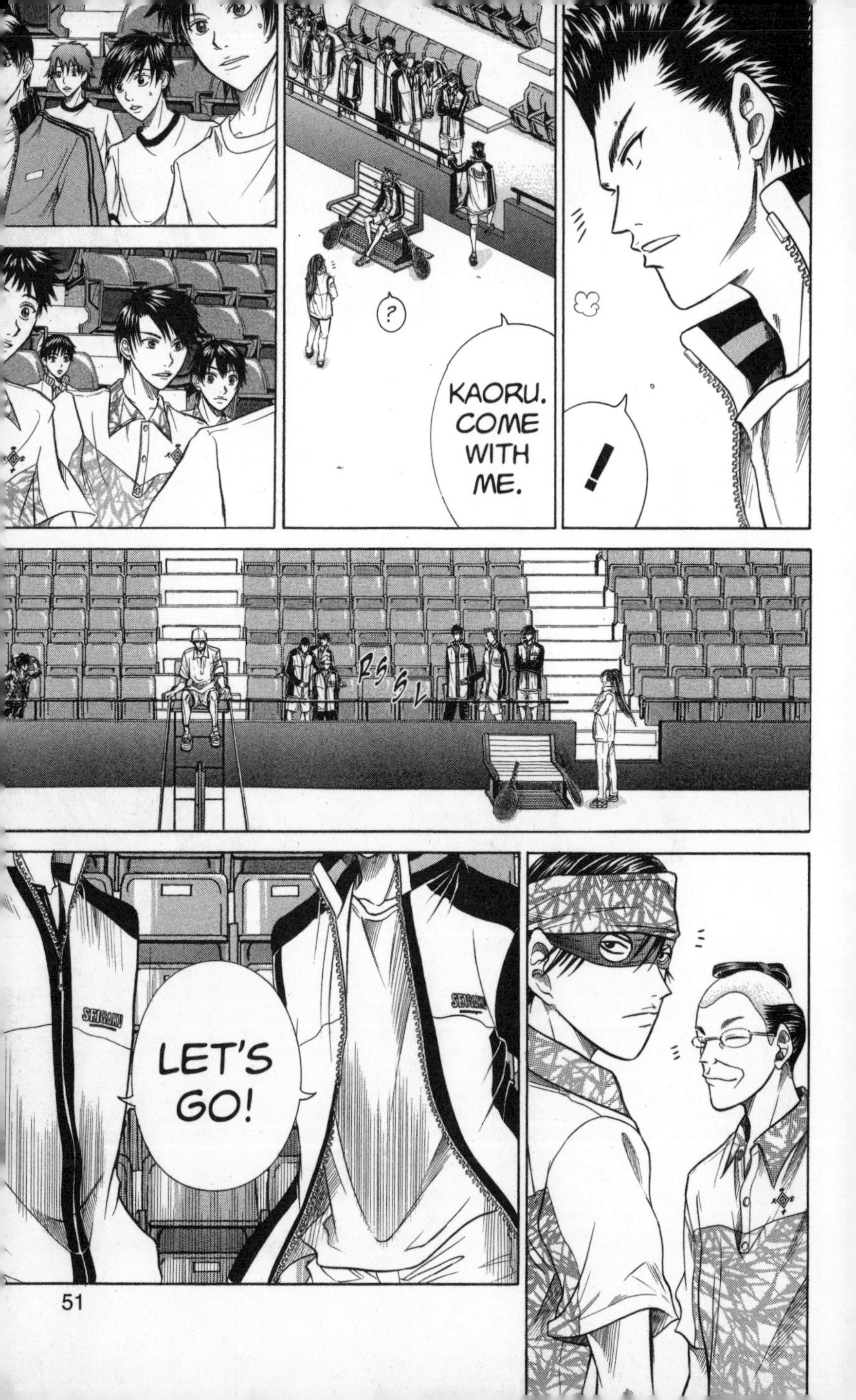
!
KAORU. COME WITH ME.
?
RSSL
LET'S GO!
SEIGAKU
SEIGAKU

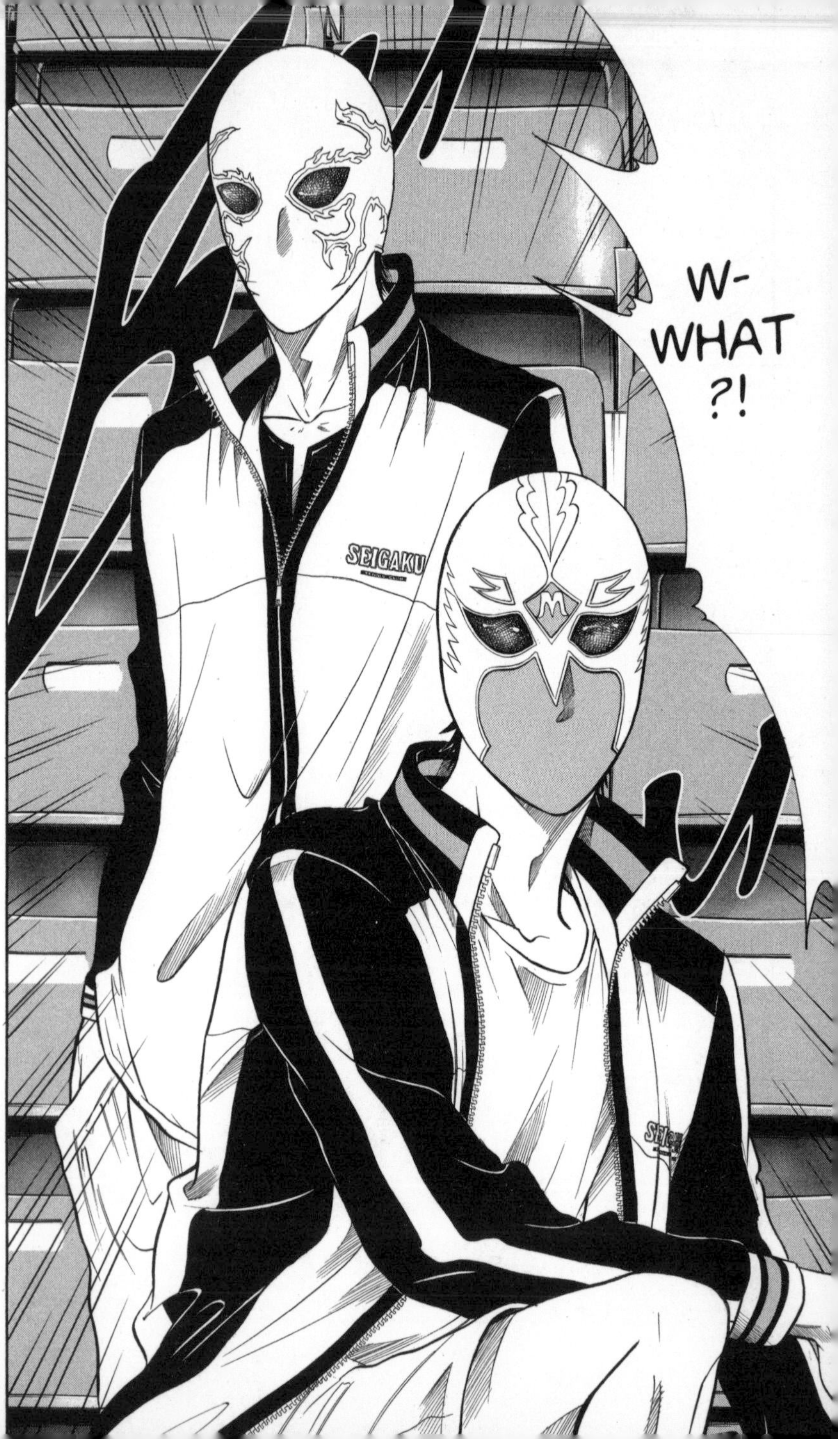
W-
WHAT
?!
SEIGAKU

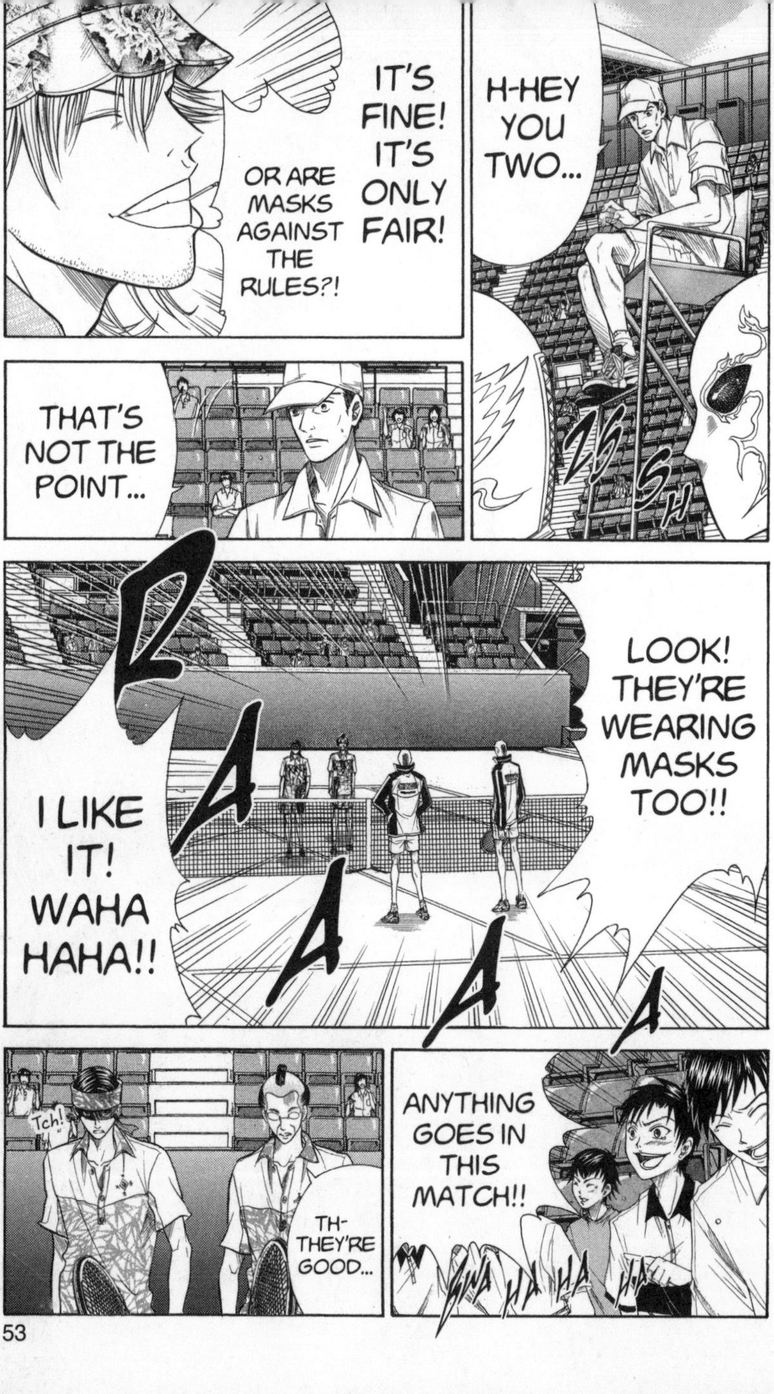
H-HEY YOU TWO...
IT'S FINE! IT'S ONLY FAIR!
OR ARE MASKS AGAINST THE RULES?!
THAT'S NOT THE POINT...
LOOK! THEY'RE WEARING MASKS TOO!!
RAAAAA
I LIKE IT! WAHAHAHA!!
ANYTHING GOES IN THIS MATCH!!
WAHAHAHA
TH-THEY'RE GOOD...
Tch!

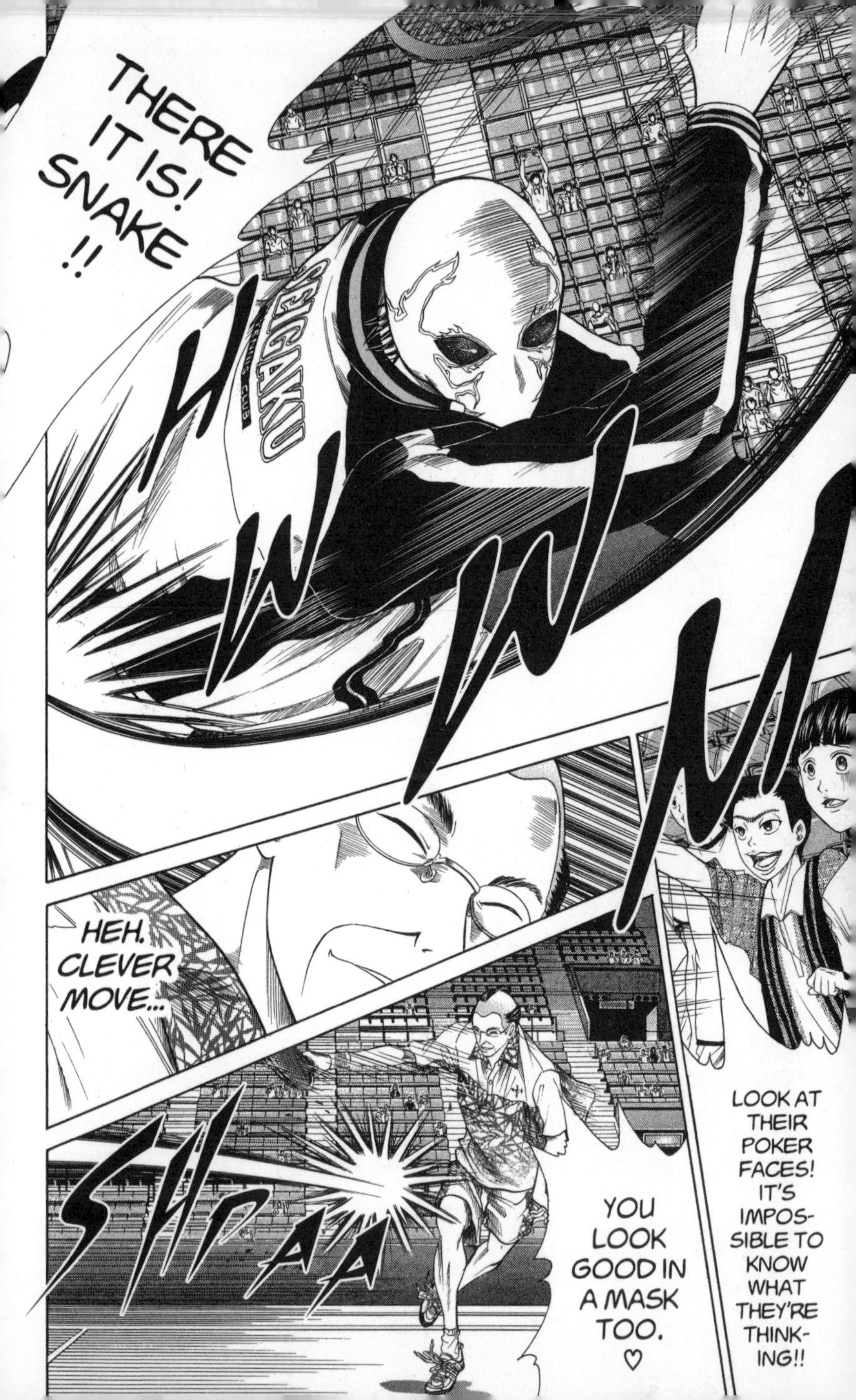
THERE IT IS! SNAKE!!
HWWM
LOOK AT THEIR POKER FACES! IT'S IMPOS-SIBLE TO KNOW WHAT THEY'RE THINK-ING!!
HEH. CLEVER MOVE...
YOU LOOK GOOD IN A MASK TOO. ♡
SHPAA

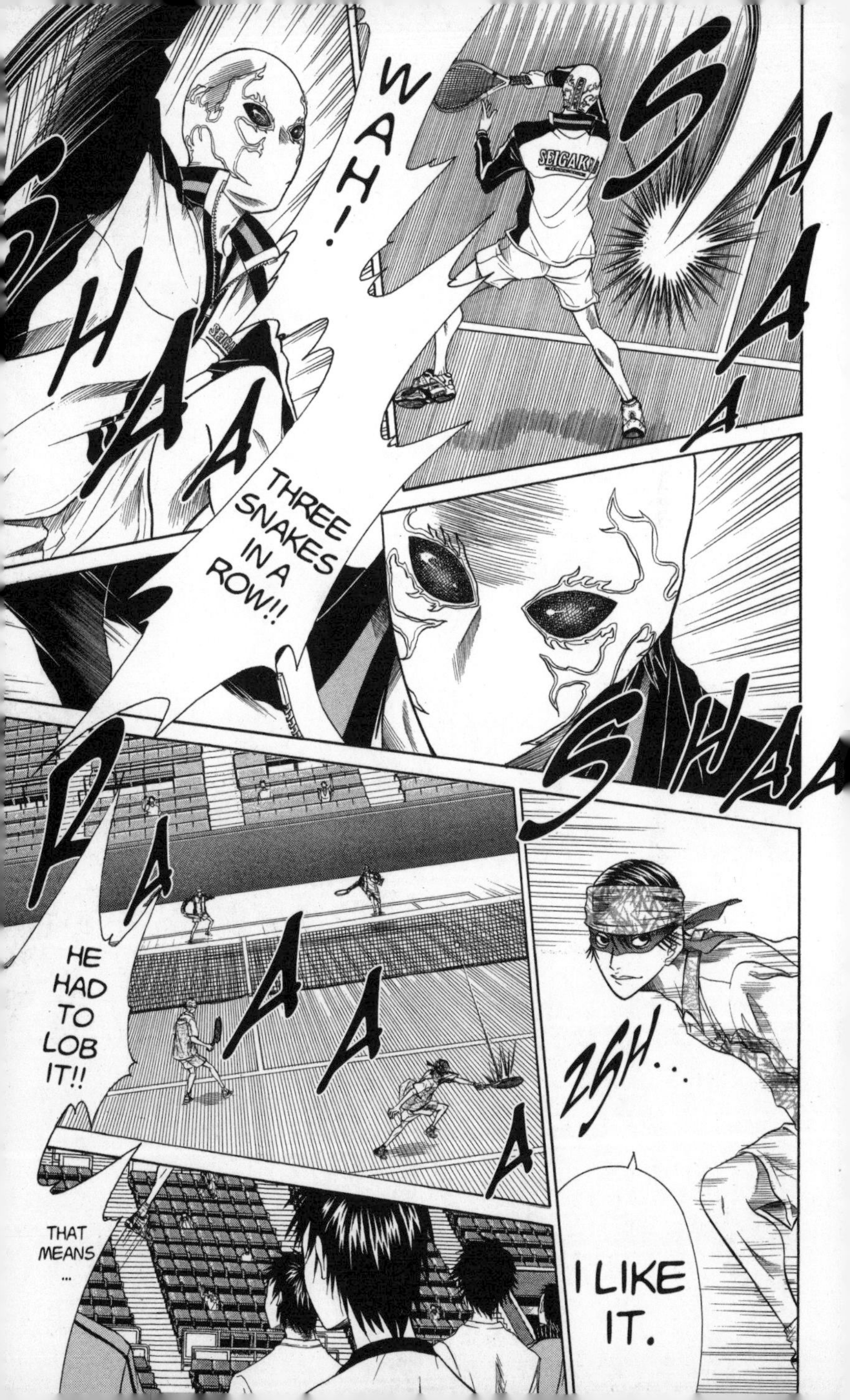
SHAAA
WAH!
SHAAAA
THREE SNAKES IN A ROW!!
SHAA
DAAAAA
ZSH...
I LIKE IT.
HE HAD TO LOB IT!!
THAT MEANS ...

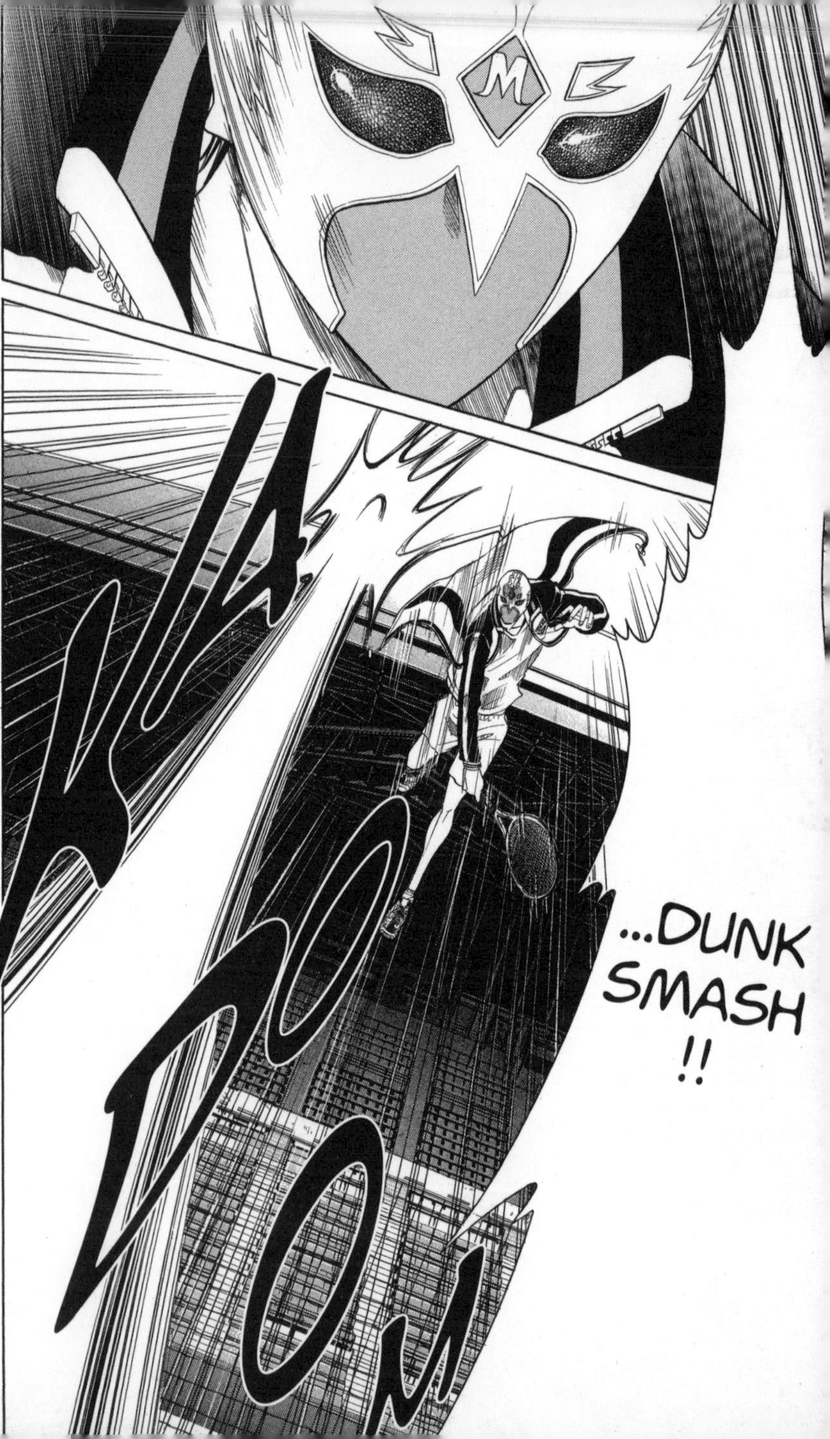
...DUNK SMASH !!

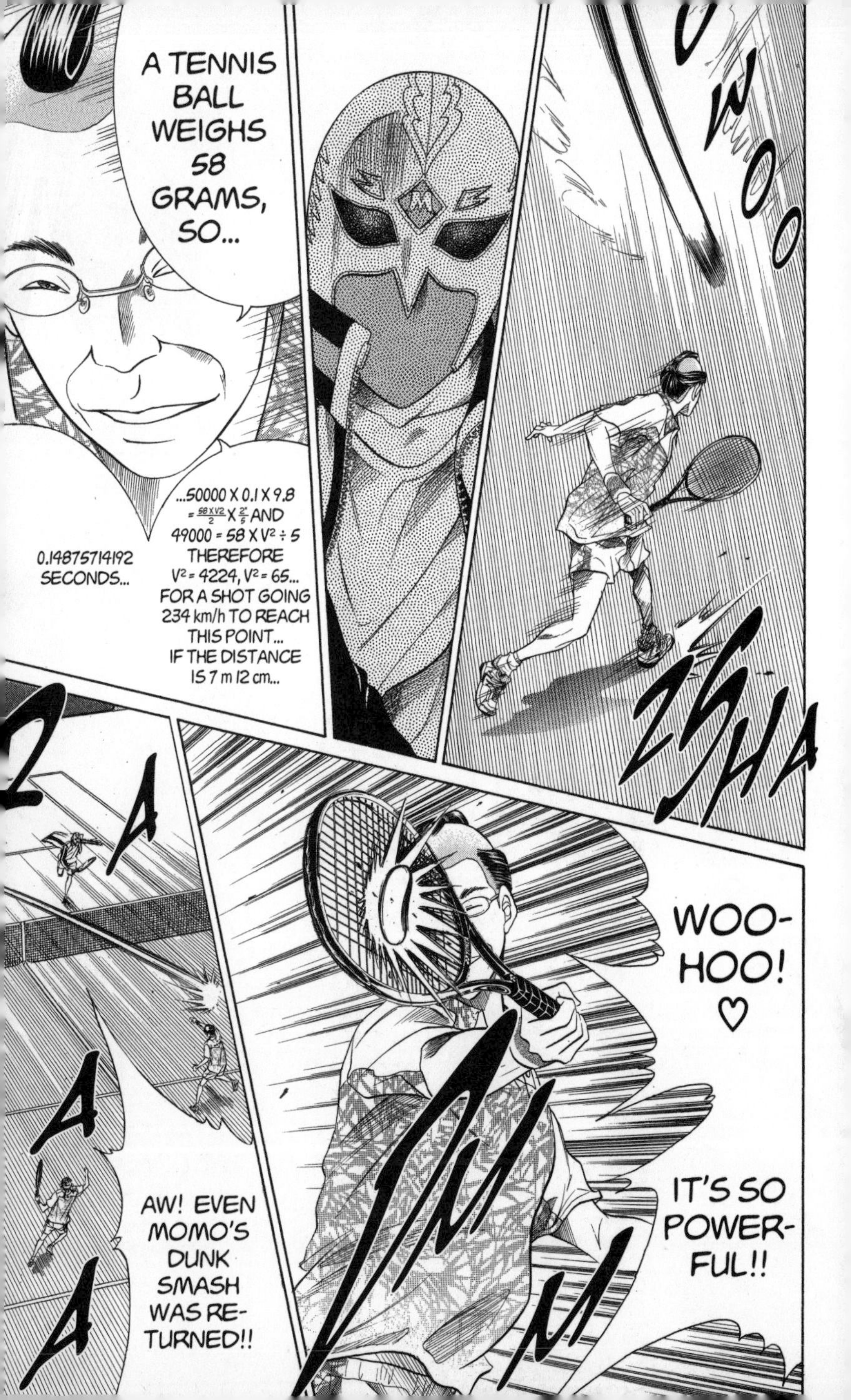
ZSHA
A TENNIS BALL WEIGHS 58 GRAMS, SO...
...50000 X 0.1 X 9.8 = 58XV2/2 X 2²/5 AND 49000 = 58 X V² ÷ 5 THEREFORE V² = 4224, V² = 65... FOR A SHOT GOING 234 km/h TO REACH THIS POINT... IF THE DISTANCE IS 7 m 12 cm...
0.14875714192 SECONDS...
WOO-HOO! ♡
IT'S SO POWER-FUL!!
AW! EVEN MOMO'S DUNK SMASH WAS RE-TURNED!!

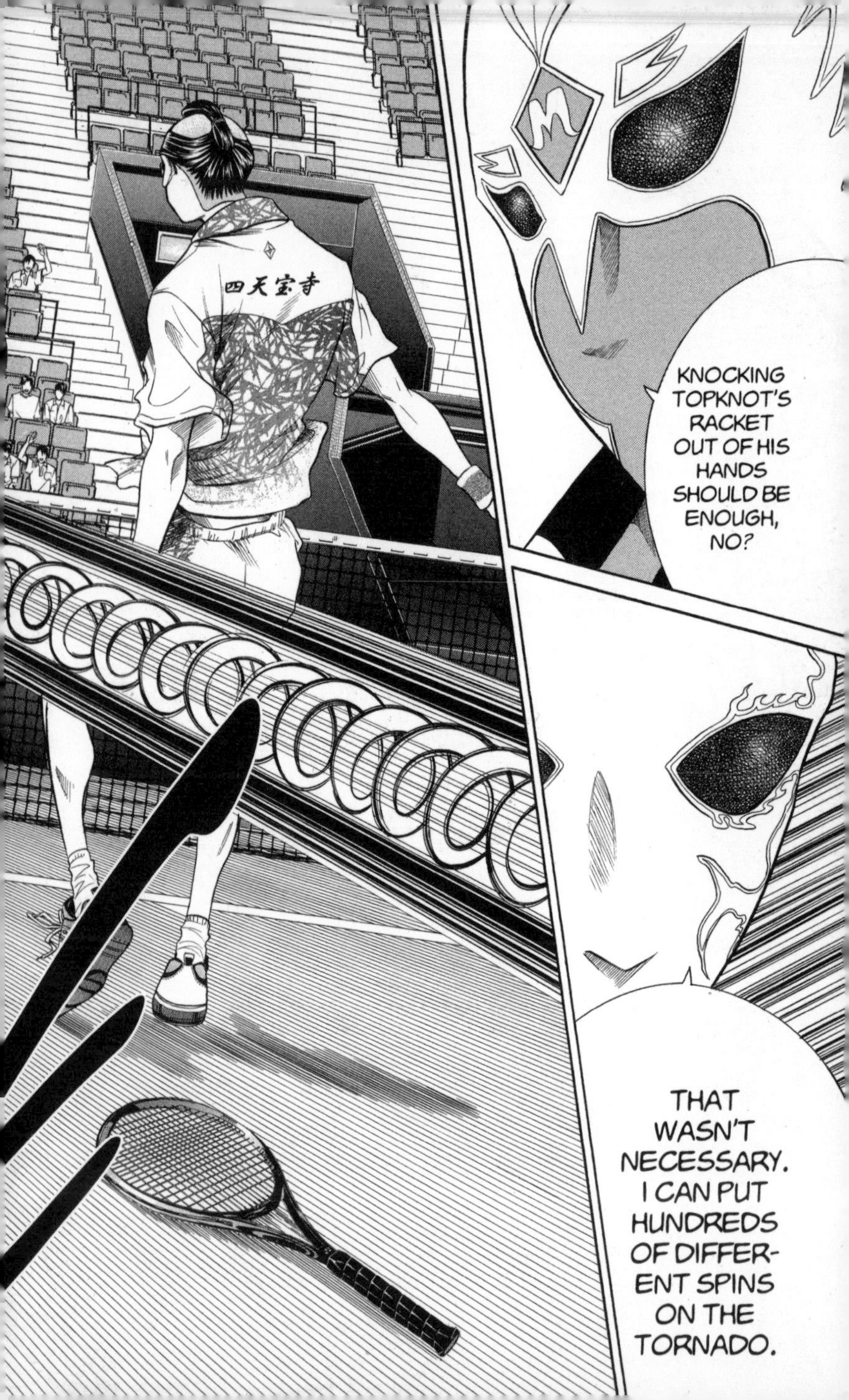

四天宝寺
KNOCKING TOPKNOT'S RACKET OUT OF HIS HANDS SHOULD BE ENOUGH, NO?
THAT WASN'T NECESSARY. I CAN PUT HUNDREDS OF DIFFER-ENT SPINS ON THE TORNADO.

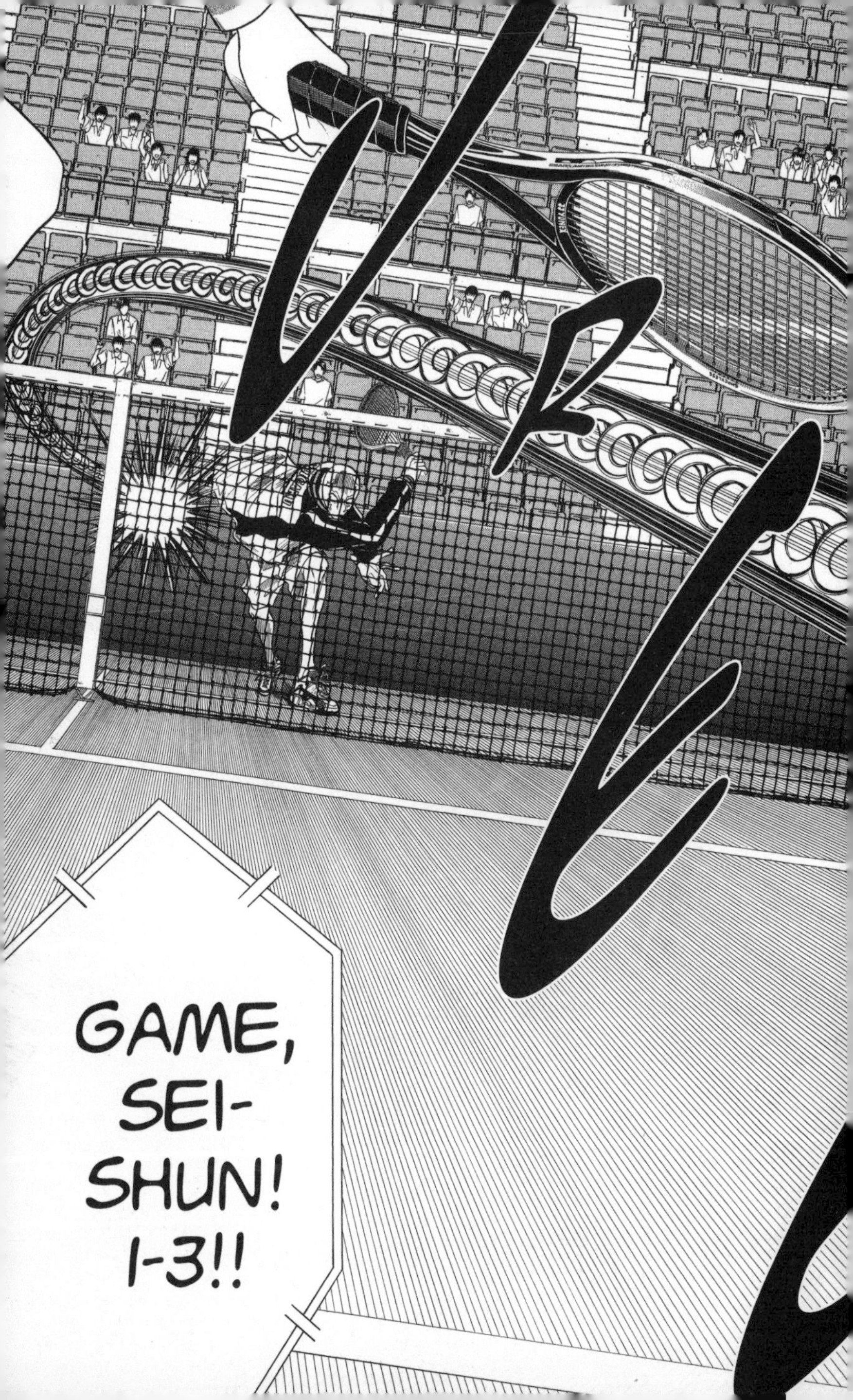
GAME, SEI-SHUN! 1-3!!

テニスの王子様

THE PRINCE OF TENNIS

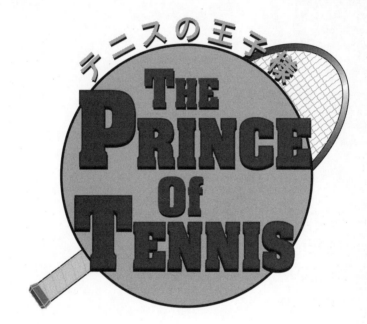

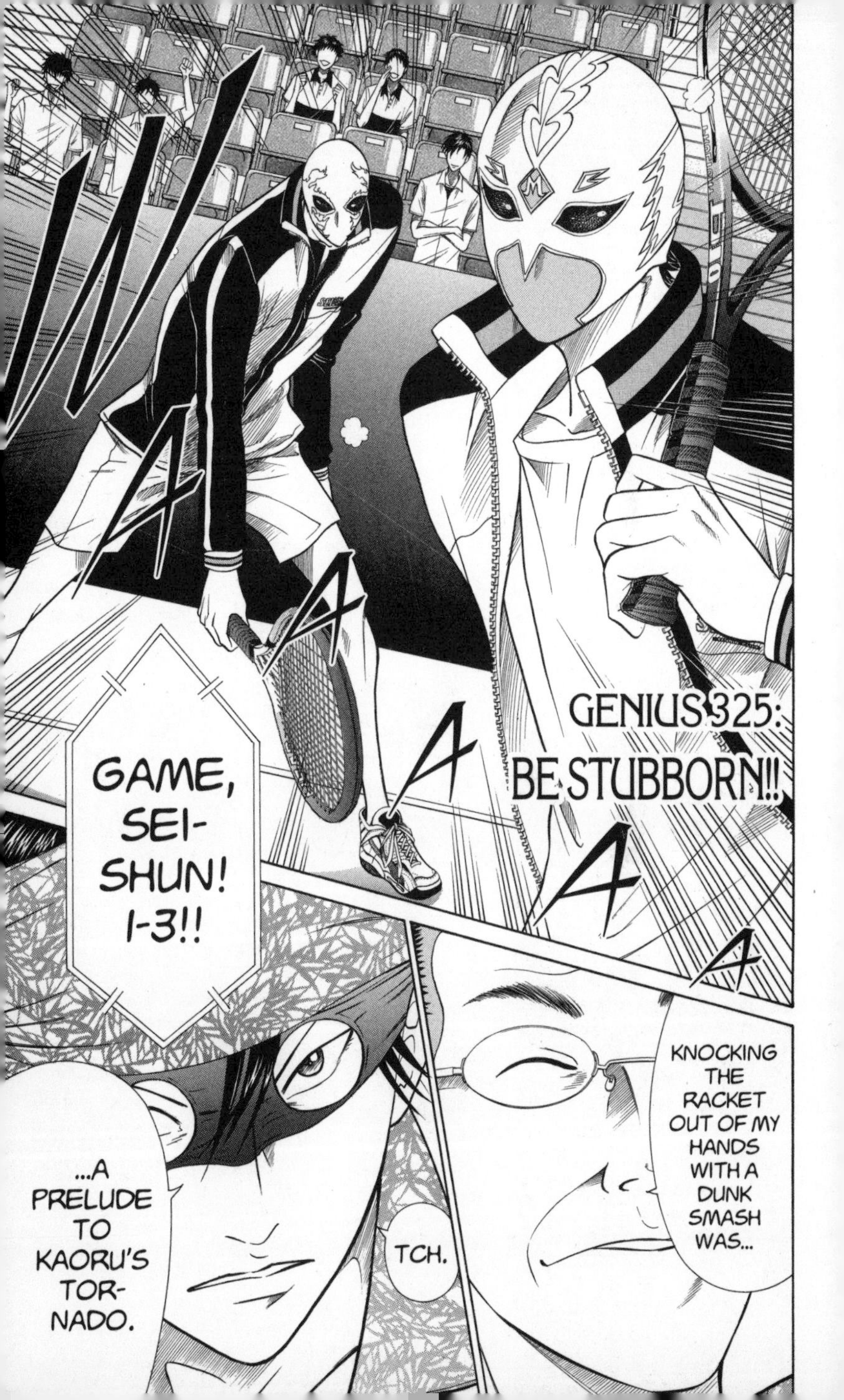
GENIUS 325:
BE STUBBORN!!
WAAAAA
GAME, SEI-SHUN! 1-3!!
KNOCKING THE RACKET OUT OF MY HANDS WITH A DUNK SMASH WAS...
TCH.
...A PRELUDE TO KAORU'S TOR-NADO.

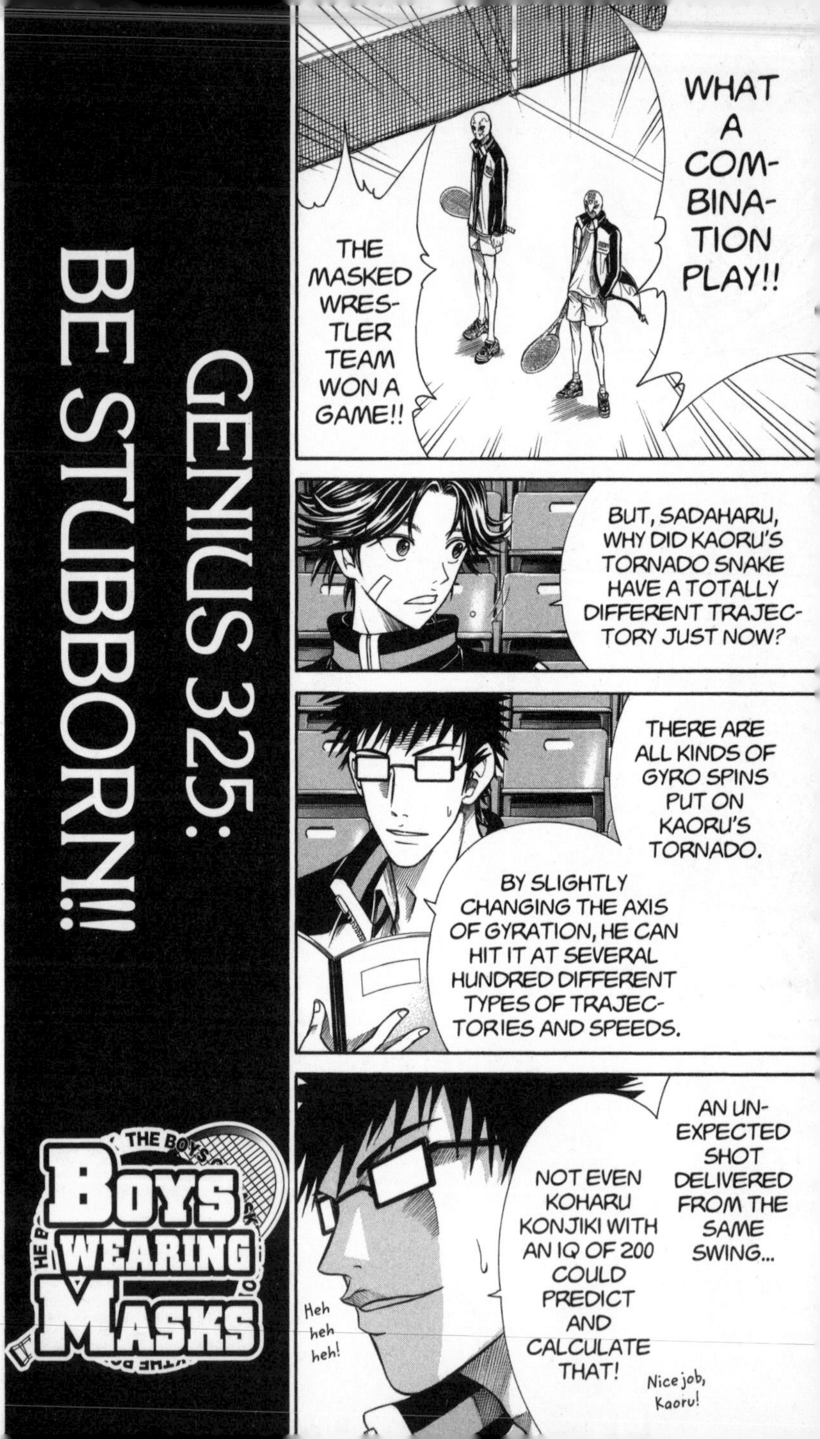
WHAT A COMBINATION PLAY!!
THE MASKED WRESTLER TEAM WON A GAME!!
BUT, SADAHARU, WHY DID KAORU'S TORNADO SNAKE HAVE A TOTALLY DIFFERENT TRAJECTORY JUST NOW?
THERE ARE ALL KINDS OF GYRO SPINS PUT ON KAORU'S TORNADO.
BY SLIGHTLY CHANGING THE AXIS OF GYRATION, HE CAN HIT IT AT SEVERAL HUNDRED DIFFERENT TYPES OF TRAJECTORIES AND SPEEDS.
AN UNEXPECTED SHOT DELIVERED FROM THE SAME SWING...
NOT EVEN KOHARU KONJIKI WITH AN IQ OF 200 COULD PREDICT AND CALCULATE THAT!
Heh heh heh!
Nice job, Kaoru!

GENIUS 325: BE STUBBORN!!!

BOYS WEARING MASKS

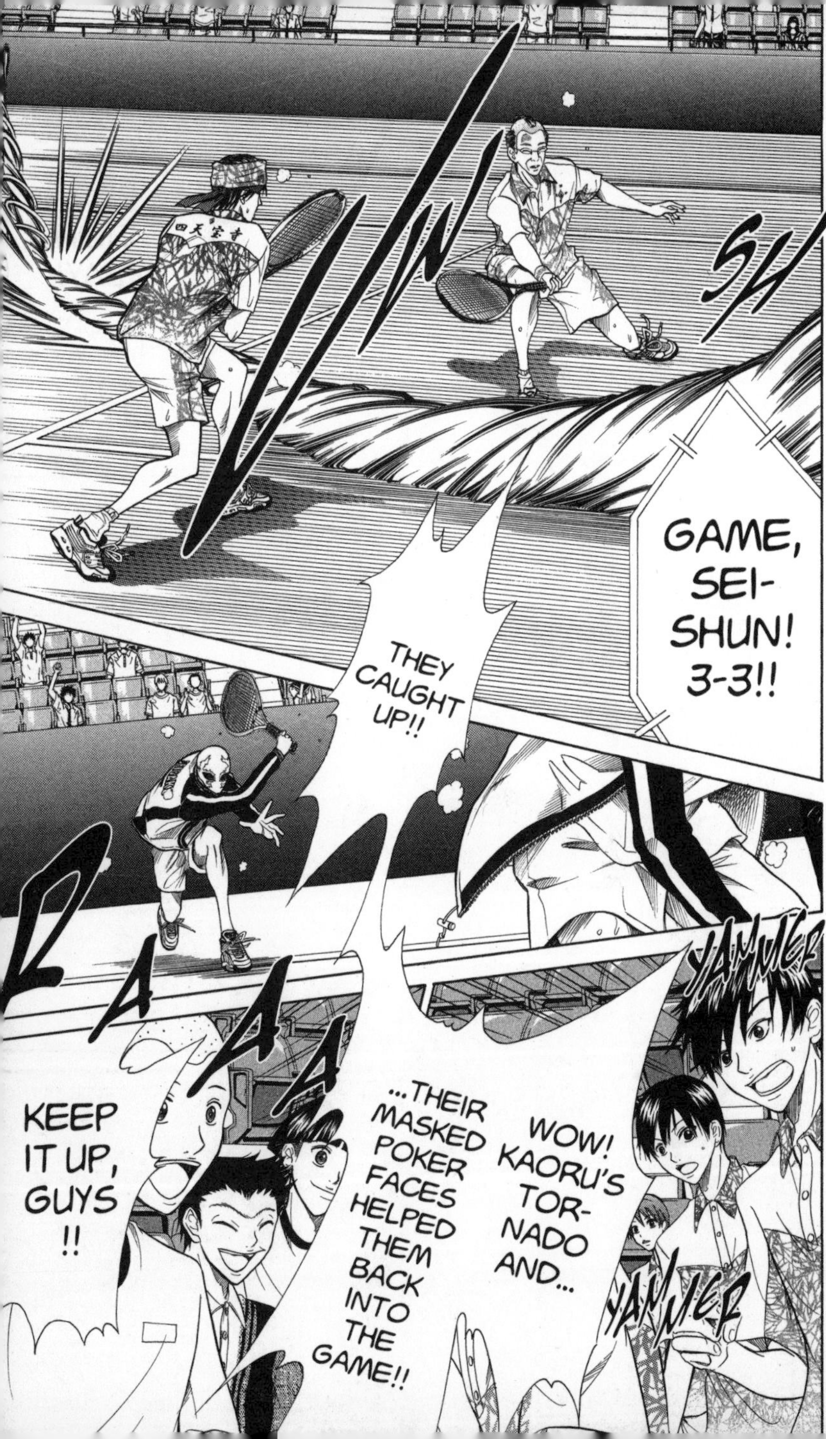
SH
GAME, SEI-SHUN! 3-3!!
THEY CAUGHT UP!!
DAAA
YAMMER
WOW! KAORU'S TOR-NADO AND...
...THEIR MASKED POKER FACES HELPED THEM BACK INTO THE GAME!!
KEEP IT UP, GUYS!!
YAMMER

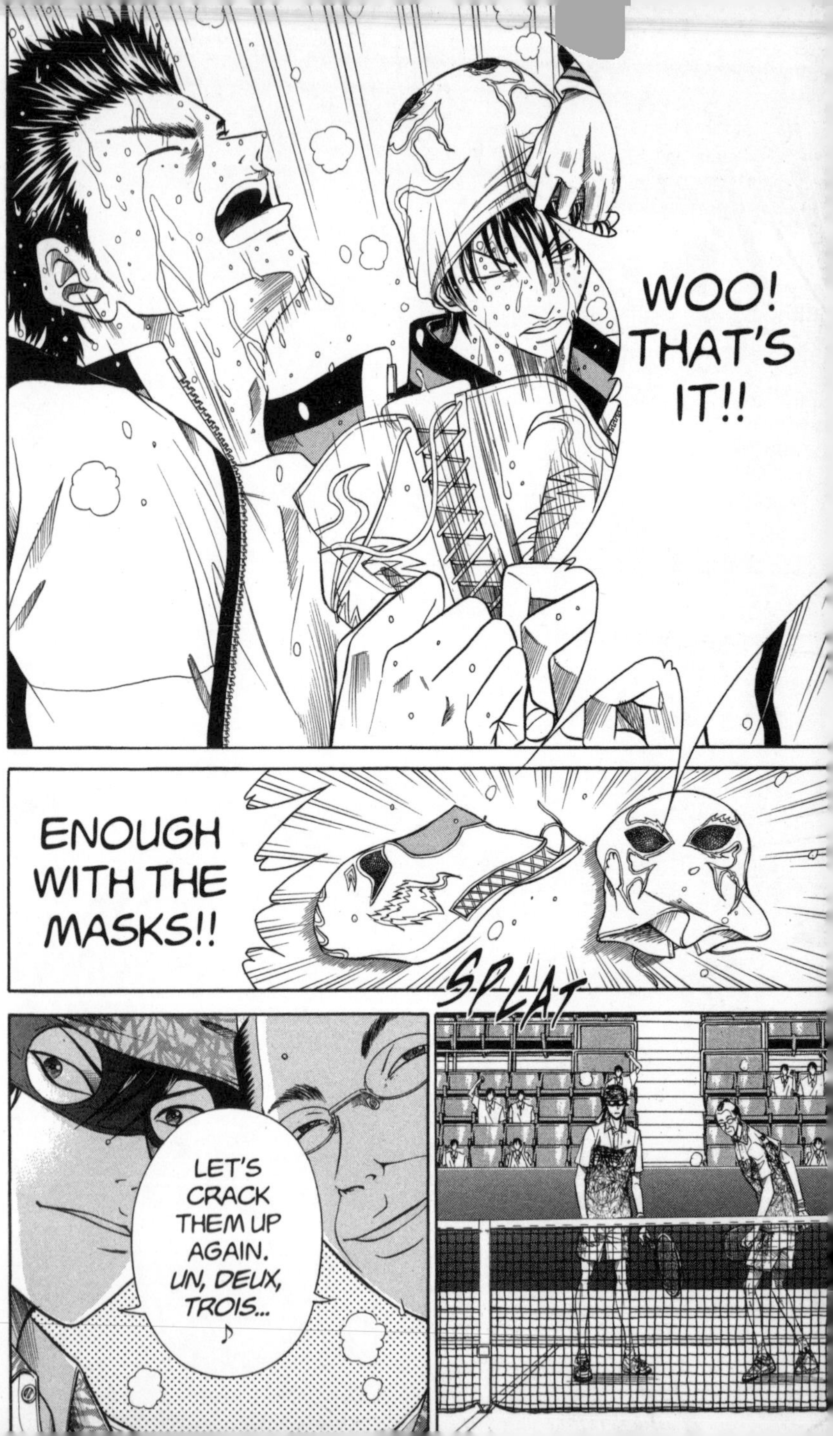
WOO! THAT'S IT!!
ENOUGH WITH THE MASKS!!
SPLAT
LET'S CRACK THEM UP AGAIN. UN, DEUX, TROIS... ♪

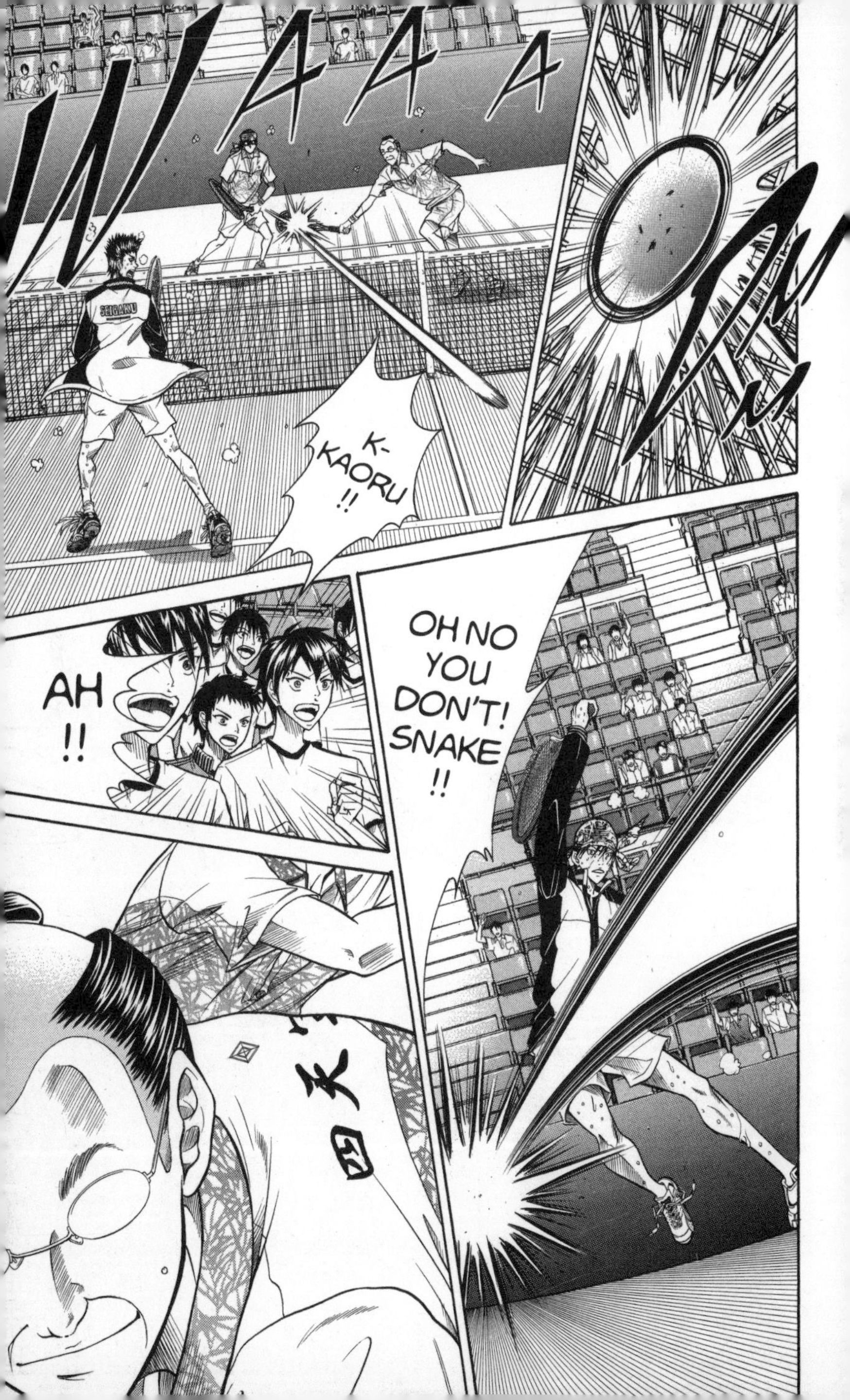
WAAA
K-KAORU!!
OH NO YOU DON'T! SNAKE!!
AH!!

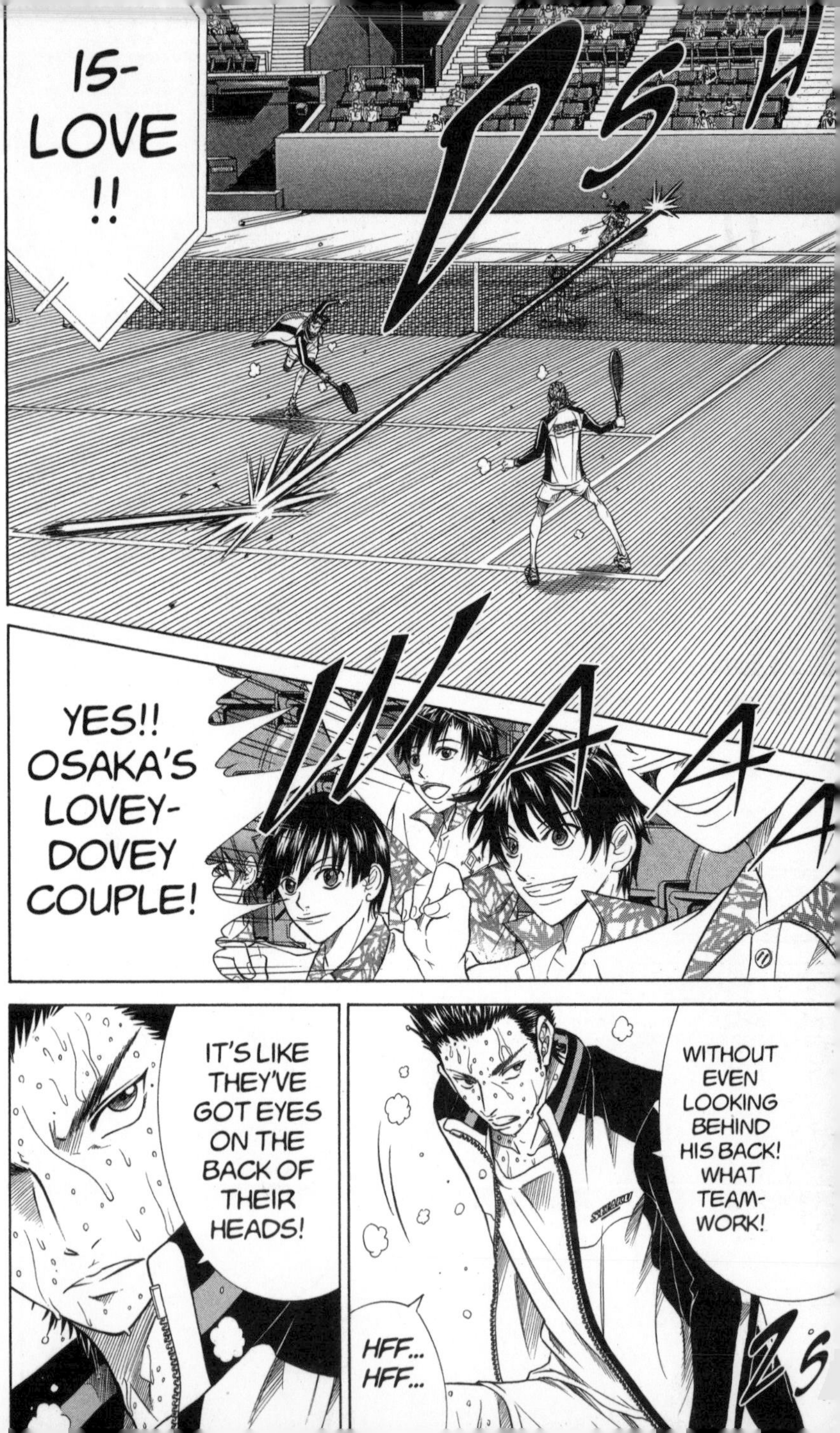
DSH
15-LOVE!!
WAAAA
YES!! OSAKA'S LOVEY-DOVEY COUPLE!
WITHOUT EVEN LOOKING BEHIND HIS BACK! WHAT TEAM-WORK!
HFF... HFF...
IT'S LIKE THEY'VE GOT EYES ON THE BACK OF THEIR HEADS!

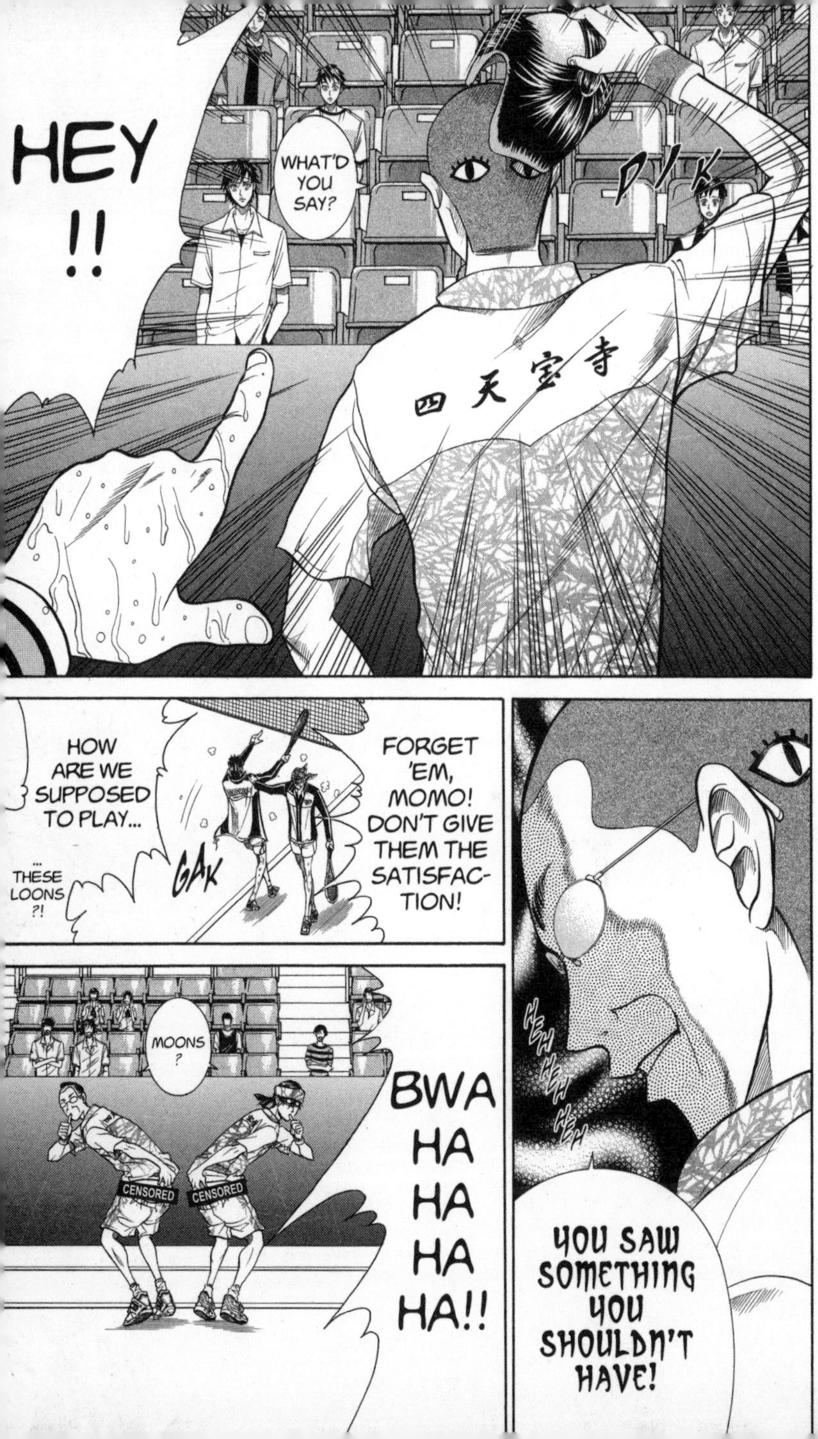
DOK
WHAT'D YOU SAY?
HEY!!
四天宝寺
HEH HEH HEH
YOU SAW SOMETHING YOU SHOULDN'T HAVE!
FORGET 'EM, MOMO! DON'T GIVE THEM THE SATISFACTION!
GAK
HOW ARE WE SUPPOSED TO PLAY...
...THESE LOONS?!
BWA HA HA HA HA!!
MOONS?
CENSORED
CENSORED

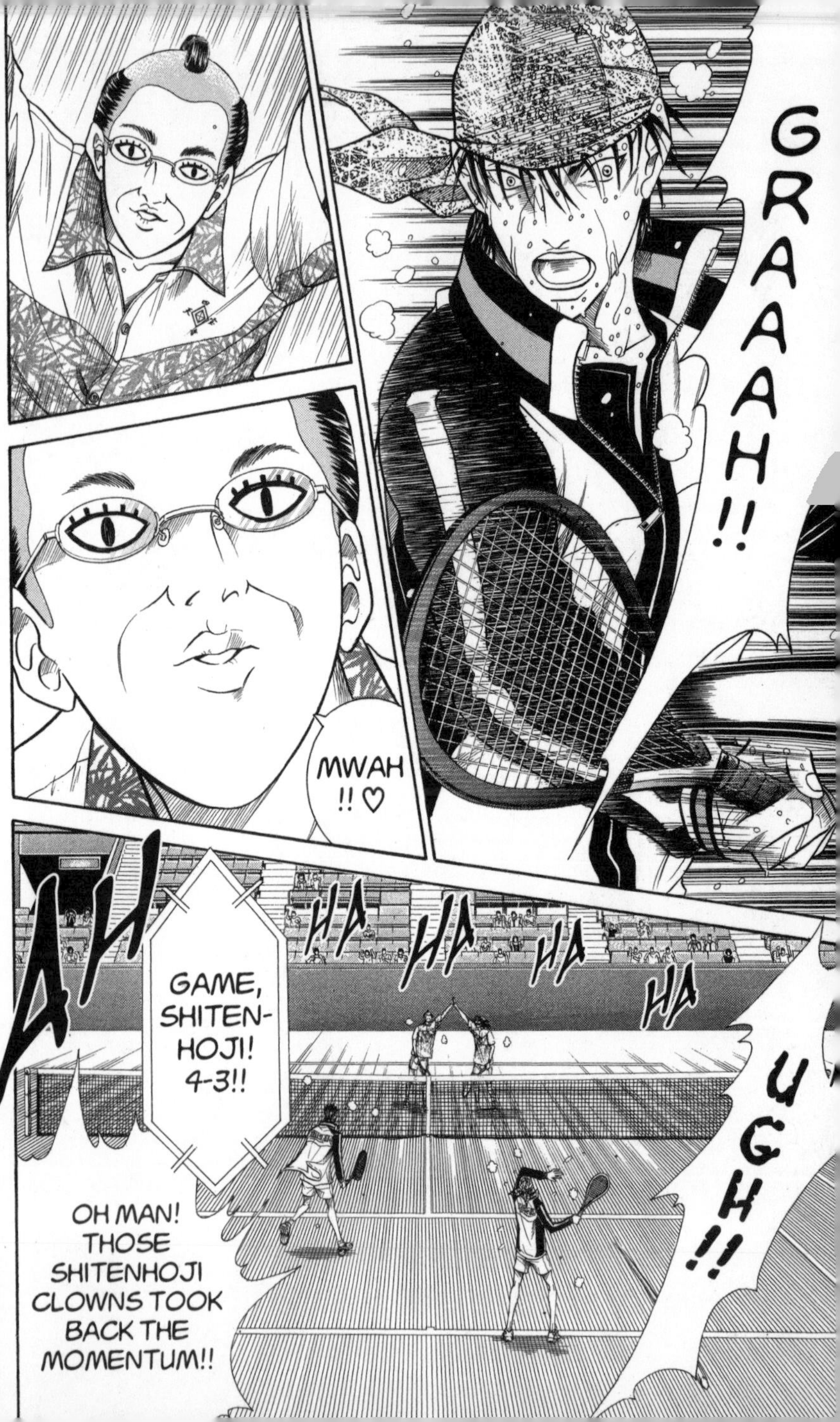
GRAAAAH!!
MWAH!! ♡
UGH!!
AH
HA HA HA HA
GAME, SHITEN-HOJI! 4-3!!
OH MAN! THOSE SHITENHOJI CLOWNS TOOK BACK THE MOMENTUM!!

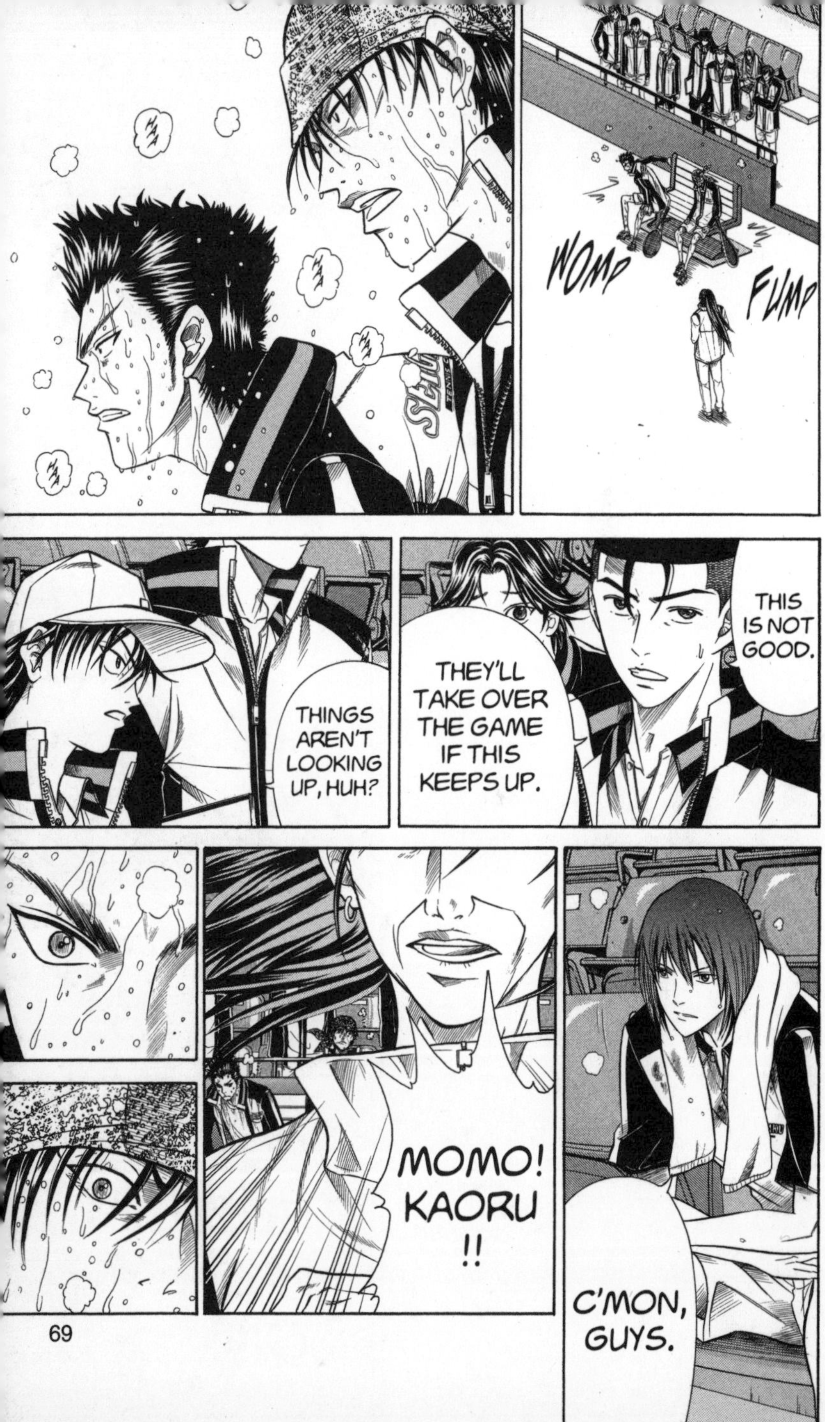
WOMP
FUMP
THIS IS NOT GOOD.
THEY'LL TAKE OVER THE GAME IF THIS KEEPS UP.
THINGS AREN'T LOOKING UP, HUH?
C'MON, GUYS.
MOMO! KAORU!!

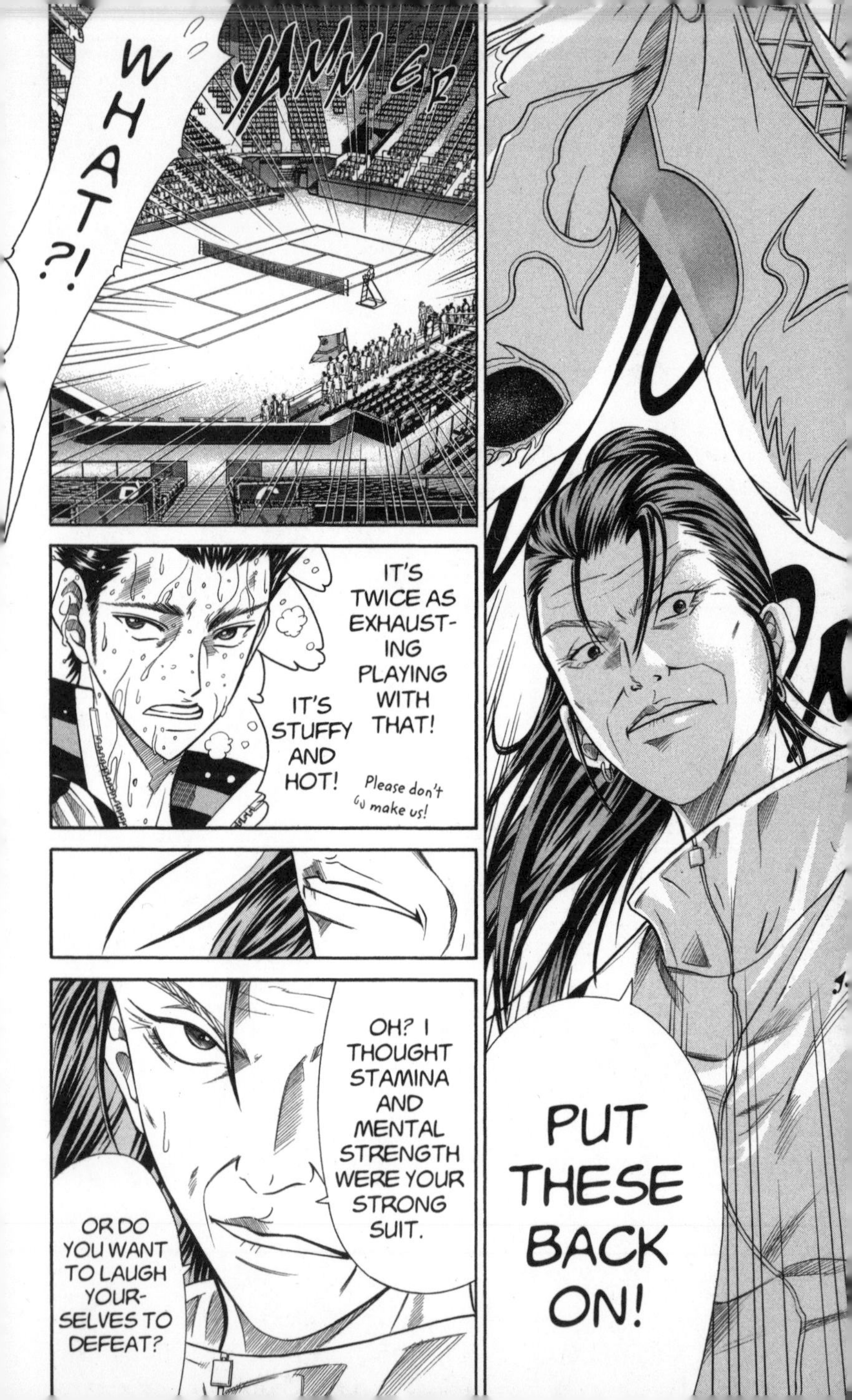
PUT THESE BACK ON!
WHAT?!
YAMMER
IT'S TWICE AS EXHAUST-ING PLAYING WITH THAT!
IT'S STUFFY AND HOT!
Please don't make us!
OH? I THOUGHT STAMINA AND MENTAL STRENGTH WERE YOUR STRONG SUIT.
OR DO YOU WANT TO LAUGH YOUR-SELVES TO DEFEAT?

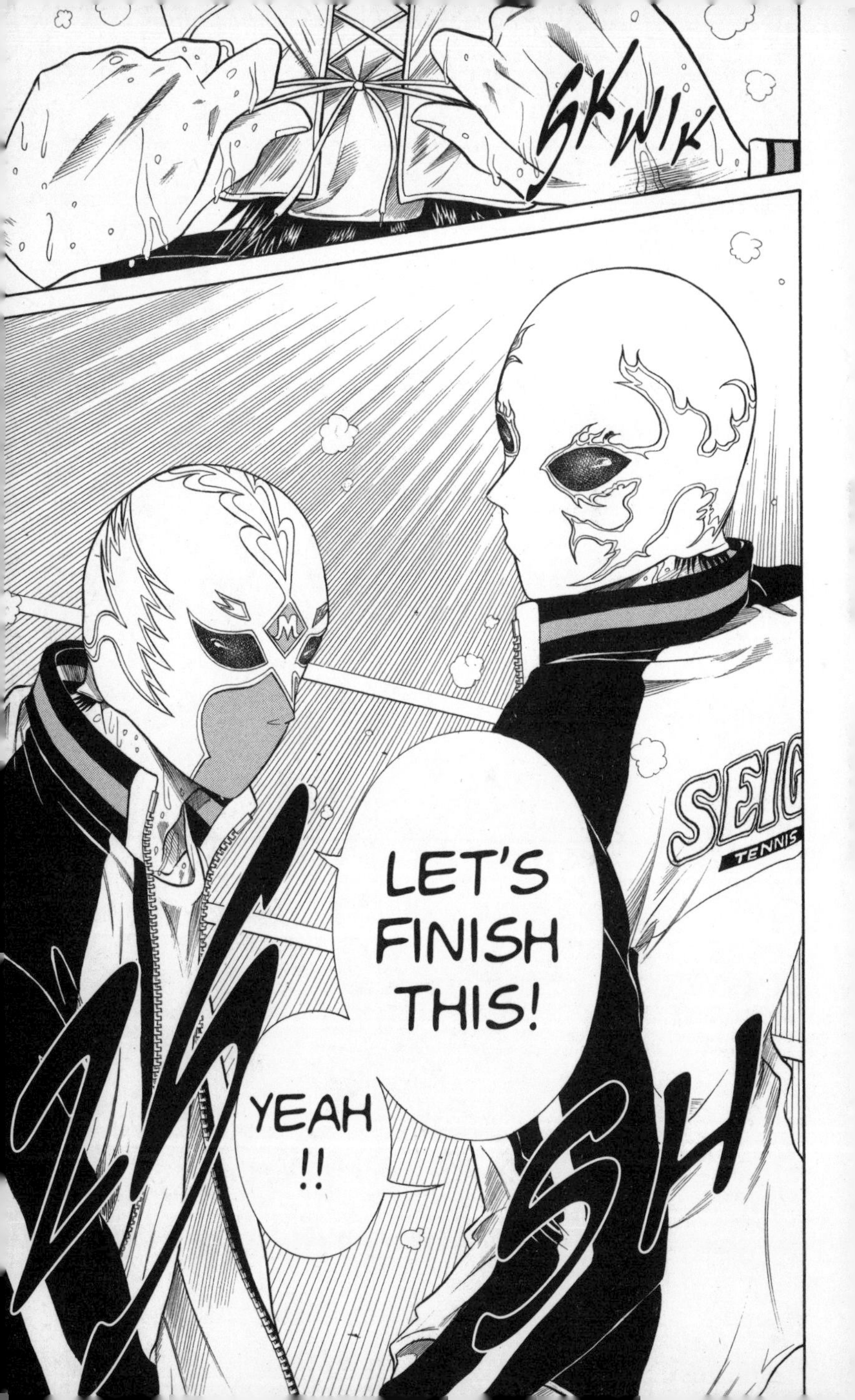
SKWIK
SEIG
TENNIS
LET'S FINISH THIS!
YEAH !!

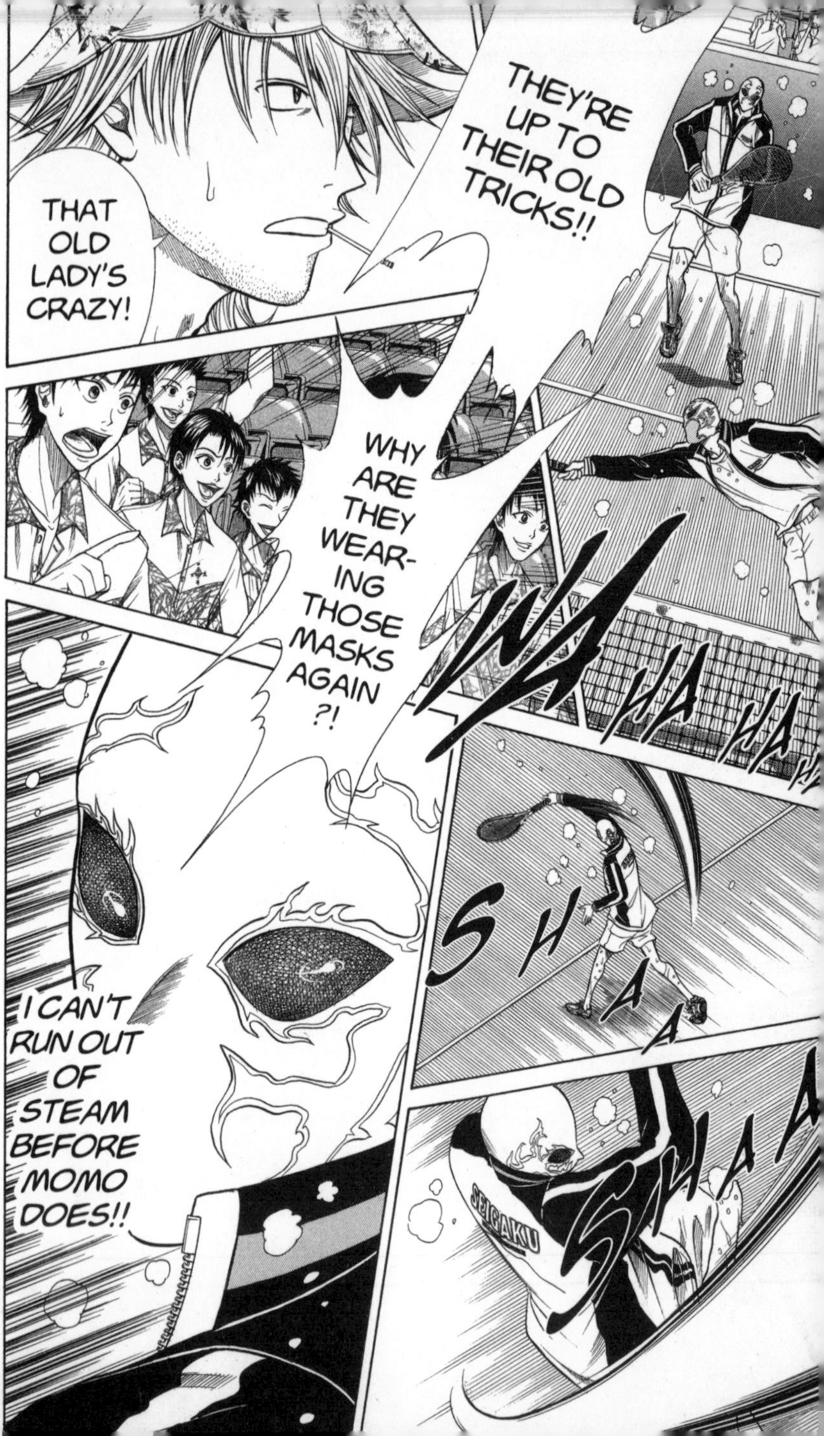
THEY'RE UP TO THEIR OLD TRICKS!!
THAT OLD LADY'S CRAZY!
WAHAHAHA
WHY ARE THEY WEARING THOSE MASKS AGAIN?!
SHAA
SHAA
I CAN'T RUN OUT OF STEAM BEFORE MOMO DOES!!

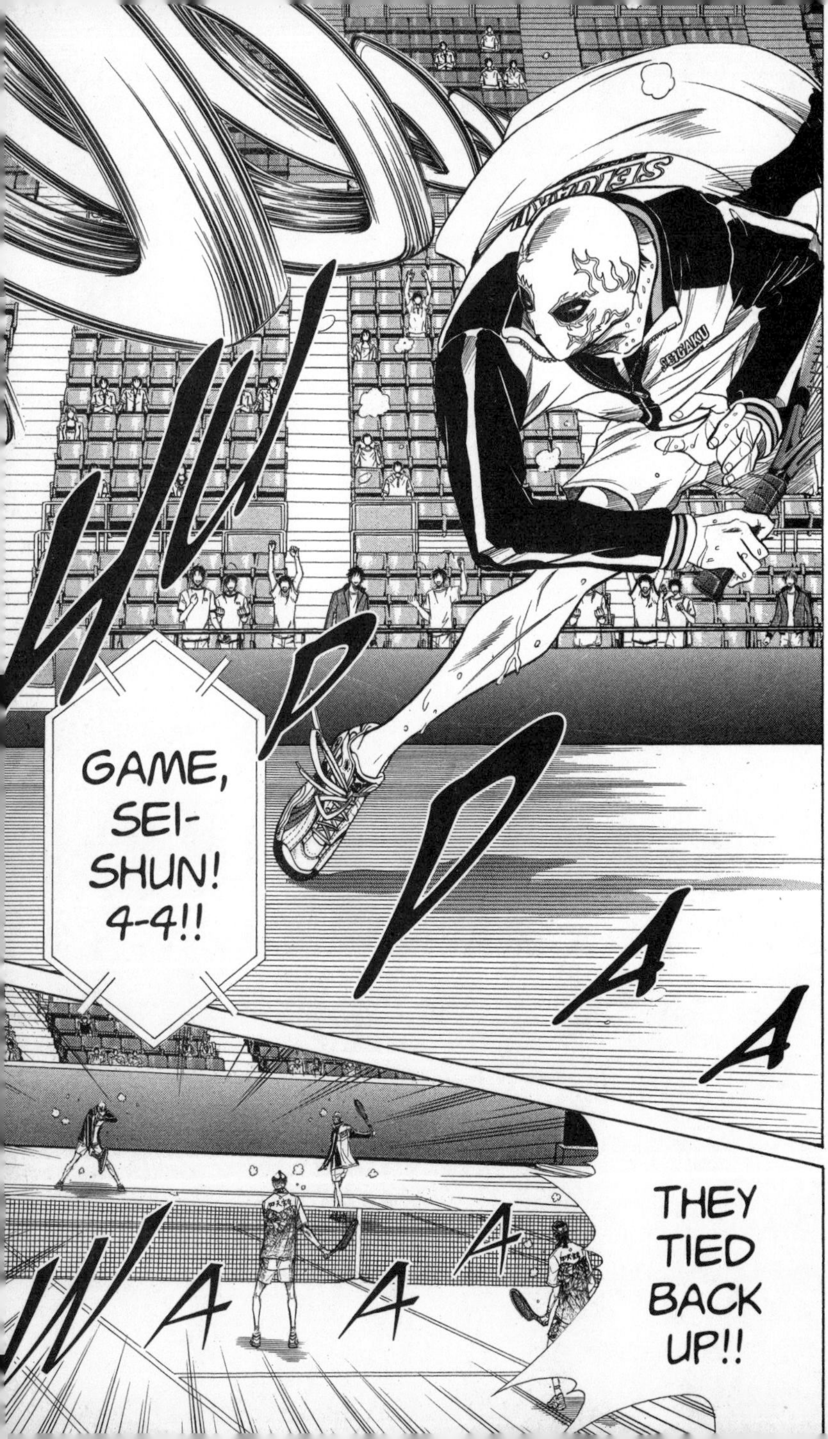
SEIGAKU
WAAAAA
GAME, SEI-SHUN! 4-4!!
THEY TIED BACK UP!!
WAAA

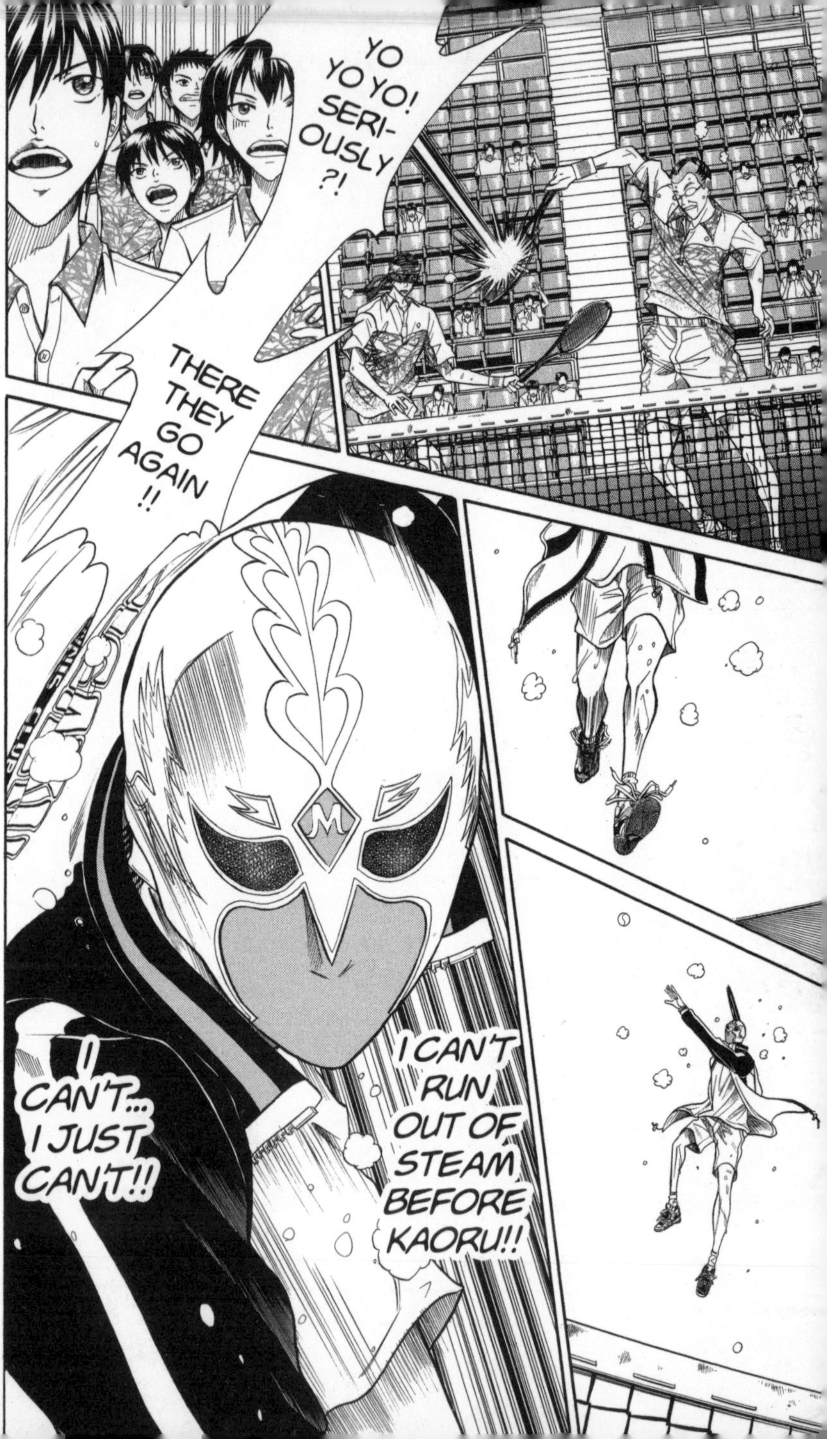
YO YO YO! SERI-OUSLY?!
THERE THEY GO AGAIN!!
I CAN'T RUN OUT OF STEAM BEFORE KAORU!!
I CAN'T... I JUST CAN'T!!

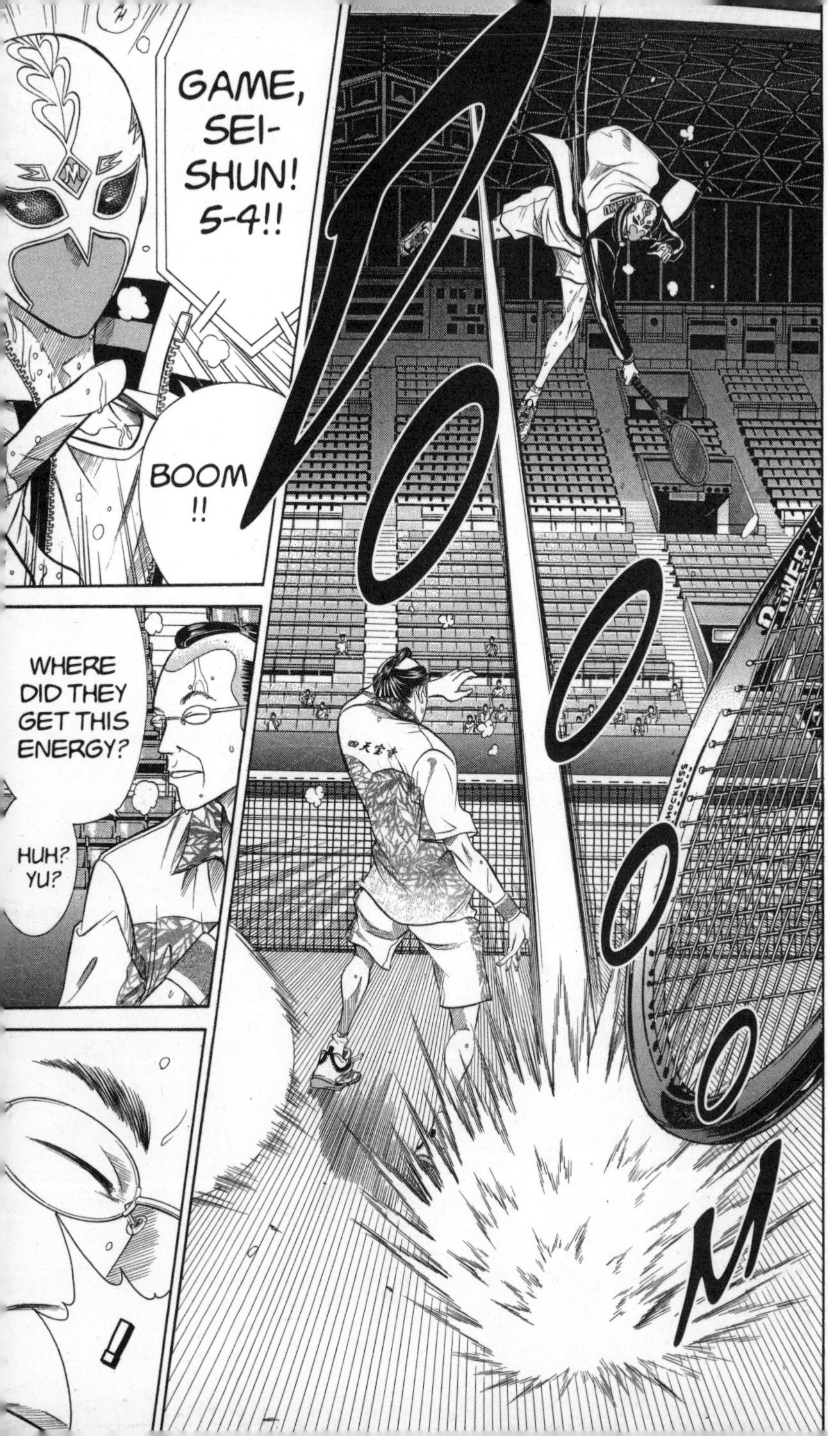

GAME, SEI-SHUN! 5-4!!
BOOM !!
WHERE DID THEY GET THIS ENERGY?
HUH? YU?
!

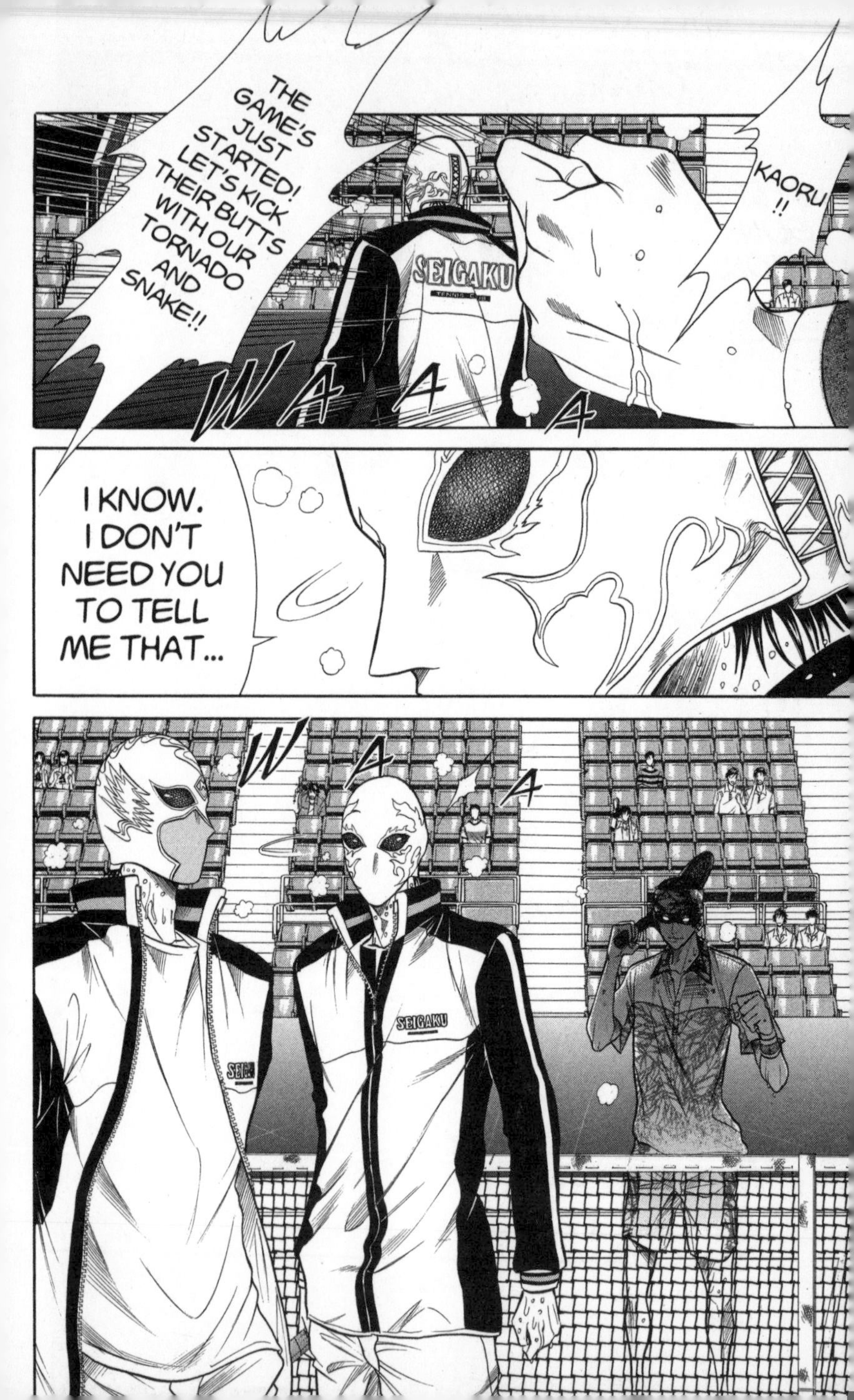
KAORU!!
THE GAME'S JUST STARTED! LET'S KICK THEIR BUTTS WITH OUR TORNADO AND SNAKE!!
WAAA
I KNOW. I DON'T NEED YOU TO TELL ME THAT...
WAAA
SEIGAKU

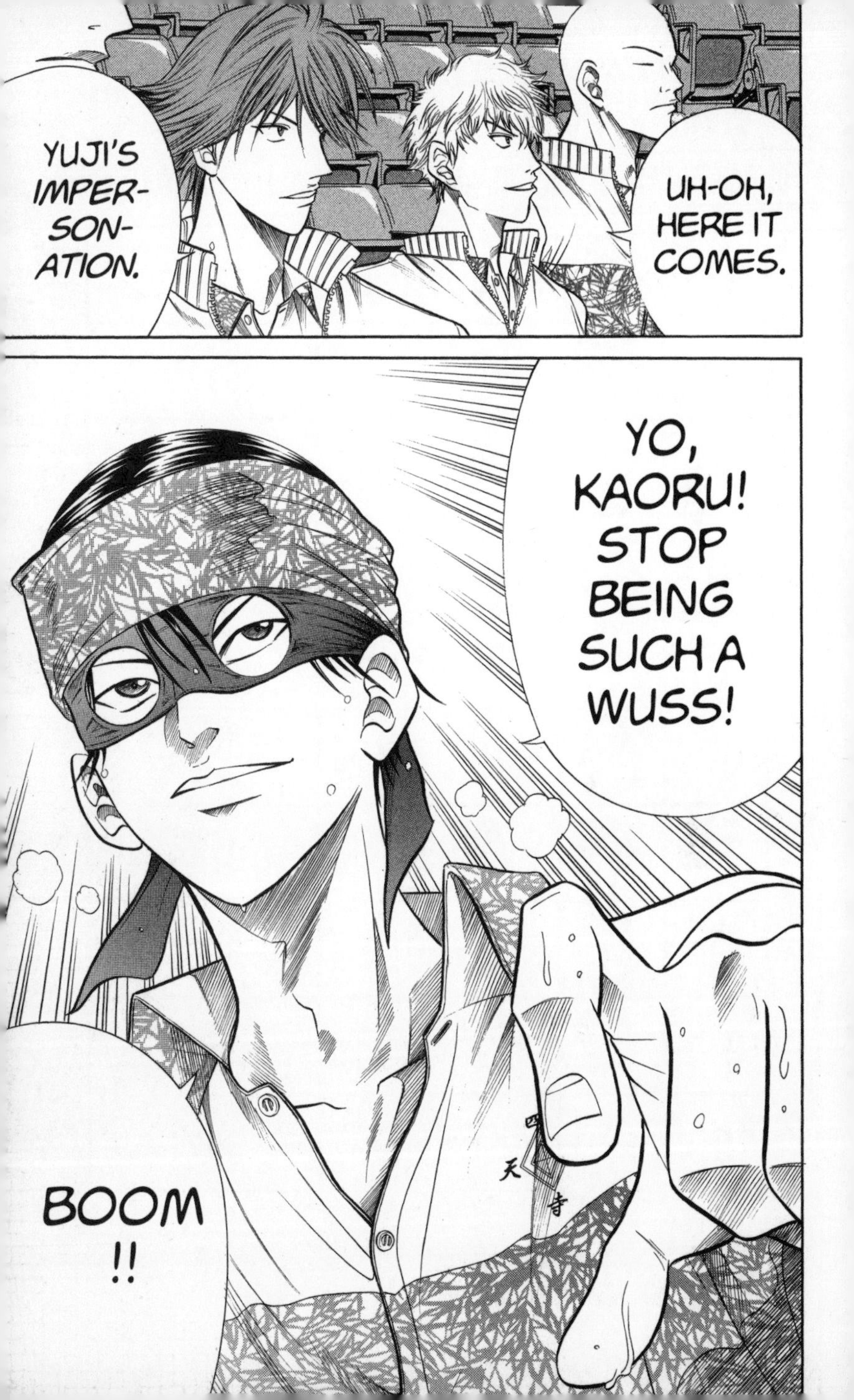
UH-OH, HERE IT COMES.
YUJI'S IMPERSONATION.
YO, KAORU! STOP BEING SUCH A WUSS!
BOOM!!

4TH CHARACTER POPULARITY POLL RESULTS!! ①

92,680 TOTAL VOTES!! THANK YOU FOR ALL YOUR VOTES!!

1ST	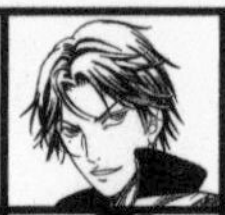	KEIGO ATOBE	12913
2ND	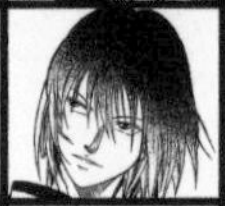	SHUSUKE FUJI	6116
3RD	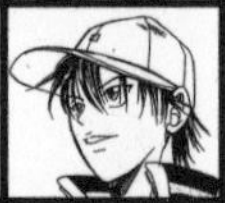	RYOMA ECHIZEN	5596
4TH	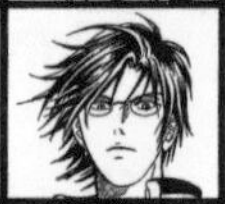	KUNIMITSU TEZUKA	5089
5TH	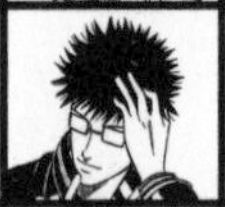	SADAHARU INUI	4917
6TH	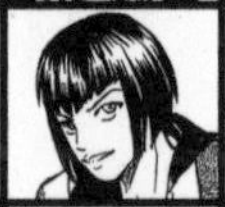	GAKUTO MUKAHI	4381
7TH	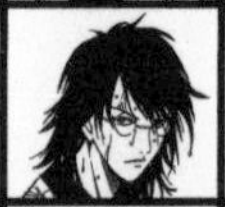	YUSHI OSHITARI	3719
8TH	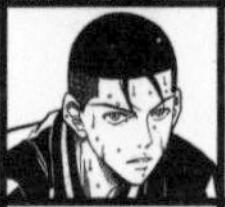	SHUICHIRO OISHI	3661
9TH	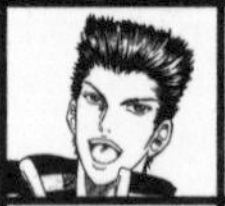	TAKESHI MOMOSHIRO	3189
10TH	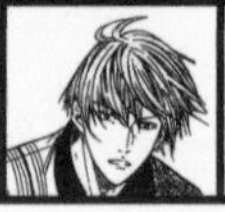	WAKASHI HIYOSHI	3021

CONTINUED ON PAGE 96

GENIUS 326: IMPERSONATION PRINCE
~KOHARU'S CRAZY ABOUT YUJI HITOJI~

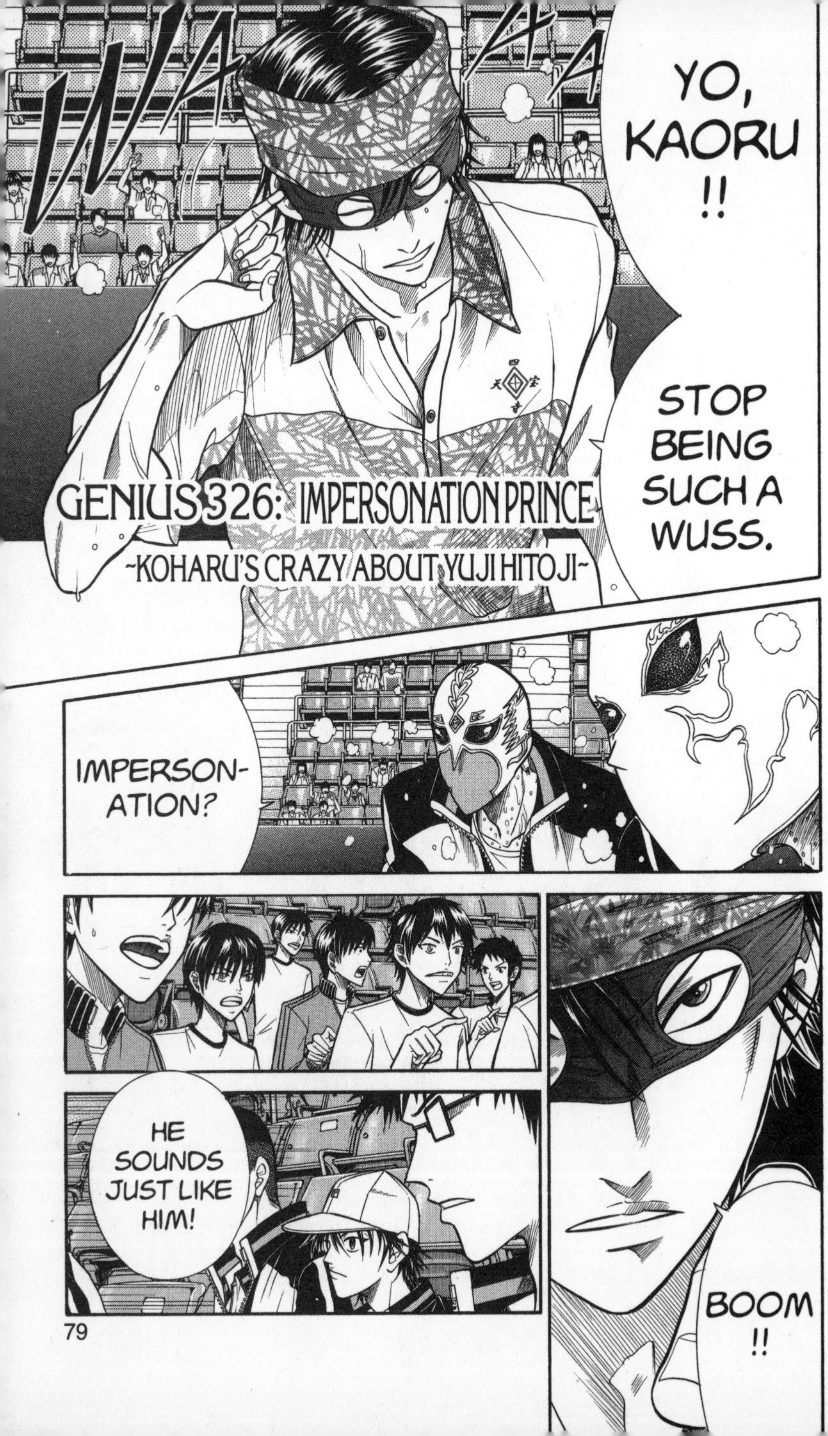
WAAA
YO, KAORU!!
STOP BEING SUCH A WUSS.
IMPERSON-ATION?
BOOM!!
HE SOUNDS JUST LIKE HIM!

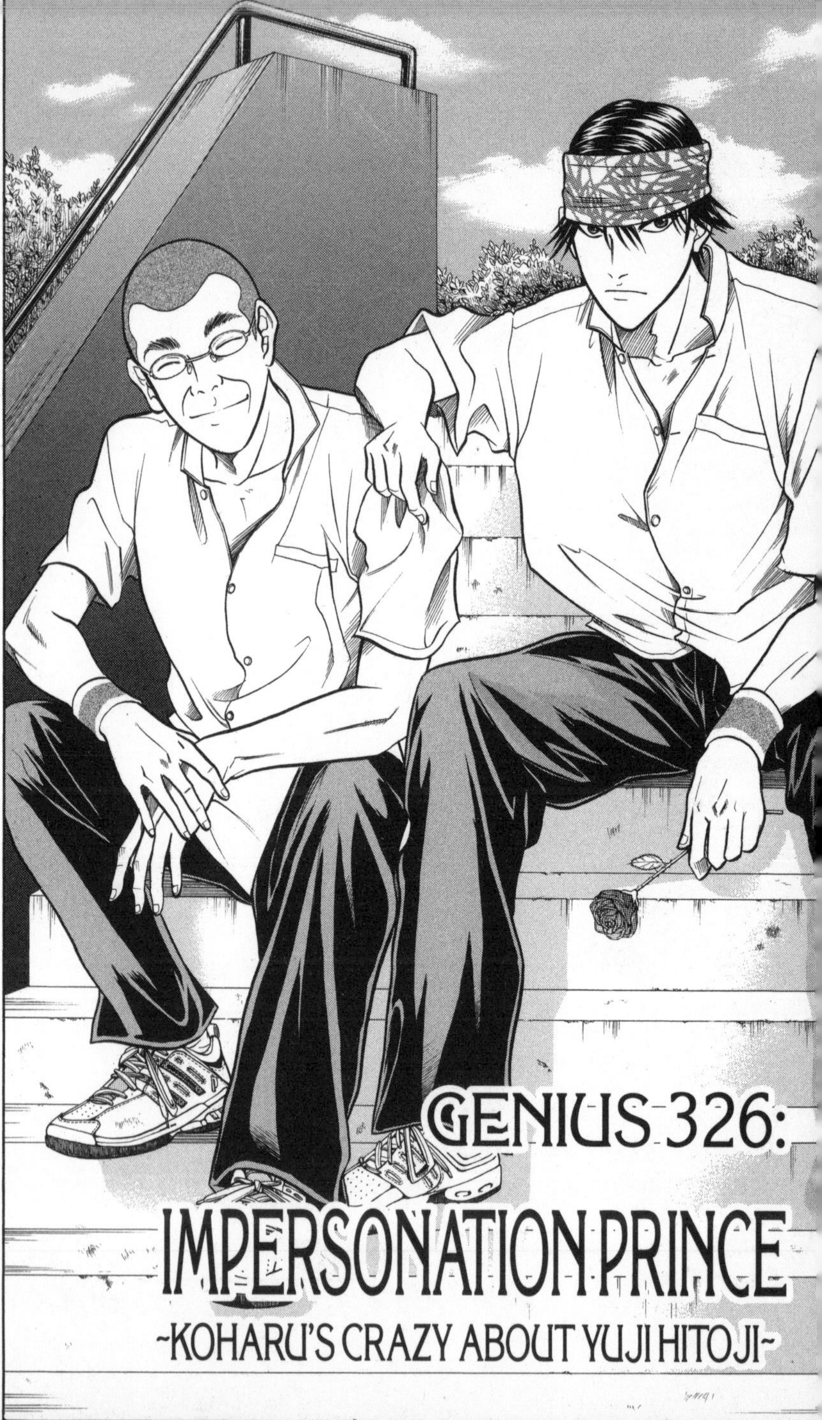
GENIUS 326:
IMPERSONATION PRINCE
~KOHARU'S CRAZY ABOUT YUJI HITOJI~

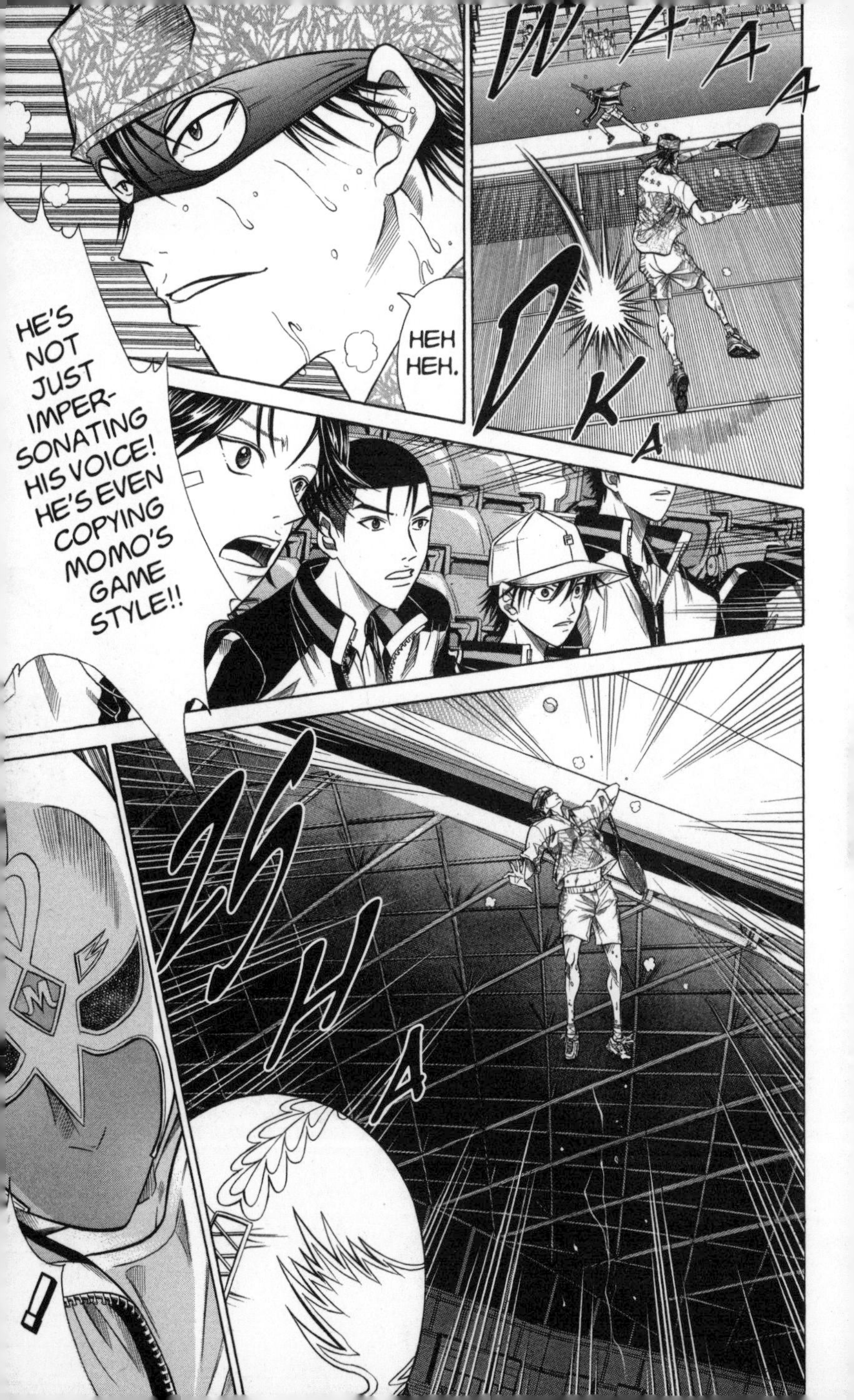
WAAA
DKA
HEH HEH.
HE'S NOT JUST IMPER-SONATING HIS VOICE! HE'S EVEN COPYING MOMO'S GAME STYLE!!
ZWA
!

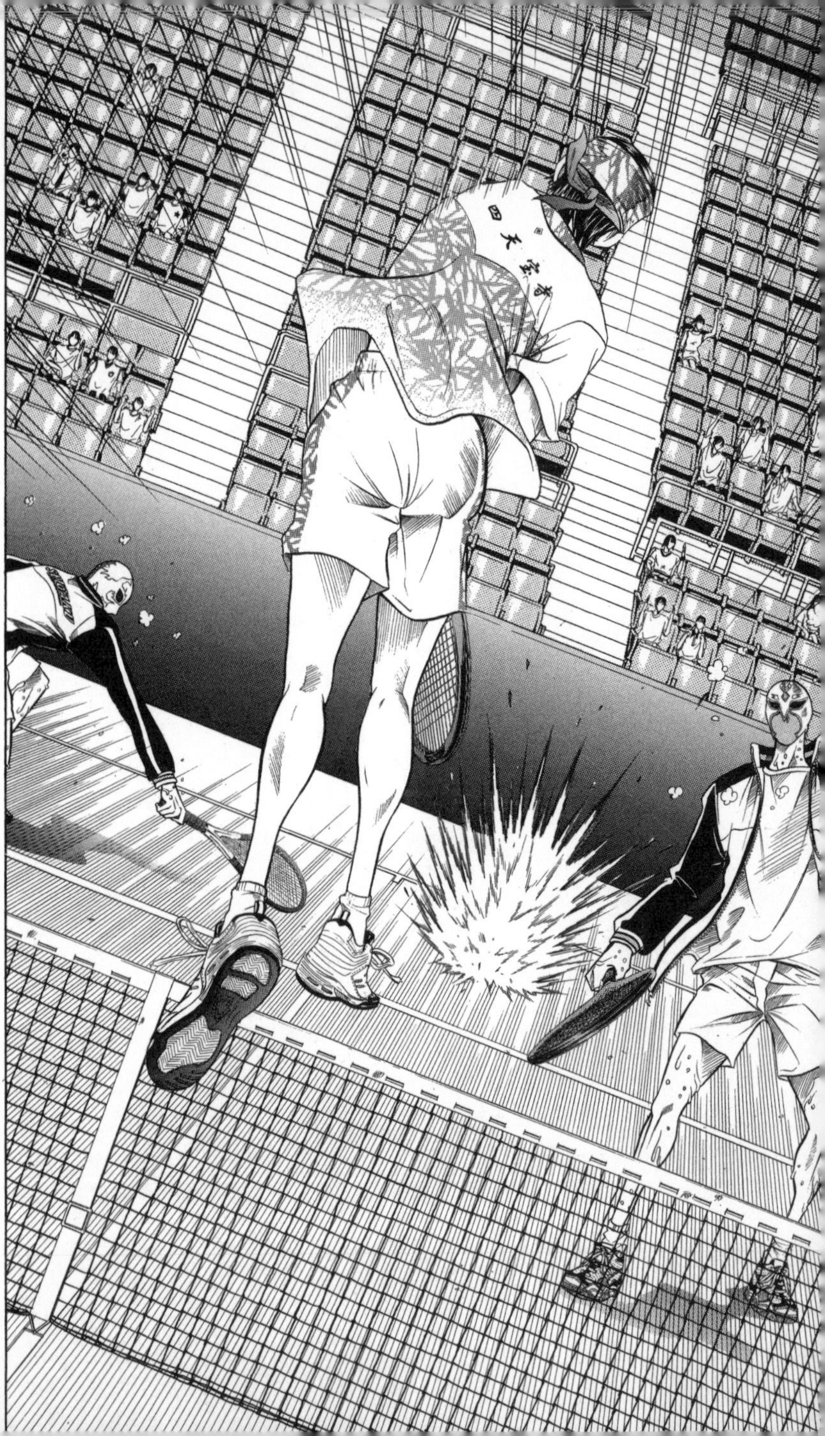
四天宝寺

READ THIS WAY

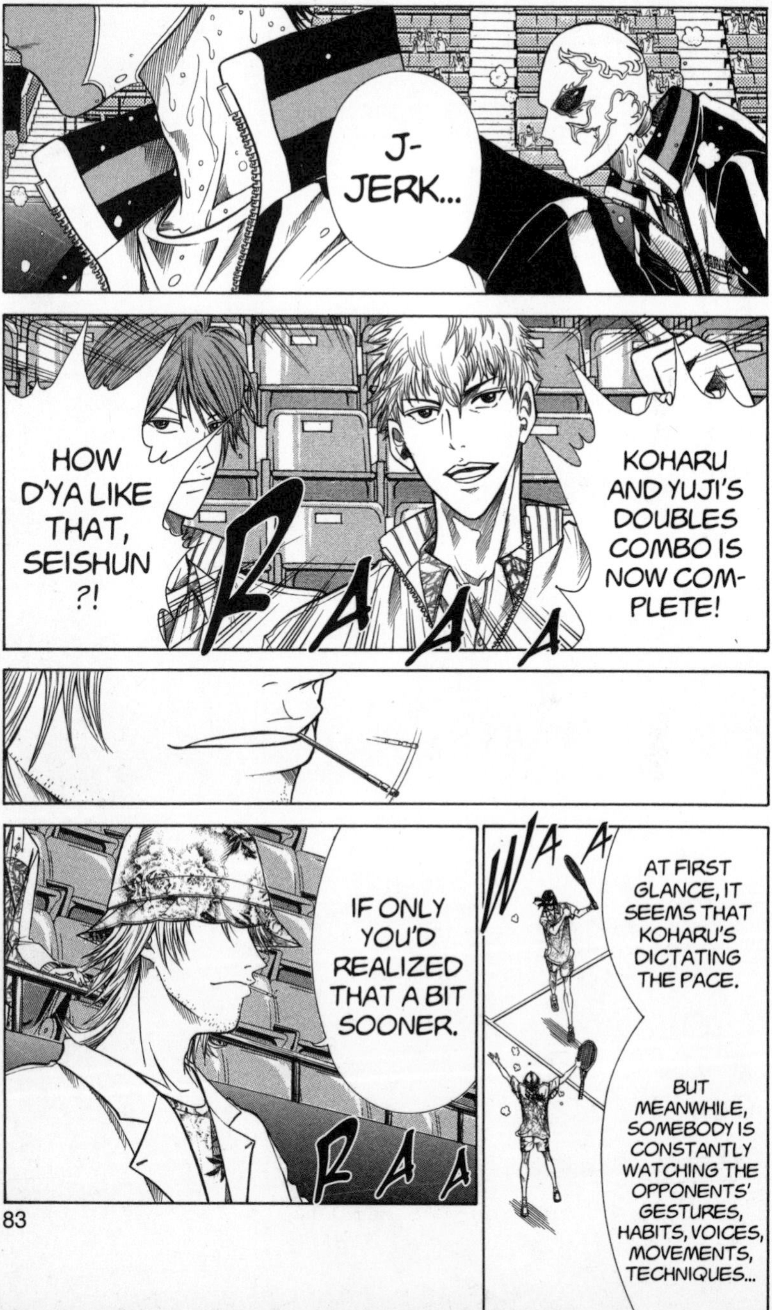
J-JERK...
KOHARU AND YUJI'S DOUBLES COMBO IS NOW COMPLETE!
HOW D'YA LIKE THAT, SEISHUN?!
RAAA
WAA
AT FIRST GLANCE, IT SEEMS THAT KOHARU'S DICTATING THE PACE.
BUT MEANWHILE, SOMEBODY IS CONSTANTLY WATCHING THE OPPONENTS' GESTURES, HABITS, VOICES, MOVEMENTS, TECHNIQUES...
IF ONLY YOU'D REALIZED THAT A BIT SOONER.
RAA

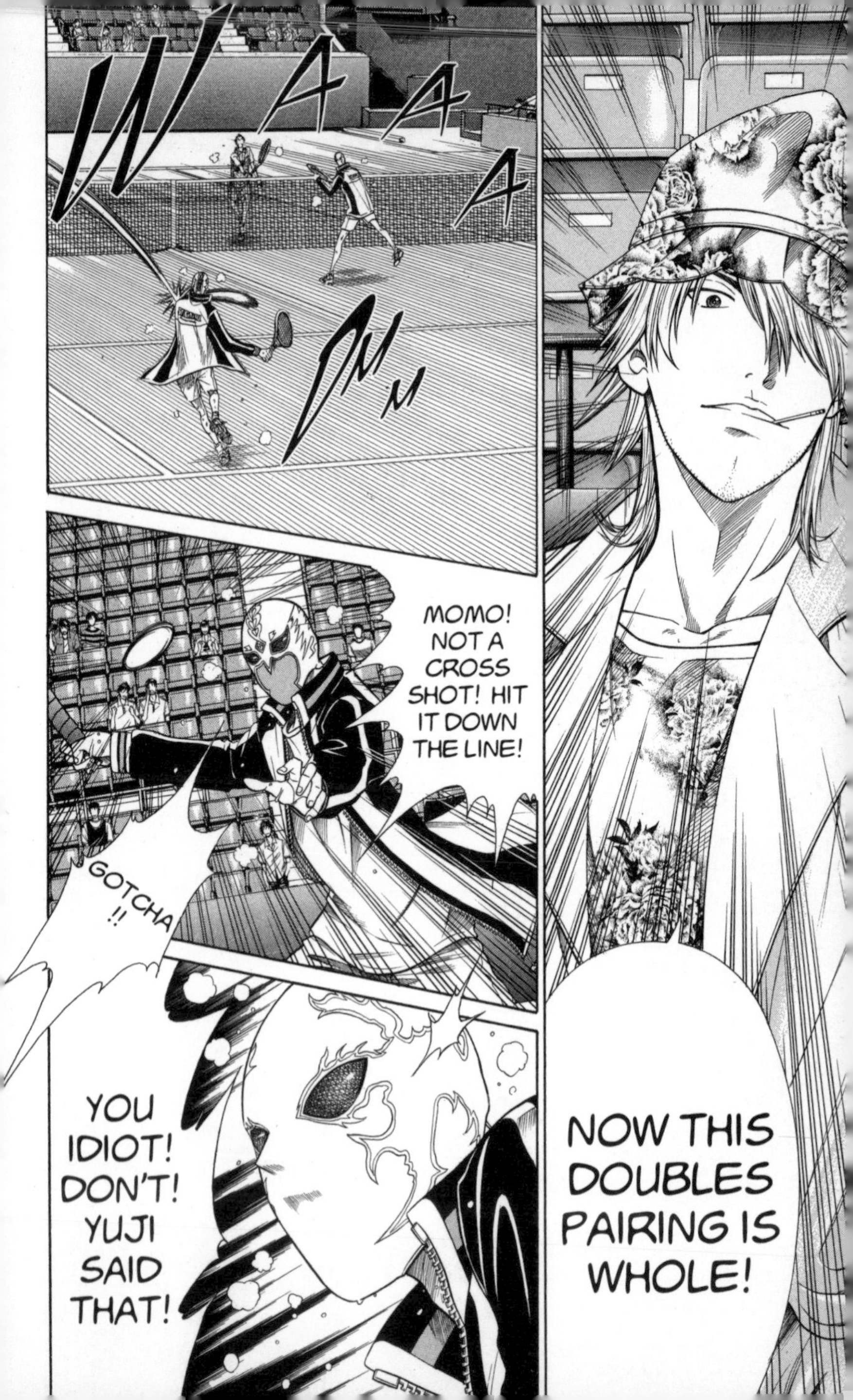
NOW THIS DOUBLES PAIRING IS WHOLE!
WAAAA
DMM
MOMO! NOT A CROSS SHOT! HIT IT DOWN THE LINE!
GOTCHA!!
YOU IDIOT! DON'T! YUJI SAID THAT!

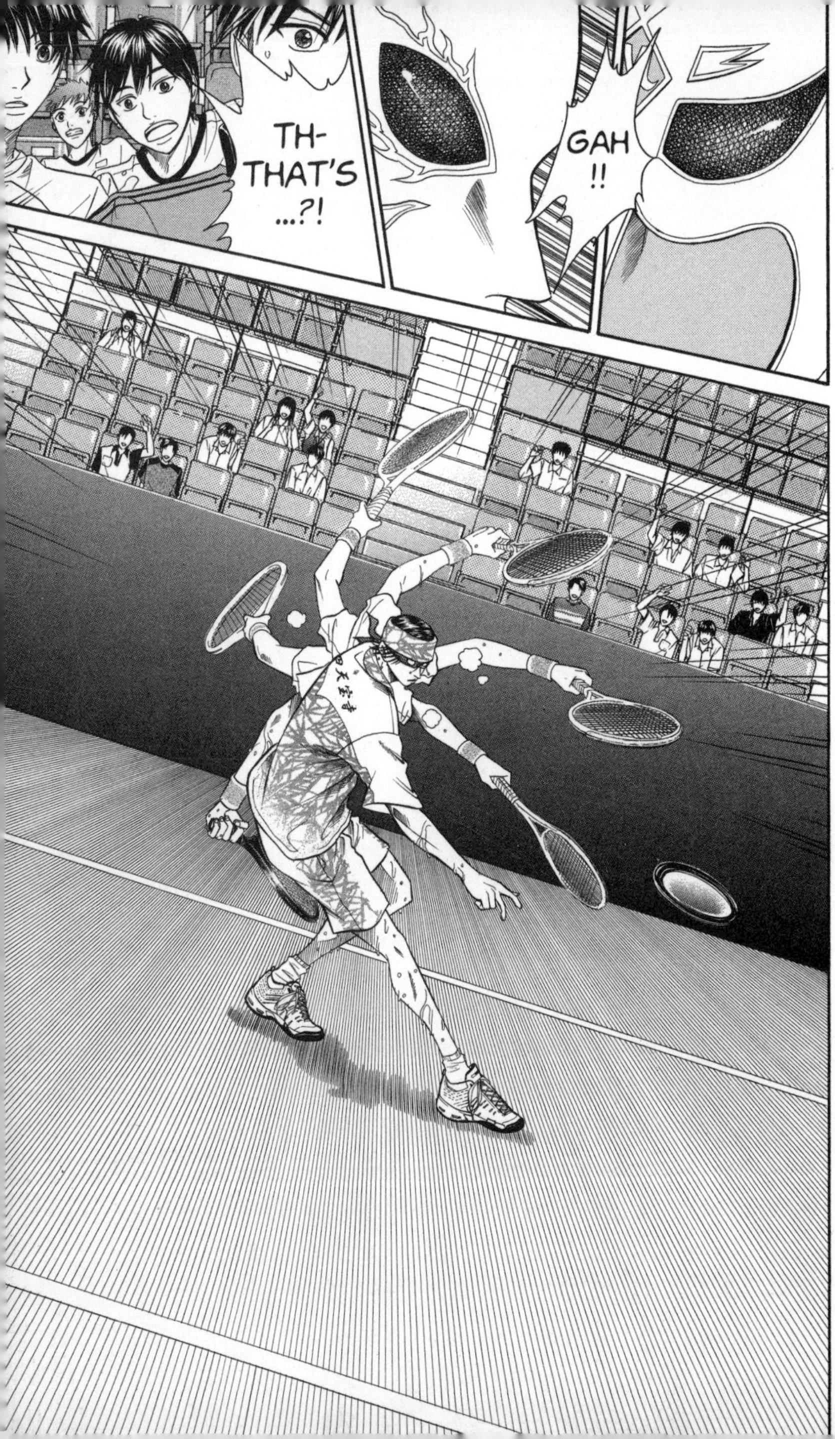
GAH !!
TH- THAT'S ...?!

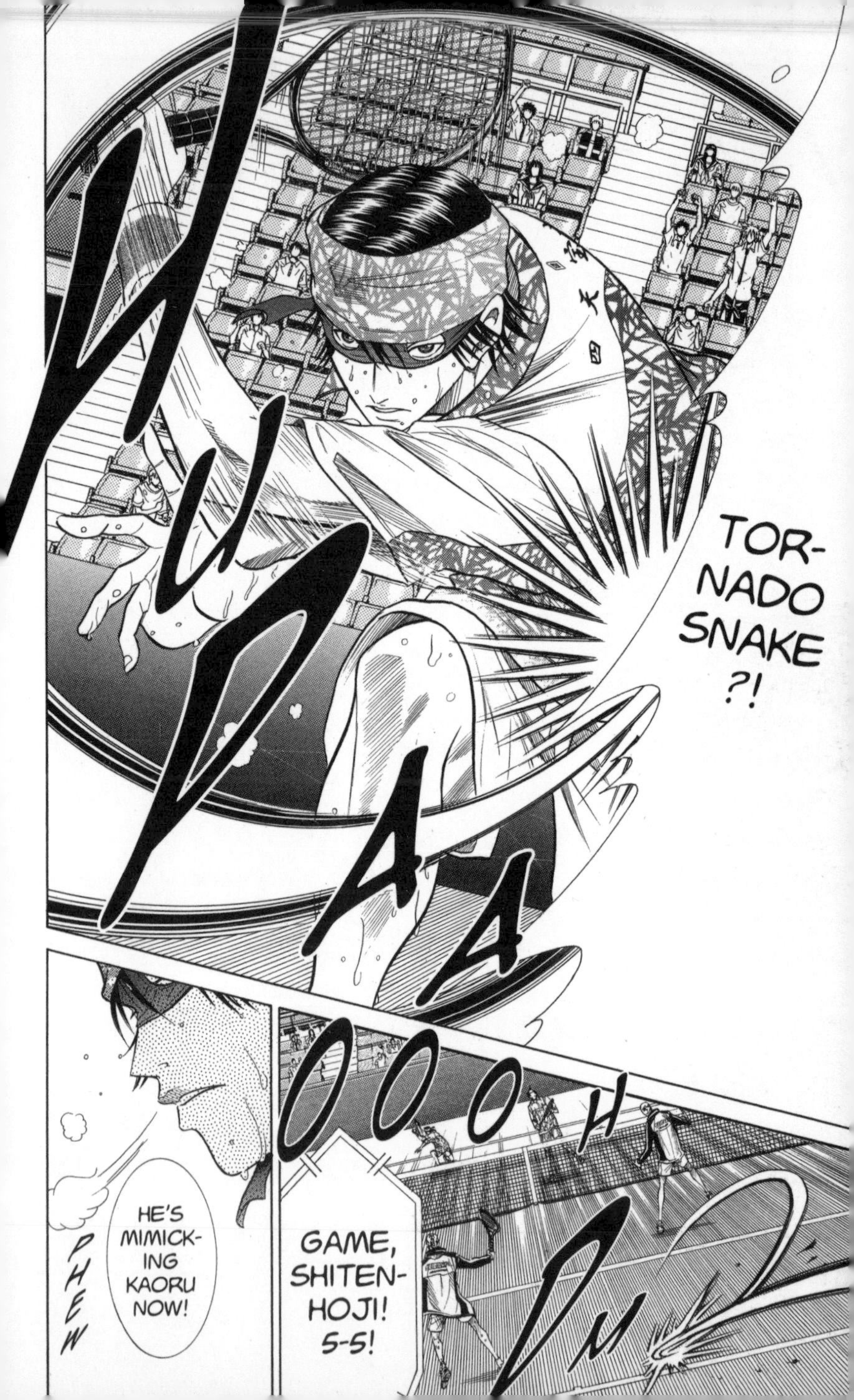
TOR-NADO SNAKE ?!
GAME, SHITEN-HOJI! 5-5!
HE'S MIMICK-ING KAORU NOW!
PHEW

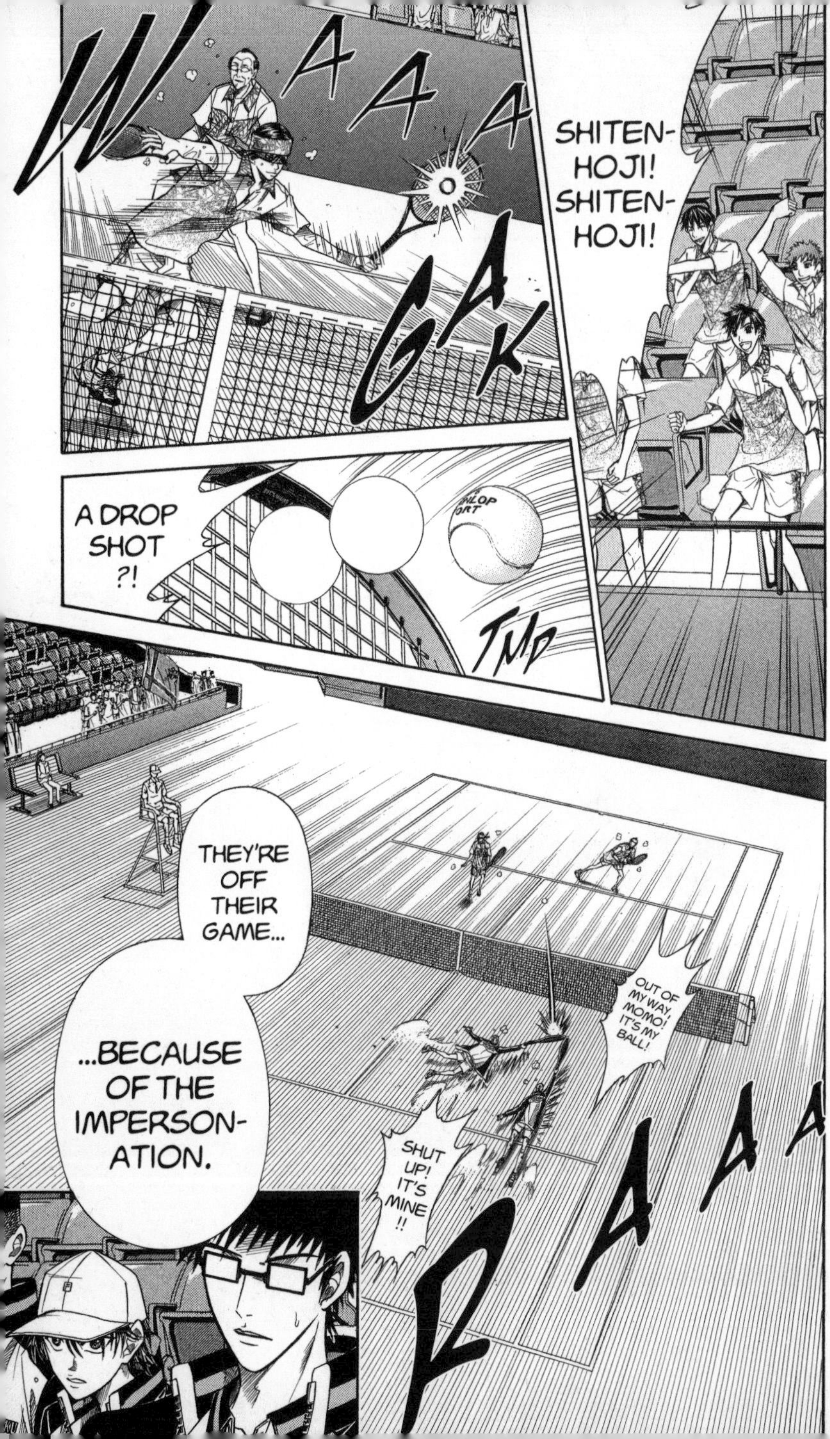
SHITEN-HOJI! SHITEN-HOJI!
WAAAA
GAK
A DROP SHOT ?!
TMP
OUT OF MY WAY, MOMO! IT'S MY BALL!
SHUT UP! IT'S MINE !!
RAAAA
THEY'RE OFF THEIR GAME...
...BECAUSE OF THE IMPERSON-ATION.

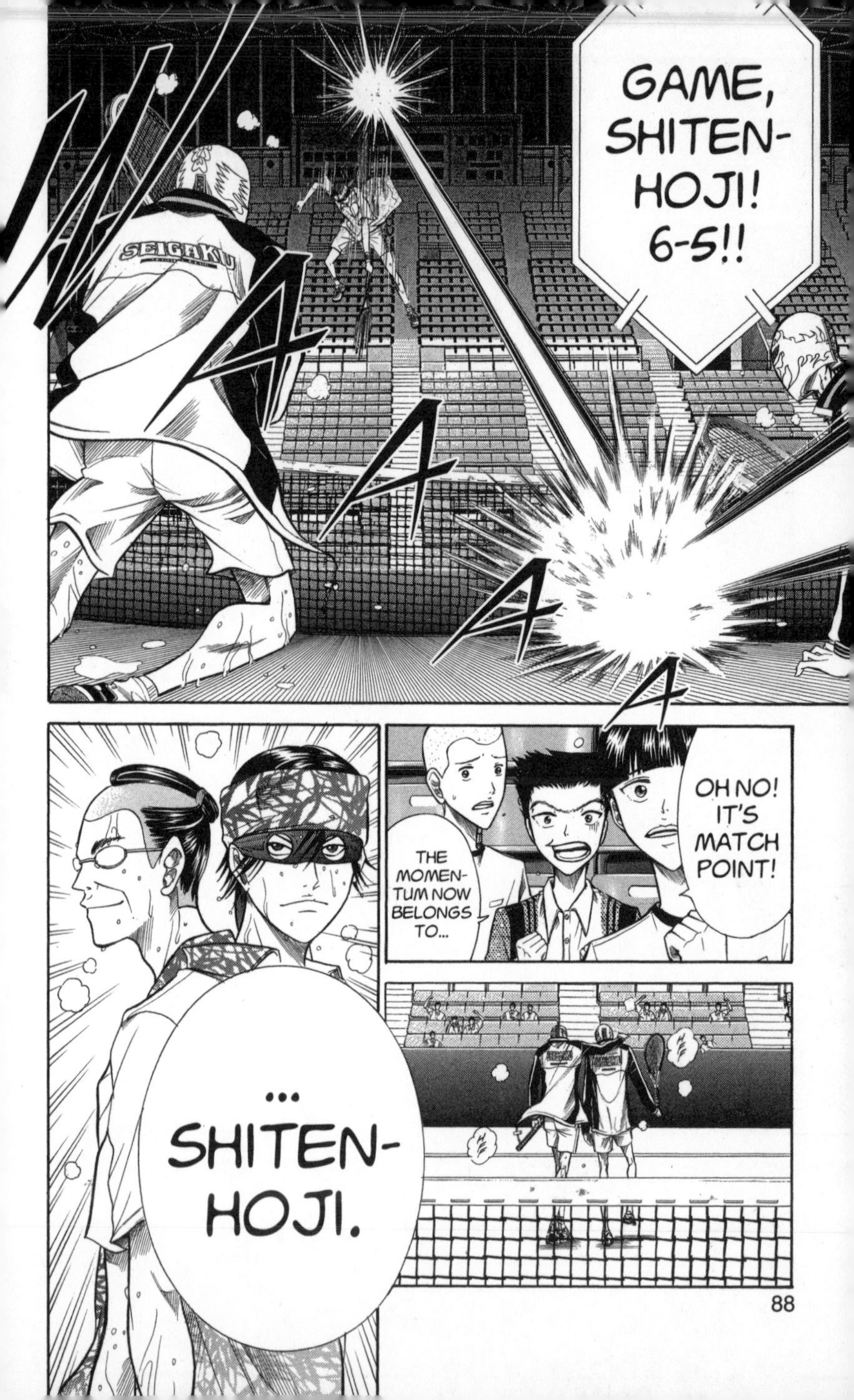
GAME, SHITEN-HOJI! 6-5!!
OH NO! IT'S MATCH POINT!
THE MOMENTUM NOW BELONGS TO...
...SHITEN-HOJI.

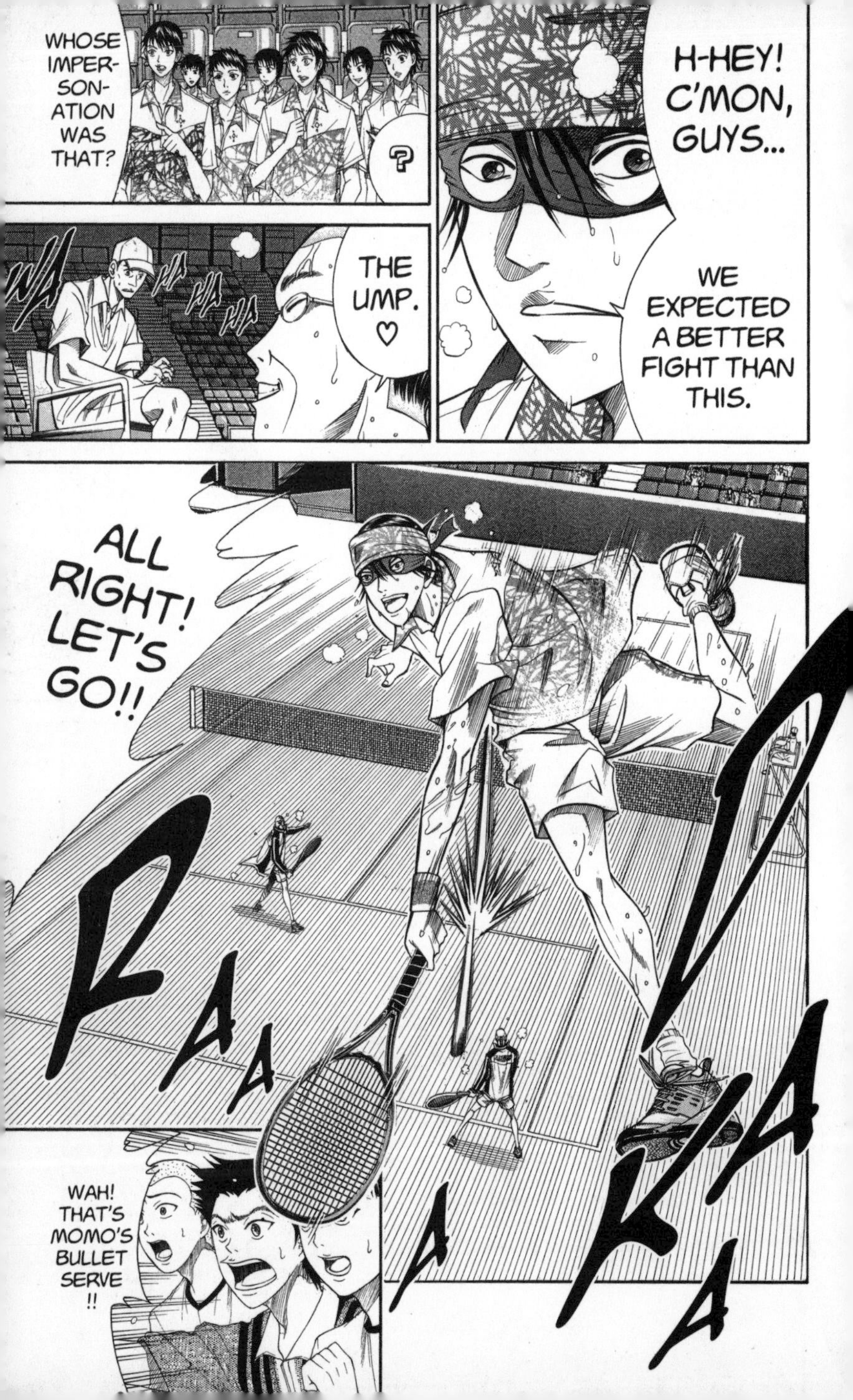
H-HEY! C'MON, GUYS...
WE EXPECTED A BETTER FIGHT THAN THIS.
WHOSE IMPERSON-ATION WAS THAT?
?
THE UMP. ♡
ALL RIGHT! LET'S GO!!
KAAA
RAAA
WAH! THAT'S MOMO'S BULLET SERVE !!

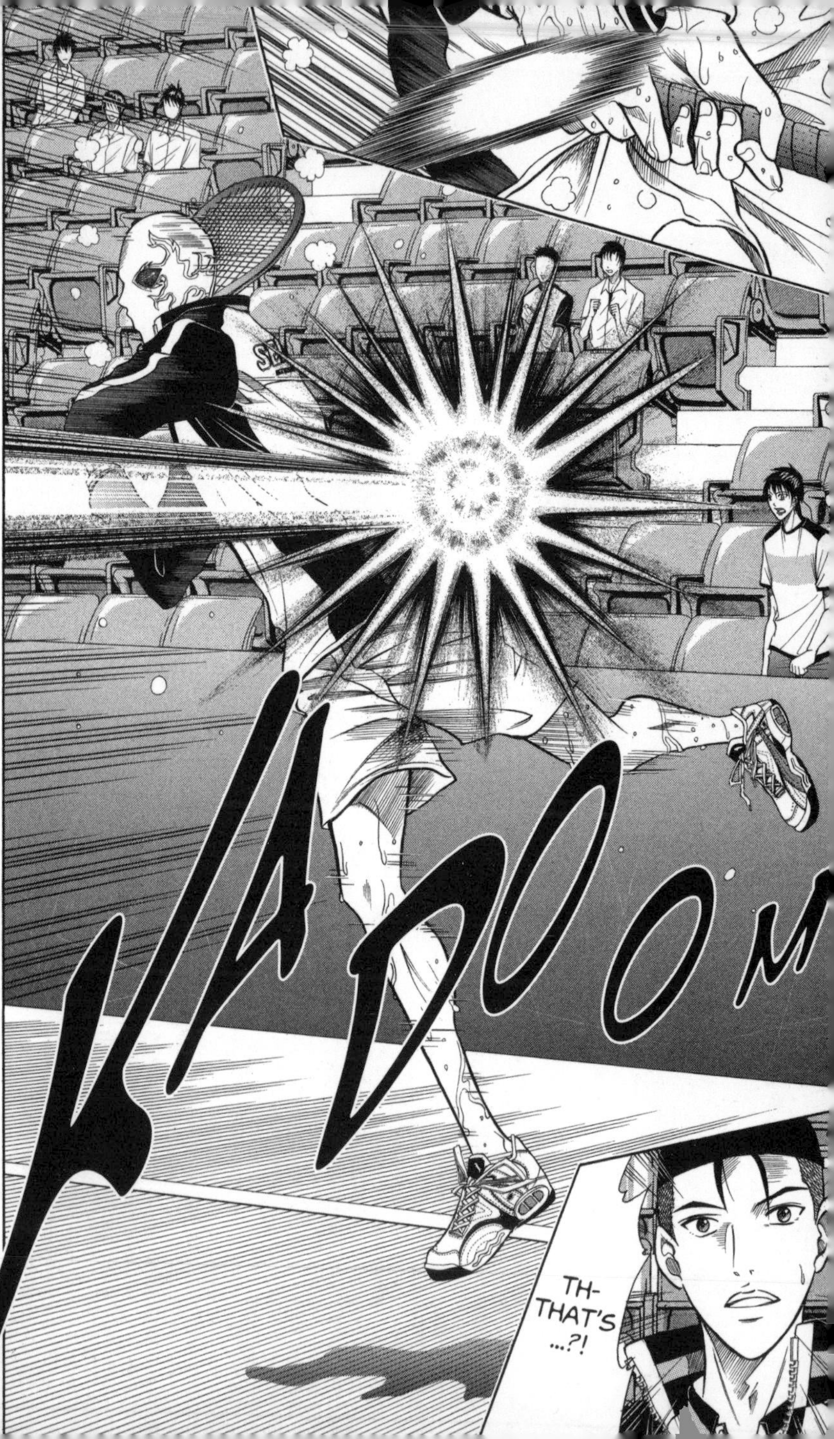
KA-BOOM
TH-THAT'S ...?!

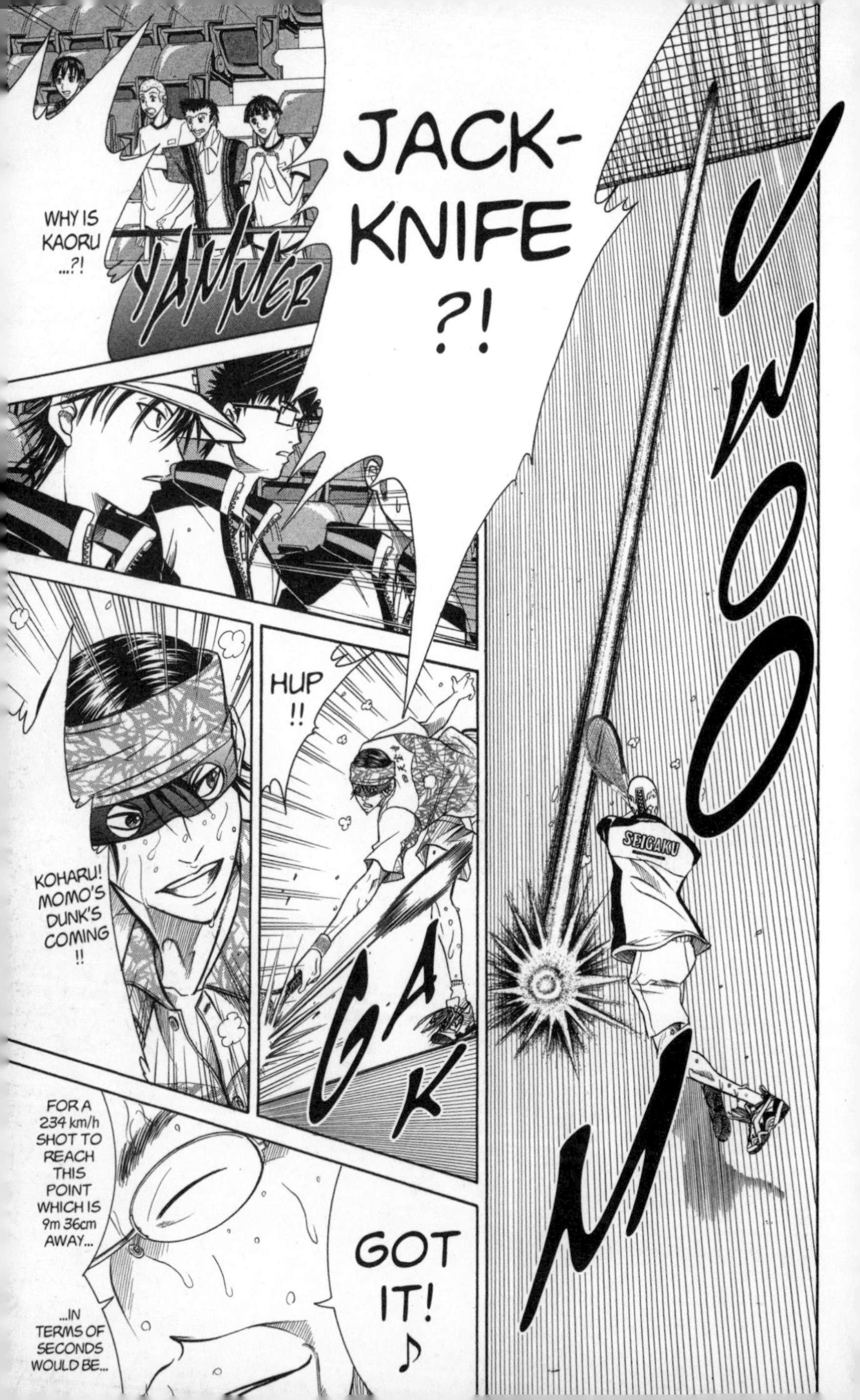
YAMMER
WHY IS KAORU ...?!
HUP !!
JACK-KNIFE ?!
GAK
KOHARU! MOMO'S DUNK'S COMING !!
GOT IT! ♪
FOR A 234 km/h SHOT TO REACH THIS POINT WHICH IS 9m 36cm AWAY...
...IN TERMS OF SECONDS WOULD BE...

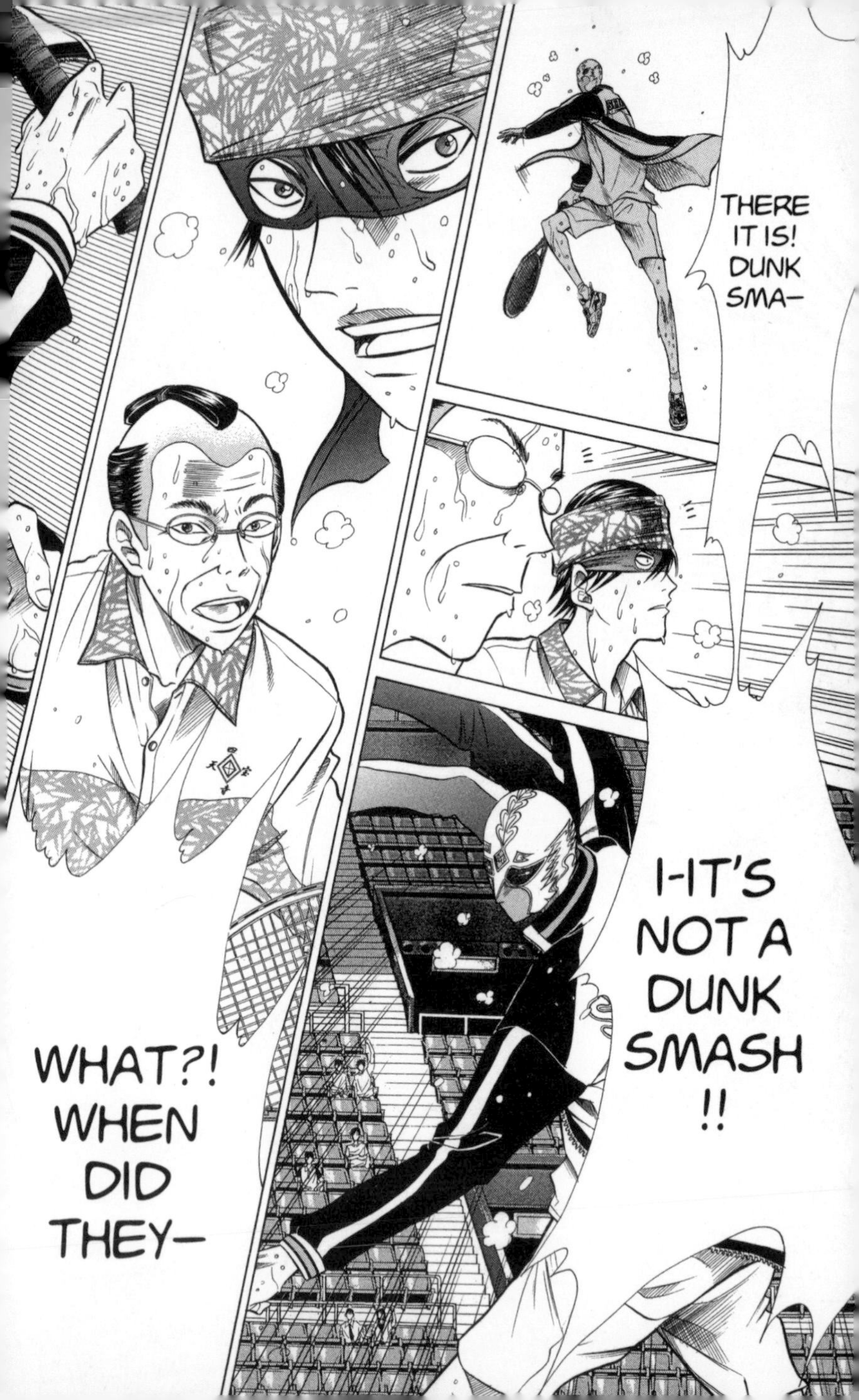
THERE IT IS! DUNK SMA-
I-IT'S NOT A DUNK SMASH !!
WHAT?! WHEN DID THEY-

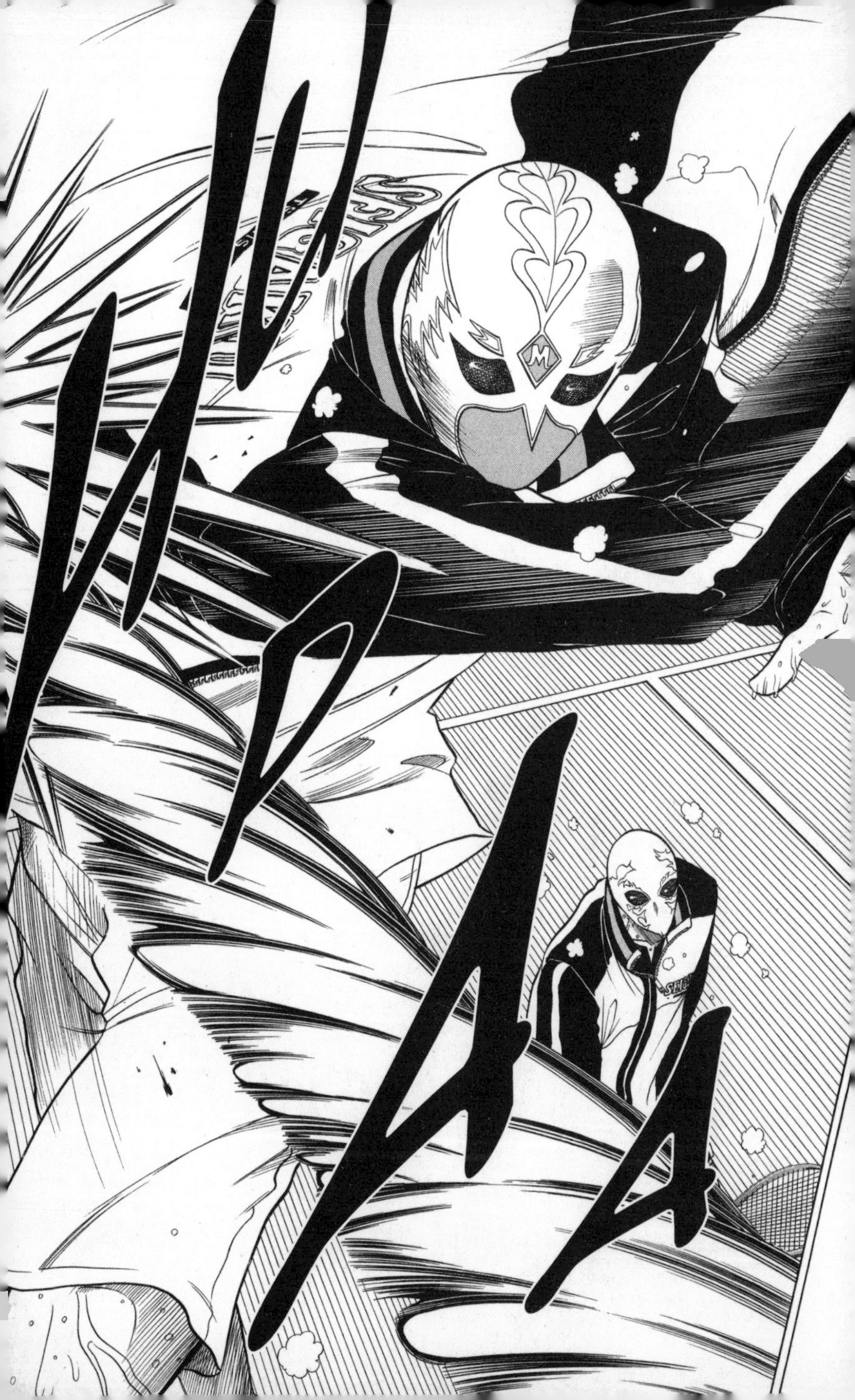

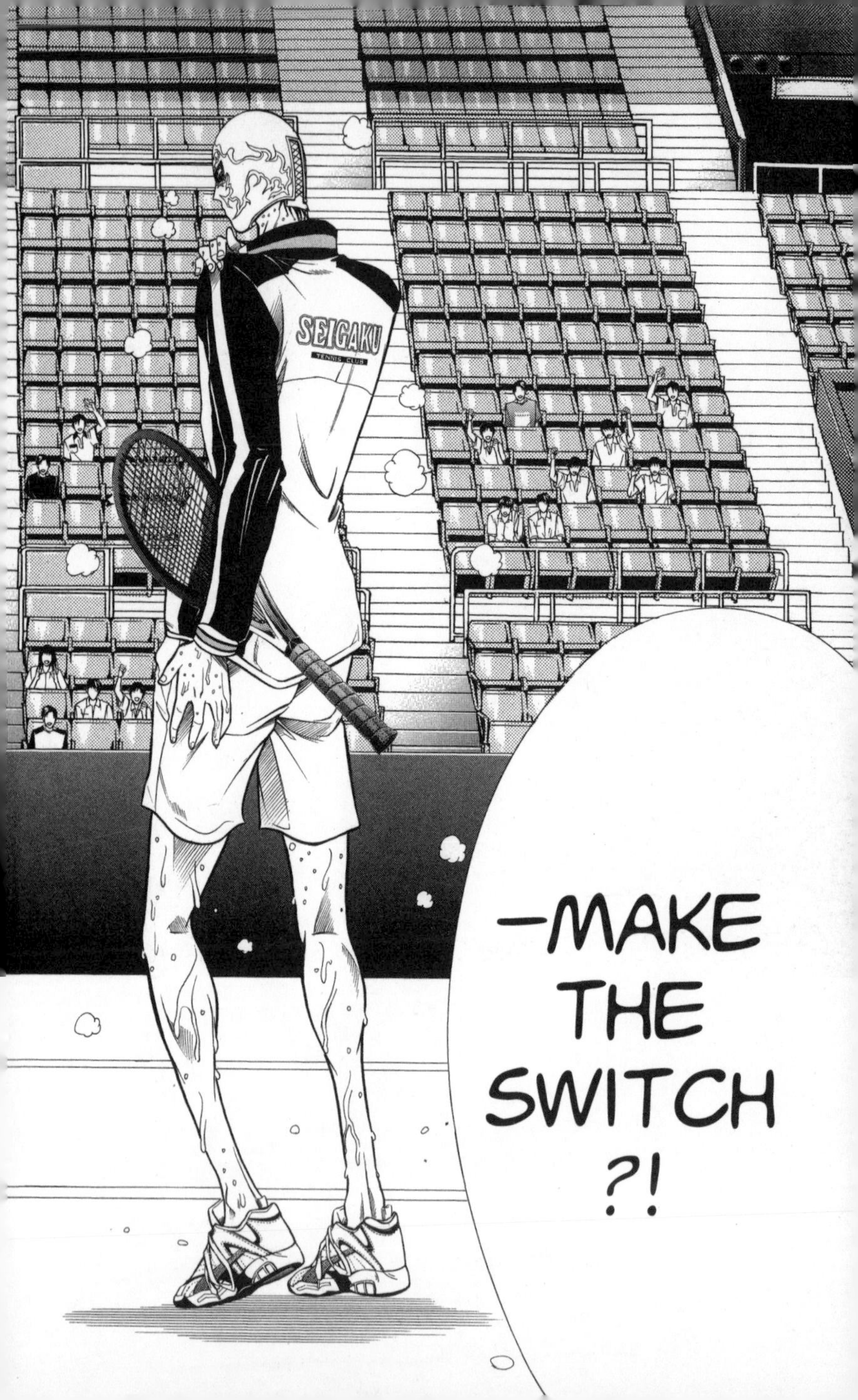
SEIGAKU
TENNIS CLUB
—MAKE THE SWITCH?!

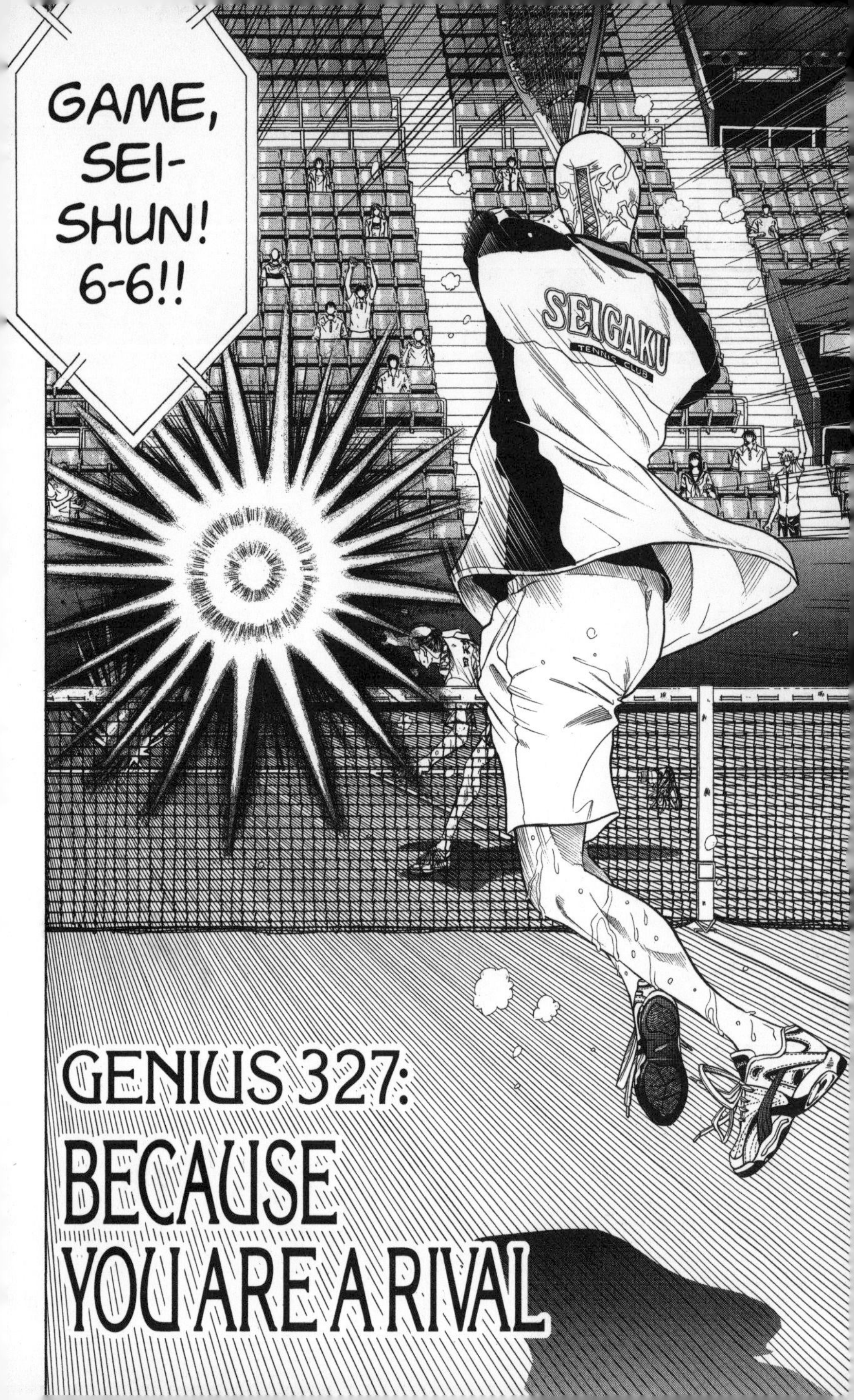
GAME, SEI-SHUN! 6-6!!
SEIGAKU
TENNIS CLUB
GENIUS 327:
BECAUSE YOU ARE A RIVAL

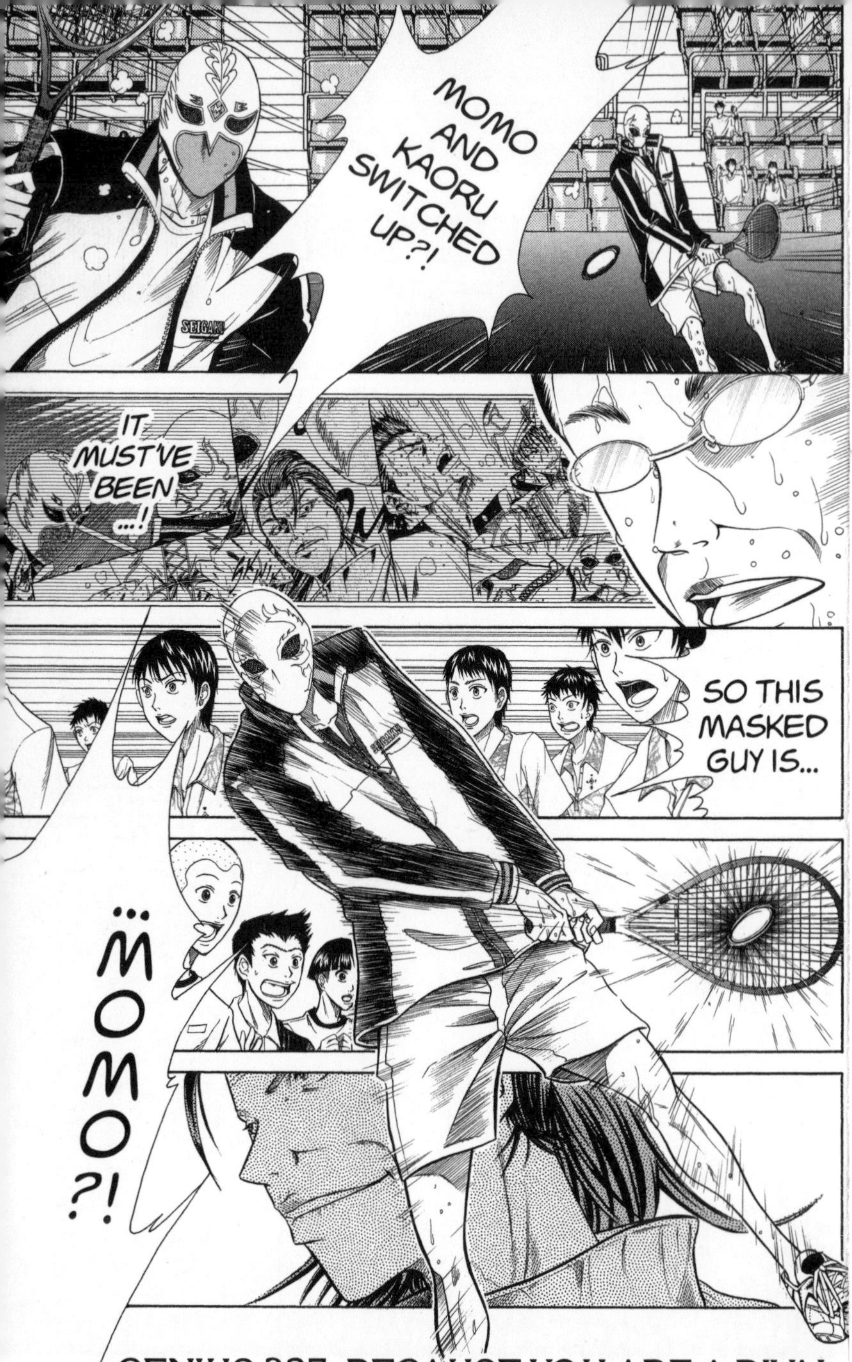
MOMO AND KAORU SWITCHED UP?!
IT MUST'VE BEEN ...!
SO THIS MASKED GUY IS...
...MOMO?!
SEIGAKU

GENIUS 327: BECAUSE YOU ARE A RIVAL

4TH CHARACTER POPULARITY POLL RESULTS!! ②

11TH	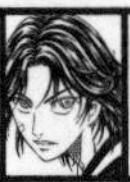	EIJI KIKUMARU	2897	21ST	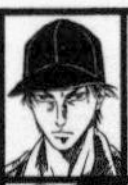	GENICHIRO SANADA	1247
12TH	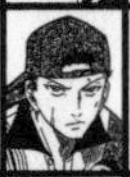	RYO SHISHIDO	2503	22ND	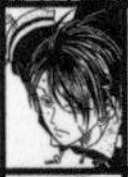	AKIRA KAMIO	1178
13TH	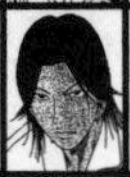	YOSHIRO AKAZAWA	2218	23RD	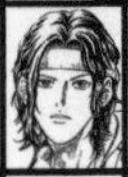	SEIICHI YUKIMURA	1036
13TH	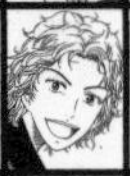	JIRO AKUTAGAWA	2218	24TH	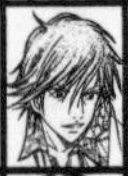	KURANOSUKE SHIRAISHI	1029
15TH	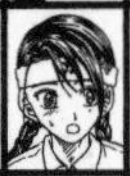	SAKUNO RYUZAKI	2146	25TH	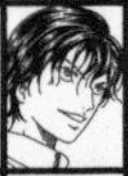	HAJIME MIZUKI	953
16TH	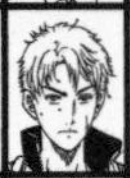	CHOTARO OHTORI	1796	26TH	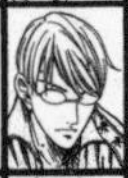	HIROSHI YAGYU	892
17TH	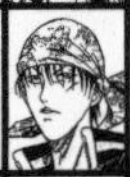	KAORU KAIDO	1750	27TH	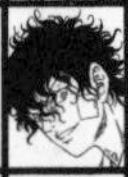	AKAYA KIRIHARA	770
18TH	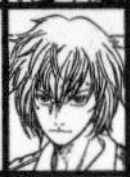	BUNTA MARUI	1641	28TH	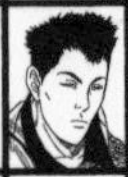	MUNEHIRO KABAJI	733
19TH	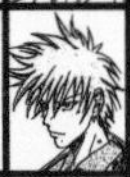	MASAHARU NIO	1310	29TH	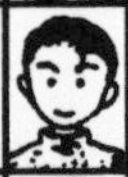	TAKESHI KONOMI	718
20TH	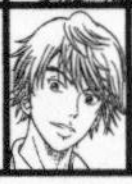	KIYOSUMI SENGOKU	1265	30TH	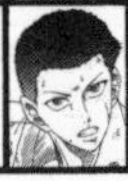	YUTA FUJI	694

CONTINUES ON PAGE 114

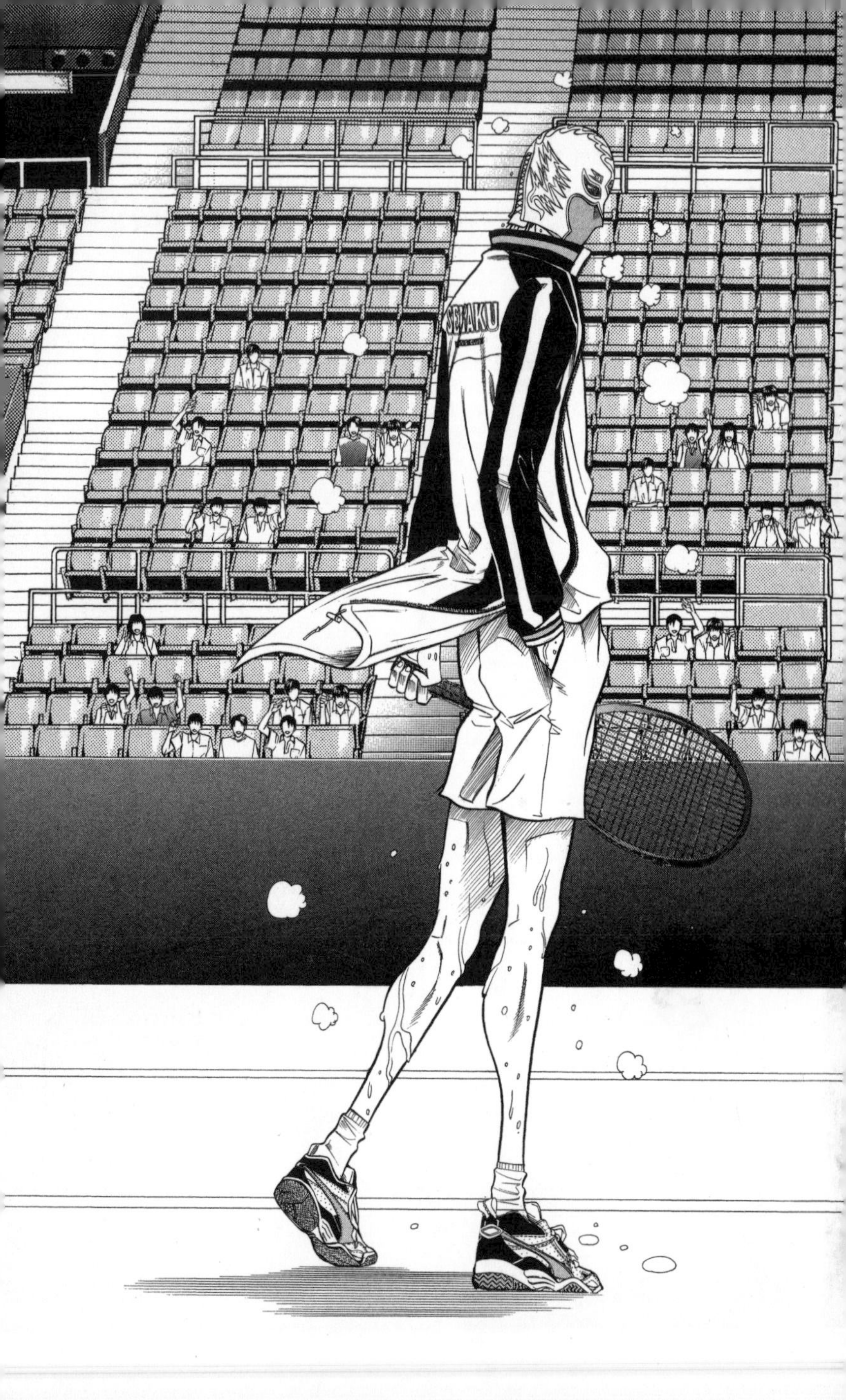

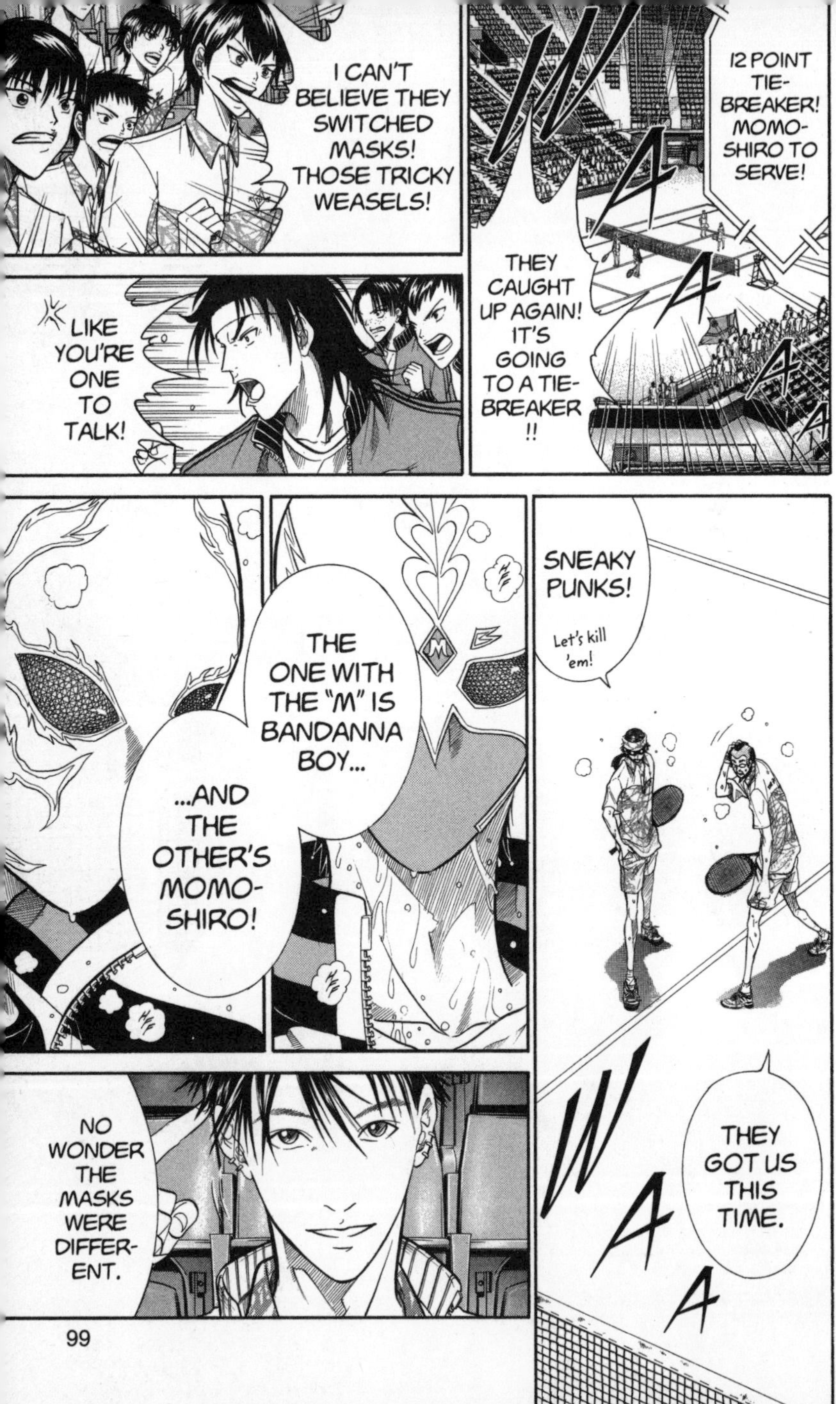
WAAAA
12 POINT TIE-BREAKER! MOMO-SHIRO TO SERVE!
THEY CAUGHT UP AGAIN! IT'S GOING TO A TIE-BREAKER !!
I CAN'T BELIEVE THEY SWITCHED MASKS! THOSE TRICKY WEASELS!
LIKE YOU'RE ONE TO TALK!
SNEAKY PUNKS!
Let's kill 'em!
THEY GOT US THIS TIME.
WAA
THE ONE WITH THE "M" IS BANDANNA BOY...
...AND THE OTHER'S MOMO-SHIRO!
NO WONDER THE MASKS WERE DIFFERENT.

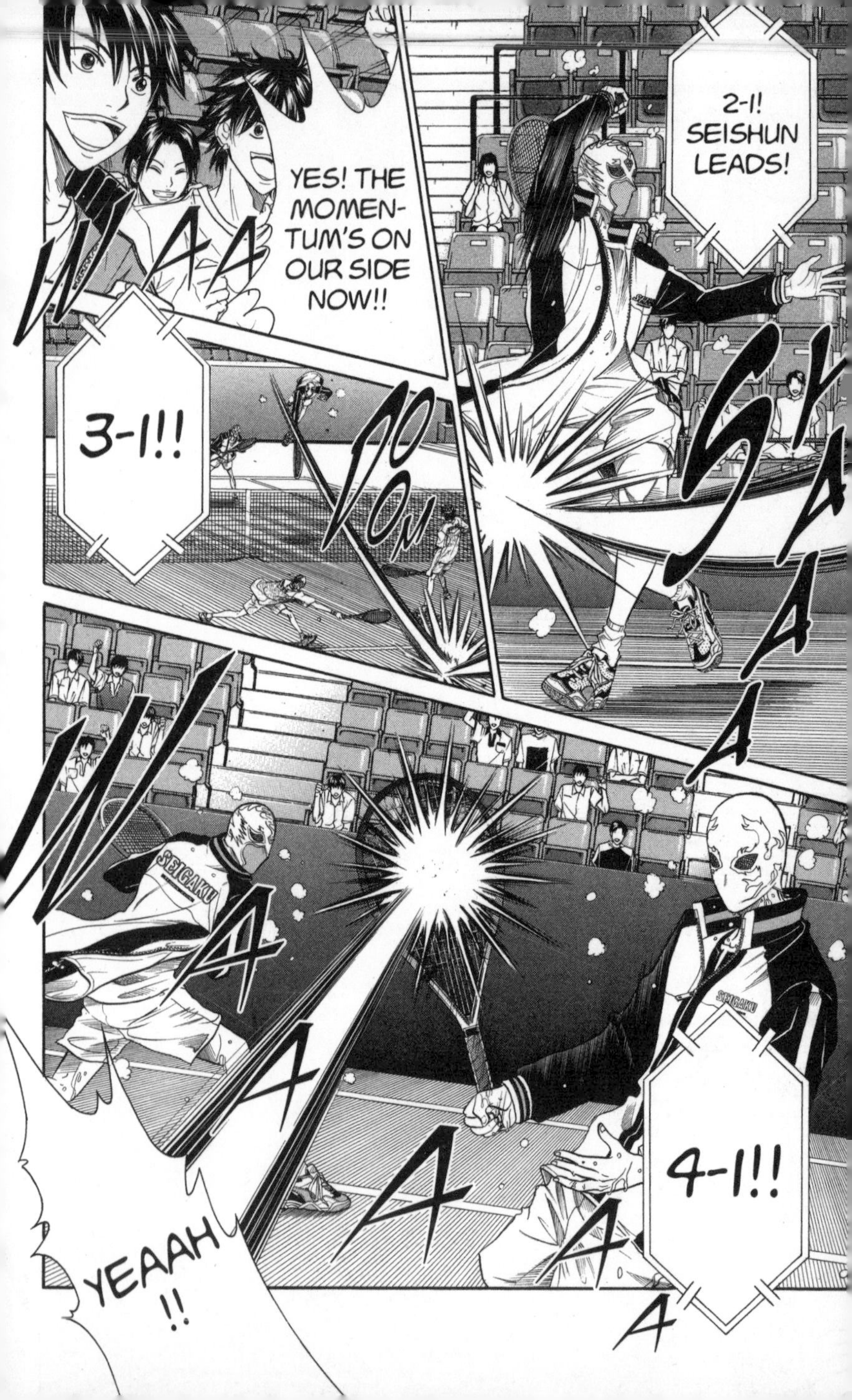
2-1! SEISHUN LEADS!
YES! THE MOMEN-TUM'S ON OUR SIDE NOW!!
WAA
3-1!!
DOOON
4-1!!
WAAAA
YEAAH!!

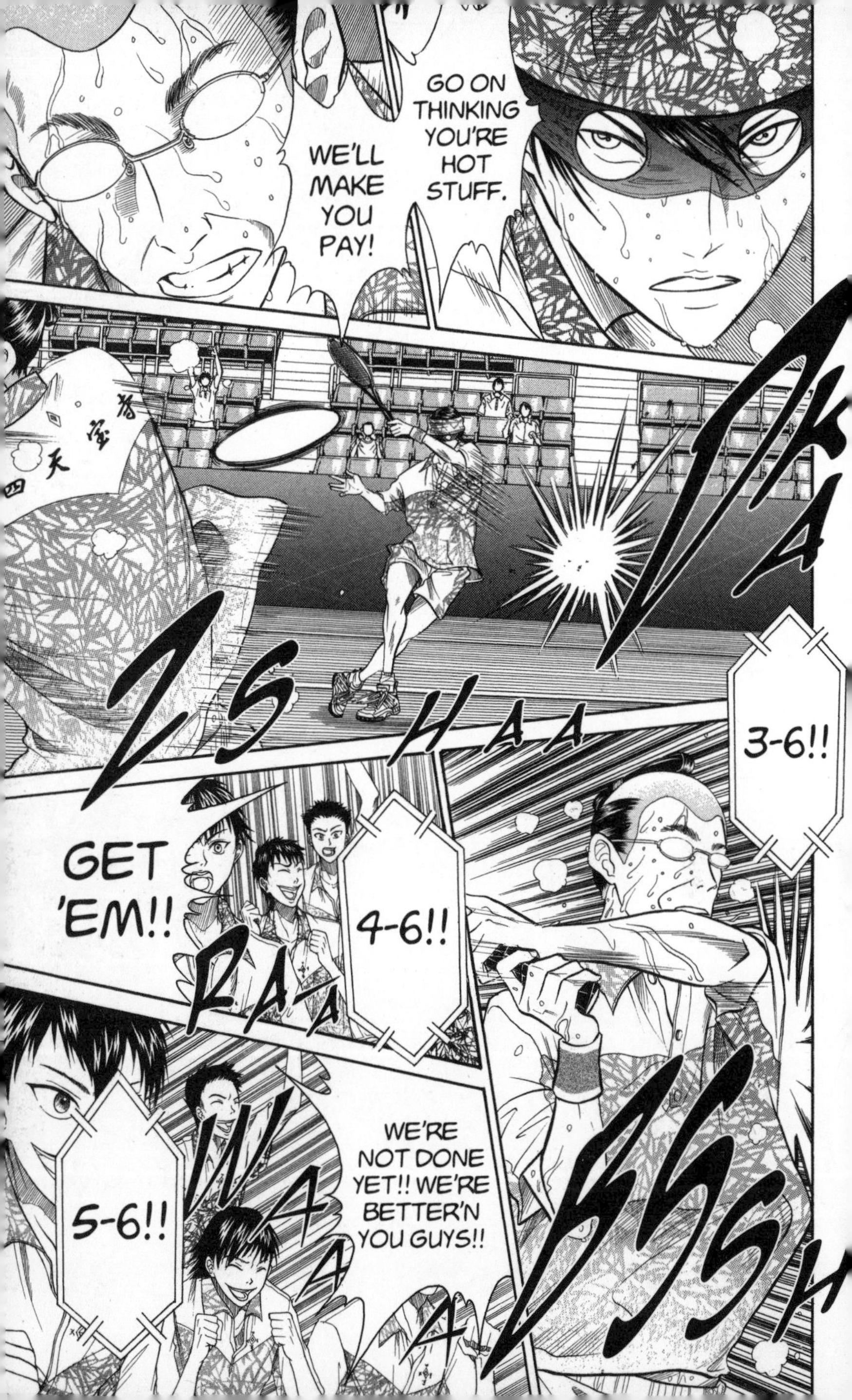
GO ON THINKING YOU'RE HOT STUFF.
WE'LL MAKE YOU PAY!
ZSHAA
3-6!!
4-6!!
GET 'EM!!
RAA
WE'RE NOT DONE YET!! WE'RE BETTER'N YOU GUYS!!
5-6!!
WAAA

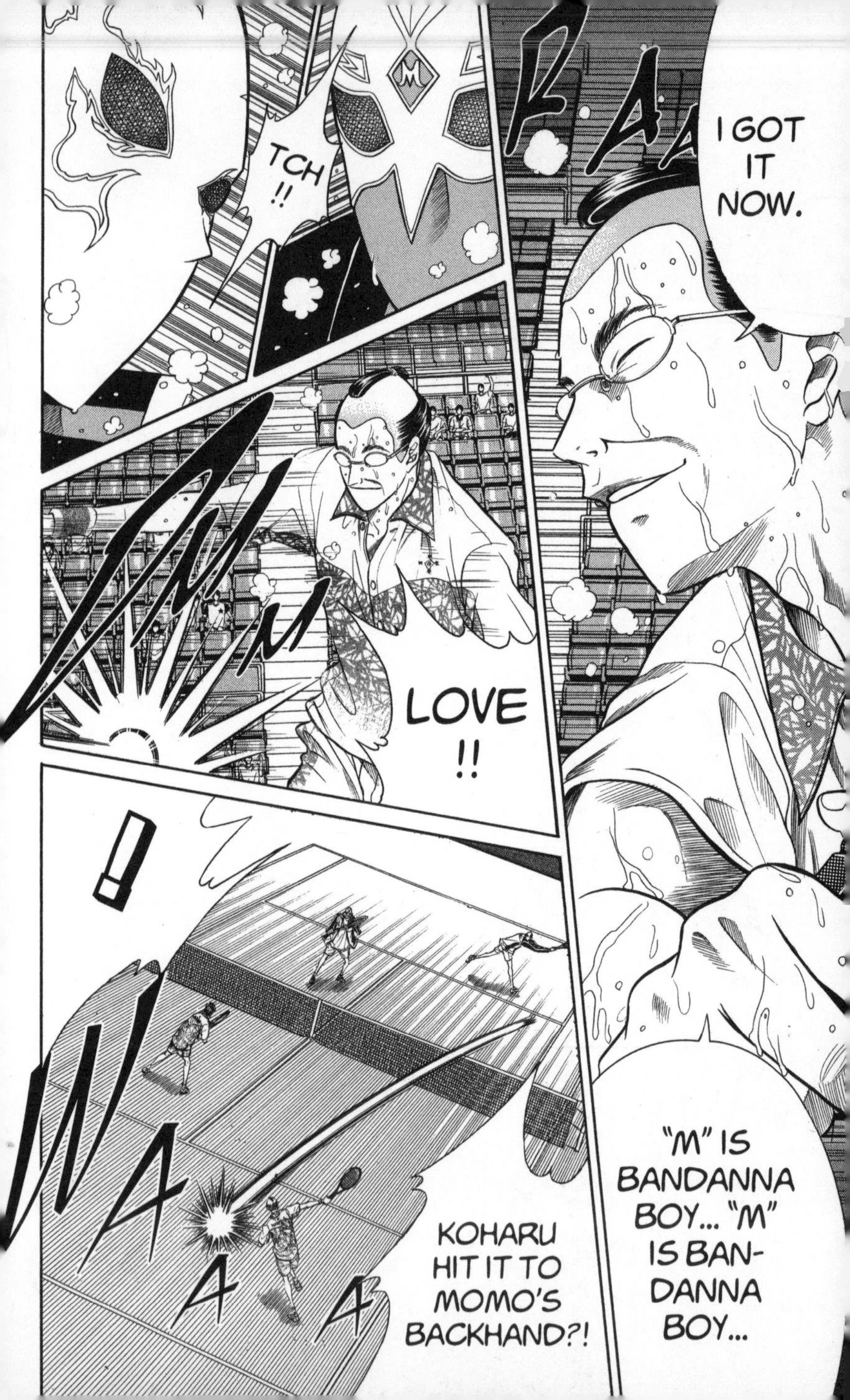
BAAA
I GOT IT NOW.
"M" IS BANDANNA BOY... "M" IS BAN-DANNA BOY...
TCH !!
LOVE !!
!
WAAAA
KOHARU HIT IT TO MOMO'S BACKHAND?!

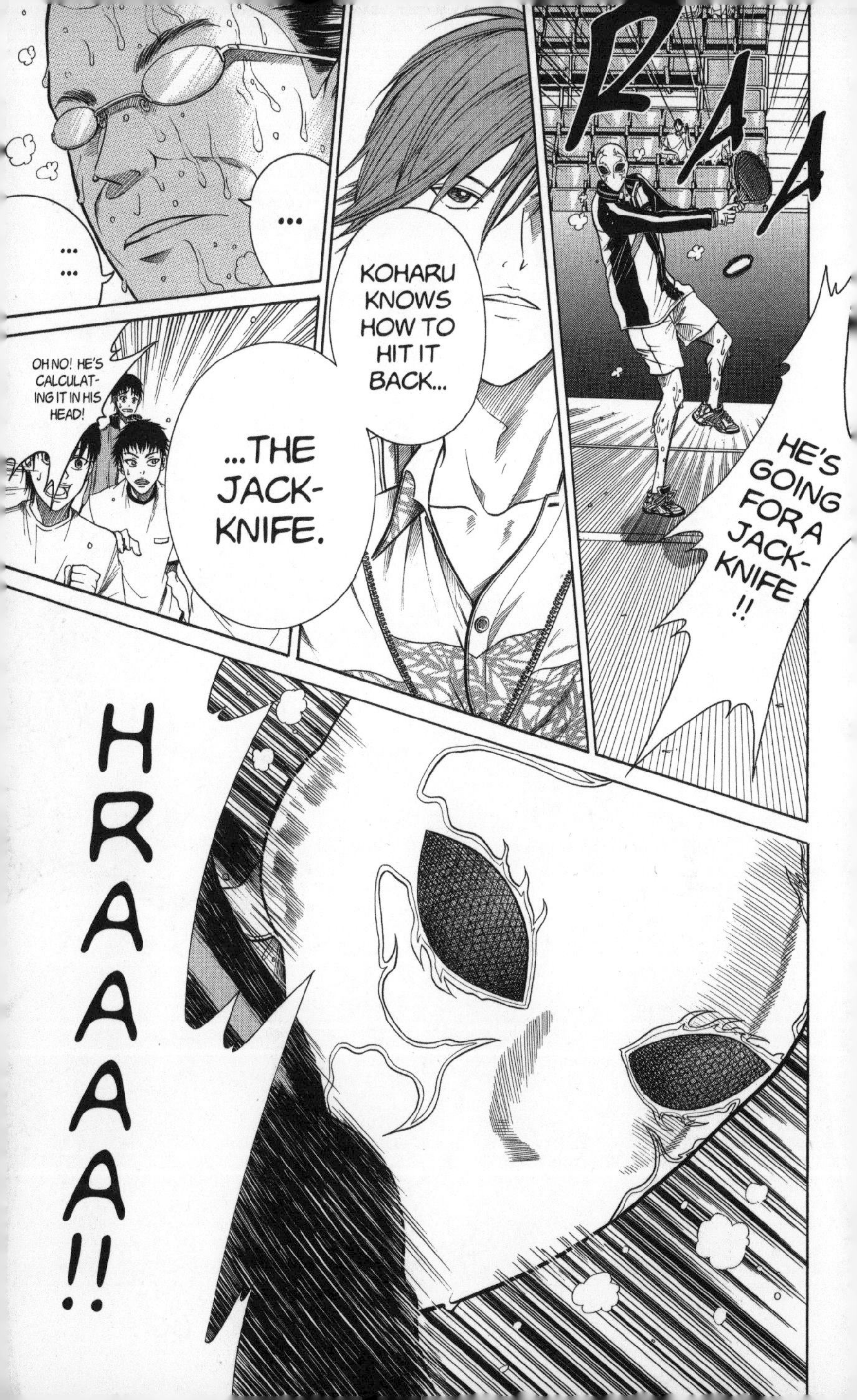
RAA
HE'S GOING FOR A JACK-KNIFE!!
KOHARU KNOWS HOW TO HIT IT BACK...
...THE JACK-KNIFE.
...
...
...
OH NO! HE'S CALCULAT-ING IT IN HIS HEAD!
HRAAAA!!

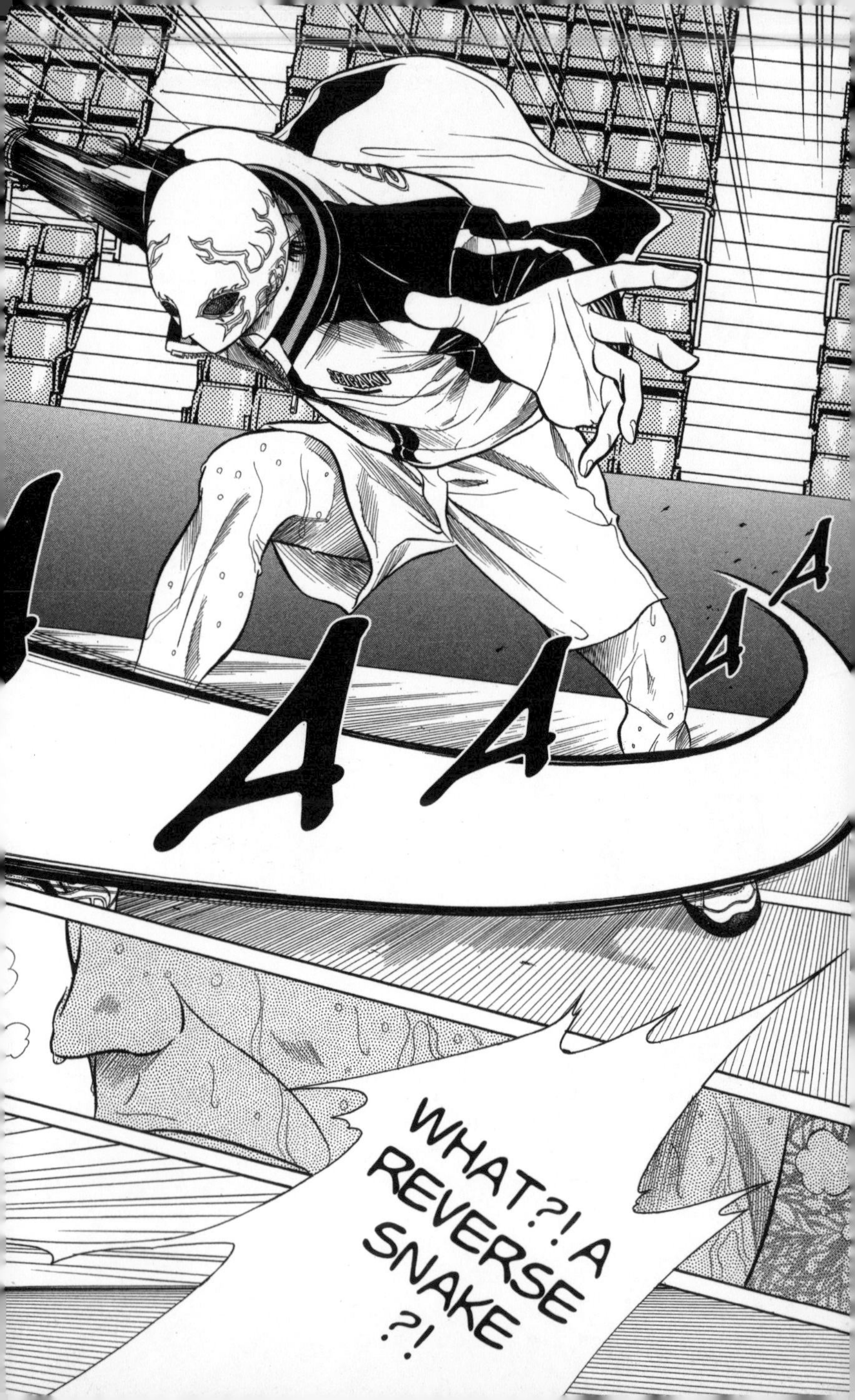
WHAT?! A REVERSE SNAKE?!

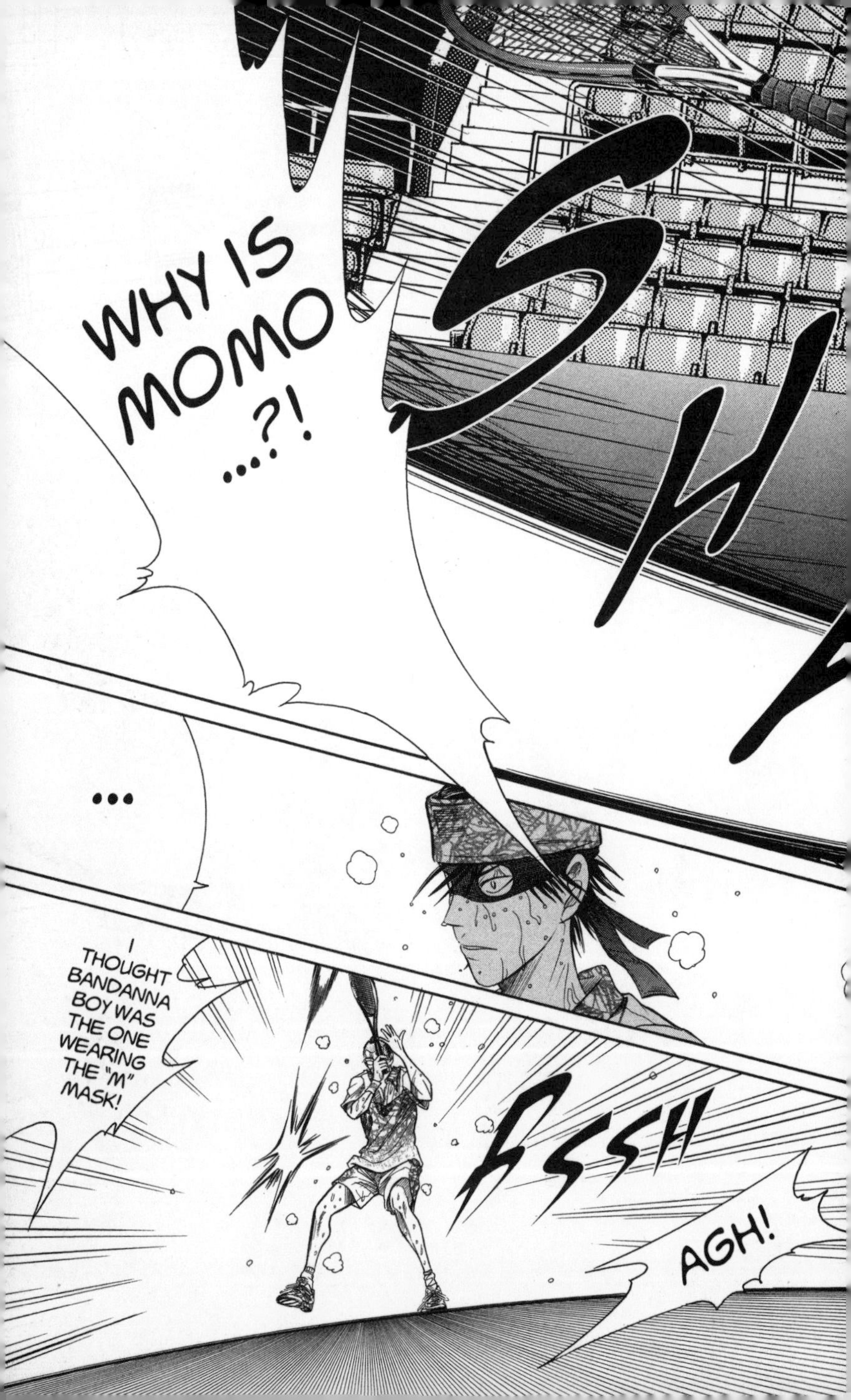
WHY IS MOMO ...?!
...
AGH!
I THOUGHT BANDANNA BOY WAS THE ONE WEARING THE "M" MASK!

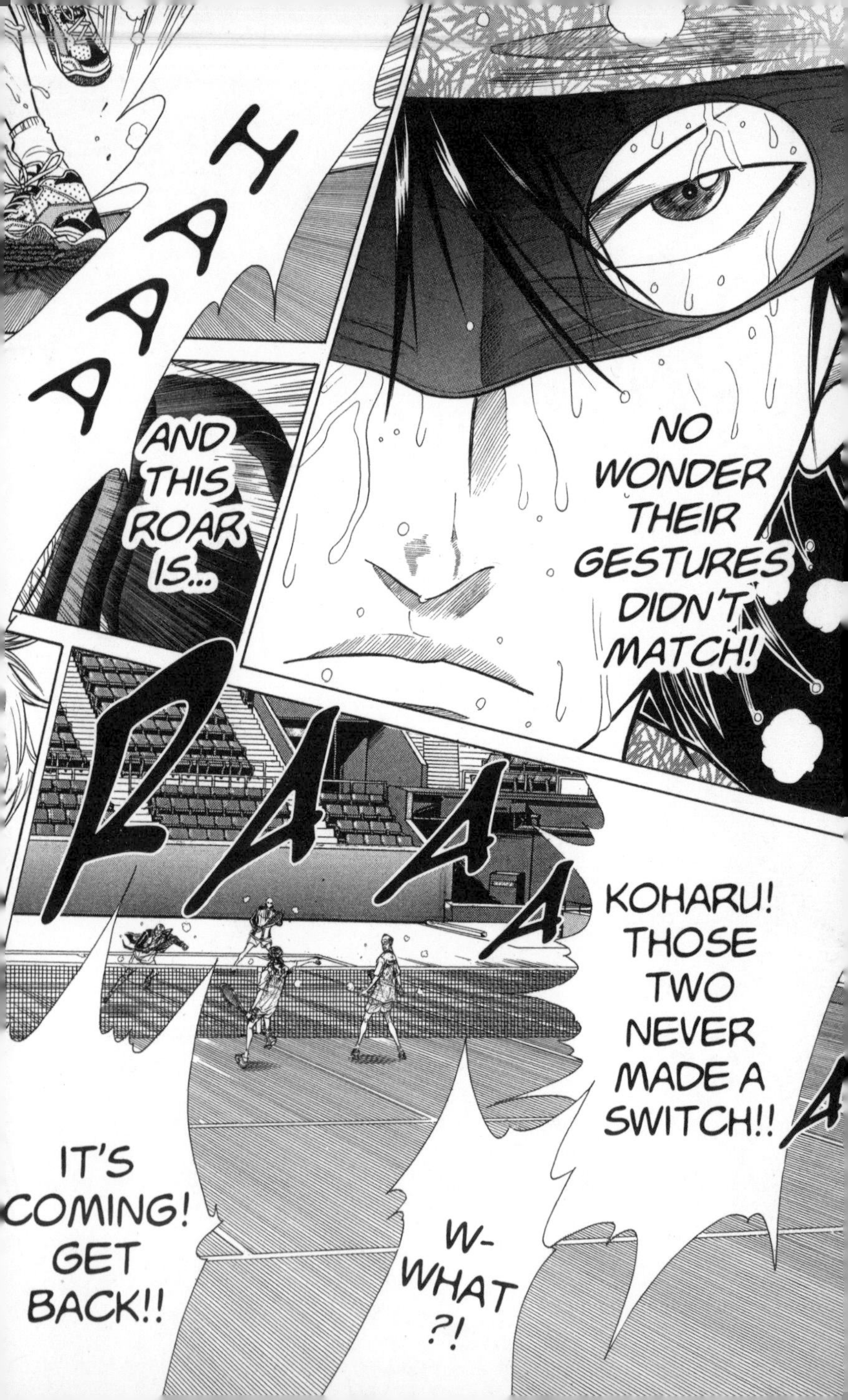
NO WONDER THEIR GESTURES DIDN'T MATCH!
HAAA
AND THIS ROAR IS...
KOHARU! THOSE TWO NEVER MADE A SWITCH!!
AAAA
W-WHAT?!
IT'S COMING! GET BACK!!

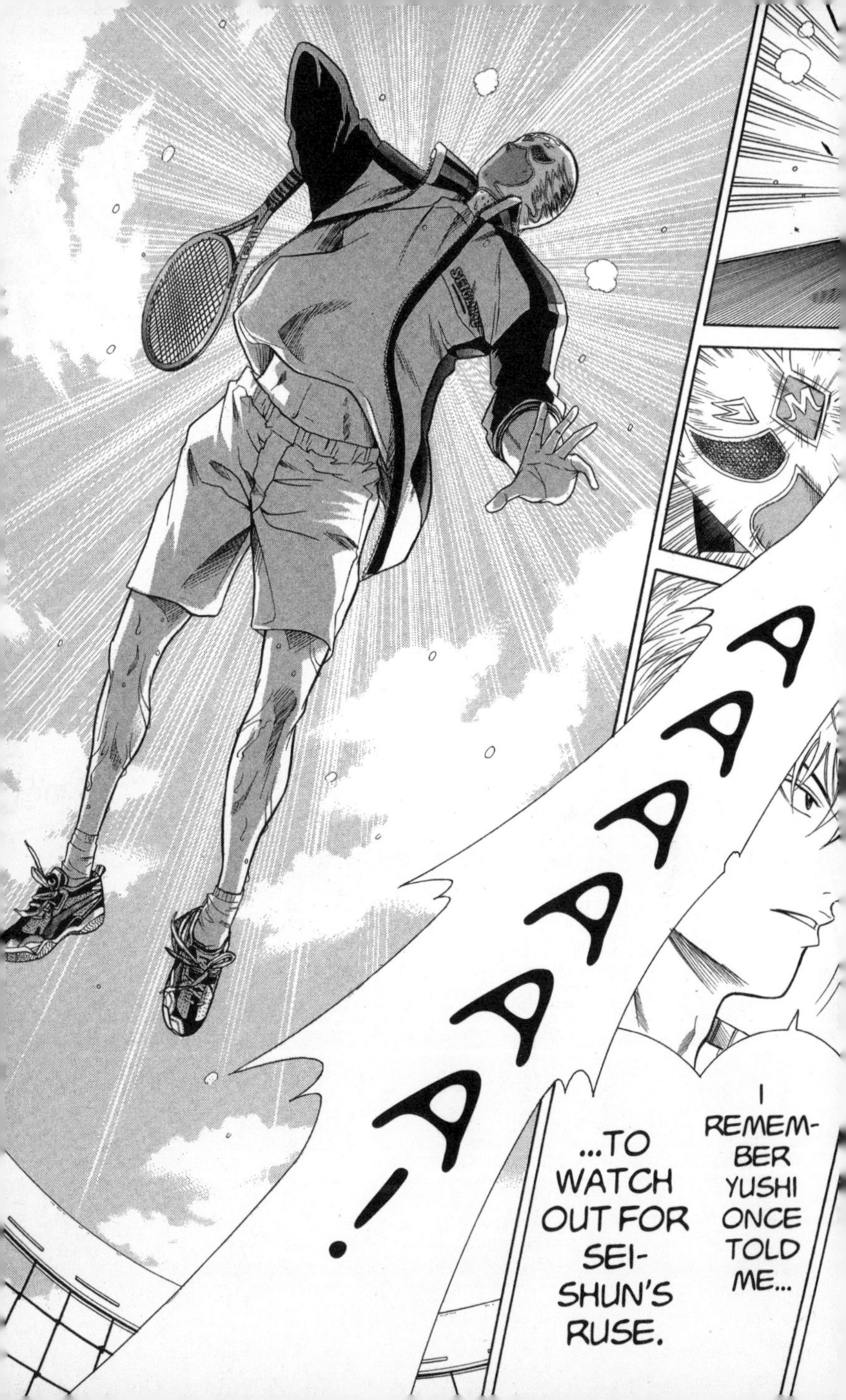

AAAAAAA!
I REMEMBER YUSHI ONCE TOLD ME...
...TO WATCH OUT FOR SEISHUN'S RUSE.

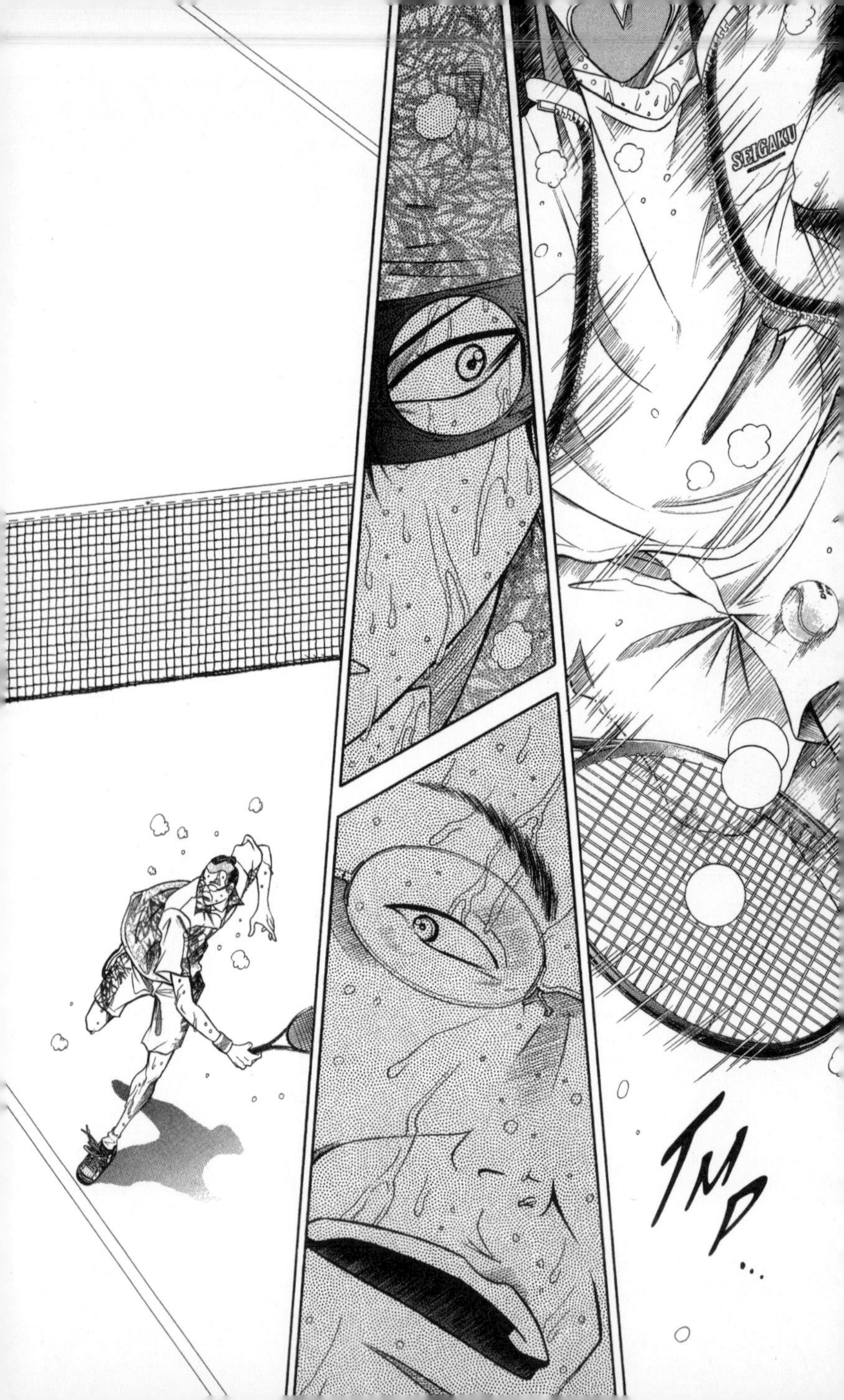
SEIGAKU
TMP...

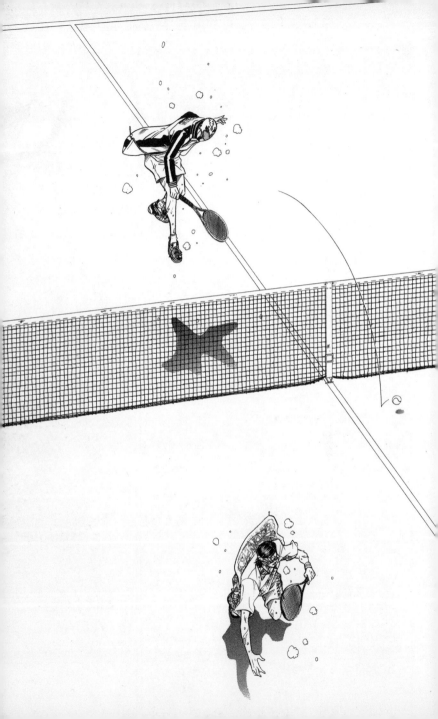

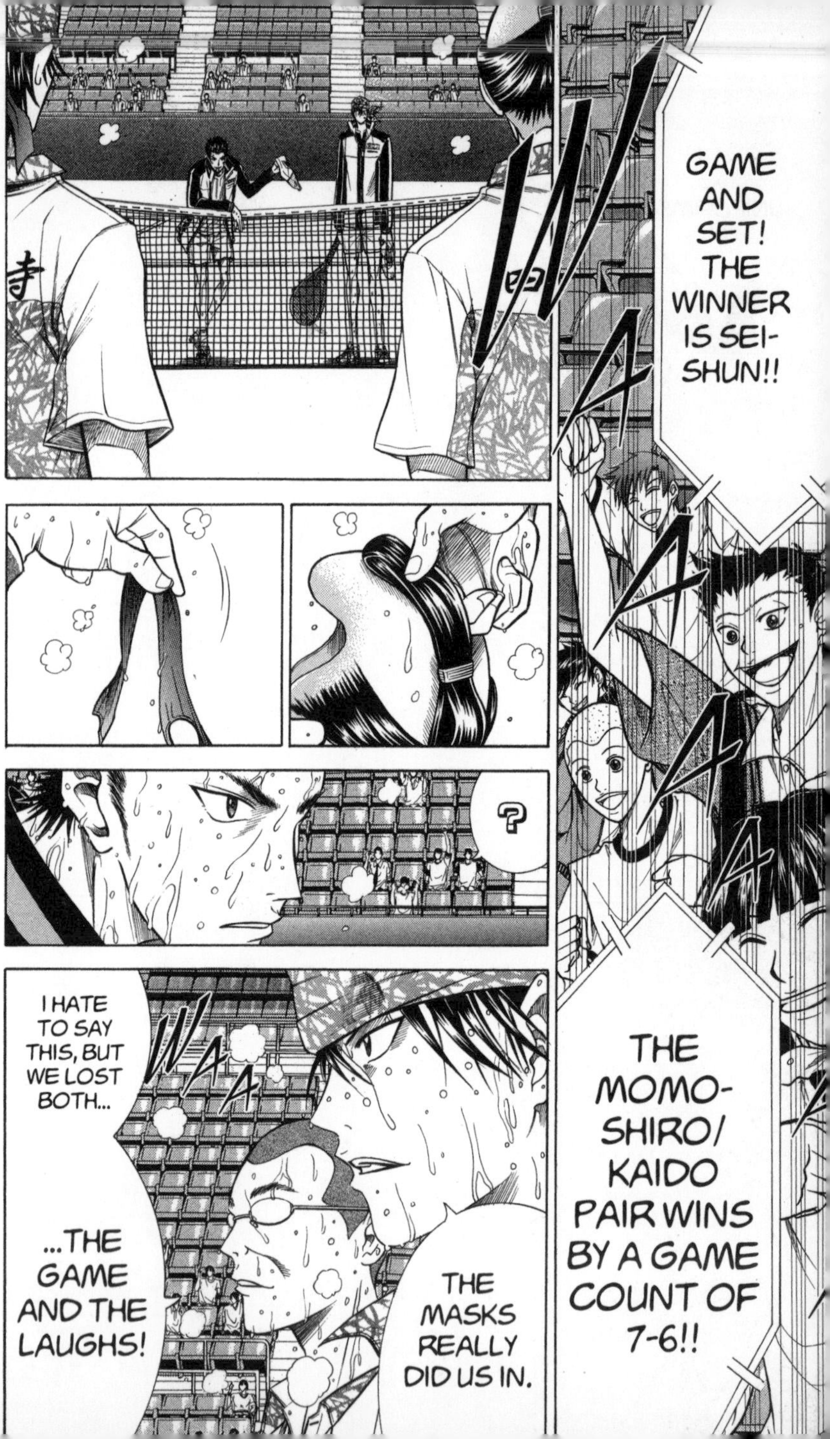
GAME AND SET! THE WINNER IS SEI-SHUN!!
WAAAA
THE MOMO-SHIRO/ KAIDO PAIR WINS BY A GAME COUNT OF 7-6!!
?
THE MASKS REALLY DID US IN.
WAA
I HATE TO SAY THIS, BUT WE LOST BOTH...
...THE GAME AND THE LAUGHS!

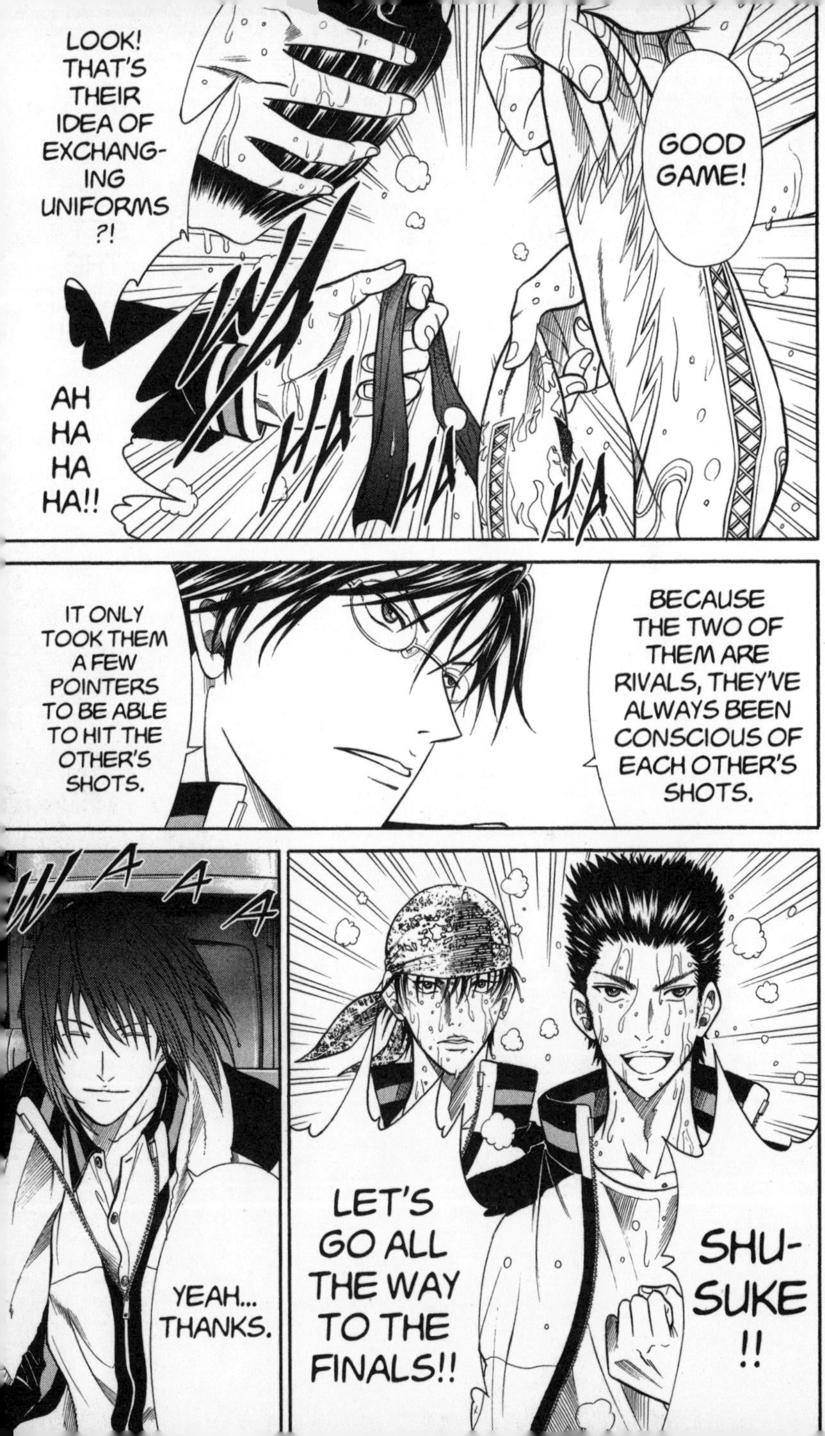
GOOD GAME!
LOOK! THAT'S THEIR IDEA OF EXCHANG-ING UNIFORMS ?!
AH HA HA HA!!
BECAUSE THE TWO OF THEM ARE RIVALS, THEY'VE ALWAYS BEEN CONSCIOUS OF EACH OTHER'S SHOTS.
IT ONLY TOOK THEM A FEW POINTERS TO BE ABLE TO HIT THE OTHER'S SHOTS.
SHU-SUKE !!
LET'S GO ALL THE WAY TO THE FINALS!!
WAAA
YEAH... THANKS.

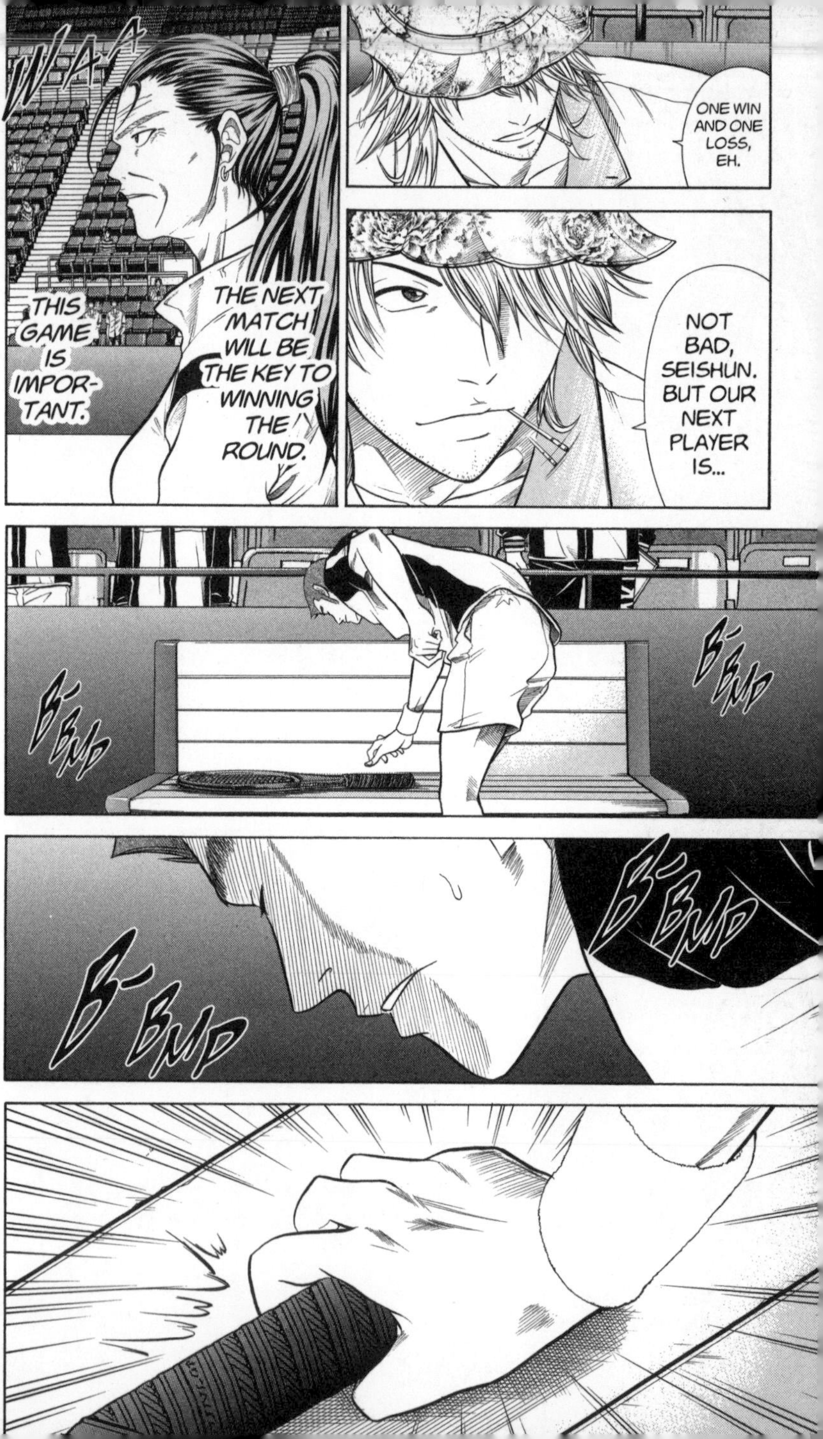
ONE WIN AND ONE LOSS, EH.
NOT BAD, SEISHUN. BUT OUR NEXT PLAYER IS...
WAA
THE NEXT MATCH WILL BE THE KEY TO WINNING THE ROUND.
THIS GAME IS IMPORTANT.
B-BMP
B-BMP
B-BMP
B-BMP

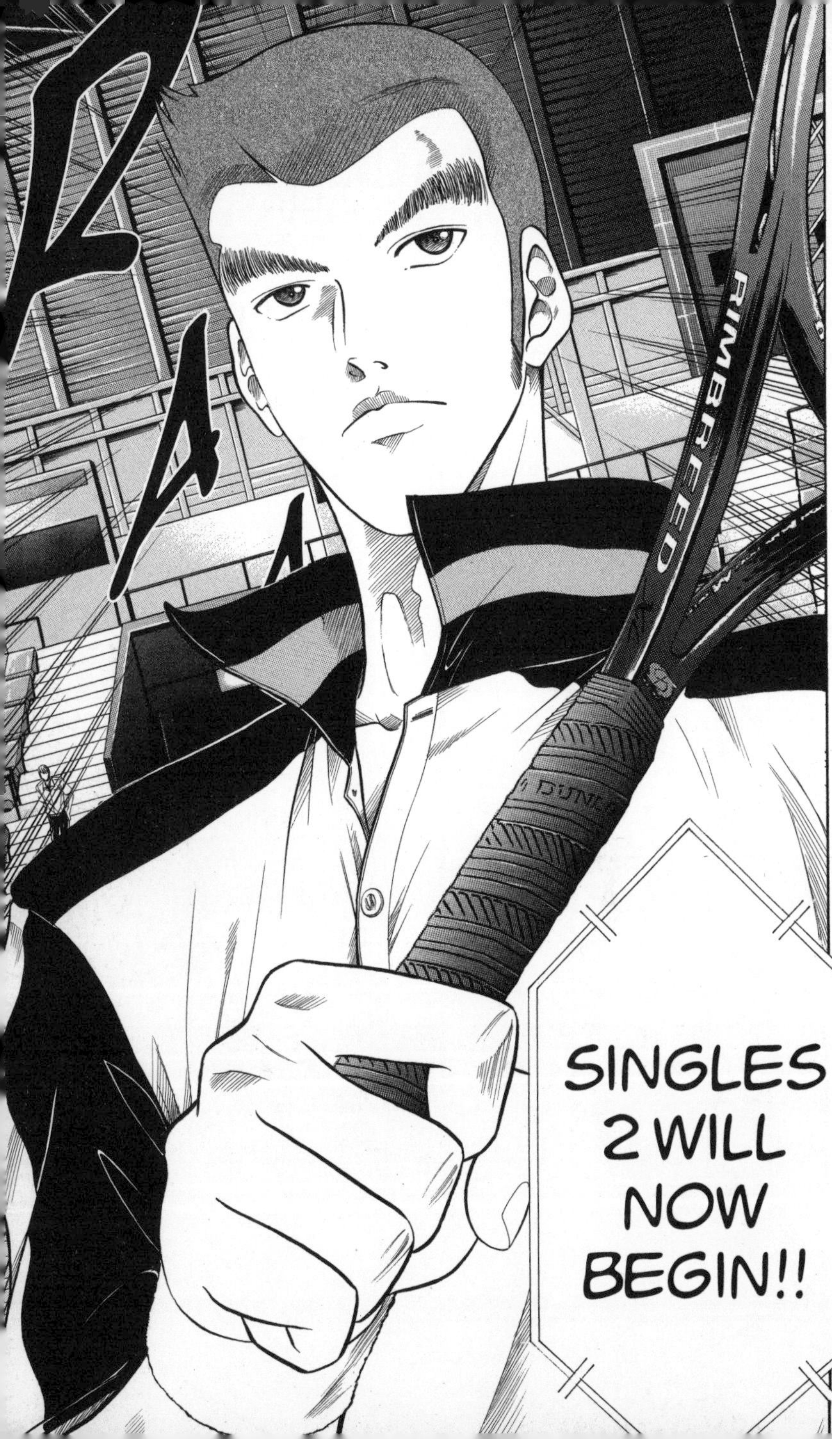
RIMBREED
SINGLES 2 WILL NOW BEGIN!!

4TH CHARACTER POPULARITY POLL RESULTS!! ③

31ST	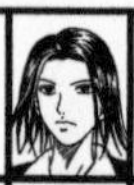	SHINJI IBU	672	41ST	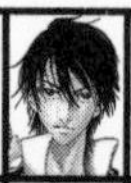	RYOGA ECHIZEN	403
32ND	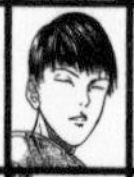	RENJI YANAGI	644	42ND	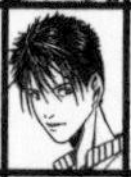	HIKARU ZAIZEN	394
33RD	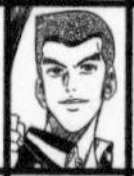	TAKASHI KAWAMURA	623	43RD	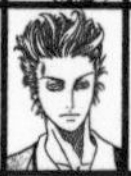	JIN AKUTSU	376
34TH	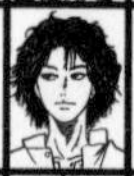	SENRI CHITOSE	522	44TH	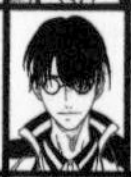	YUDAI YAMATO	309
34TH	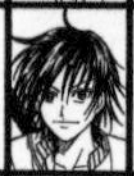	KINTARO TOYAMA	522	45TH	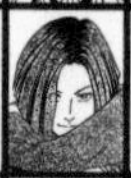	HAGINOSUKE TAKI	285
36TH	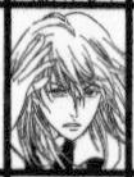	RIN HIRAKOBA	496	46TH	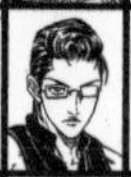	EISHIRO KITE	279
37TH	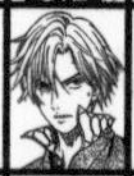	KOJIRO SAEKI	479	47TH	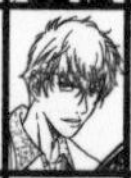	KENYA OSHITARI	268
38TH	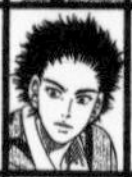	KENTARO MINAMI	472	48TH	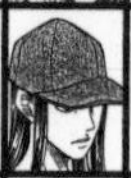	ATSUSHI KISARAZU	259
39TH	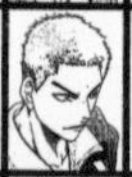	KIPPEI TACHIBANA	459	49TH	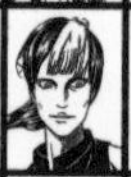	HIROSHI CHINEN	196
40TH	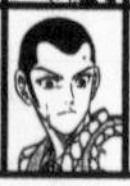	KENTARO AOI	442	50TH	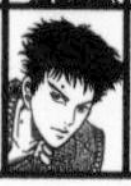	HARUKAZE KUROBANE	170

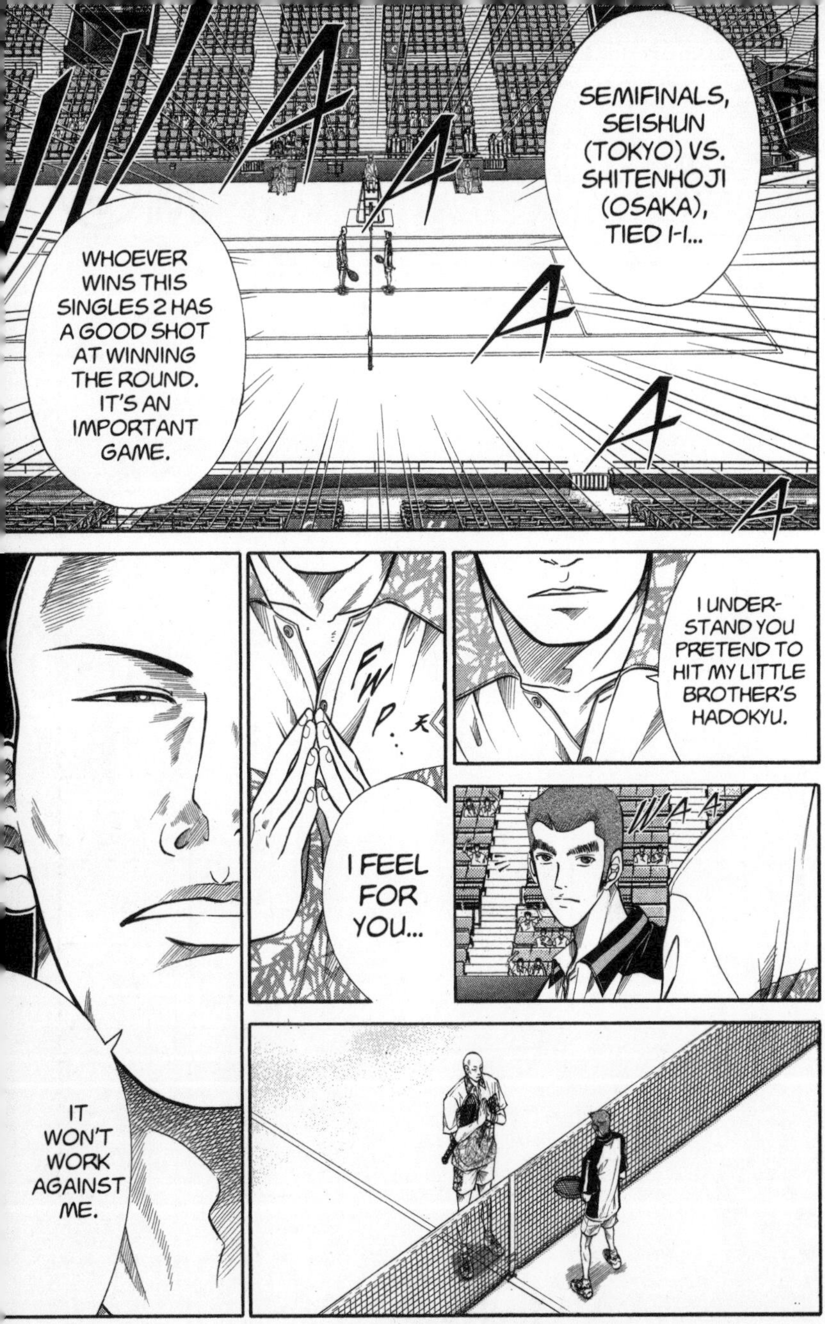
SEMIFINALS, SEISHUN (TOKYO) VS. SHITENHOJI (OSAKA), TIED 1-1...
WAAAAA
WHOEVER WINS THIS SINGLES 2 HAS A GOOD SHOT AT WINNING THE ROUND. IT'S AN IMPORTANT GAME.
I UNDER-STAND YOU PRETEND TO HIT MY LITTLE BROTHER'S HADOKYU.
FWP...
I FEEL FOR YOU...
WAA
IT WON'T WORK AGAINST ME.

GENIUS 328: ORIGINATOR

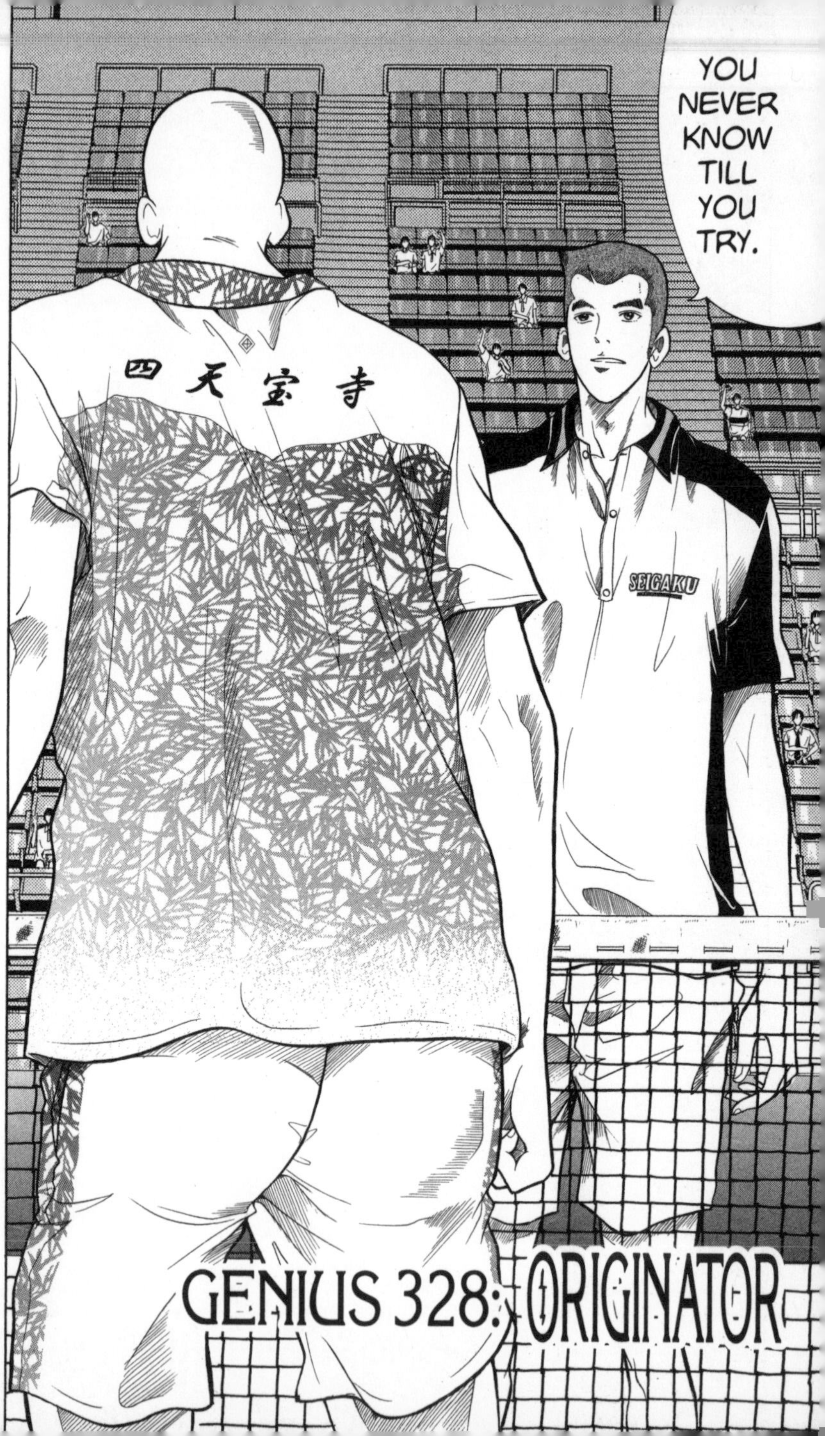
YOU NEVER KNOW TILL YOU TRY.
四天宝寺
SEIGAKU
GENIUS 328: ORIGINATOR

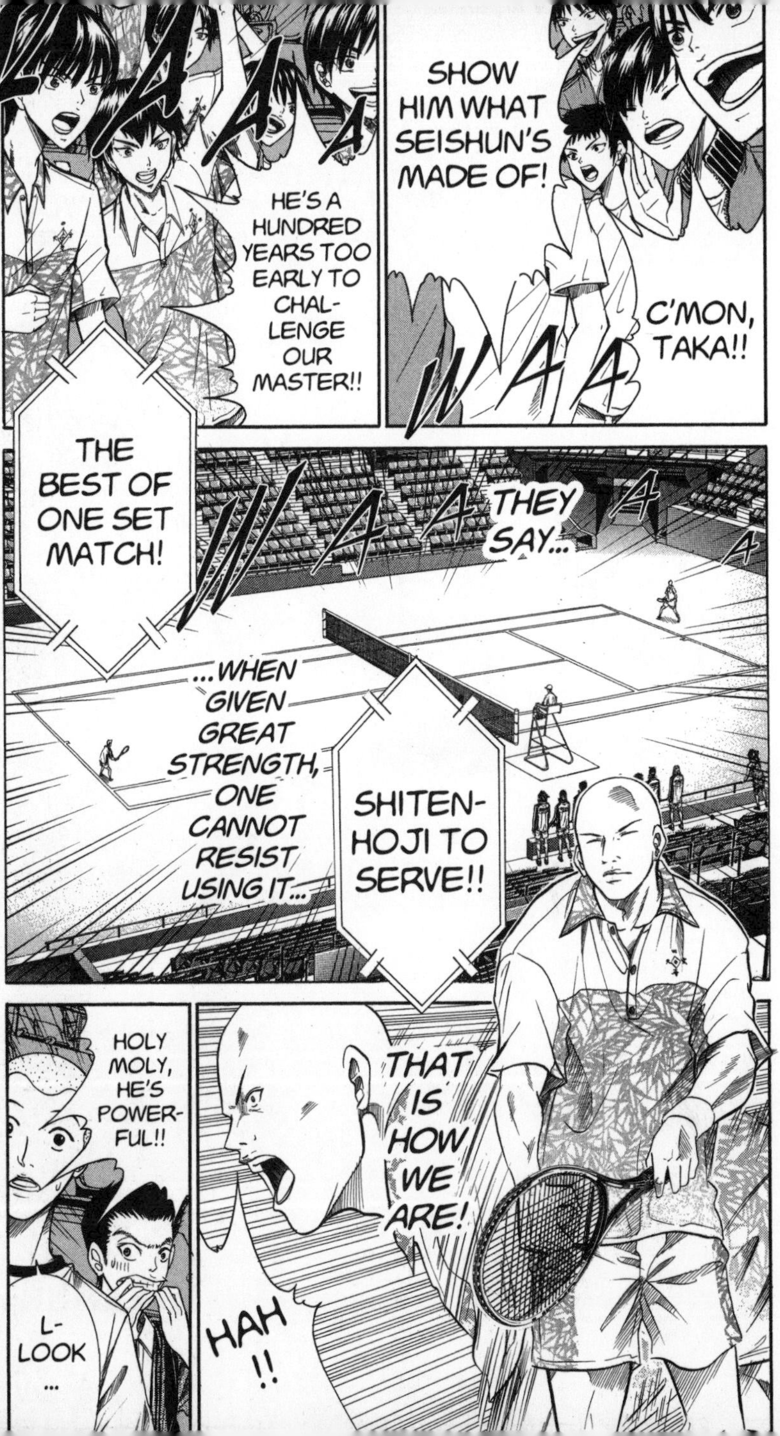
SHOW HIM WHAT SEISHUN'S MADE OF!
C'MON, TAKA!!
WAAA
HE'S A HUNDRED YEARS TOO EARLY TO CHAL-LENGE OUR MASTER!!
THE BEST OF ONE SET MATCH!
WAAA
THEY SAY...
...WHEN GIVEN GREAT STRENGTH, ONE CANNOT RESIST USING IT...
SHITEN-HOJI TO SERVE!!
THAT IS HOW WE ARE!
HAH!!
HOLY MOLY, HE'S POWER-FUL!!
L-LOOK...

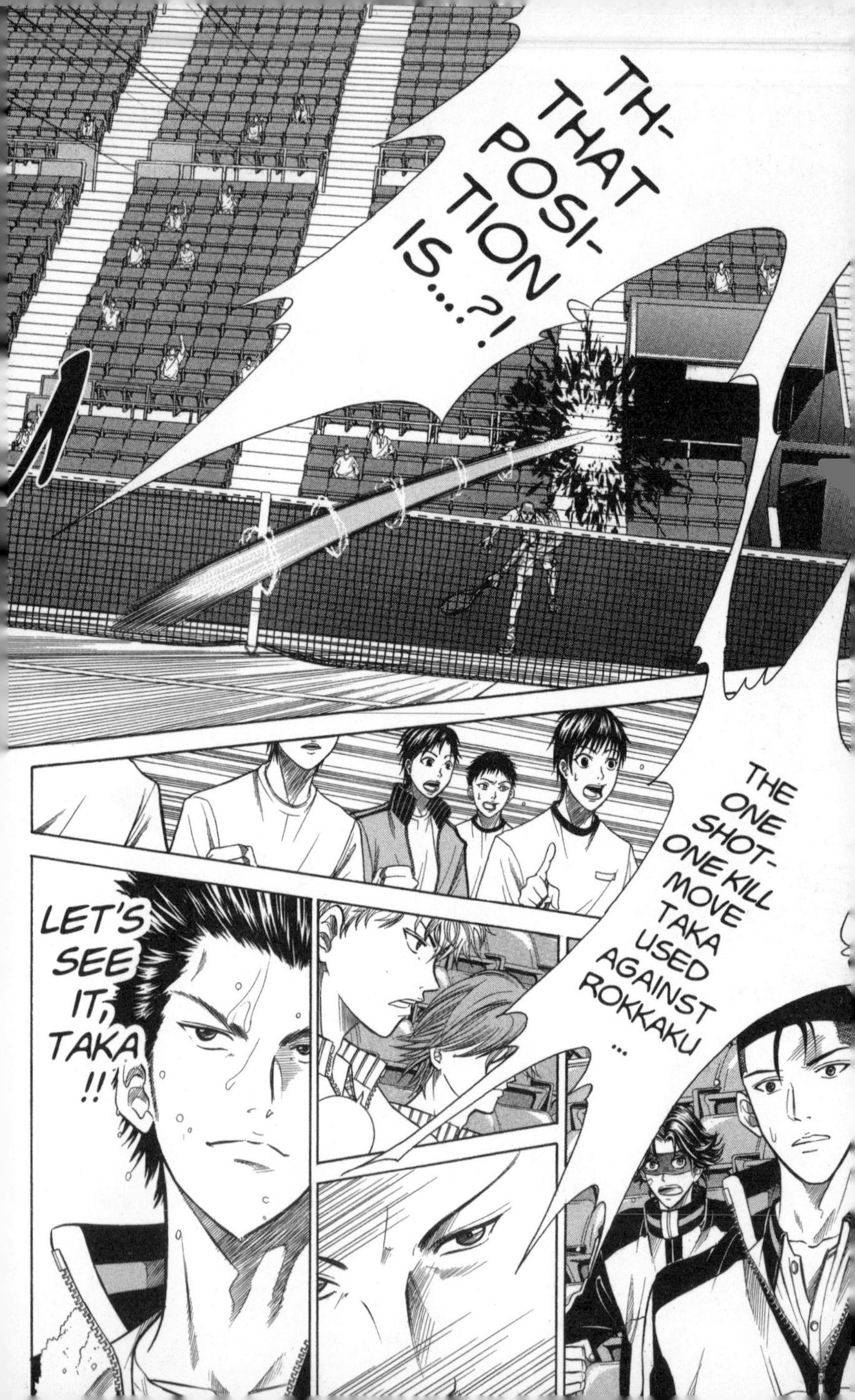
TH-THAT POSI-TION IS...?!
THE ONE SHOT-ONE KILL MOVE TAKA USED AGAINST ROKKAKU ...
LET'S SEE IT, TAKA!!

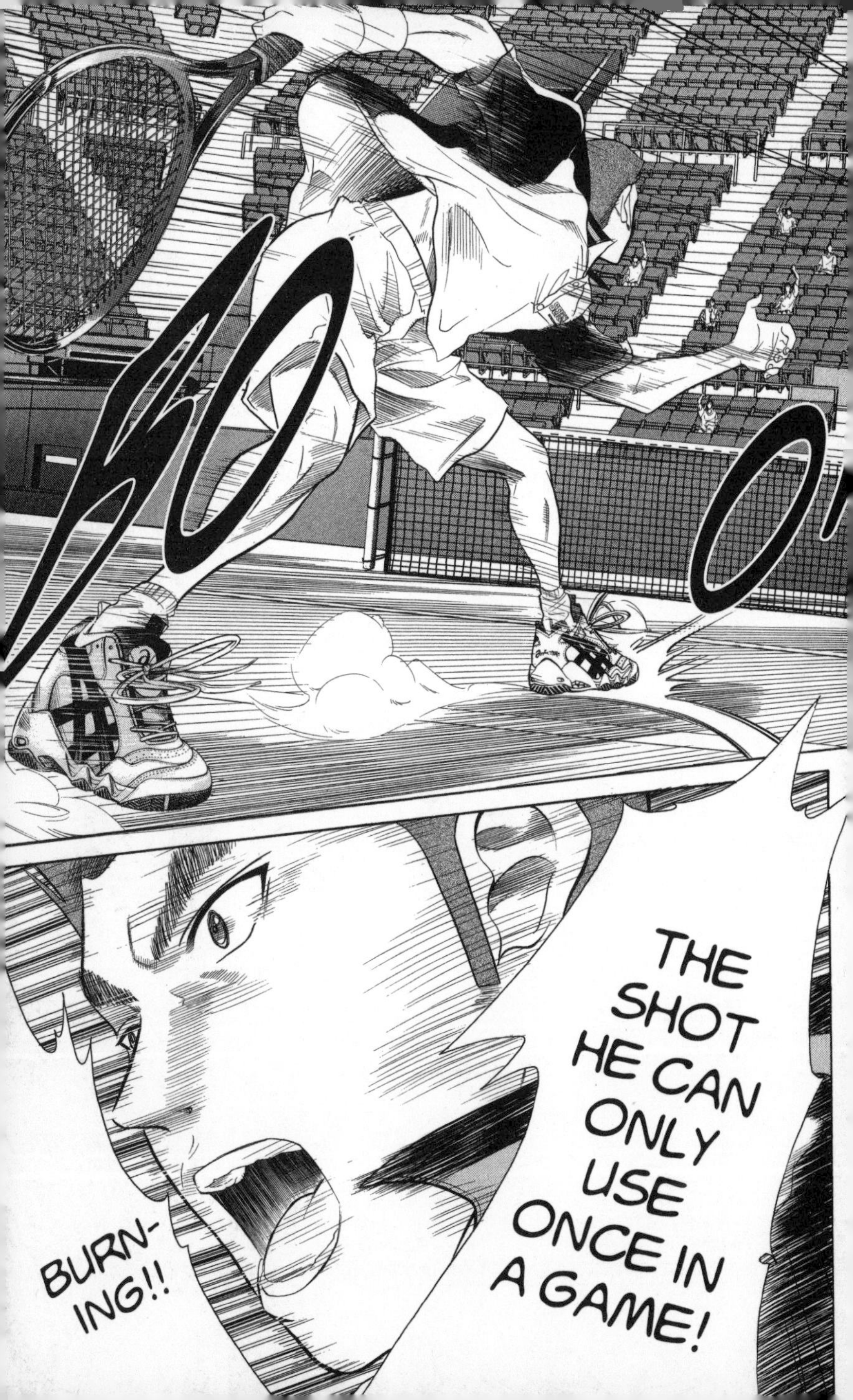
THE SHOT HE CAN ONLY USE ONCE IN A GAME!
BURNING!!

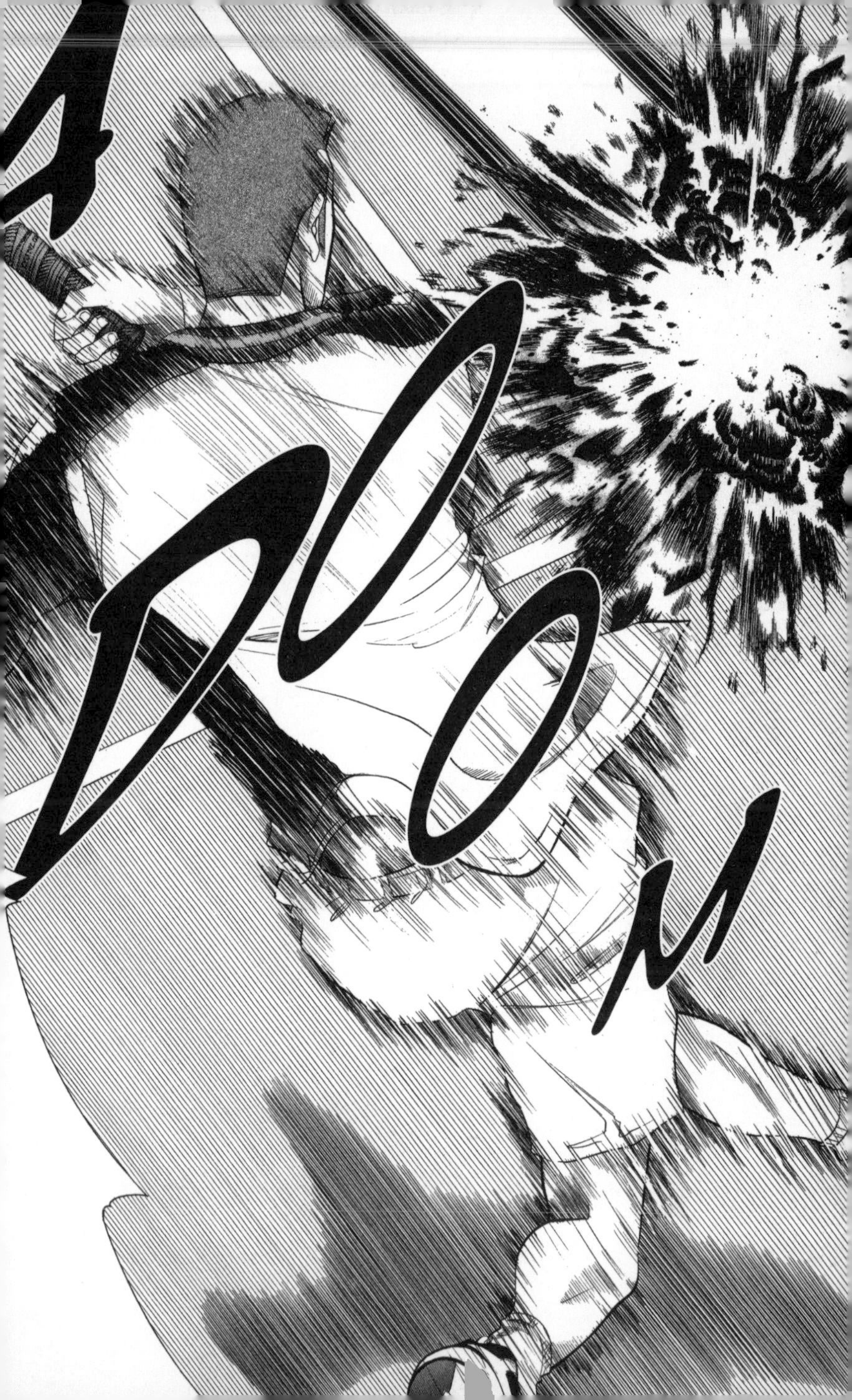

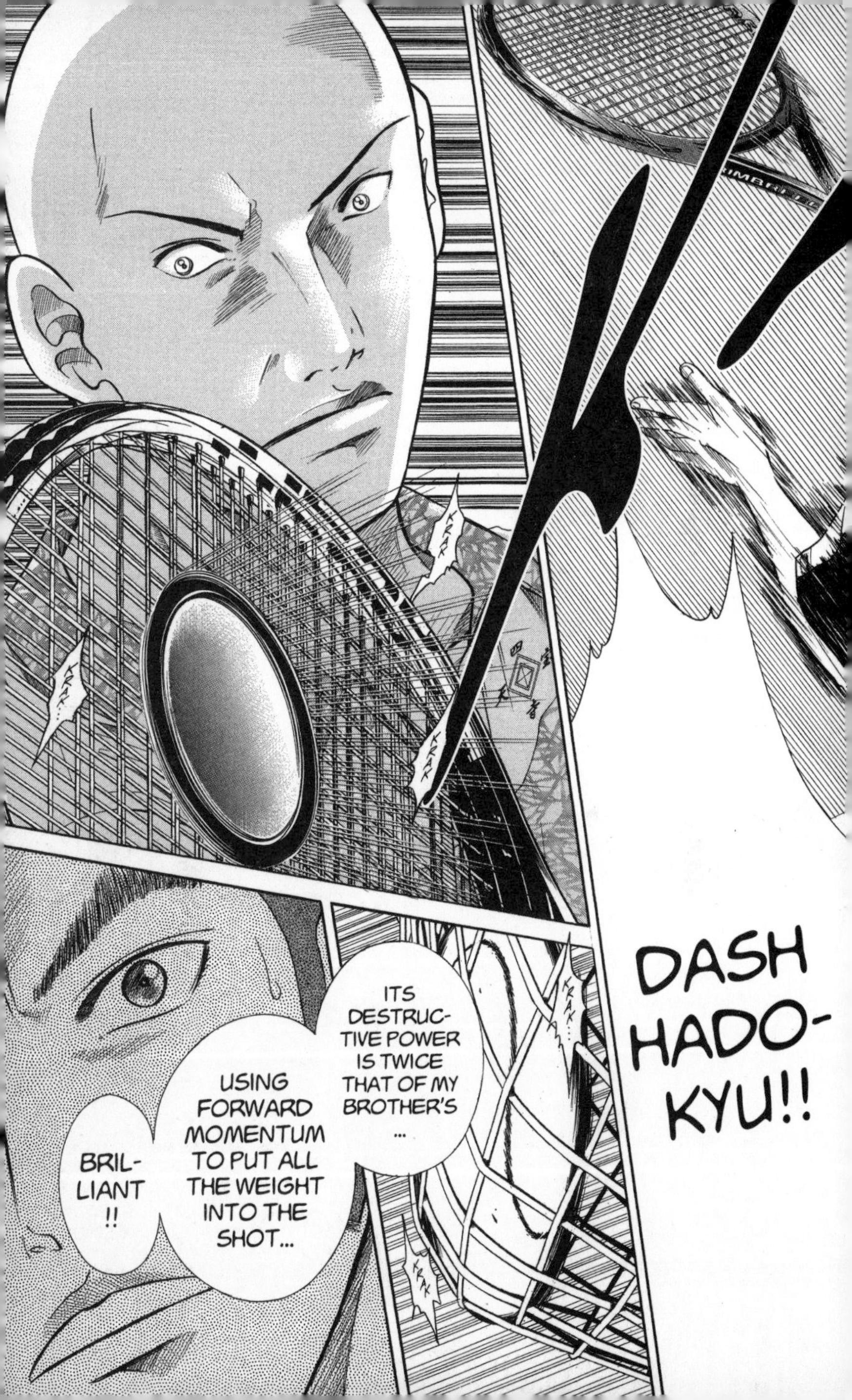
DASH HADO-KYU!!
KRAK
KRAK
KRAK
KRAK
KRAK
ITS DESTRUCTIVE POWER IS TWICE THAT OF MY BROTHER'S...
USING FORWARD MOMENTUM TO PUT ALL THE WEIGHT INTO THE SHOT...
BRILLIANT!!

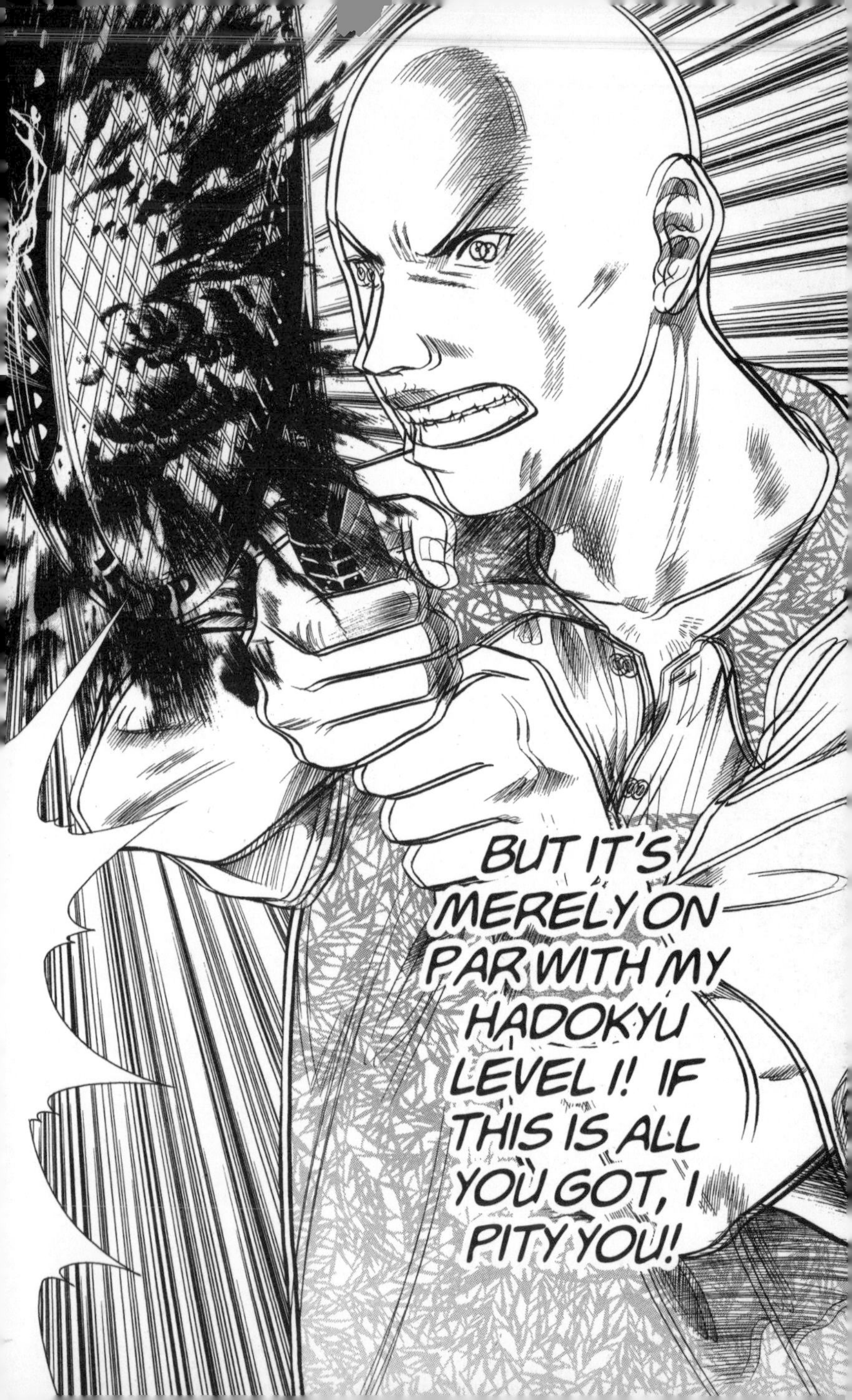
BUT IT'S MERELY ON PAR WITH MY HADOKYU LEVEL 1! IF THIS IS ALL YOU GOT, I PITY YOU!

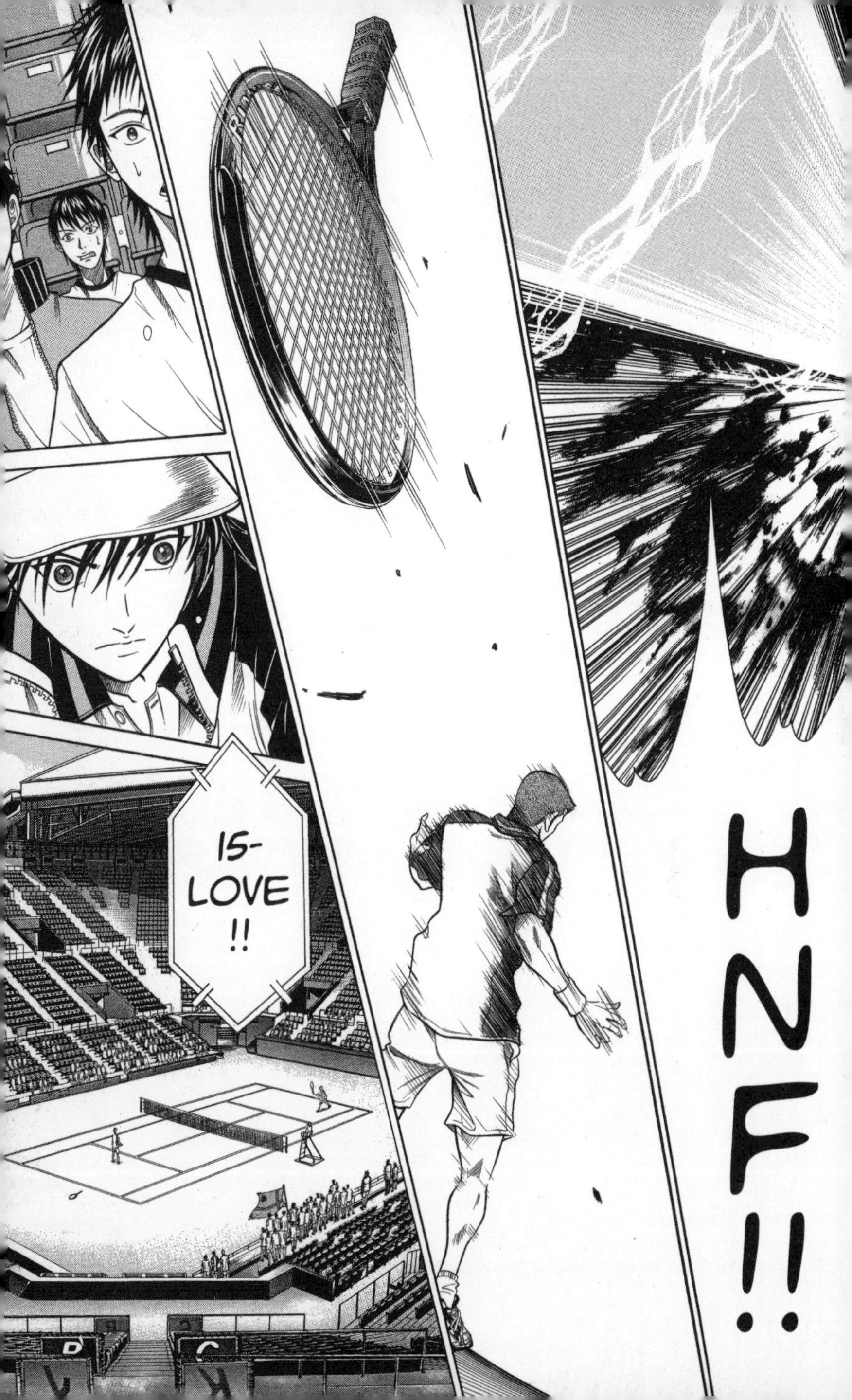
HNF!!
15-LOVE!!

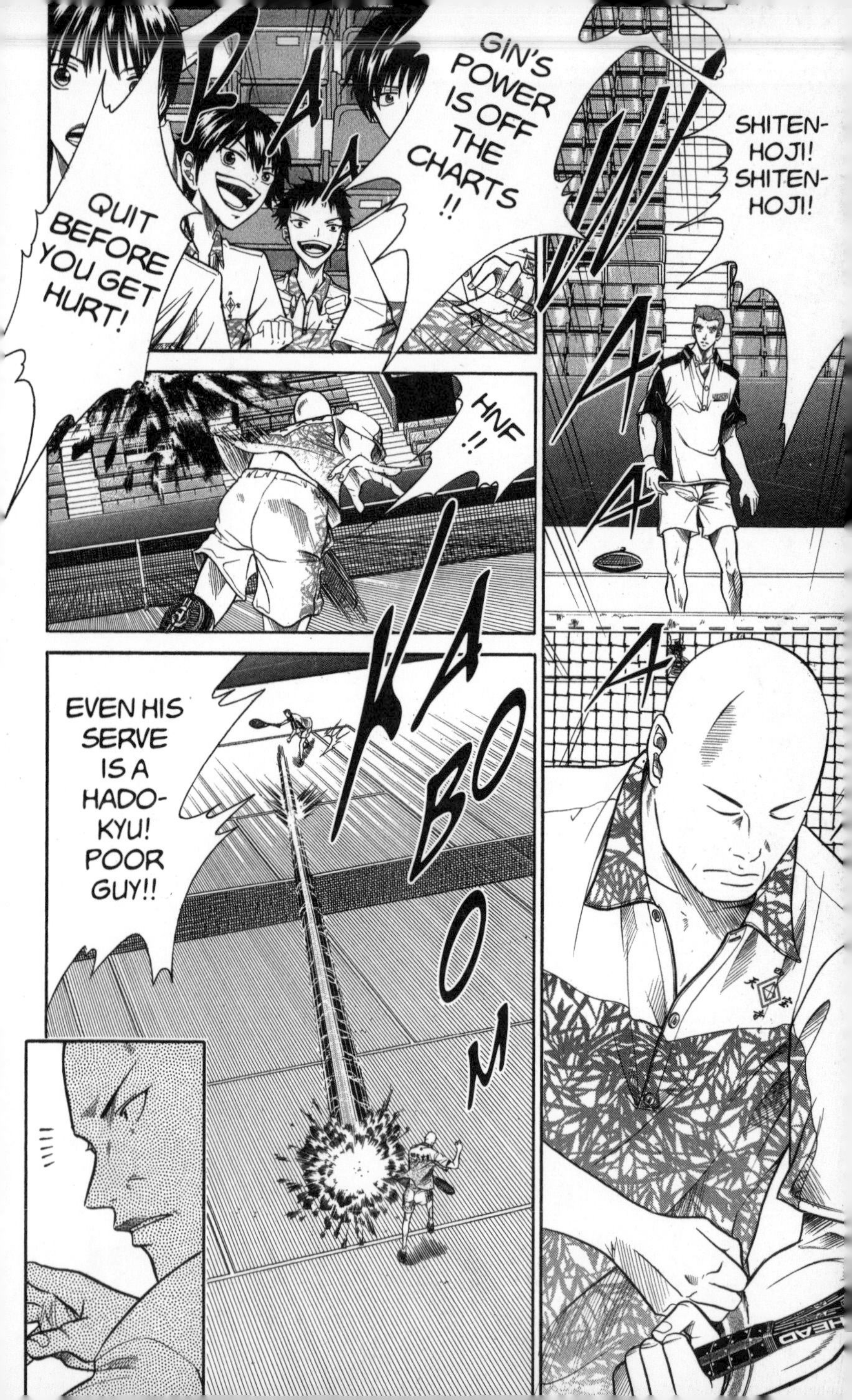
SHITEN-HOJI! SHITEN-HOJI!
GIN'S POWER IS OFF THE CHARTS!!
QUIT BEFORE YOU GET HURT!
HNF!!
EVEN HIS SERVE IS A HADO-KYU! POOR GUY!!
KABOOM

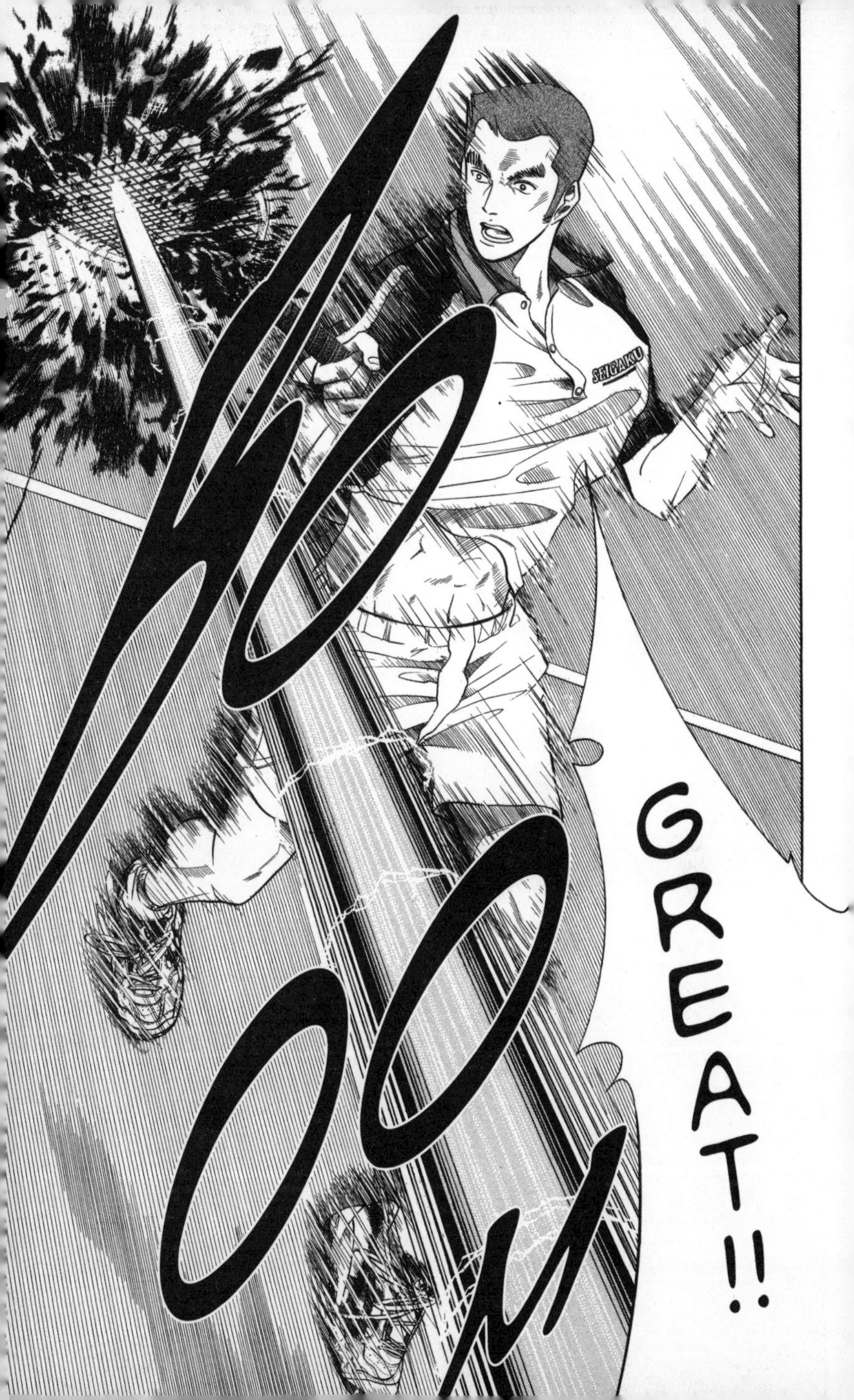
SEIGAKU
GREAT!!

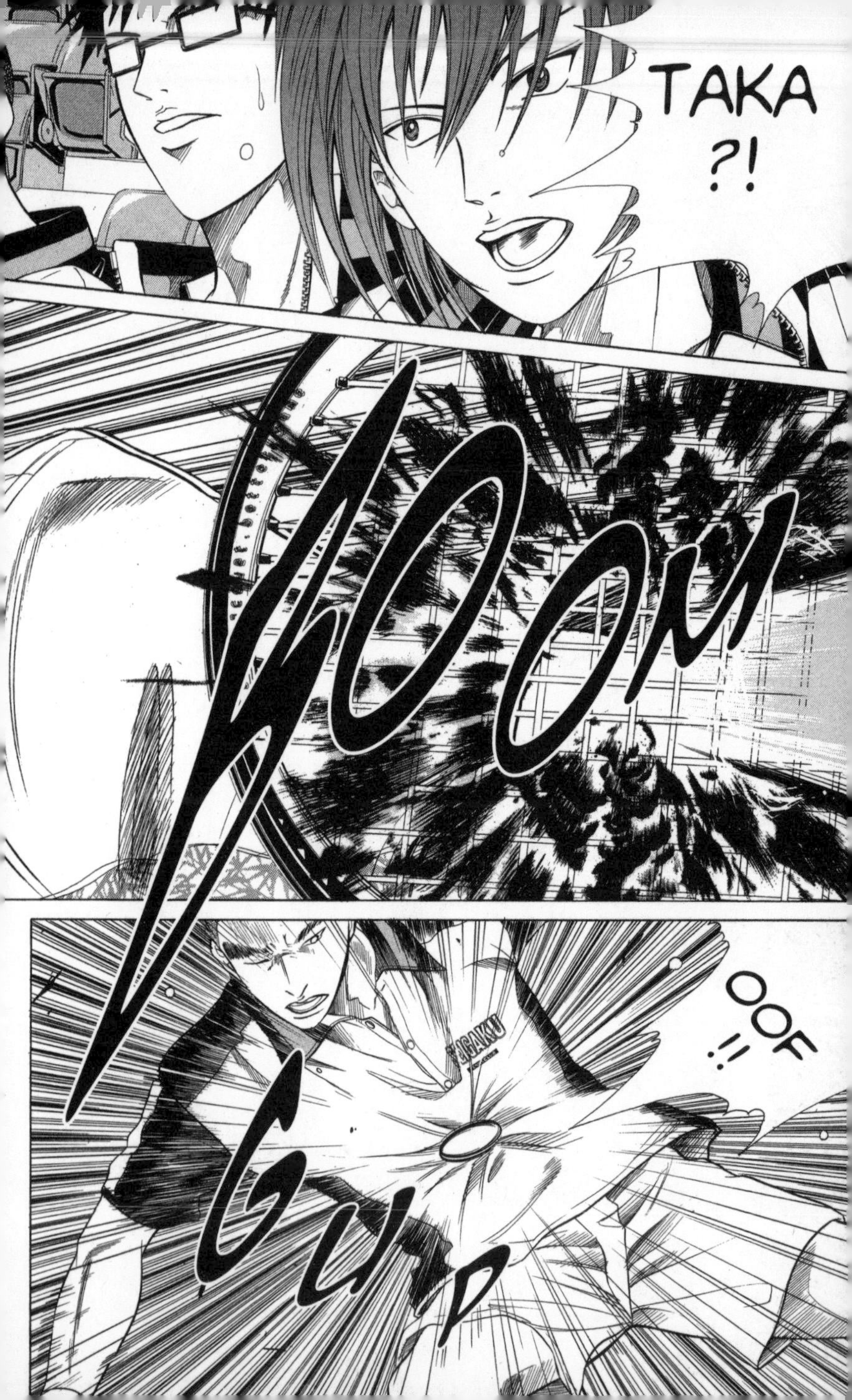
TAKA ?!
ZOOM
OOF !!
GUP

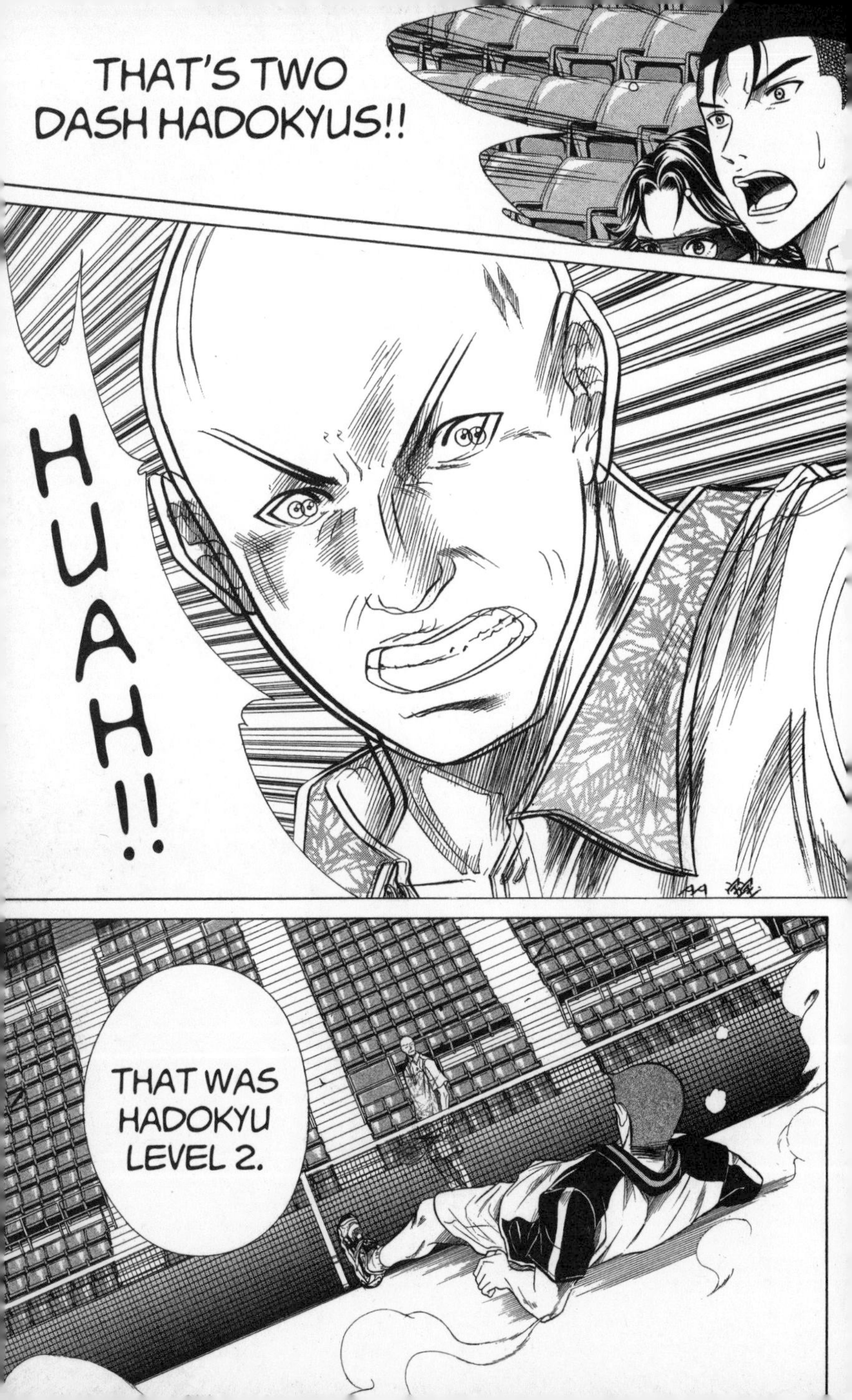
THAT'S TWO DASH HADOKYUS!!
HUAH!!
THAT WAS HADOKYU LEVEL 2.

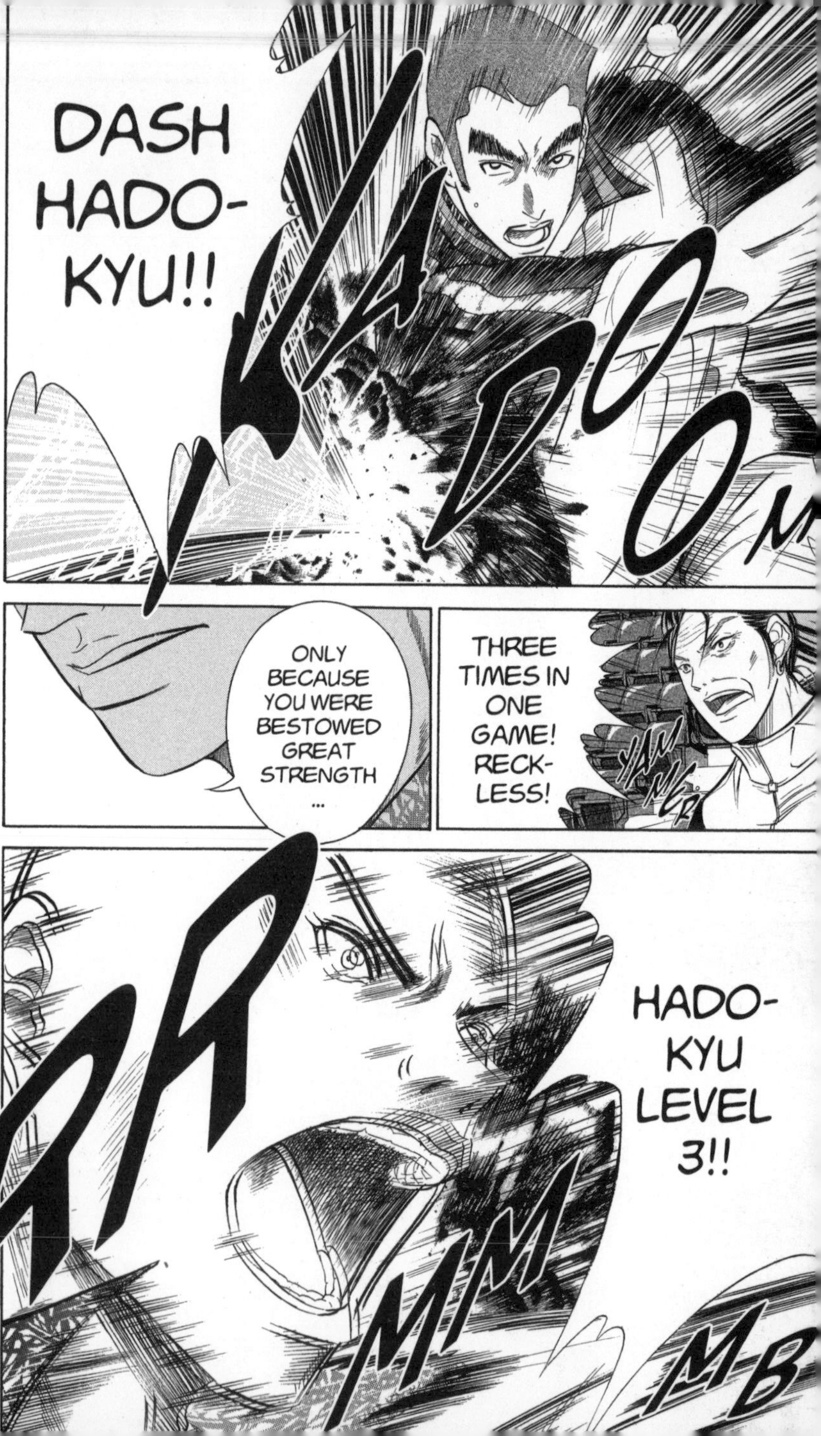
DASH HADO-KYU!!
THREE TIMES IN ONE GAME! RECKLESS!
ONLY BECAUSE YOU WERE BESTOWED GREAT STRENGTH ...
HADO-KYU LEVEL 3!!

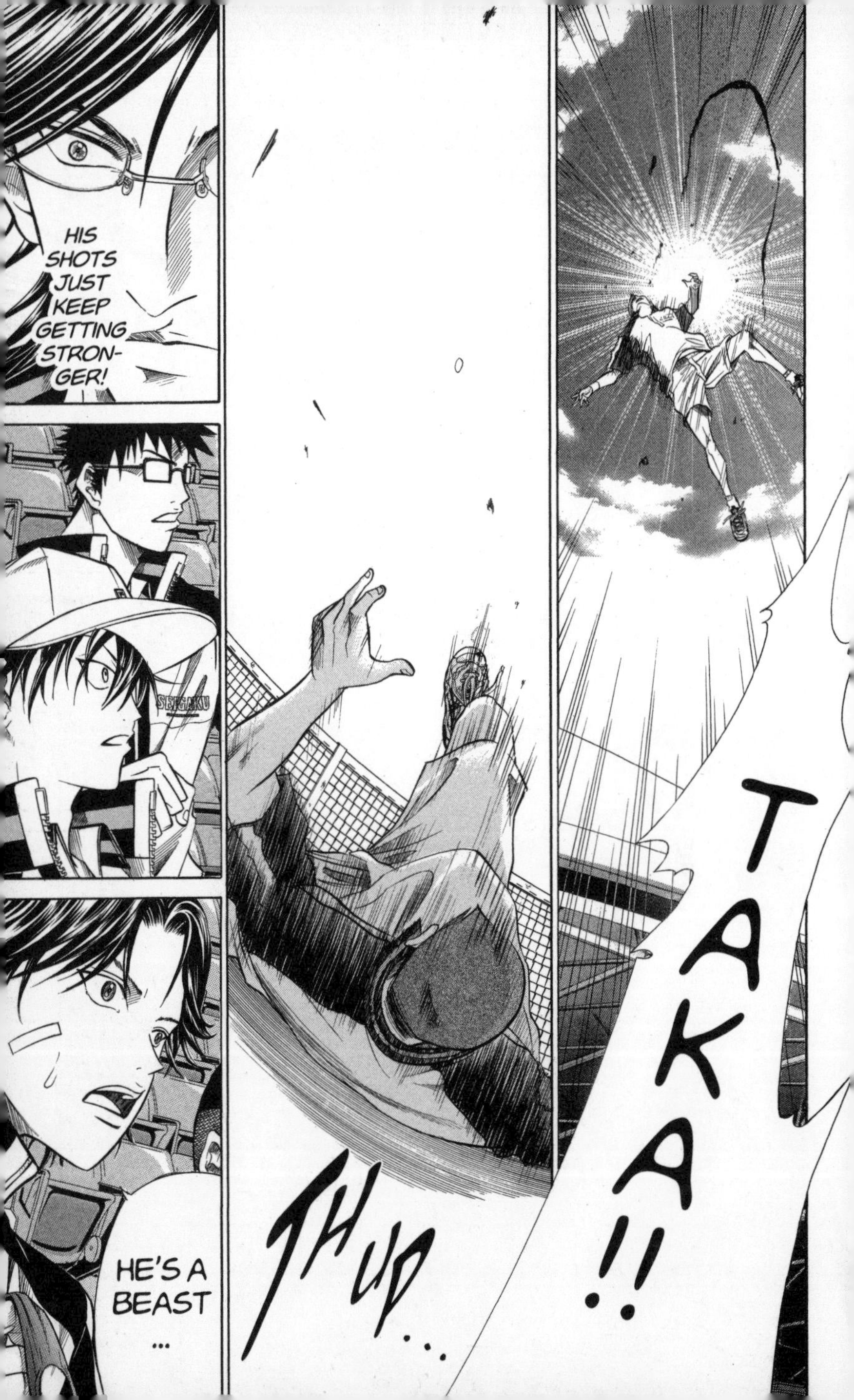
TAKA!!
THUD...
HIS SHOTS JUST KEEP GETTING STRONGER!
HE'S A BEAST...

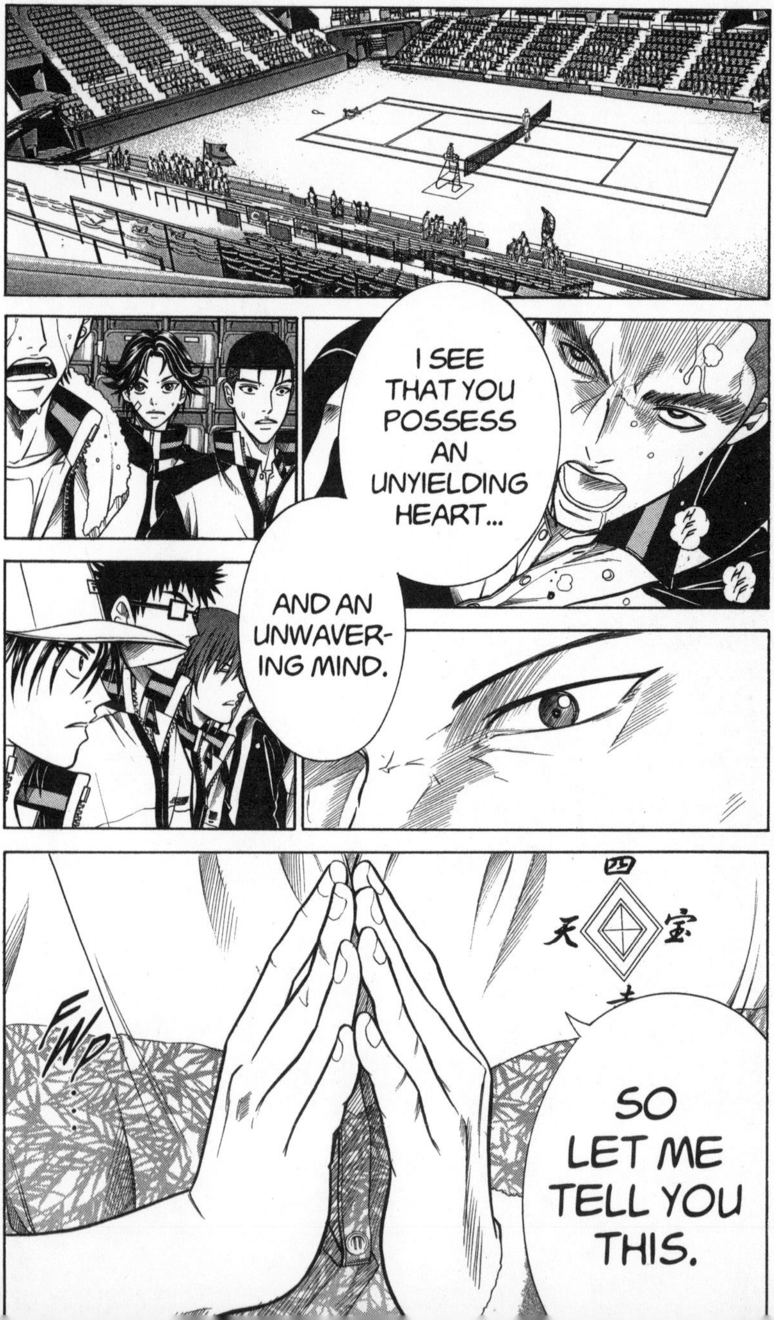
I SEE THAT YOU POSSESS AN UNYIELDING HEART...
HF
HF
AND AN UNWAVERING MIND.
四 天 宝
FWP
SO LET ME TELL YOU THIS.

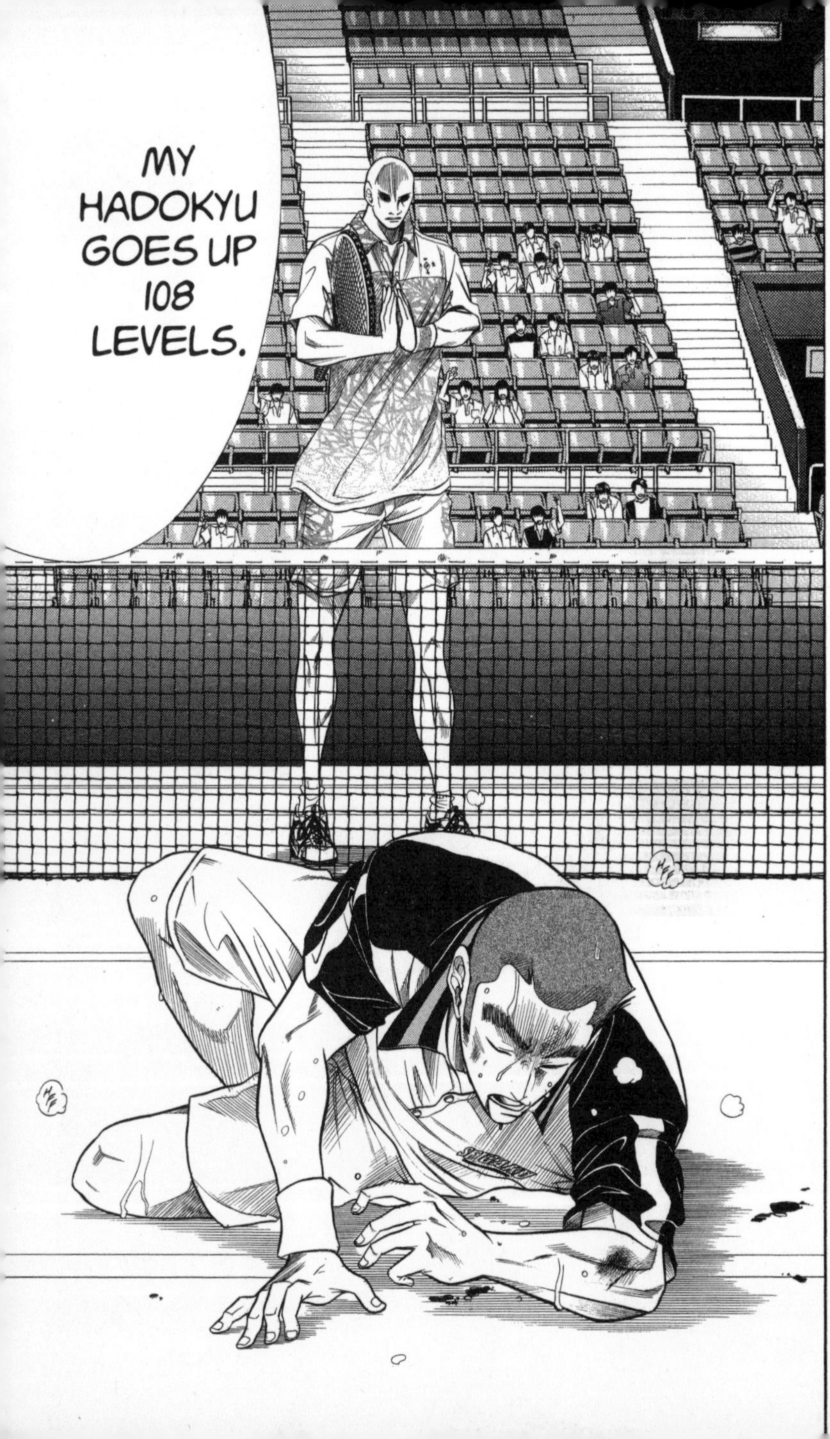
MY HADOKYU GOES UP 108 LEVELS.

テニスの王子様

THE PRINCE OF TENNIS

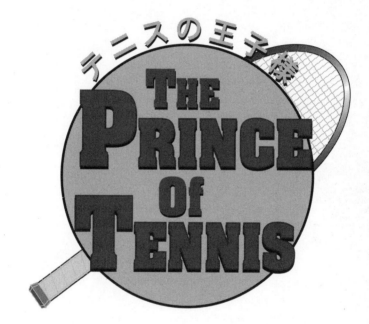

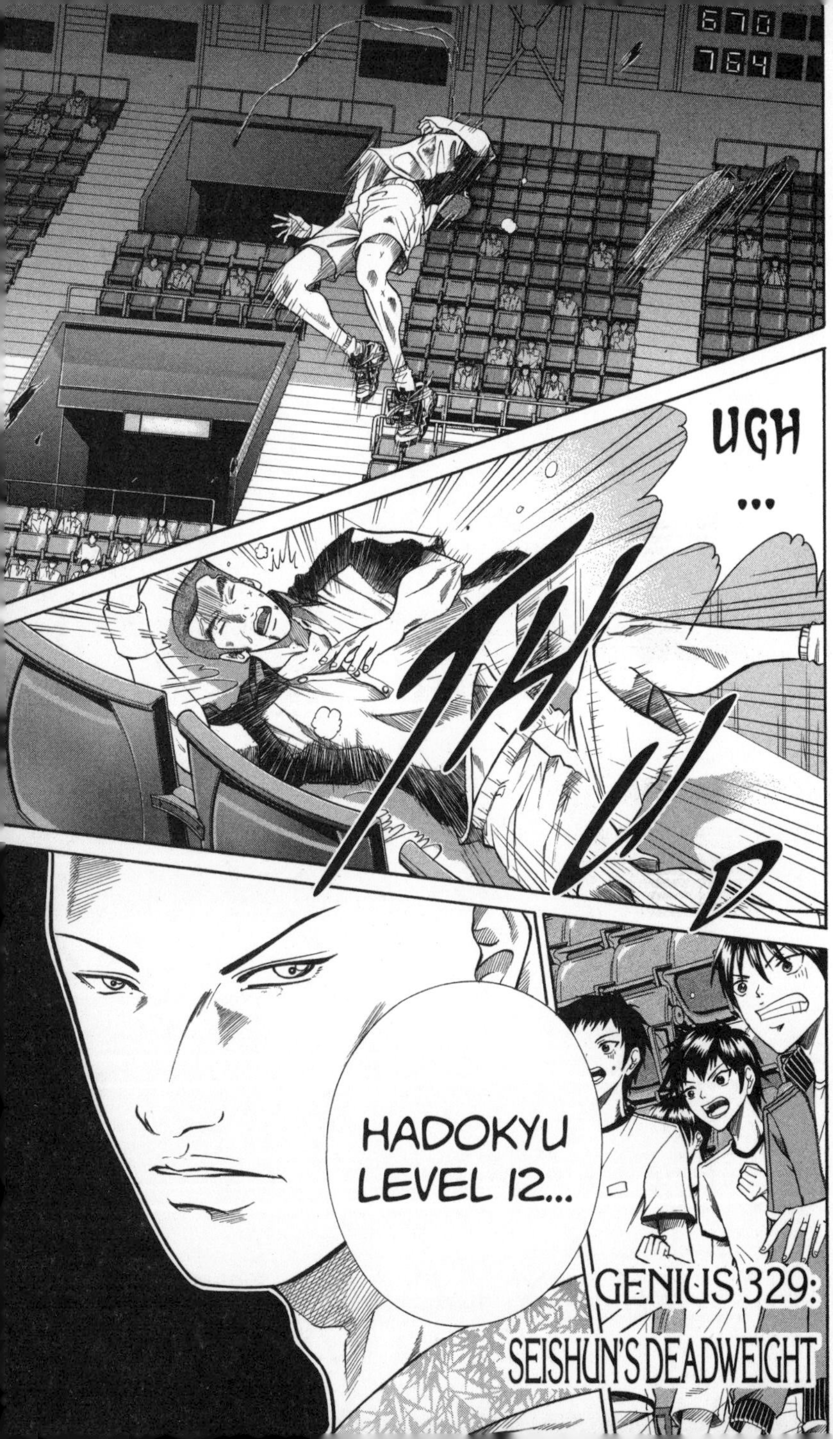
UGH
...
THUD
HADOKYU LEVEL 12...
GENIUS 329:
SEISHUN'S DEADWEIGHT

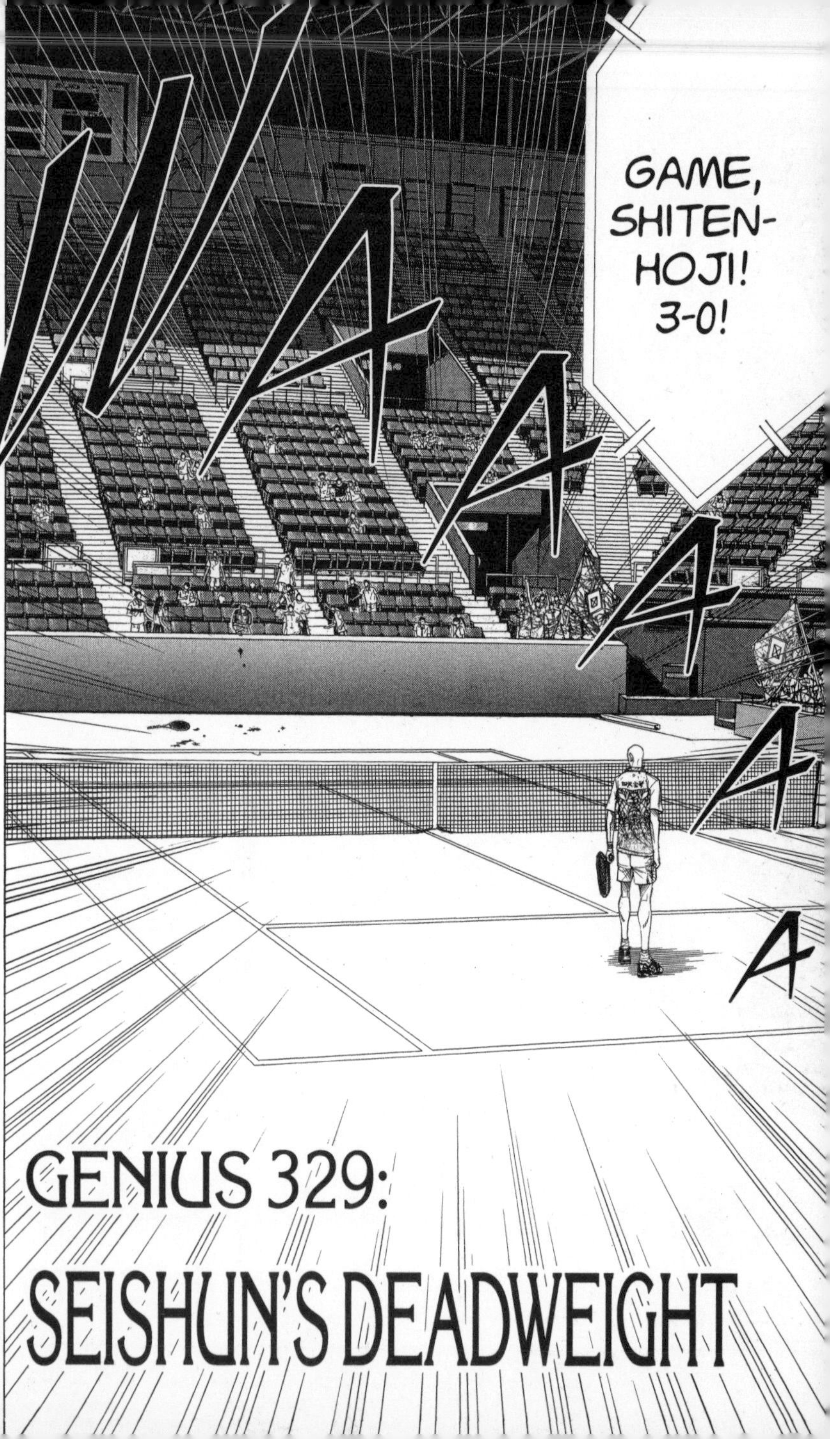
WAAAAAA
GAME, SHITEN-HOJI! 3-0!

GENIUS 329: SEISHUN'S DEADWEIGHT

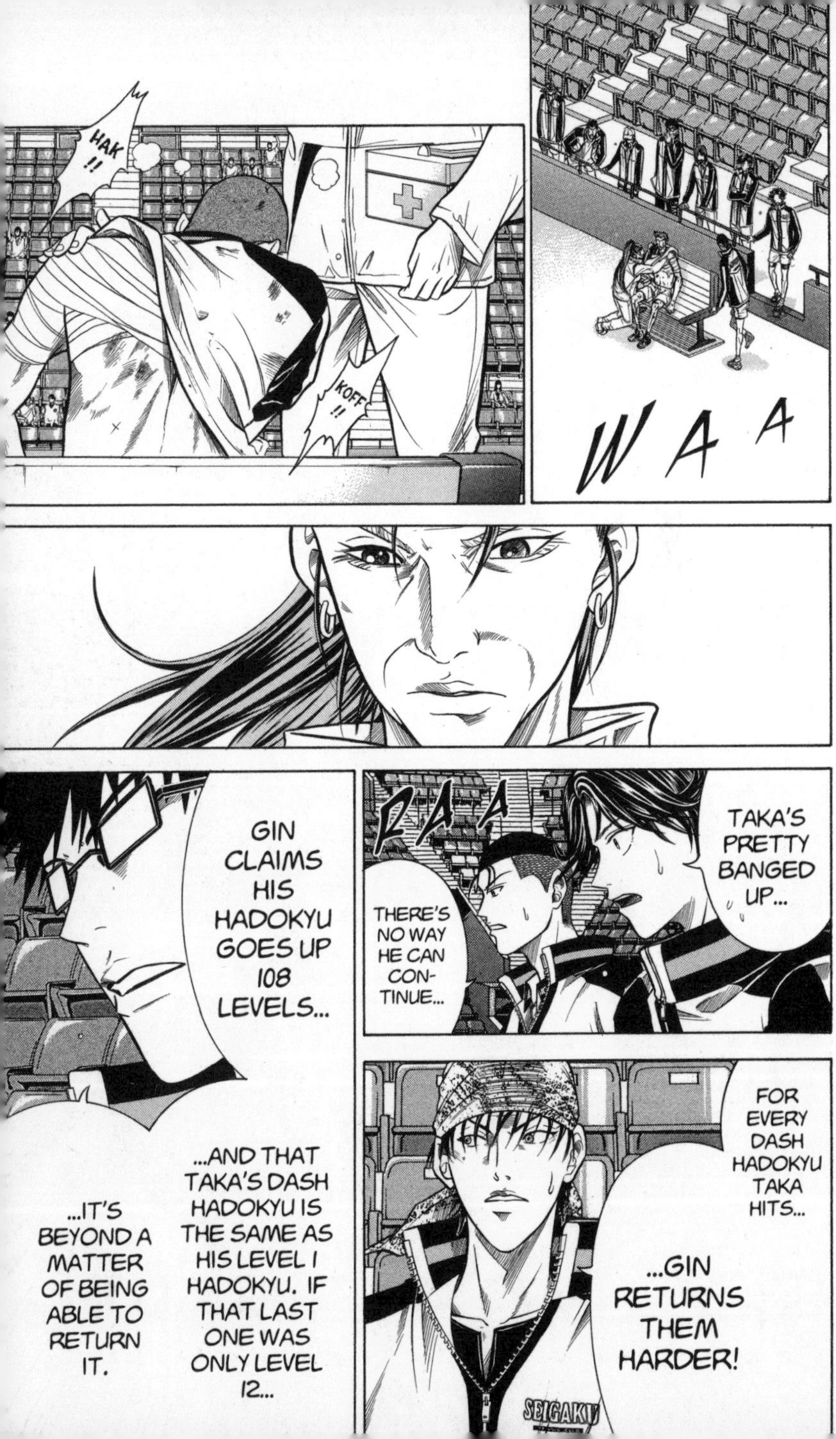
WAA
HAK!!
KOFF!!
RAA
TAKA'S PRETTY BANGED UP...
THERE'S NO WAY HE CAN CON-TINUE...
GIN CLAIMS HIS HADOKYU GOES UP 108 LEVELS...
FOR EVERY DASH HADOKYU TAKA HITS...
...GIN RETURNS THEM HARDER!
...AND THAT TAKA'S DASH HADOKYU IS THE SAME AS HIS LEVEL 1 HADOKYU. IF THAT LAST ONE WAS ONLY LEVEL 12...
...IT'S BEYOND A MATTER OF BEING ABLE TO RETURN IT.
SEIGAKU

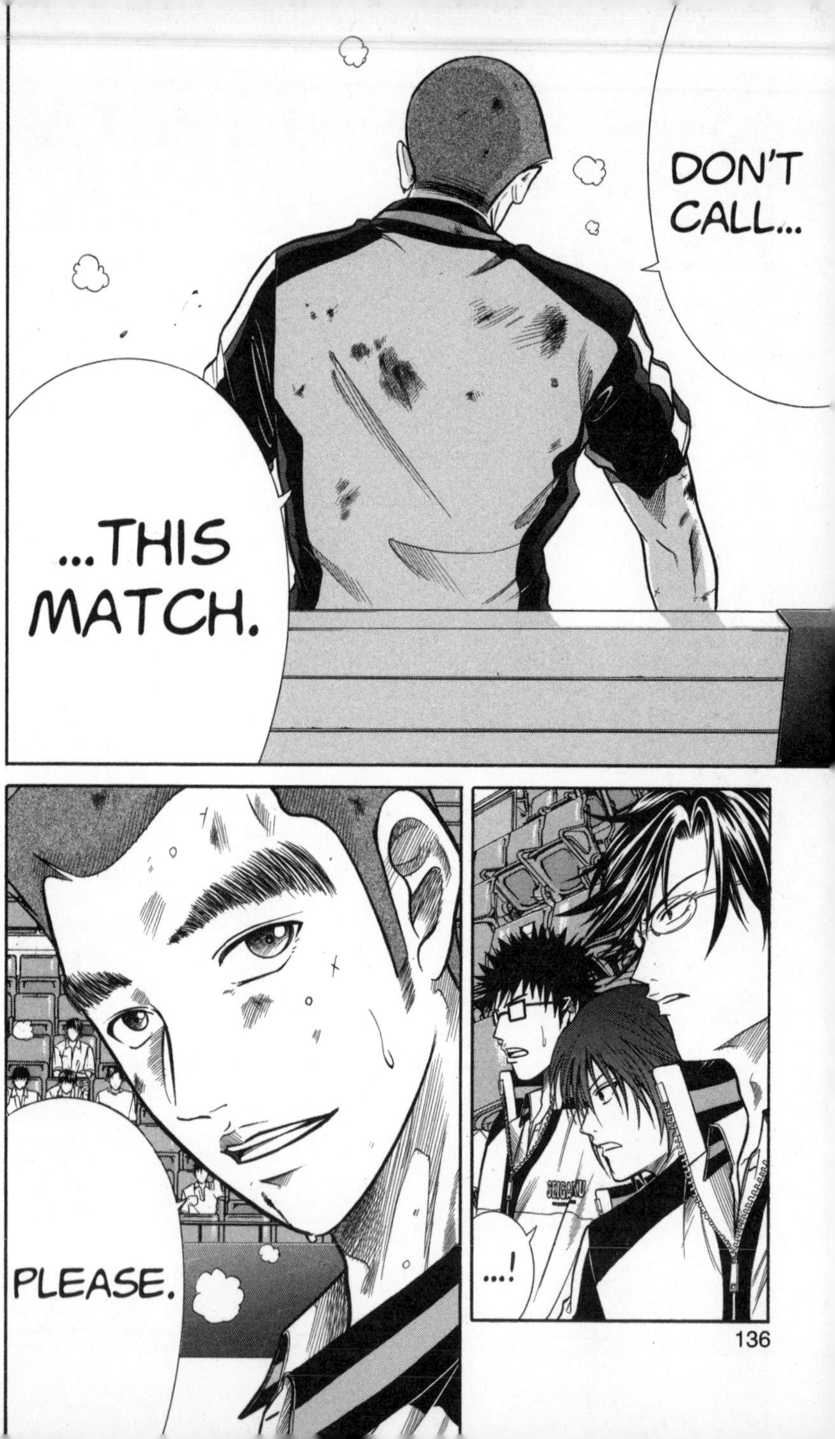
DON'T CALL...
...THIS MATCH.
...!
PLEASE.
SEIGAKU

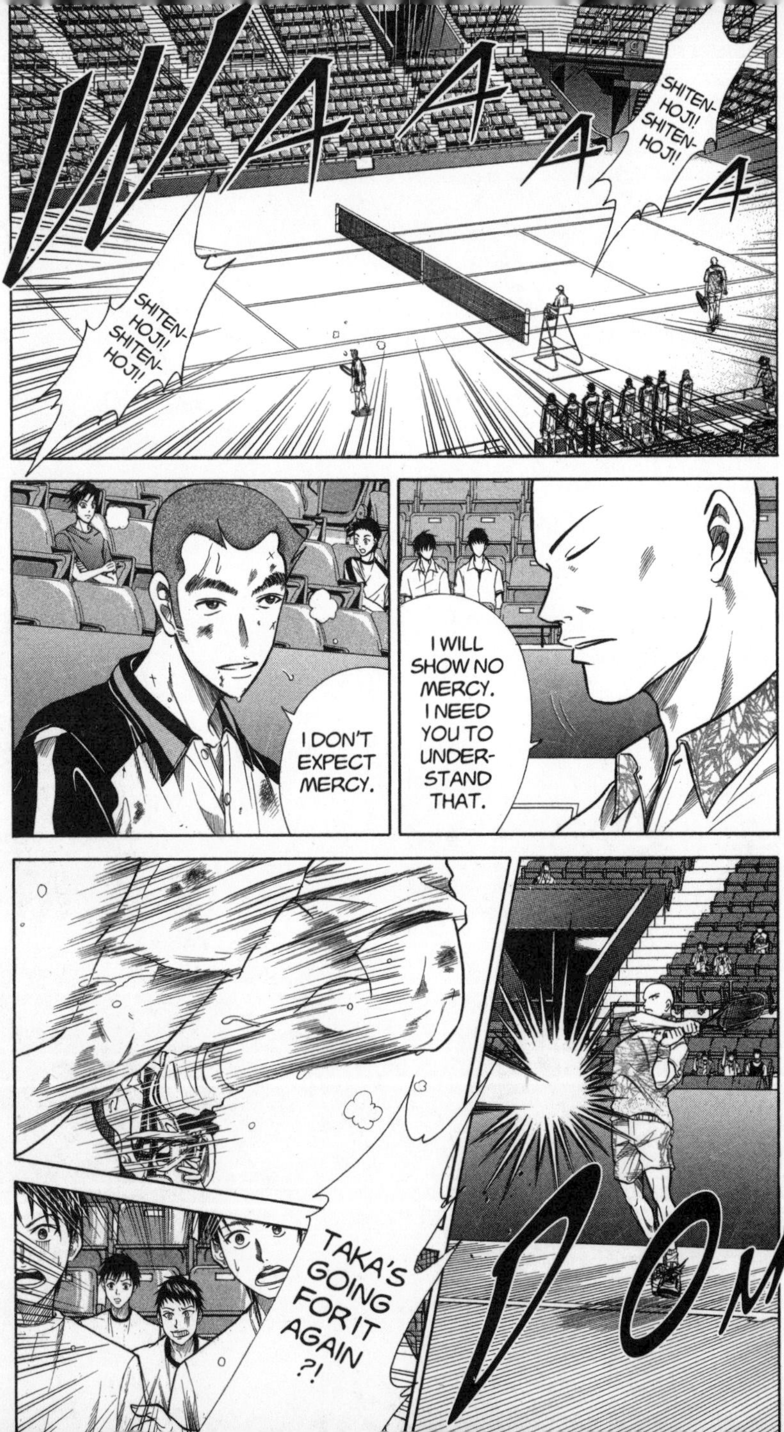
WAAAA
SHITEN-HOJI! SHITEN-HOJI!
SHITEN-HOJI! SHITEN-HOJI!
I WILL SHOW NO MERCY. I NEED YOU TO UNDERSTAND THAT.
I DON'T EXPECT MERCY.
DOM
TAKA'S GOING FOR IT AGAIN?!

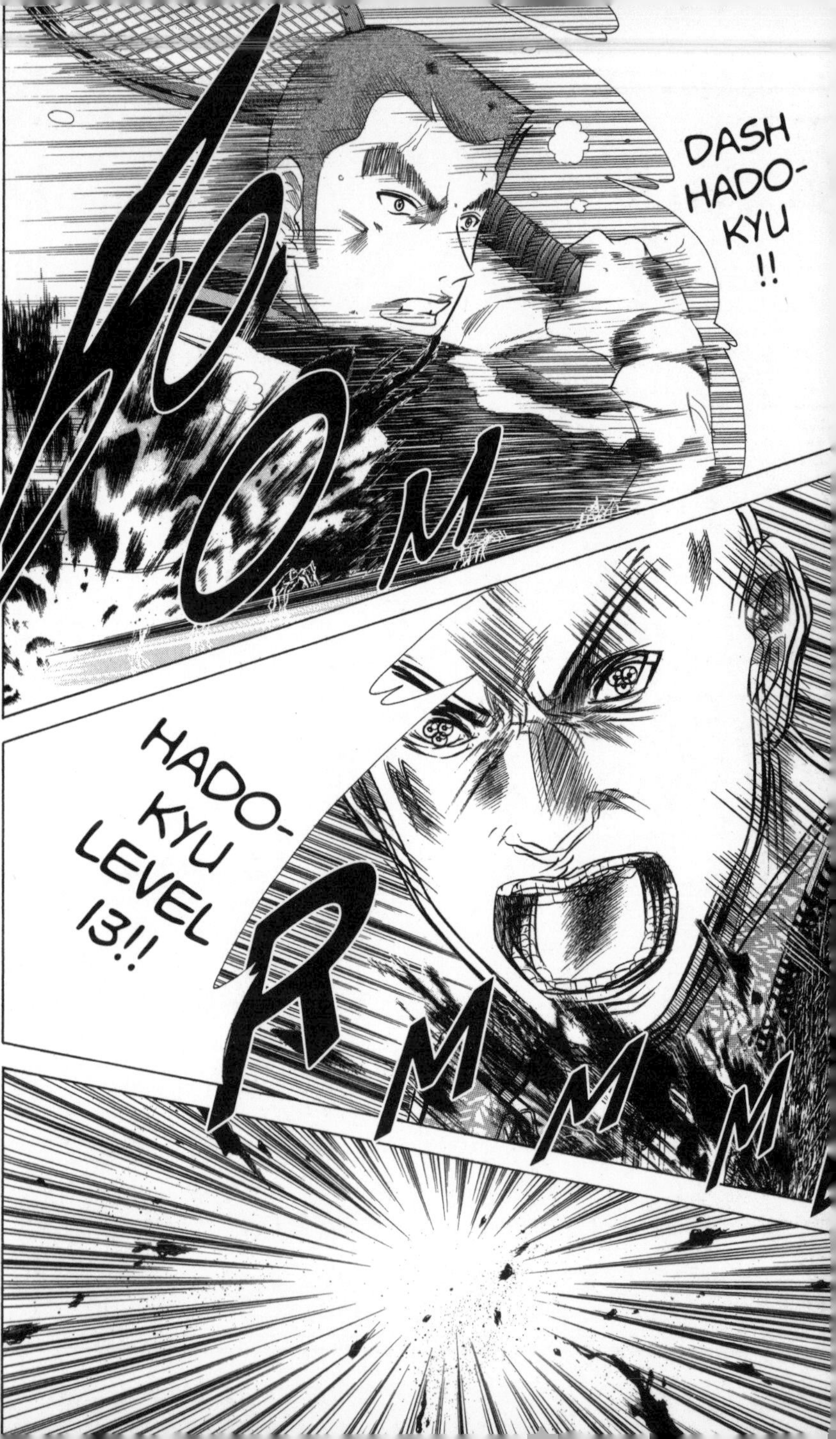
DASH HADO-KYU!!
HADO-KYU LEVEL 13!!

READ THIS WAY

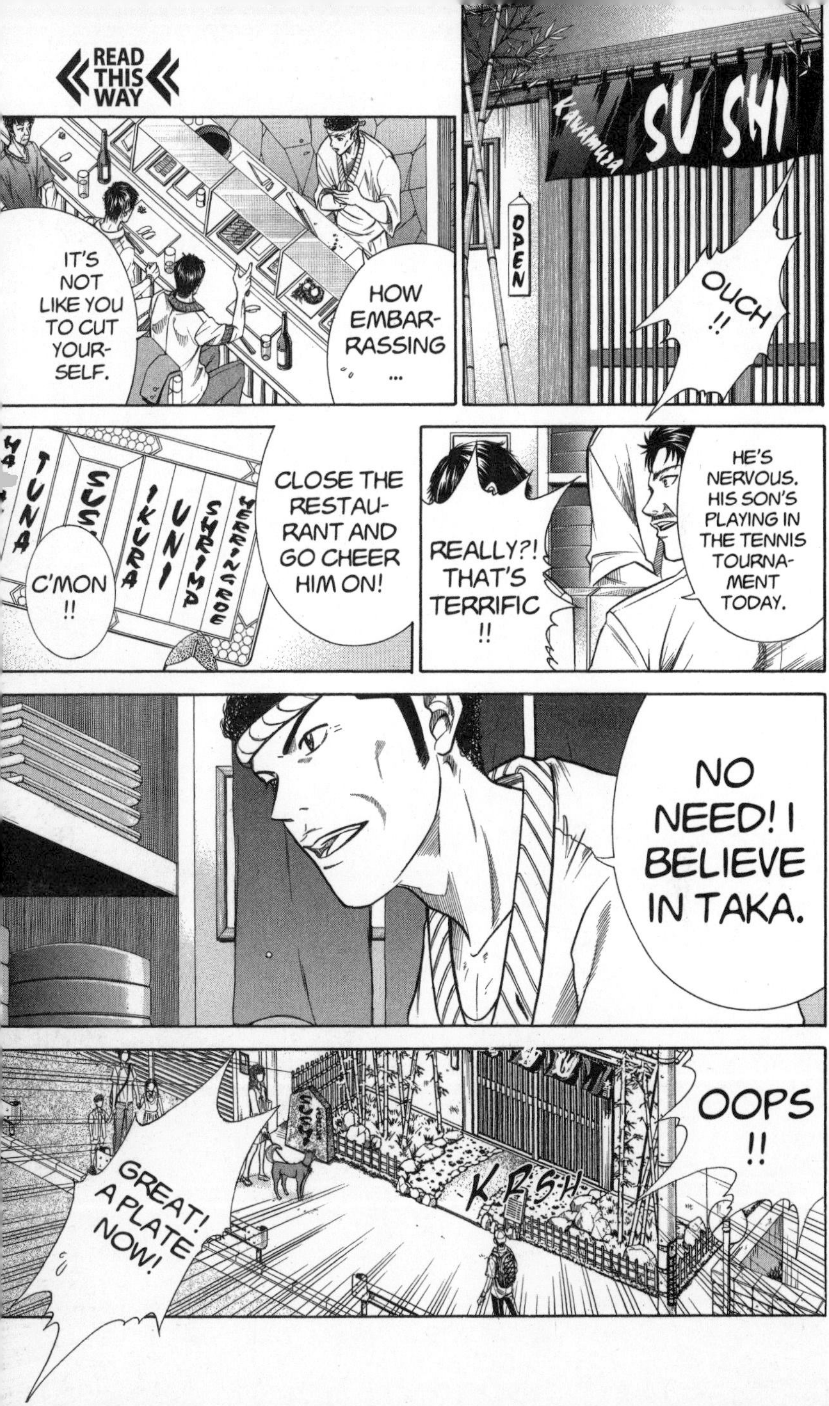
KAWAMURA
SUSHI
OPEN
OUCH!!
HOW EMBARRASSING...
IT'S NOT LIKE YOU TO CUT YOURSELF.
HE'S NERVOUS. HIS SON'S PLAYING IN THE TENNIS TOURNAMENT TODAY.
REALLY?! THAT'S TERRIFIC!!
CLOSE THE RESTAURANT AND GO CHEER HIM ON!
HERRING ROE
SHRIMP
UNI
IKURA
TUNA
C'MON!!
NO NEED! I BELIEVE IN TAKA.
OOPS!!
KRSH
GREAT! A PLATE NOW!

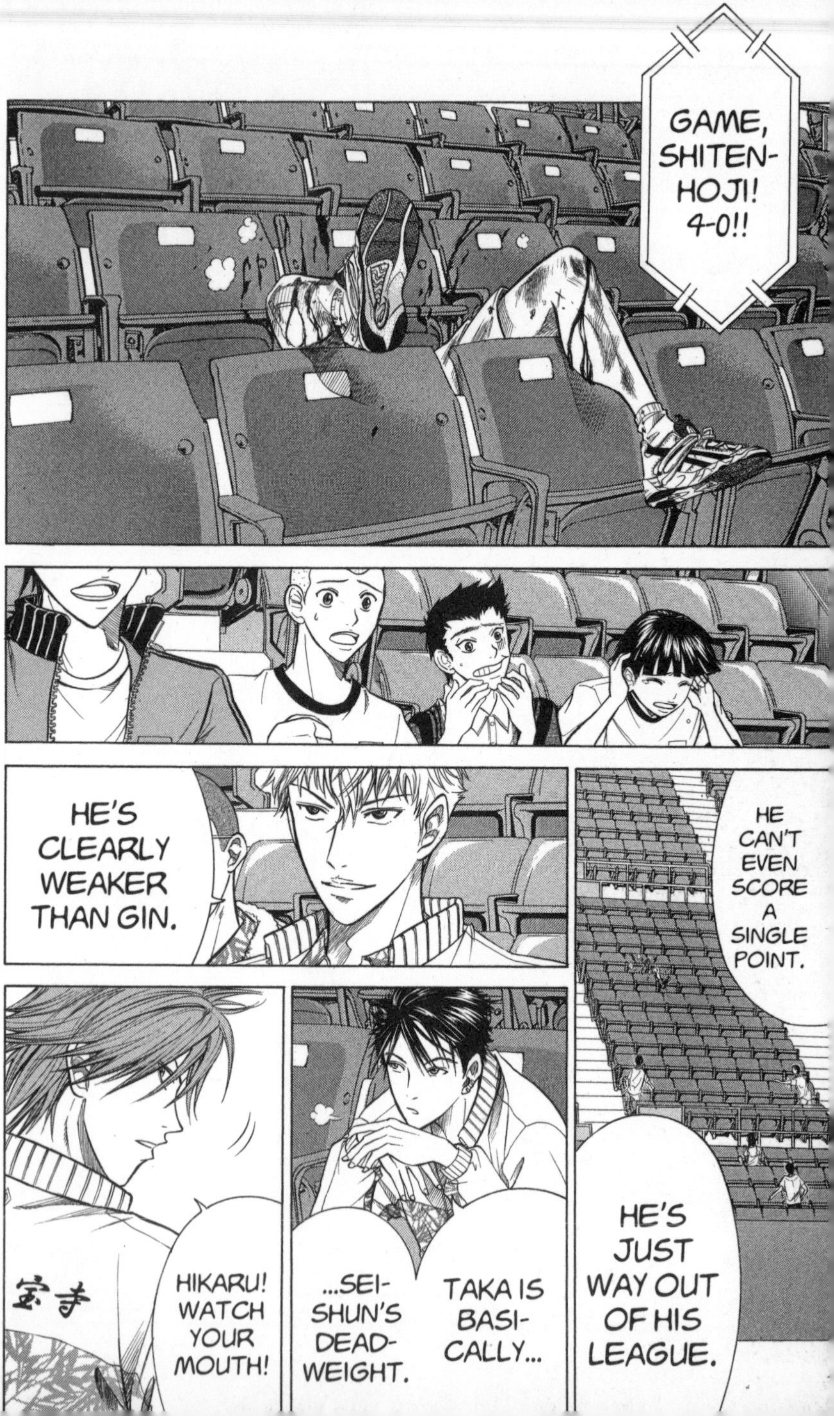
GAME, SHITEN-HOJI! 4-0!!
HE CAN'T EVEN SCORE A SINGLE POINT.
HE'S JUST WAY OUT OF HIS LEAGUE.
HE'S CLEARLY WEAKER THAN GIN.
TAKA IS BASI-CALLY...
...SEI-SHUN'S DEAD-WEIGHT.
HIKARU! WATCH YOUR MOUTH!

READ THIS WAY

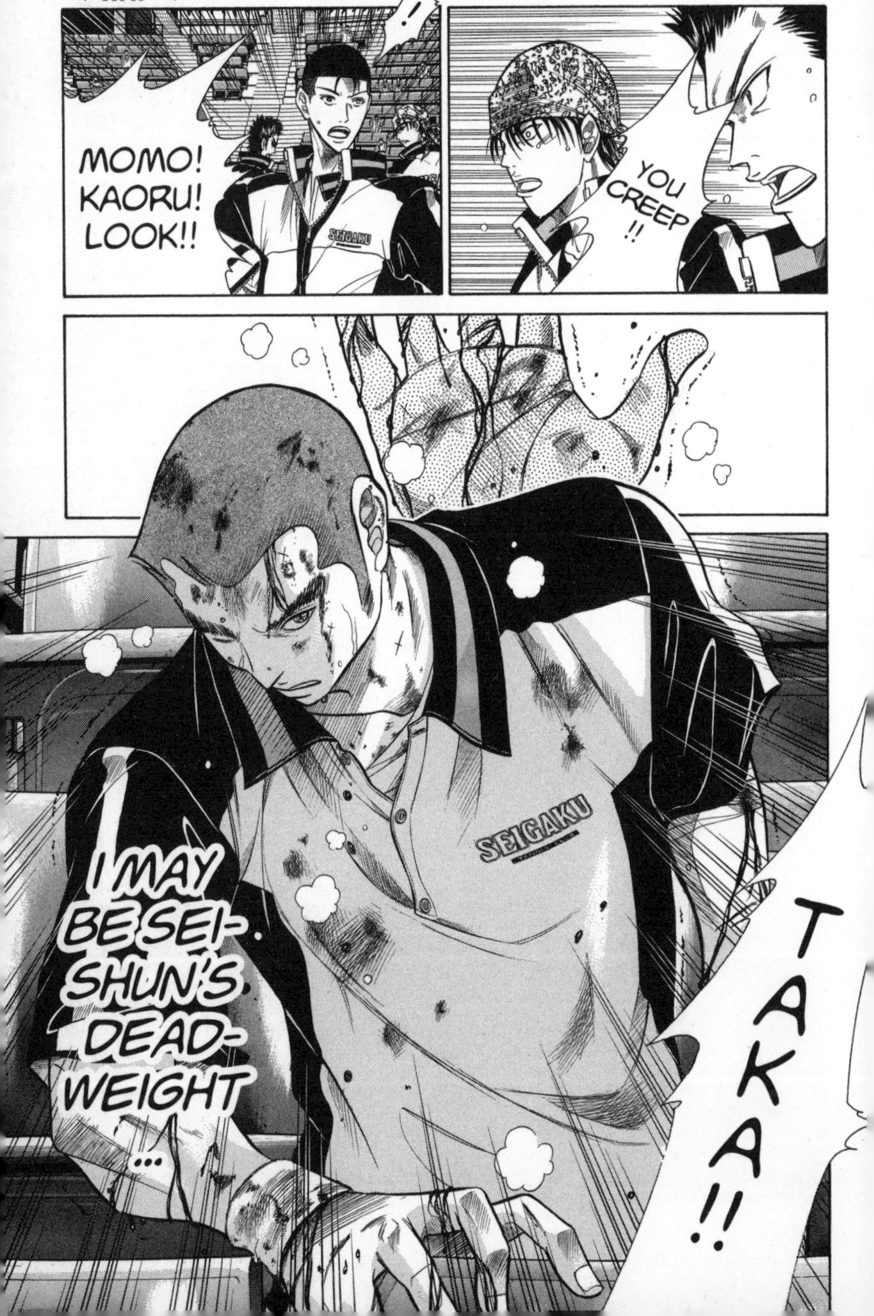
YOU CREEP!!
!
MOMO! KAORU! LOOK!!
TAKA!!
I MAY BE SEI-SHUN'S DEAD-WEIGHT...

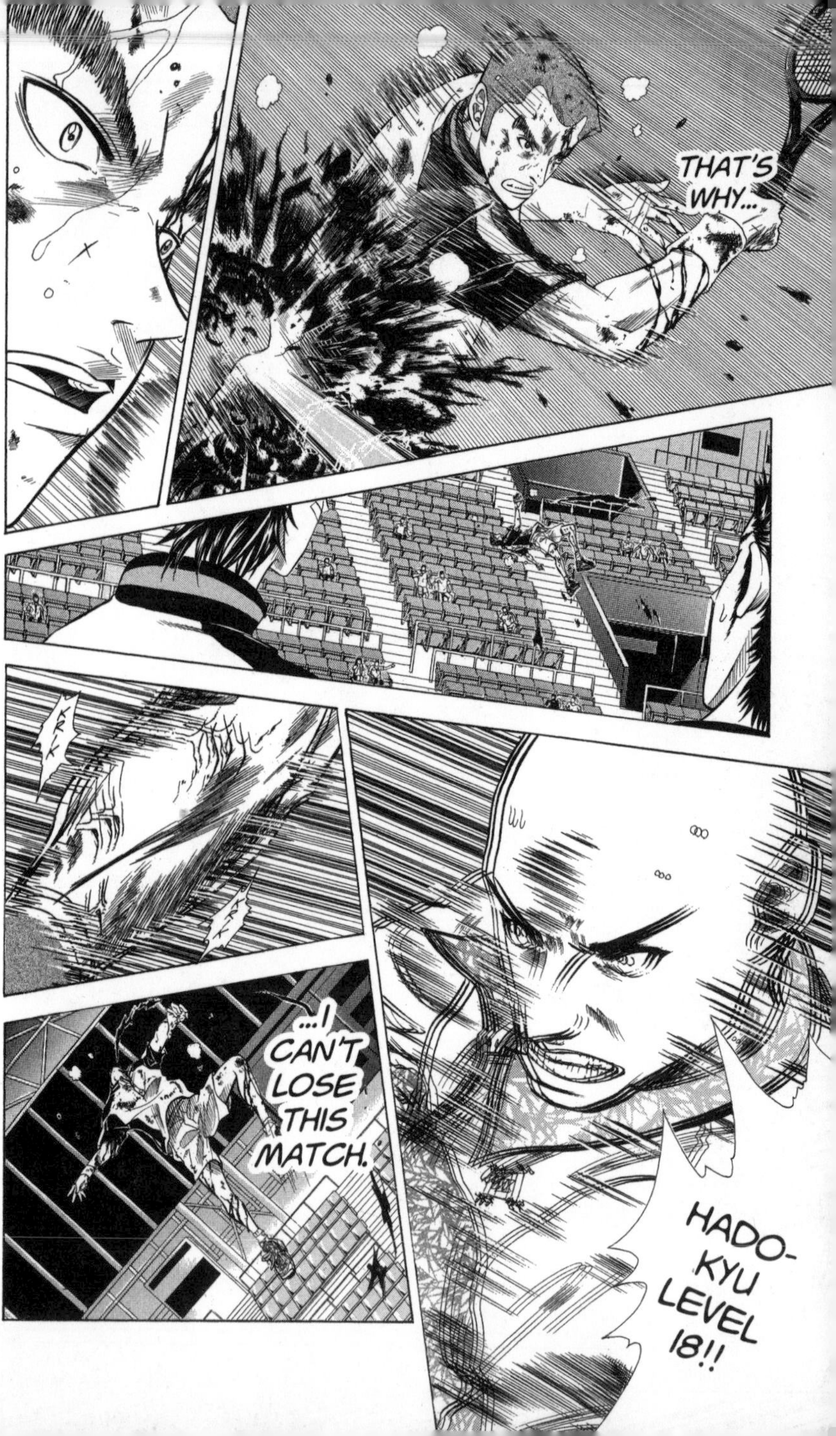
THAT'S WHY...
HADO-KYU LEVEL 18!!
KRIK
KRIK
...I CAN'T LOSE THIS MATCH.

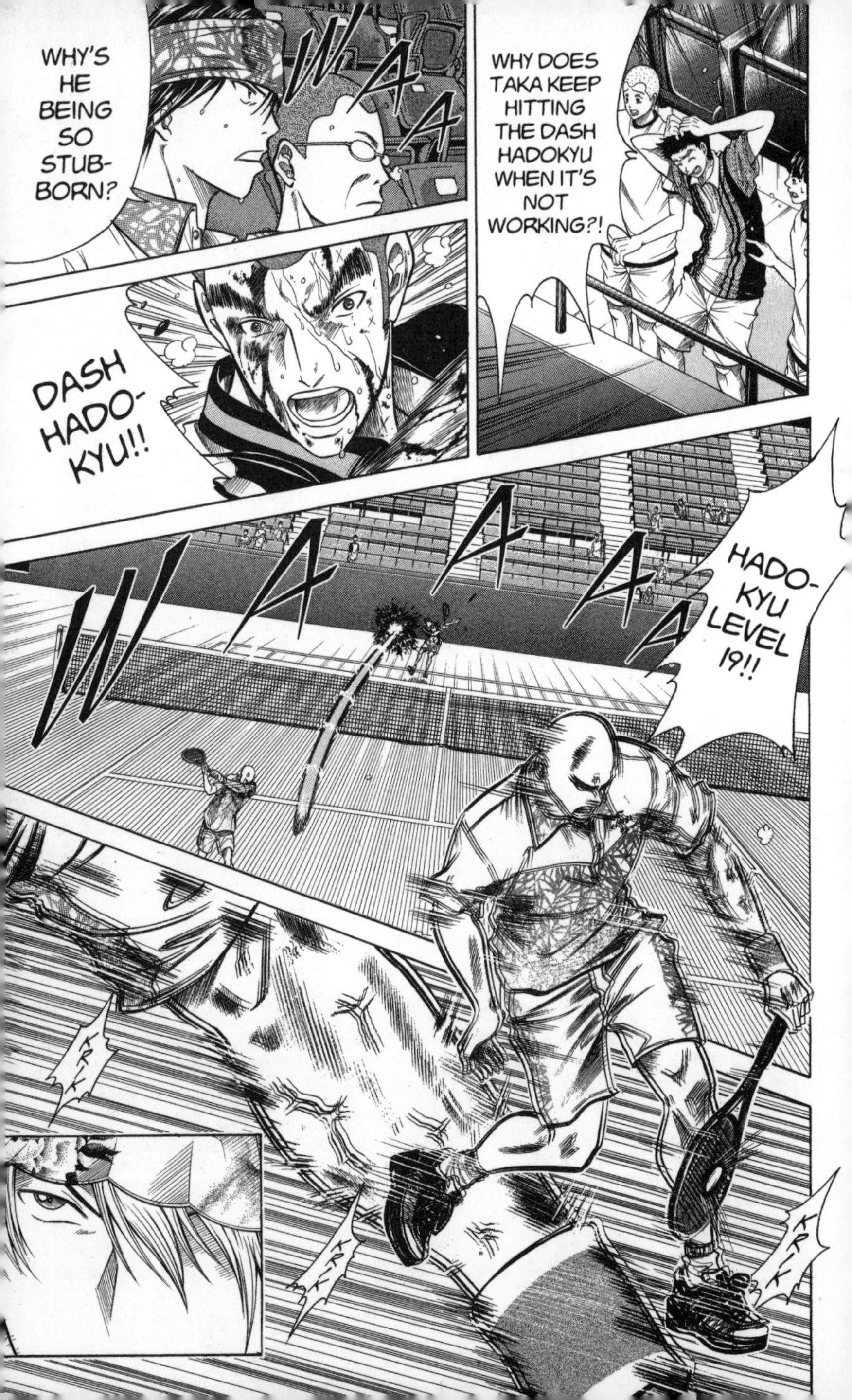
WHY DOES TAKA KEEP HITTING THE DASH HADOKYU WHEN IT'S NOT WORKING?!
WAA
WHY'S HE BEING SO STUBBORN?
DASH HADOKYU!!
HADOKYU LEVEL 19!!
WAAAA
KRIK
KRIK
KRIK

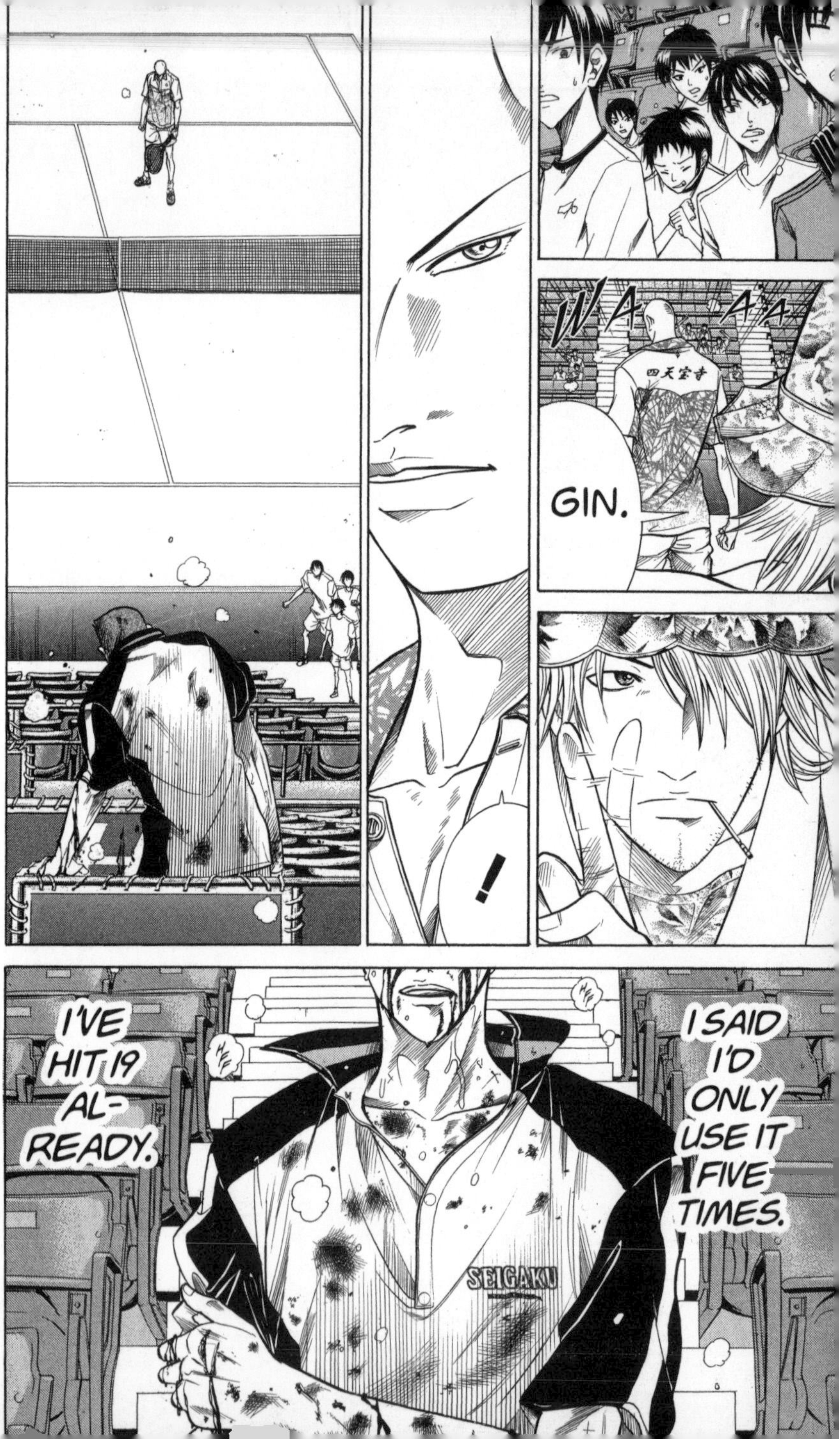
WAAA
GIN.
!
I SAID I'D ONLY USE IT FIVE TIMES.
I'VE HIT 19 AL-READY.

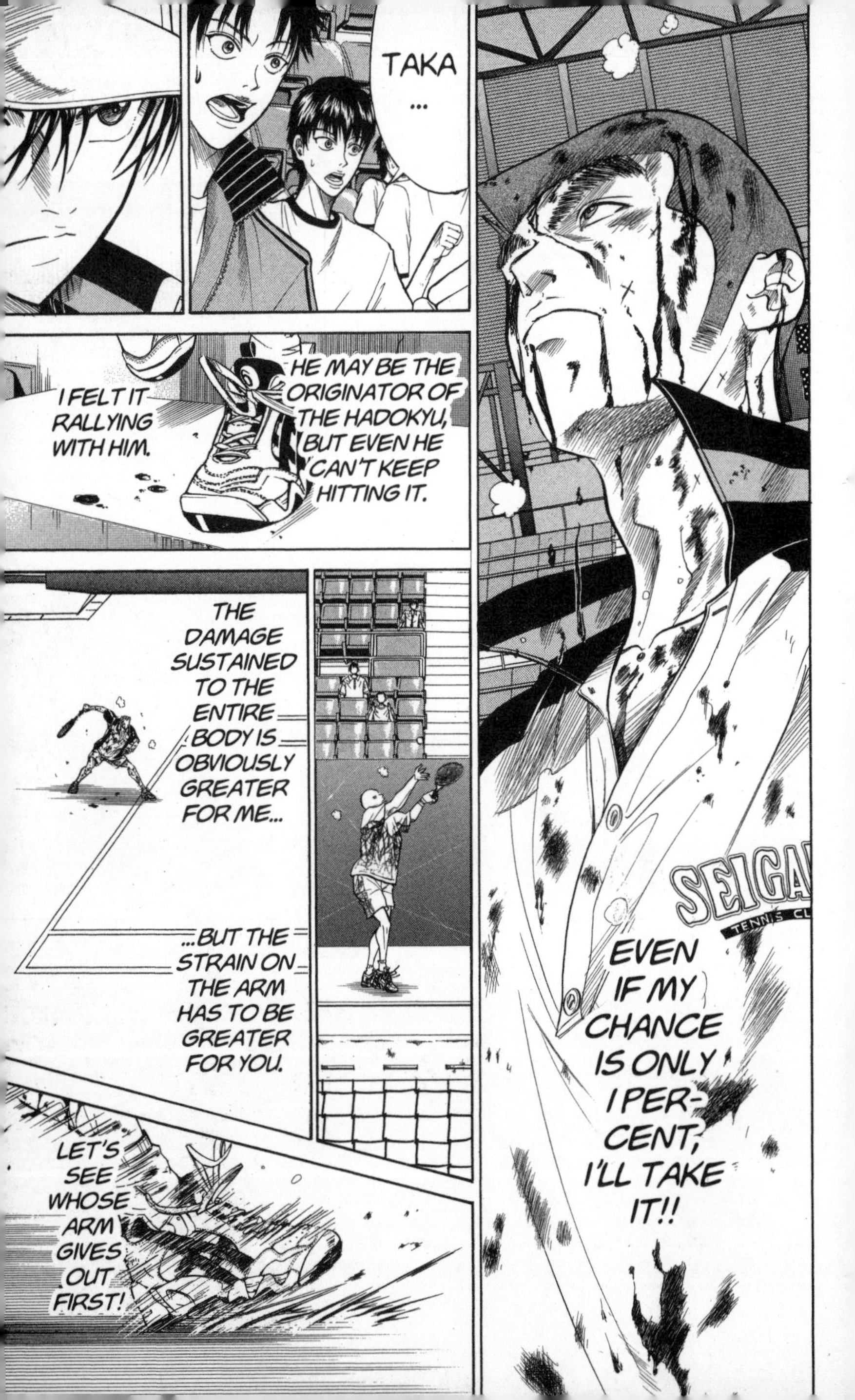

EVEN IF MY CHANCE IS ONLY 1 PERCENT, I'LL TAKE IT!!
TAKA ...
HE MAY BE THE ORIGINATOR OF THE HADOKYU, BUT EVEN HE CAN'T KEEP HITTING IT.
I FELT IT RALLYING WITH HIM.
THE DAMAGE SUSTAINED TO THE ENTIRE BODY IS OBVIOUSLY GREATER FOR ME...
...BUT THE STRAIN ON THE ARM HAS TO BE GREATER FOR YOU.
LET'S SEE WHOSE ARM GIVES OUT FIRST!
SEIGAKU
TENNIS CL

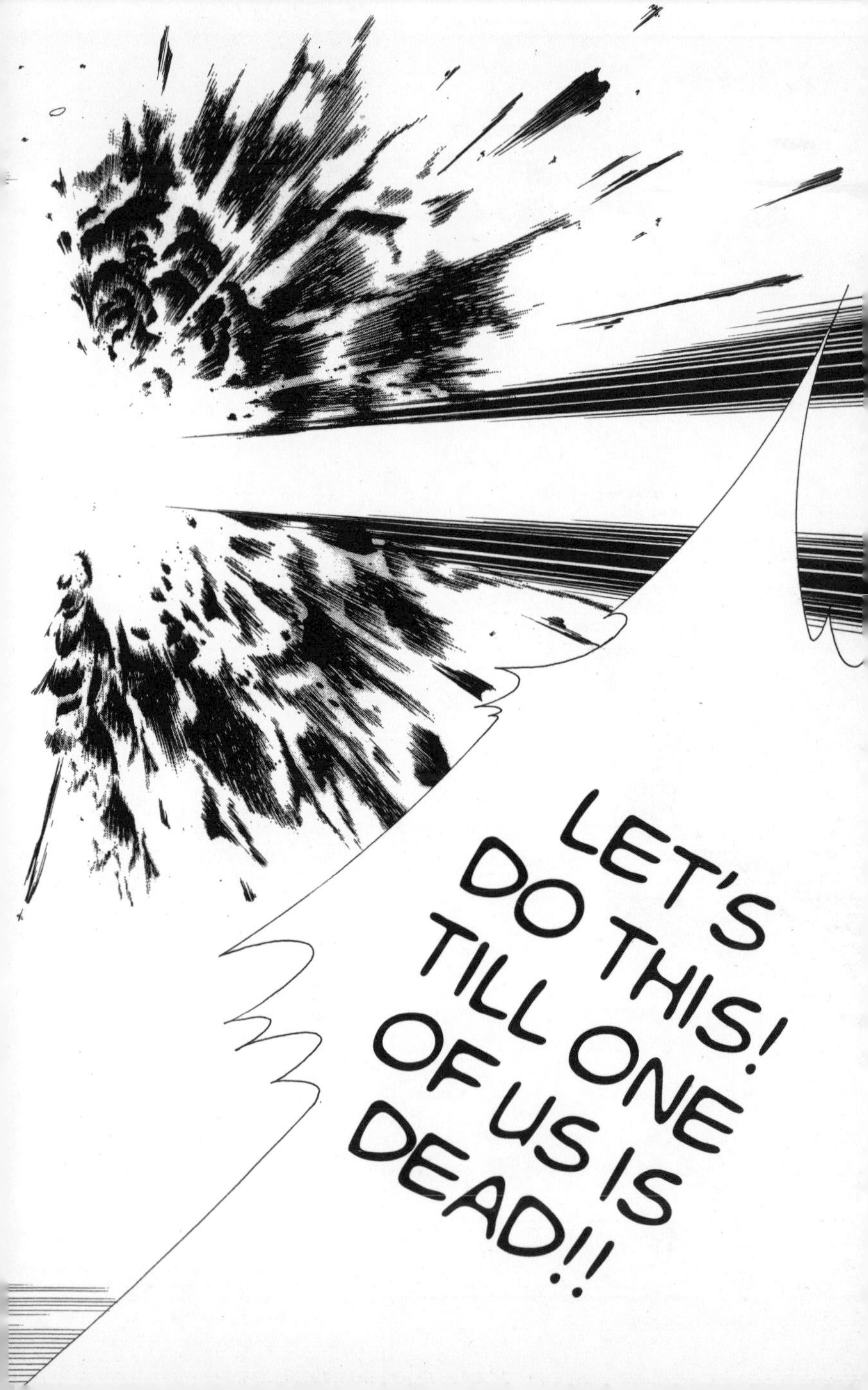
LET'S DO THIS! TILL ONE OF US IS DEAD!!

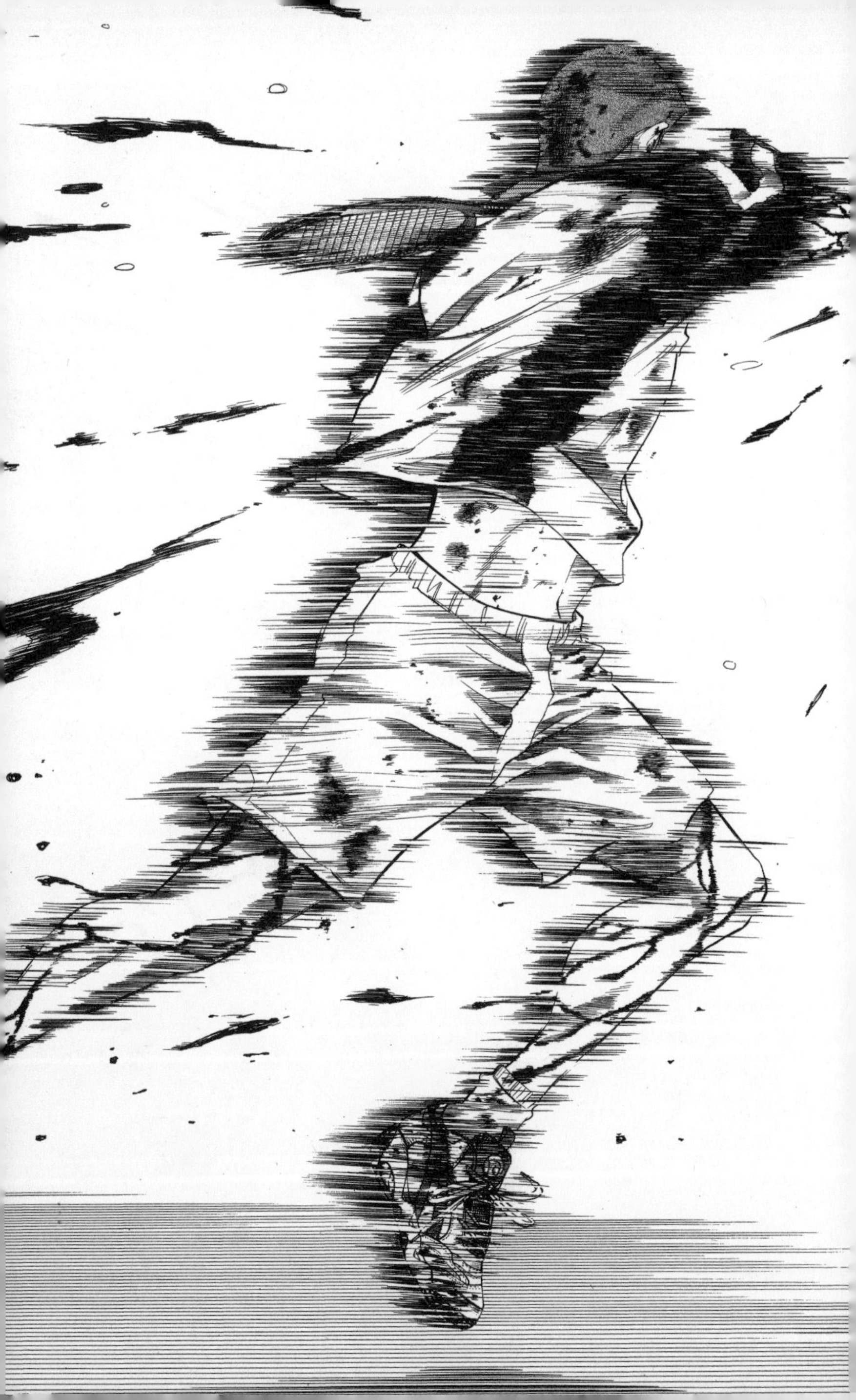

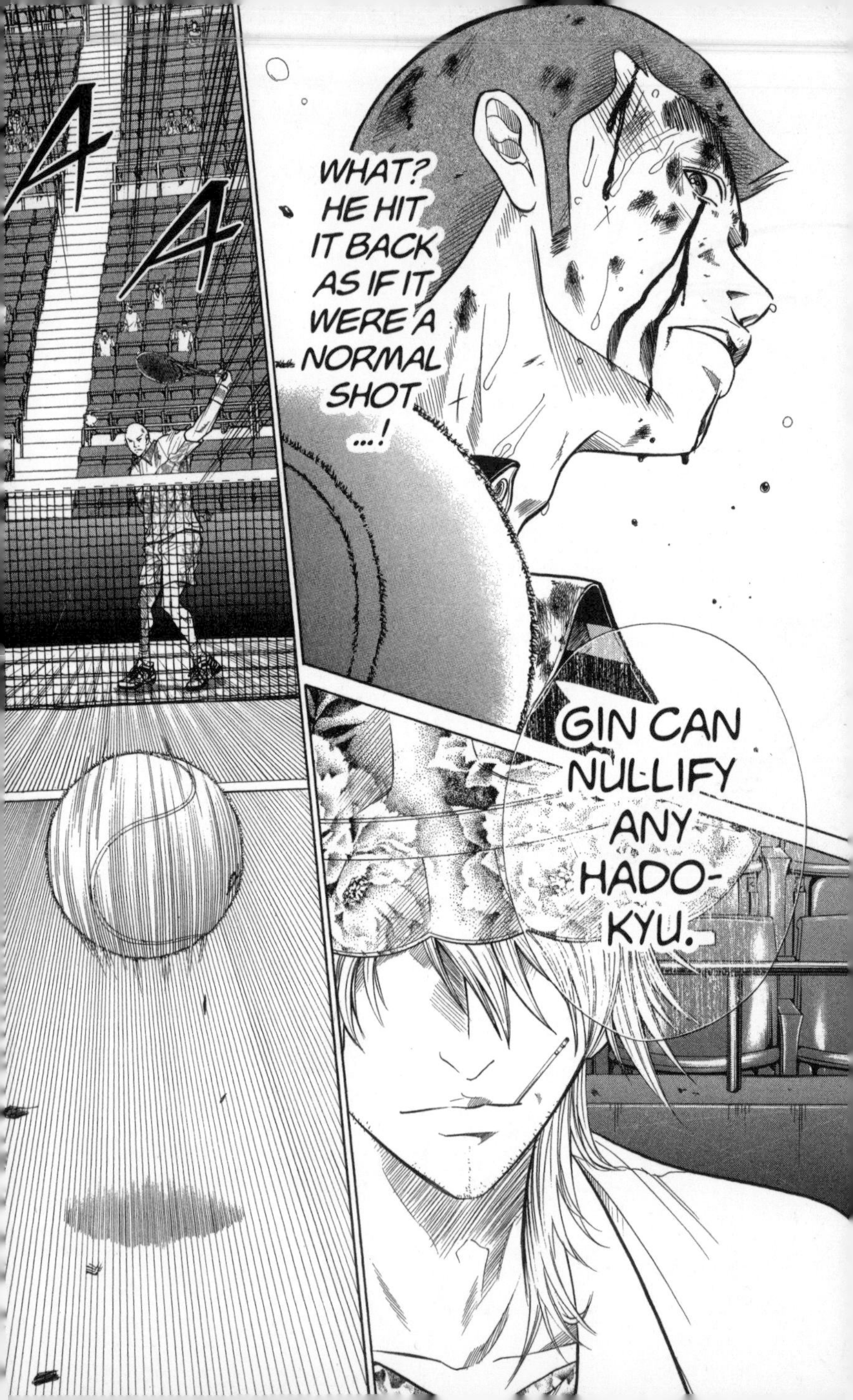
WHAT? HE HIT IT BACK AS IF IT WERE A NORMAL SHOT ...!
GIN CAN NULLIFY ANY HADO-KYU.
A
A

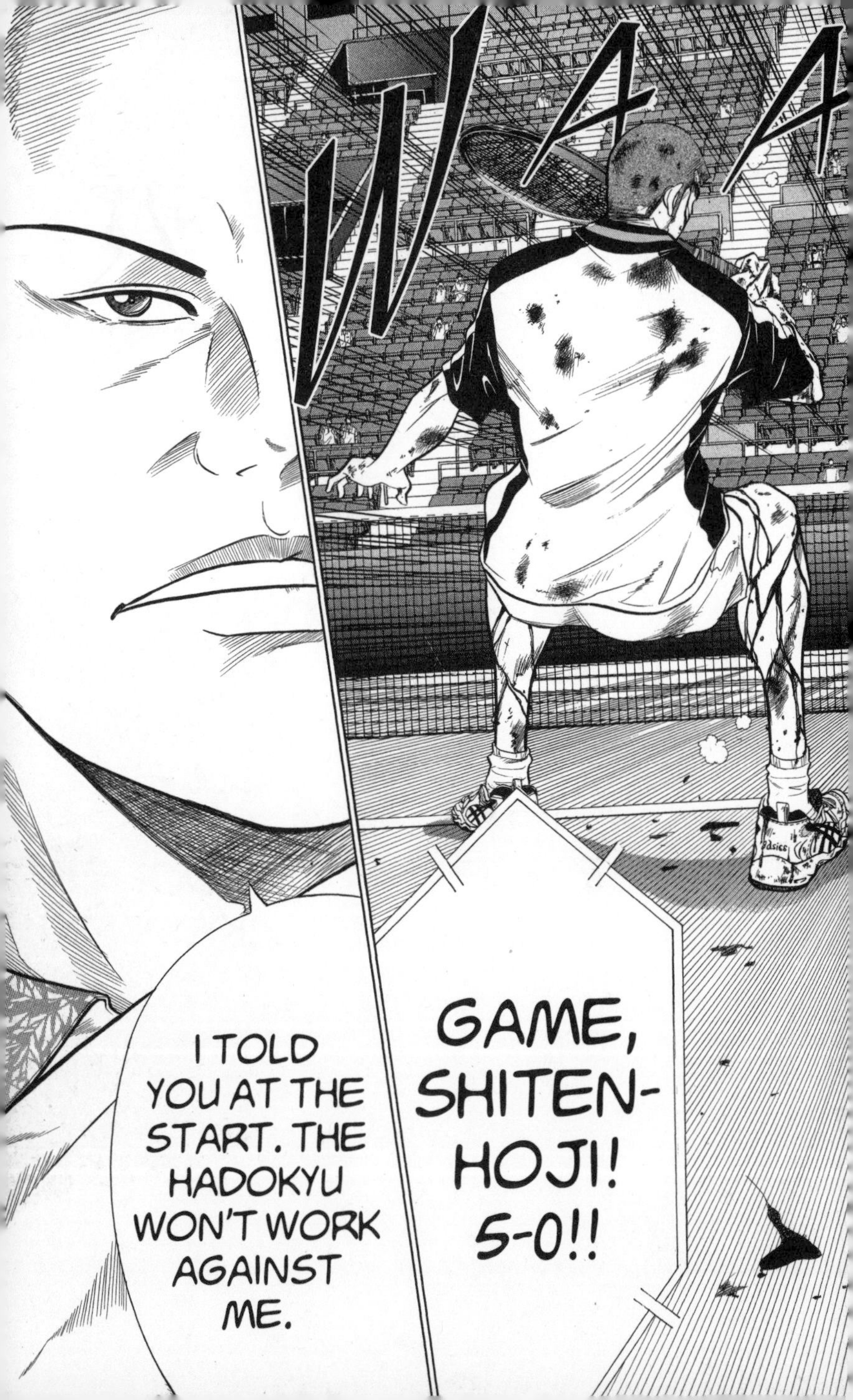
WAA
GAME, SHITEN-HOJI! 5-0!!
I TOLD YOU AT THE START. THE HADOKYU WON'T WORK AGAINST ME.

テニスの王子様

THE PRINCE OF TENNIS

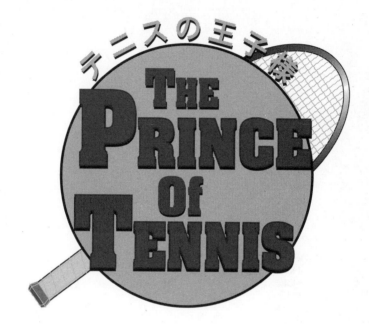

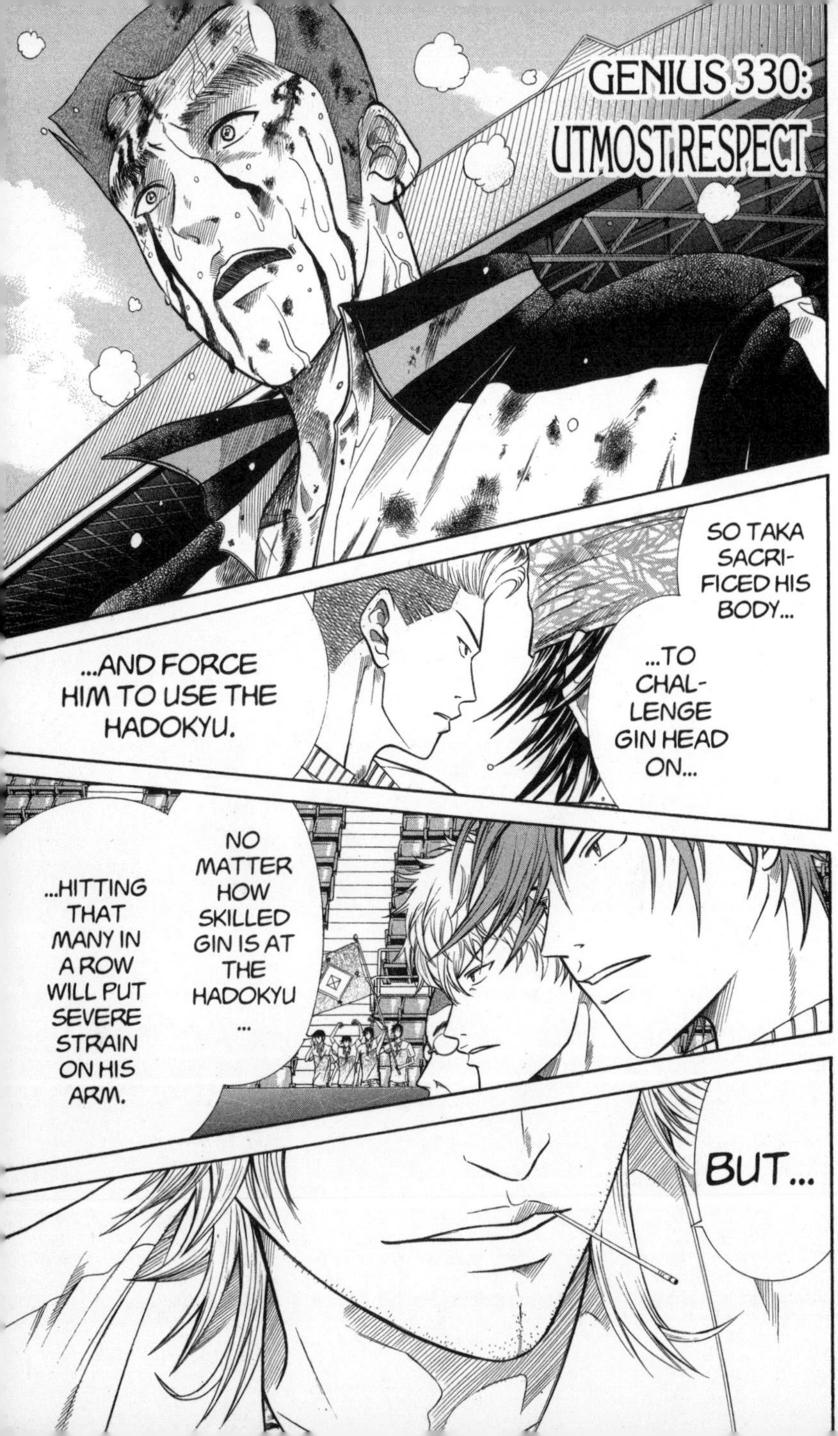
GENIUS 330: UTMOST RESPECT
SO TAKA SACRIFICED HIS BODY...
...TO CHALLENGE GIN HEAD ON...
...AND FORCE HIM TO USE THE HADOKYU.
NO MATTER HOW SKILLED GIN IS AT THE HADOKYU...
...HITTING THAT MANY IN A ROW WILL PUT SEVERE STRAIN ON HIS ARM.
BUT...

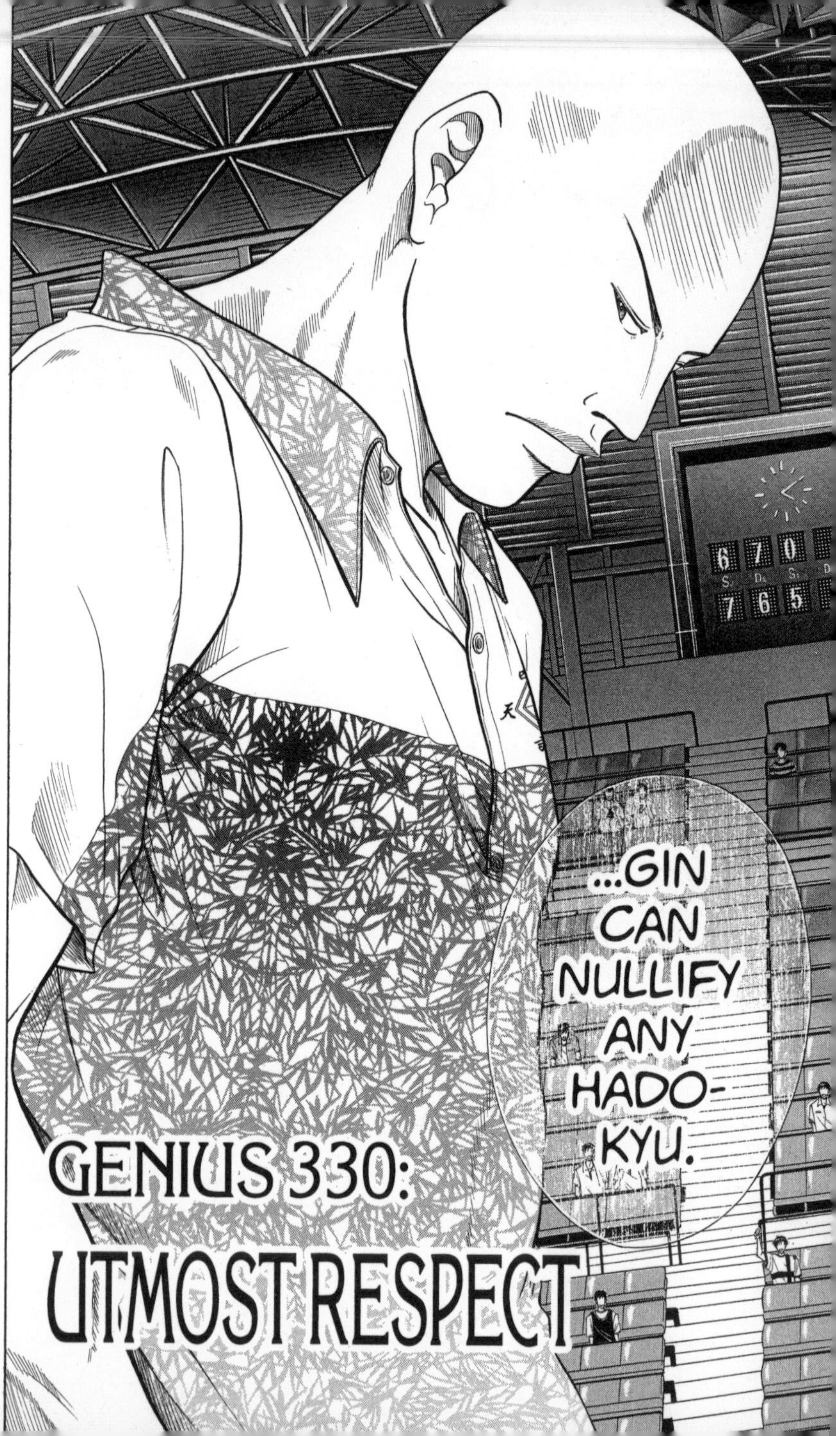
...GIN CAN NULLIFY ANY HADO-KYU.
GENIUS 330:
UTMOST RESPECT

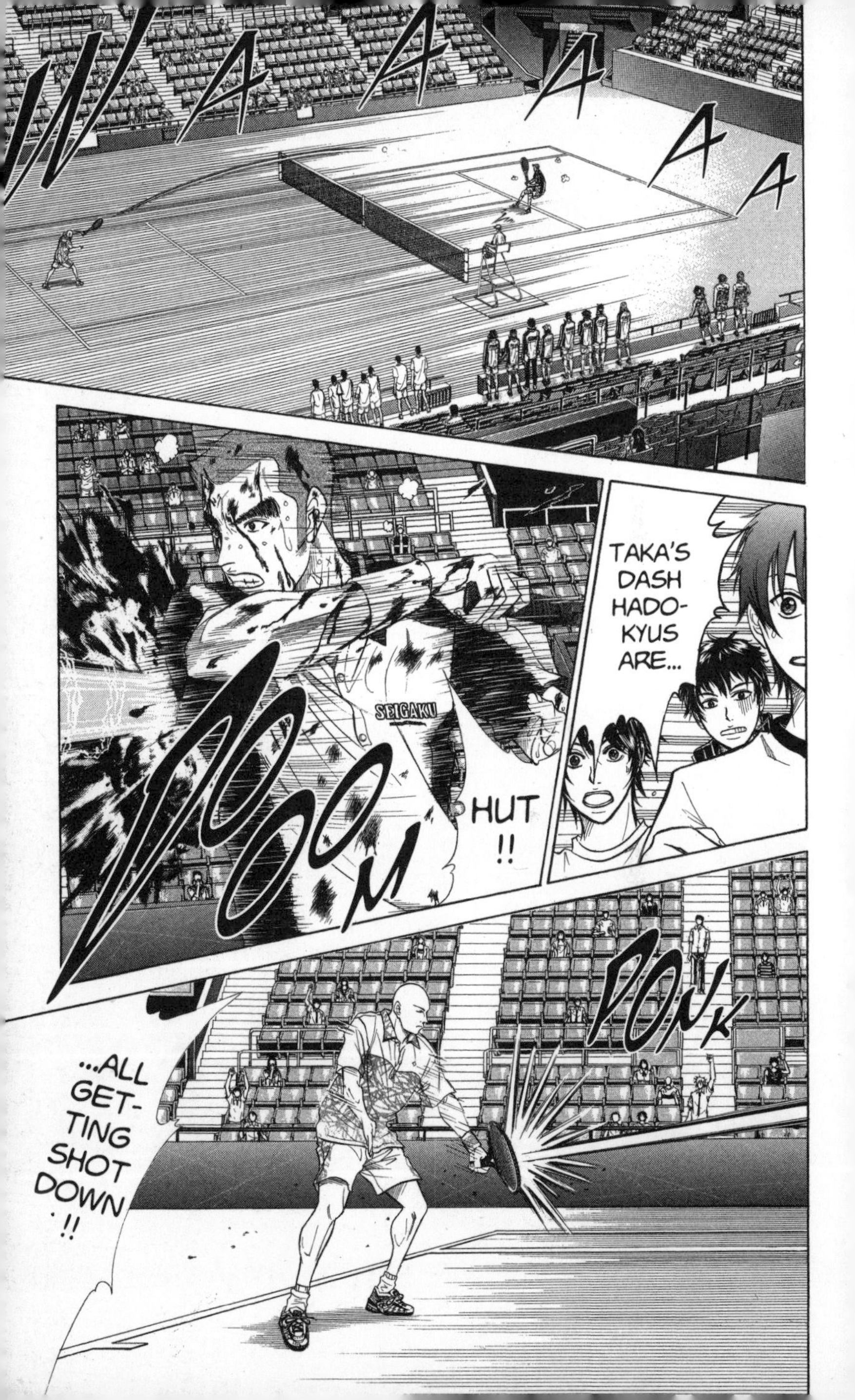
WAAAAA
TAKA'S DASH HADO-KYUS ARE...
SEIGAKU
VOOOM
HUT !!
DONK
...ALL GET-TING SHOT DOWN !!

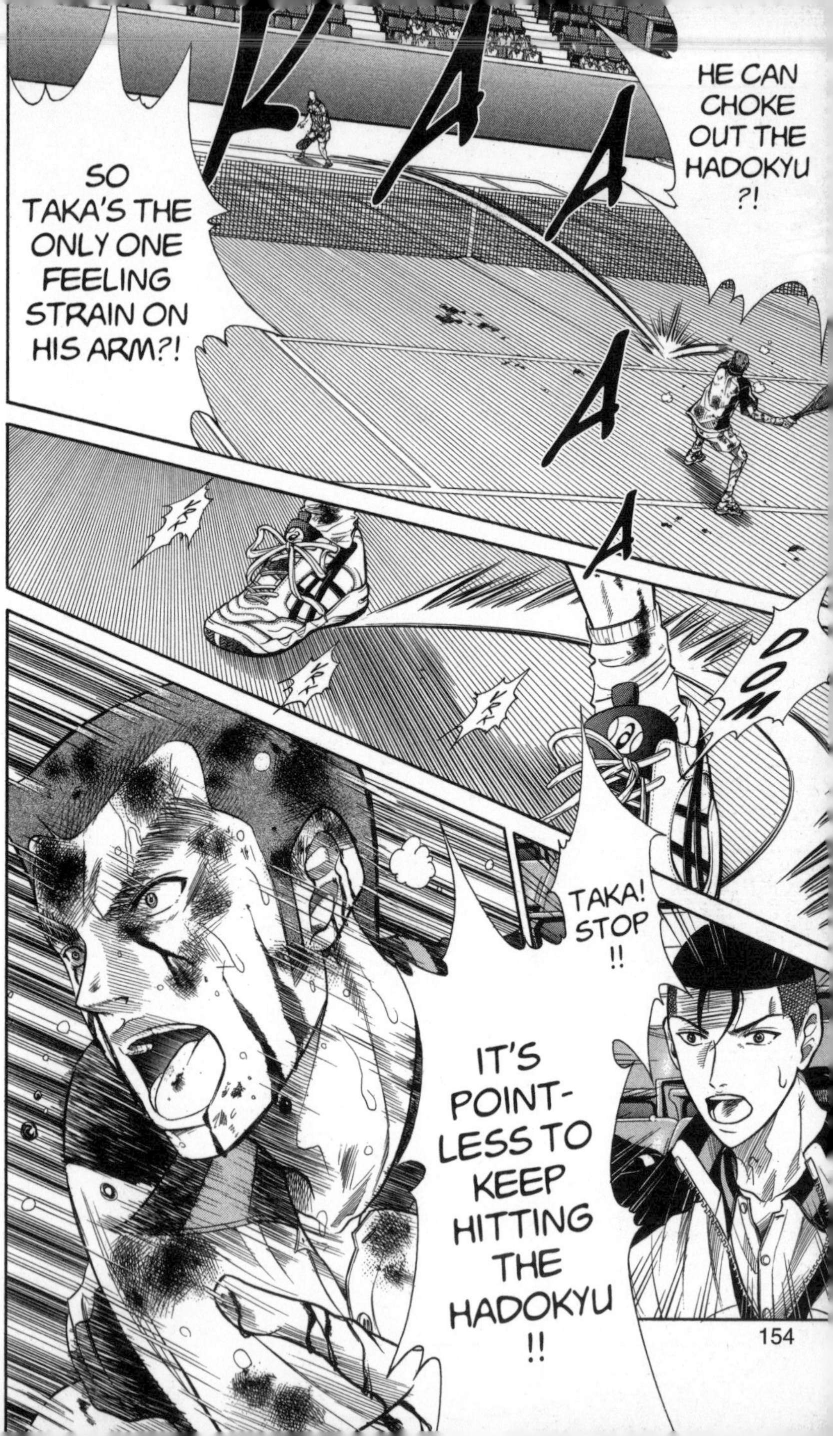
HE CAN CHOKE OUT THE HADOKYU ?!
SO TAKA'S THE ONLY ONE FEELING STRAIN ON HIS ARM?!
TAKA! STOP !!
IT'S POINT-LESS TO KEEP HITTING THE HADOKYU !!

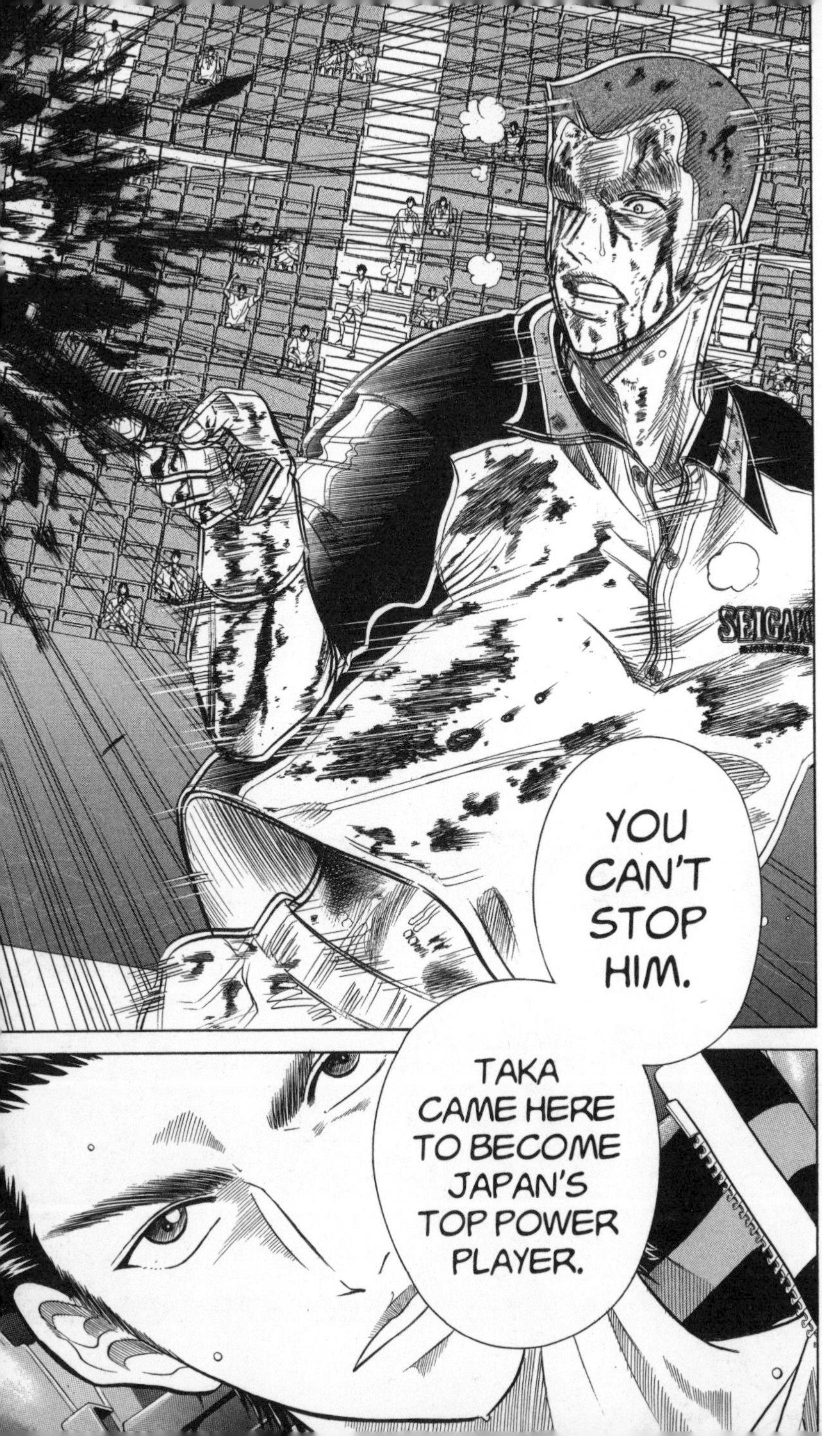
YOU CAN'T STOP HIM.
TAKA CAME HERE TO BECOME JAPAN'S TOP POWER PLAYER.

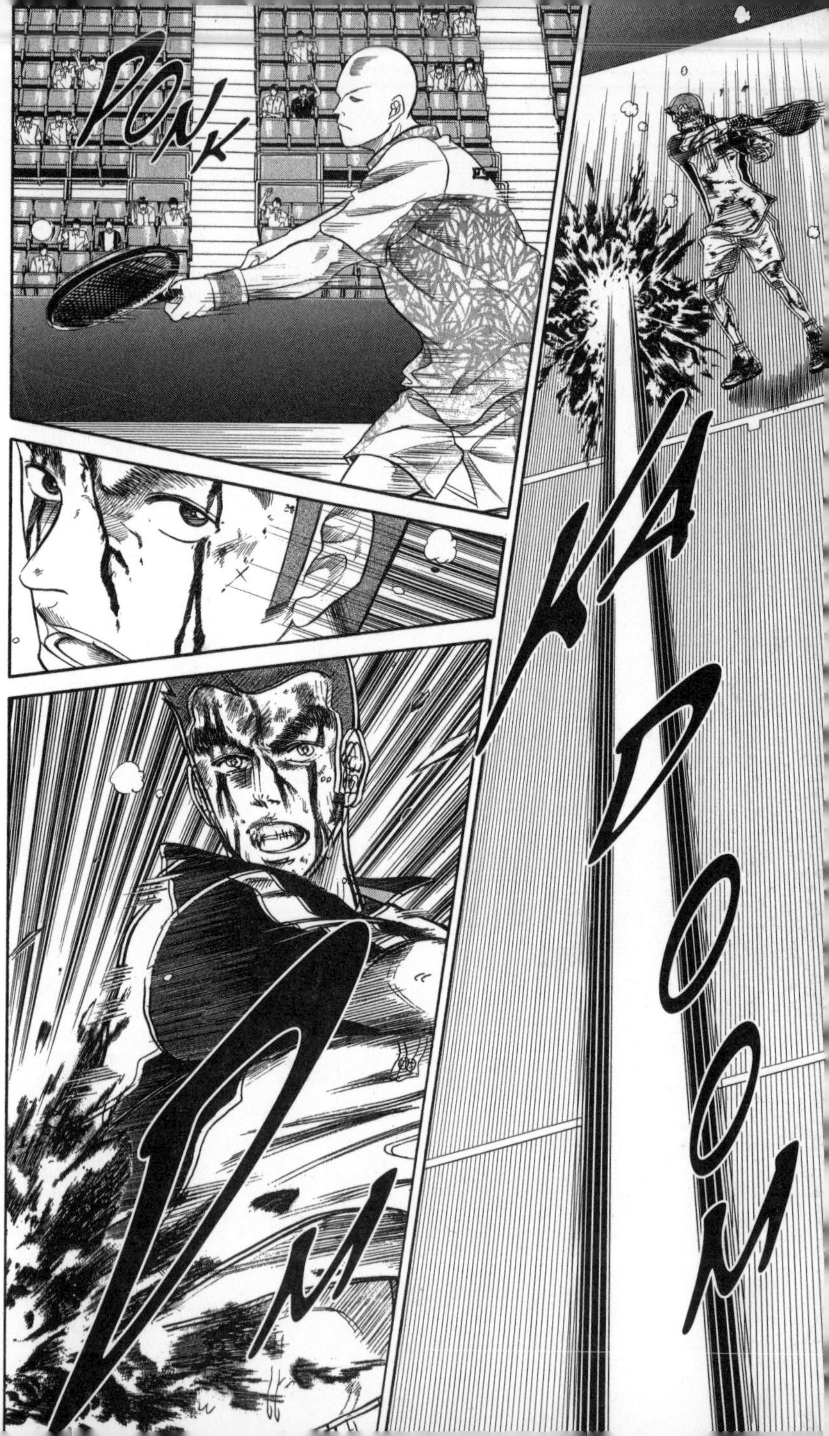
KADOOOM
DONK
VMM

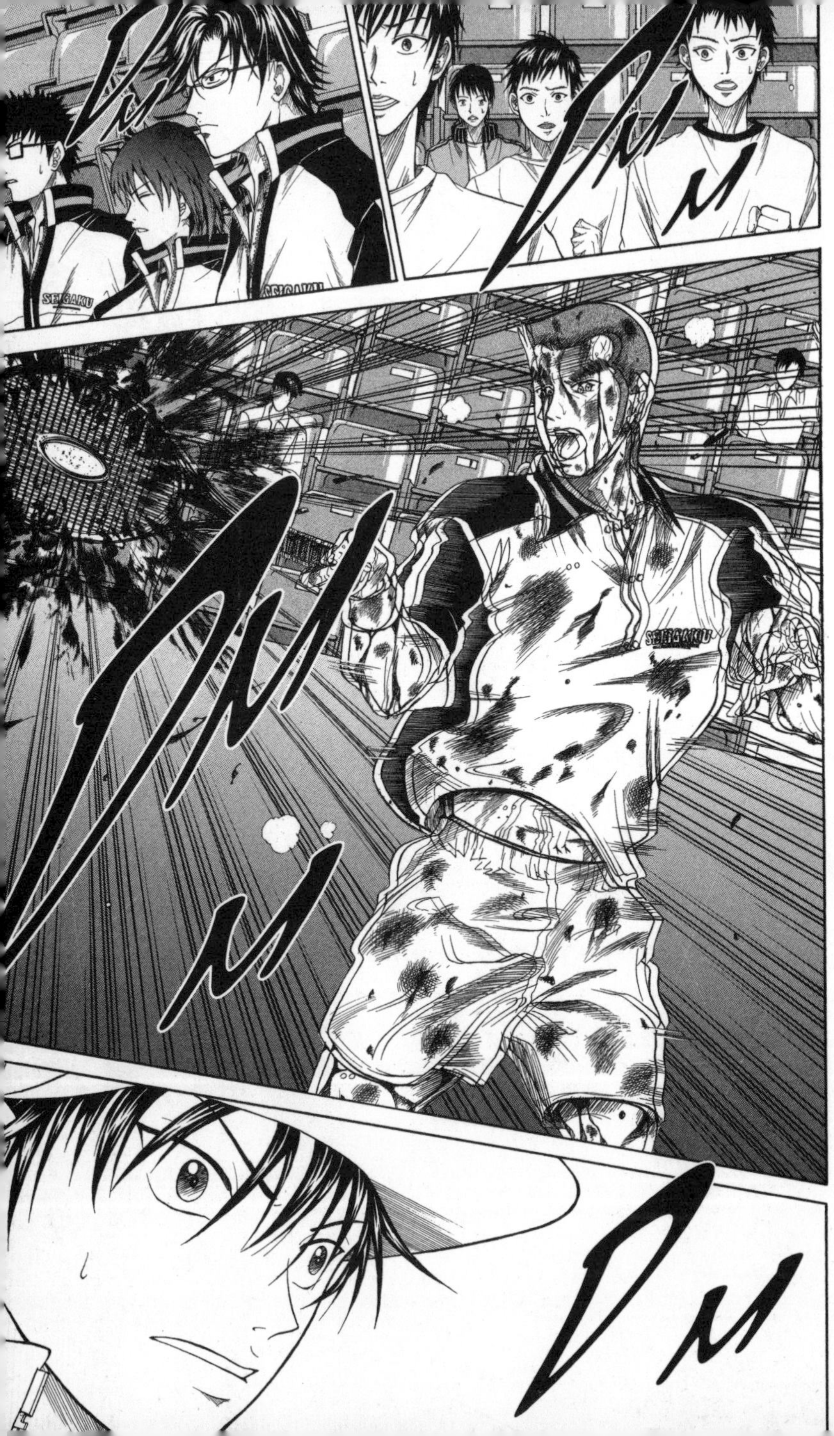

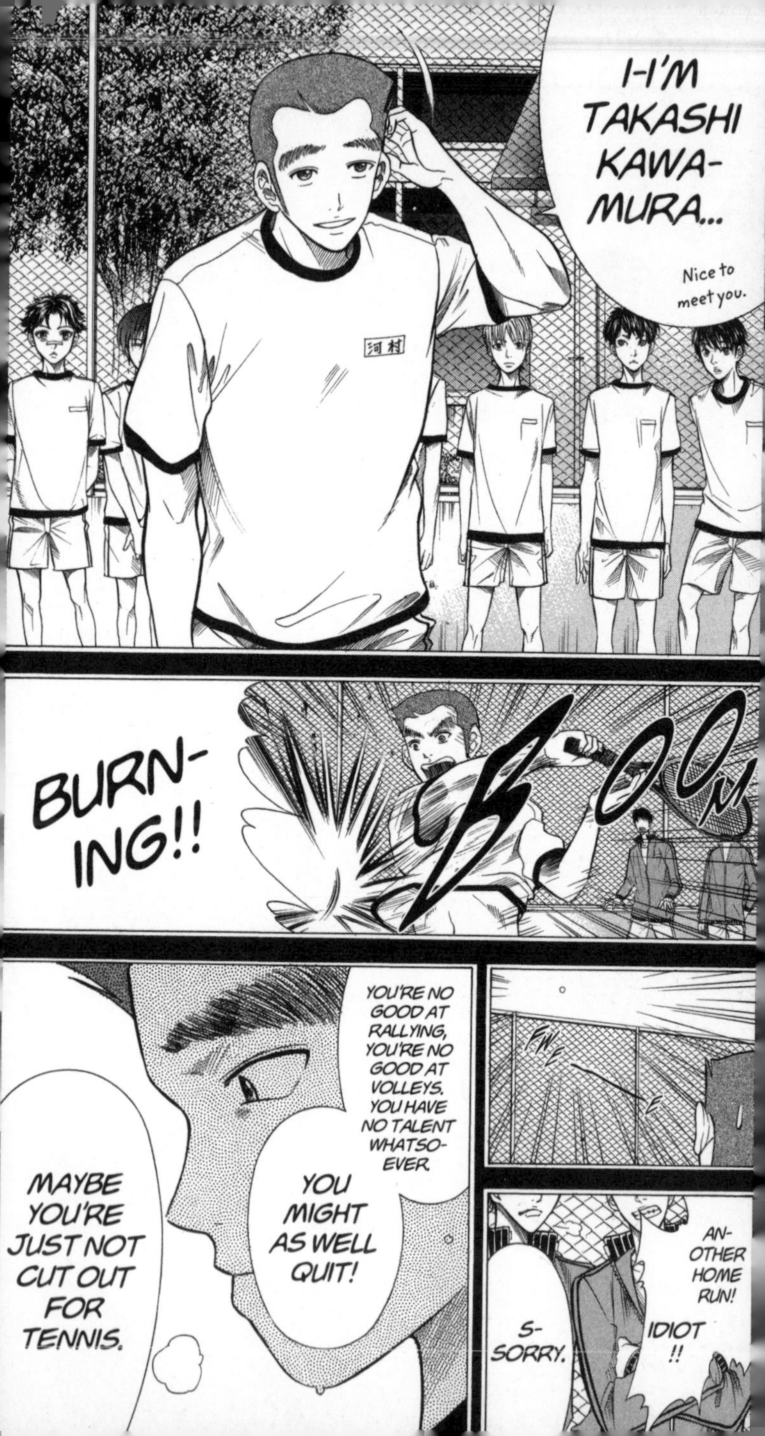
I-I'M TAKASHI KAWAMURA...
Nice to meet you.
BURNING!!
AN-OTHER HOME RUN!
IDIOT!!
S-SORRY.
YOU'RE NO GOOD AT RALLYING, YOU'RE NO GOOD AT VOLLEYS. YOU HAVE NO TALENT WHATSOEVER.
YOU MIGHT AS WELL QUIT!
MAYBE YOU'RE JUST NOT CUT OUT FOR TENNIS.

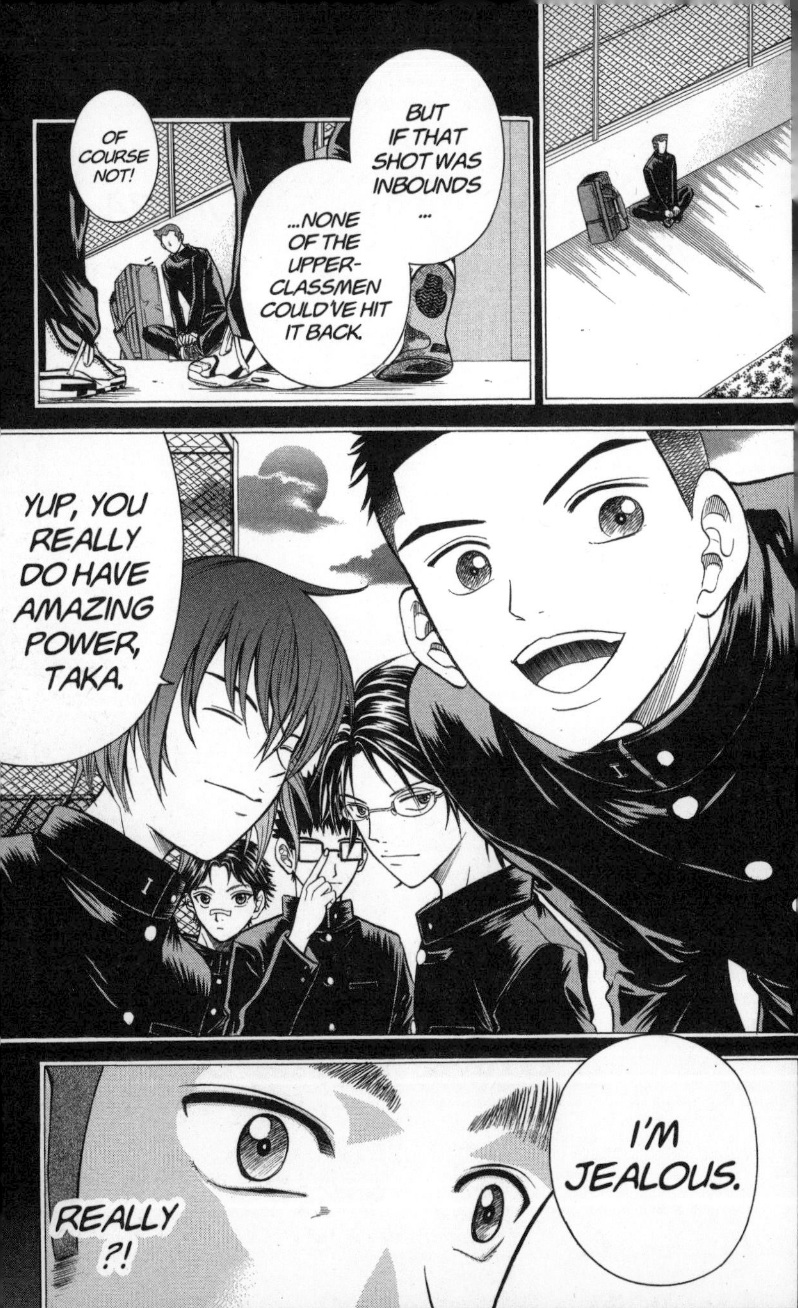
BUT IF THAT SHOT WAS INBOUNDS ...
...NONE OF THE UPPER-CLASSMEN COULD'VE HIT IT BACK.
OF COURSE NOT!
YUP, YOU REALLY DO HAVE AMAZING POWER, TAKA.
I'M JEALOUS.
REALLY ?!

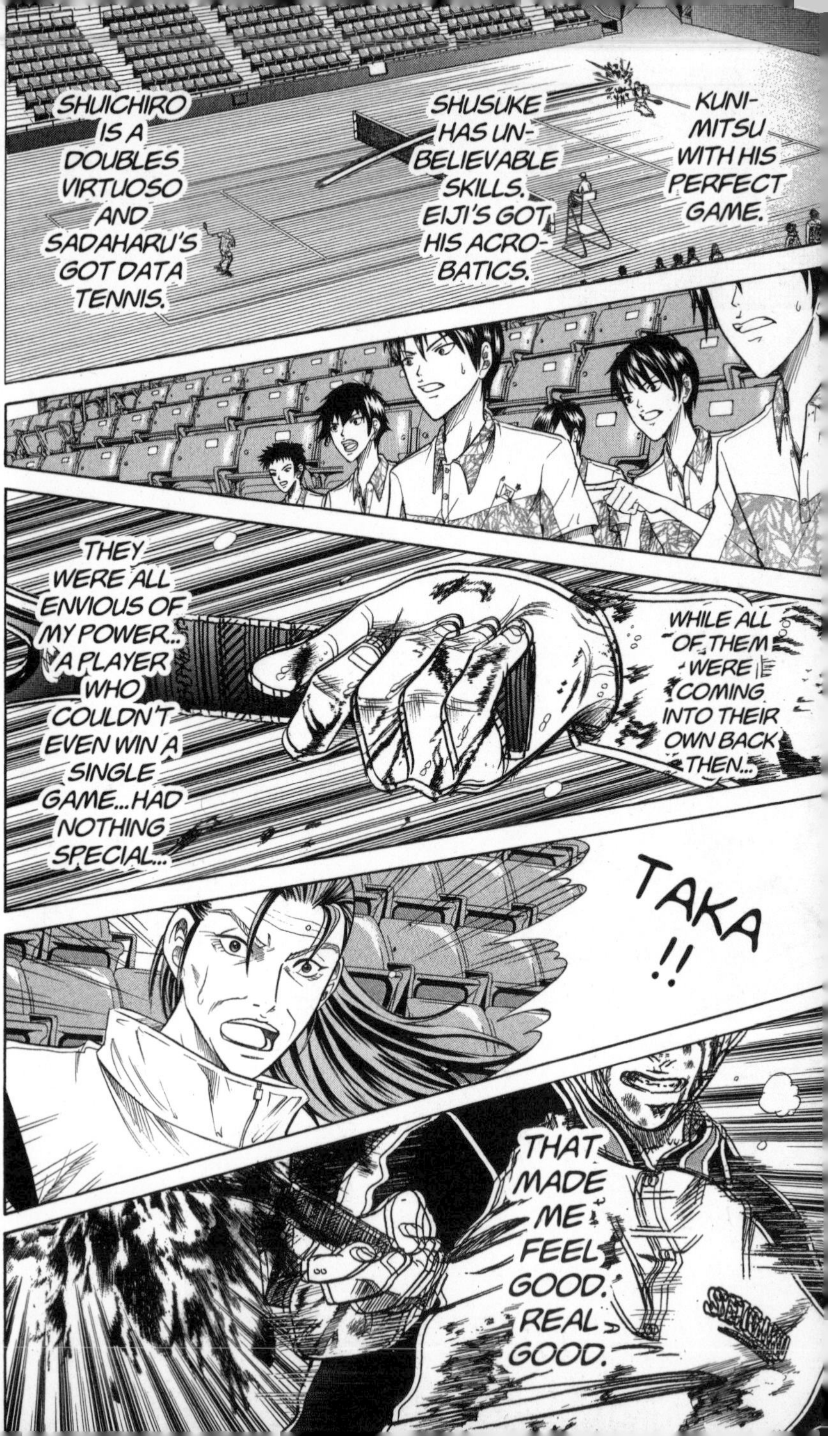
KUNIMITSU WITH HIS PERFECT GAME.
SHUSUKE HAS UNBELIEVABLE SKILLS. EIJI'S GOT HIS ACROBATICS.
SHUICHIRO IS A DOUBLES VIRTUOSO AND SADAHARU'S GOT DATA TENNIS.
WHILE ALL OF THEM WERE COMING INTO THEIR OWN BACK THEN...
THEY WERE ALL ENVIOUS OF MY POWER... A PLAYER WHO COULDN'T EVEN WIN A SINGLE GAME...HAD NOTHING SPECIAL...
TAKA !!
THAT MADE ME FEEL GOOD. REAL GOOD.

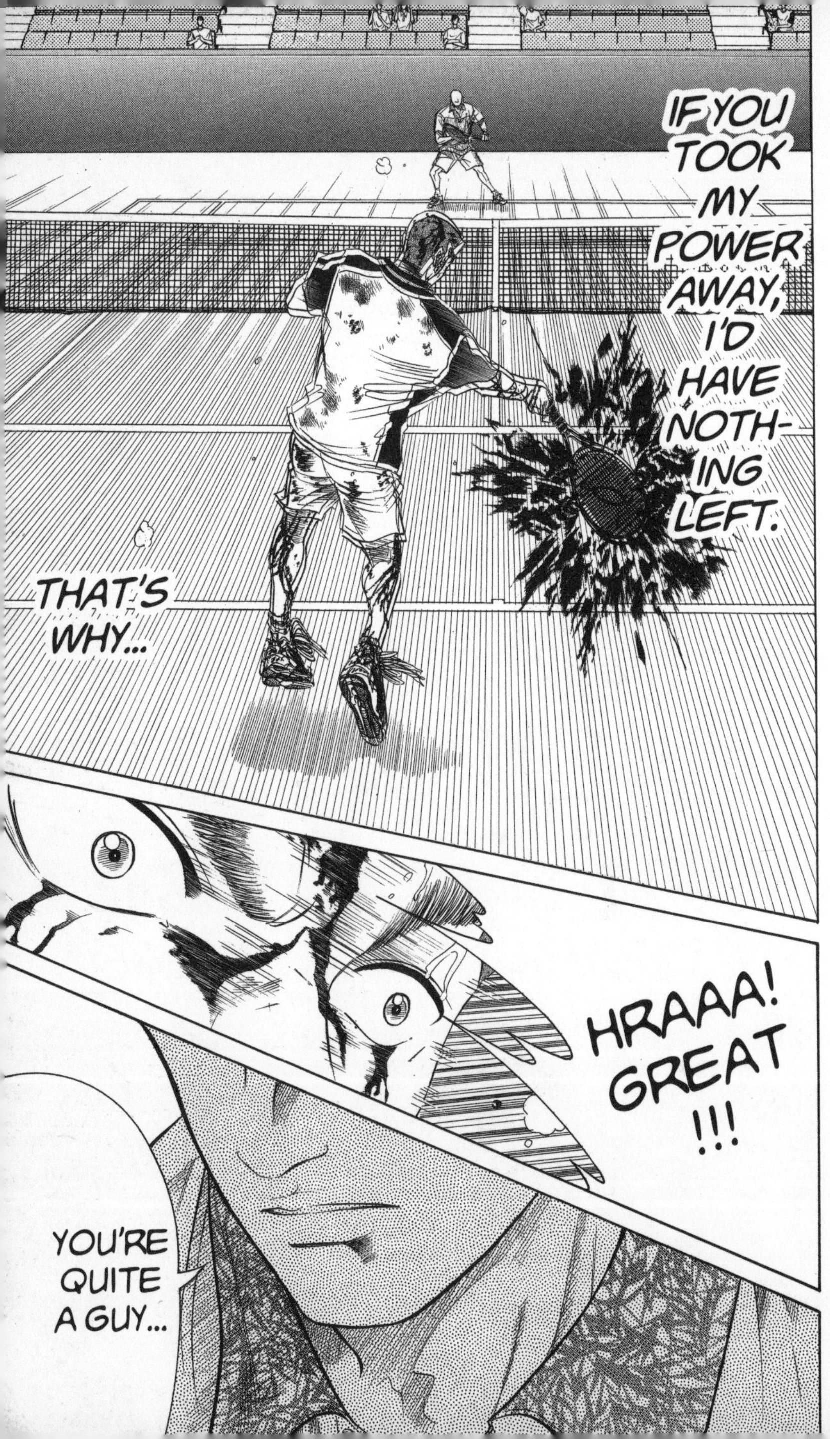
IF YOU TOOK MY POWER AWAY, I'D HAVE NOTHING LEFT.
THAT'S WHY...
HRAAA! GREAT!!!
YOU'RE QUITE A GUY...

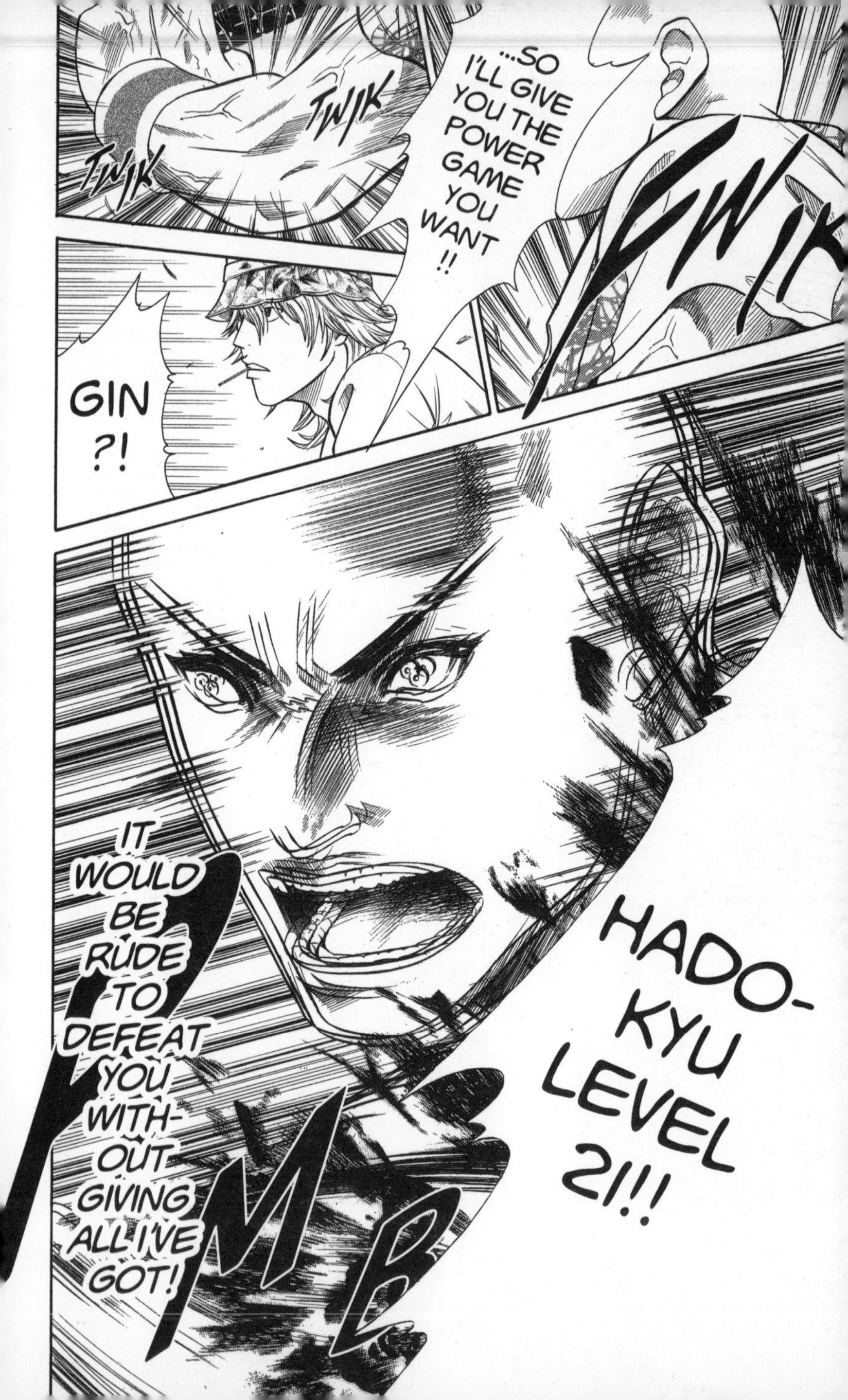

TWIK
TWIK
...SO I'LL GIVE YOU THE POWER GAME YOU WANT!!
FWIK
GIN?!
HADO-KYU LEVEL 2!!!
IT WOULD BE RUDE TO DEFEAT YOU WITHOUT GIVING ALL I'VE GOT!

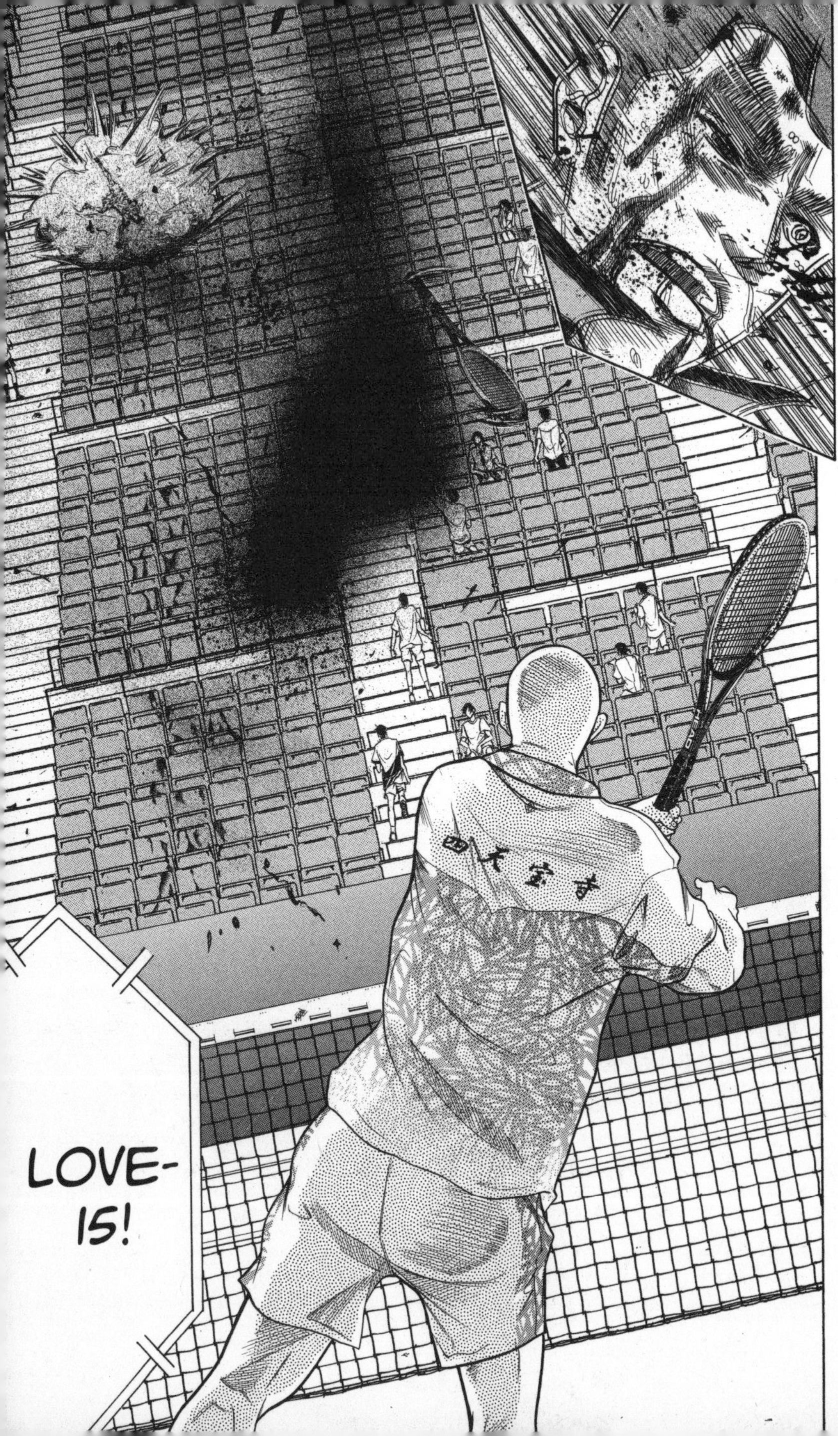
LOVE-15!

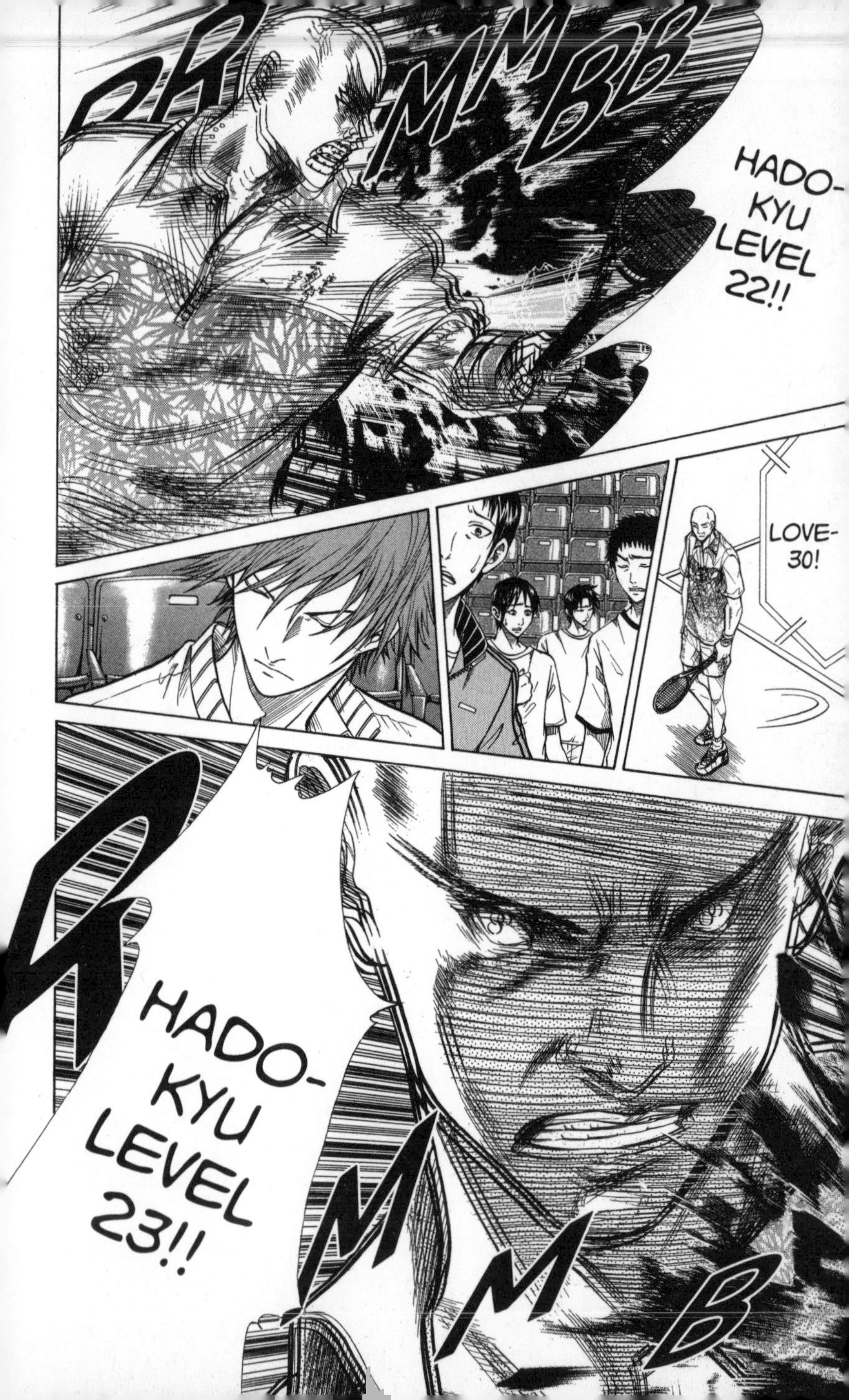
DRMMBB
HADO-KYU LEVEL 22!!
LOVE-30!
HADO-KYU LEVEL 23!!
DRMMB

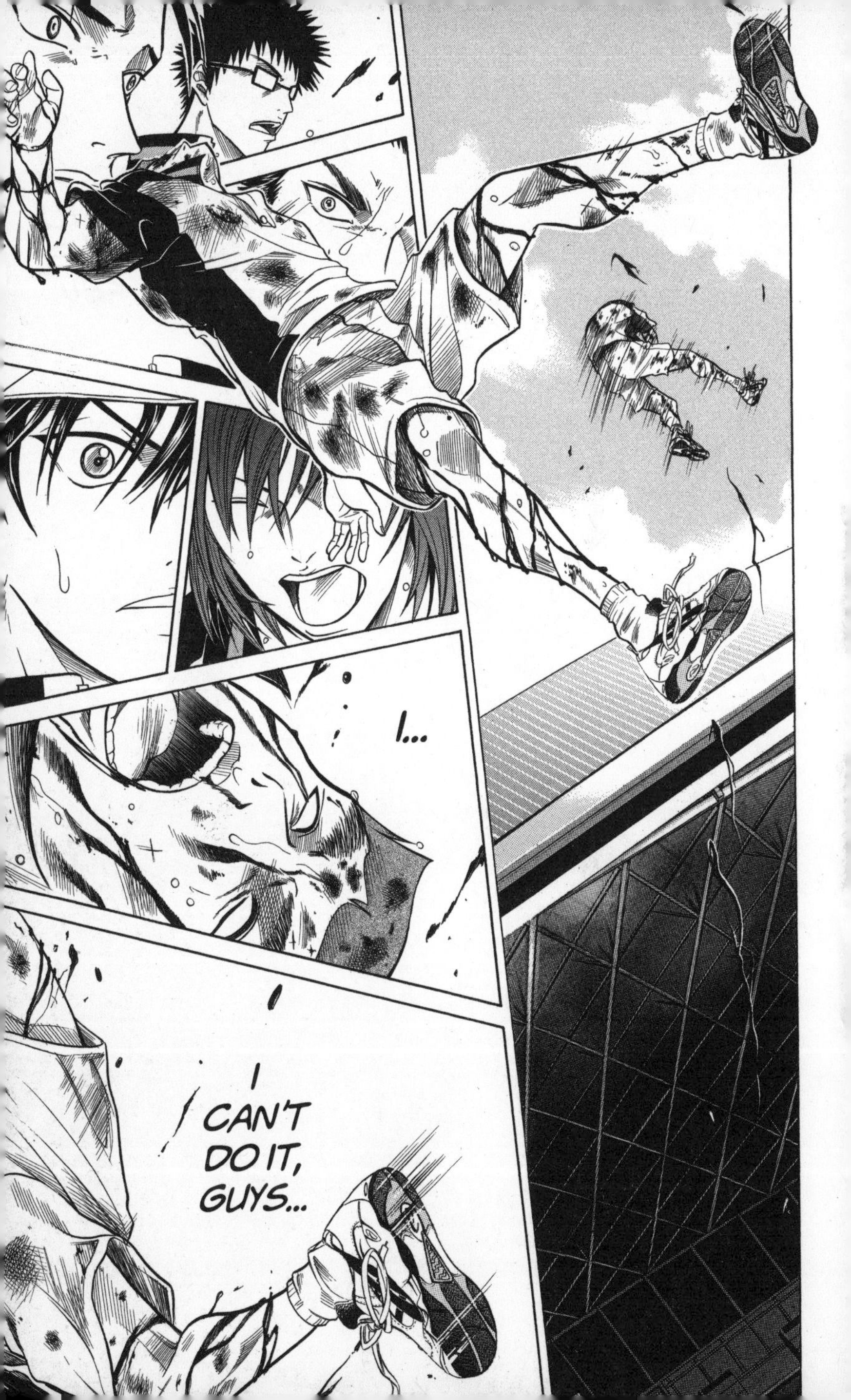
I...
I CAN'T DO IT, GUYS...

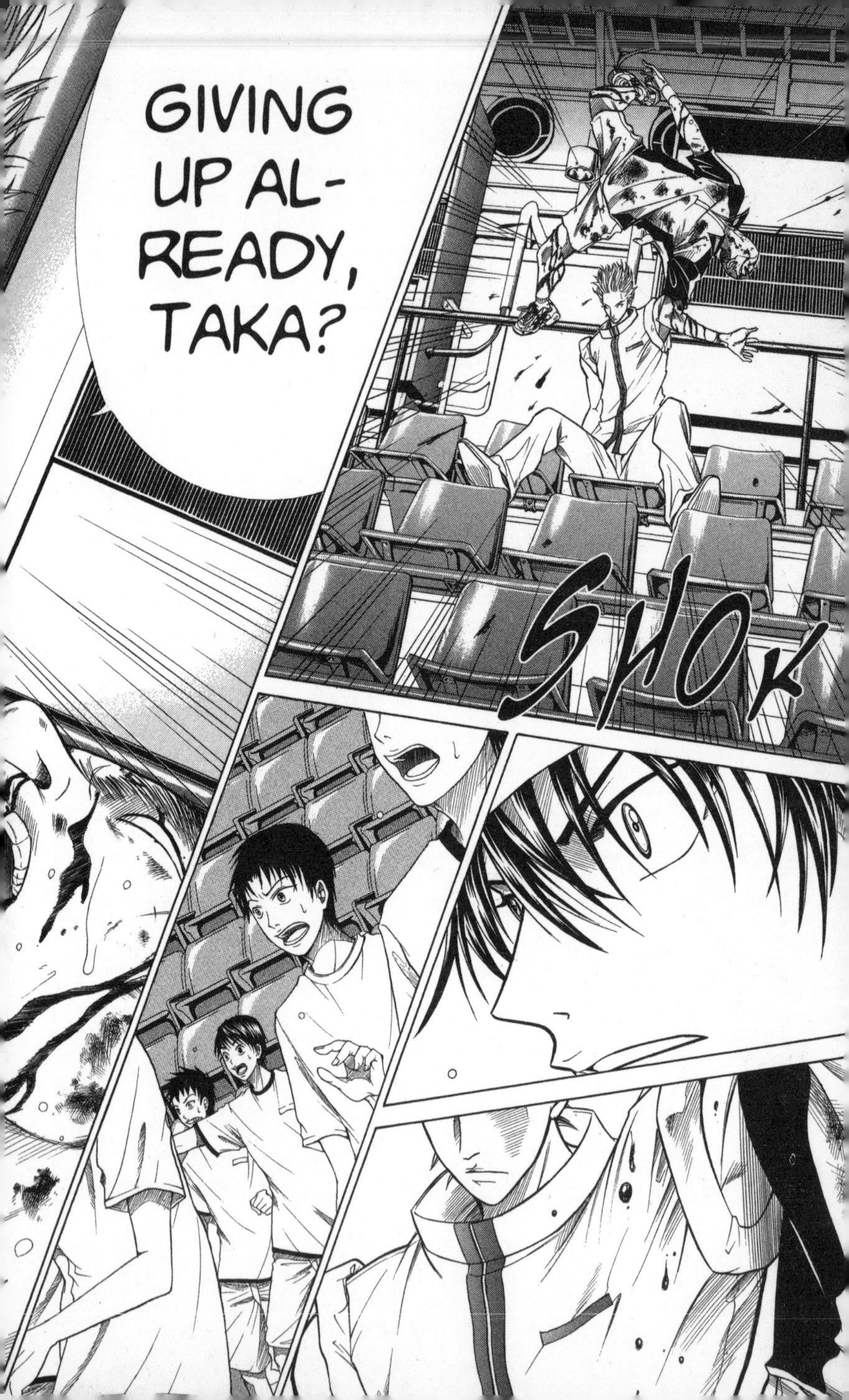
SHOK
GIVING UP AL-READY, TAKA?

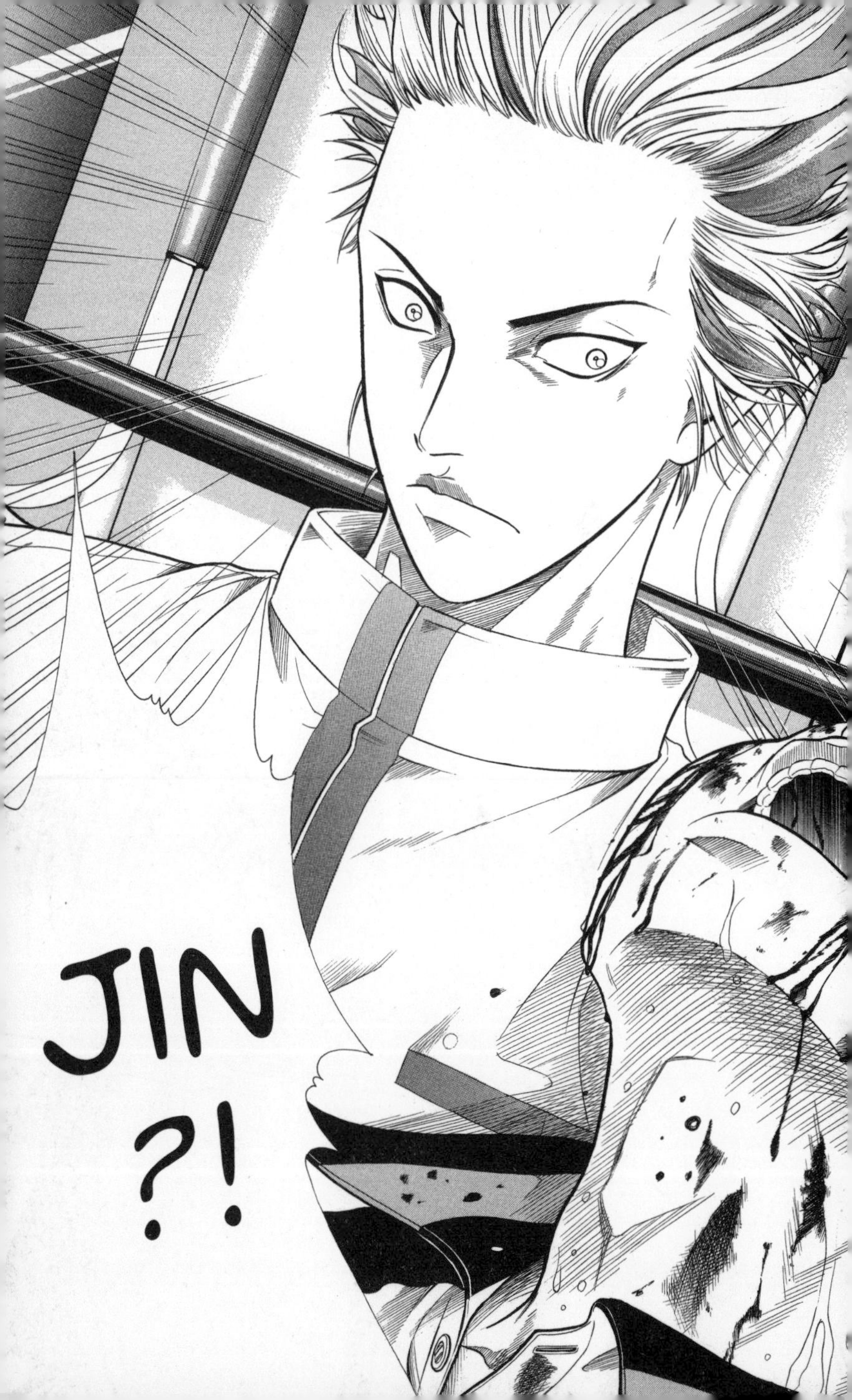
JIN
?!

テニスの王子様

THE PRINCE OF TENNIS

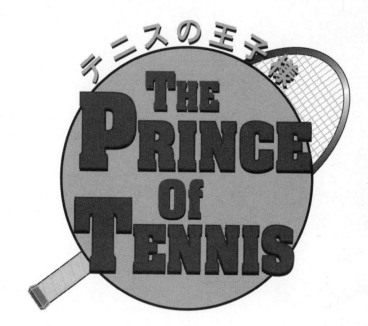

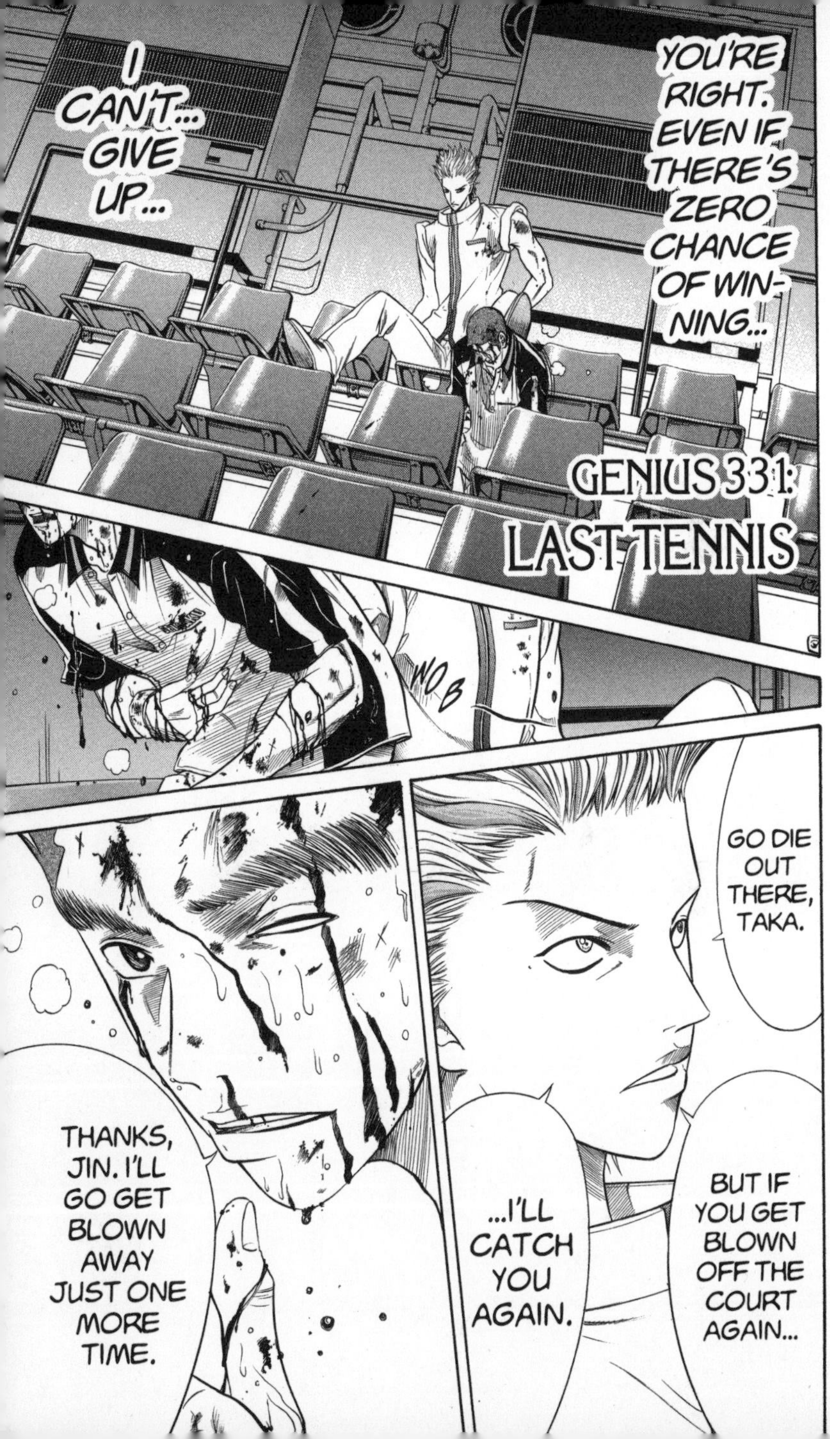
YOU'RE RIGHT. EVEN IF THERE'S ZERO CHANCE OF WIN-NING...
I CAN'T... GIVE UP...
GENIUS 331:
LAST TENNIS
GO DIE OUT THERE, TAKA.
BUT IF YOU GET BLOWN OFF THE COURT AGAIN...
...I'LL CATCH YOU AGAIN.
THANKS, JIN. I'LL GO GET BLOWN AWAY JUST ONE MORE TIME.

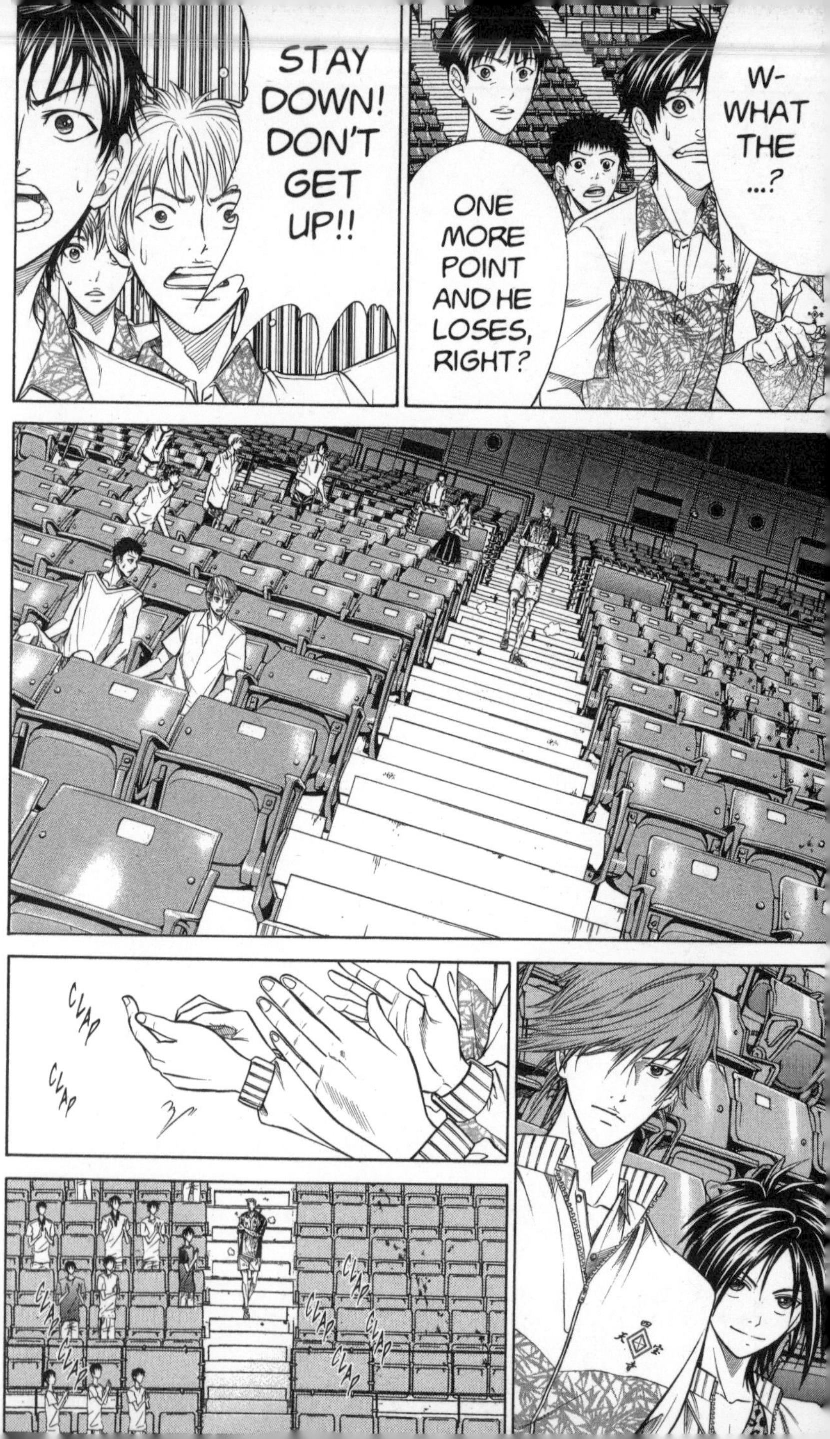
W-WHAT THE ...?
ONE MORE POINT AND HE LOSES, RIGHT?
STAY DOWN! DON'T GET UP!!
CLAP
CLAP
CLAP
CLAP
CLAP
CLAP
CLAP
CLAP

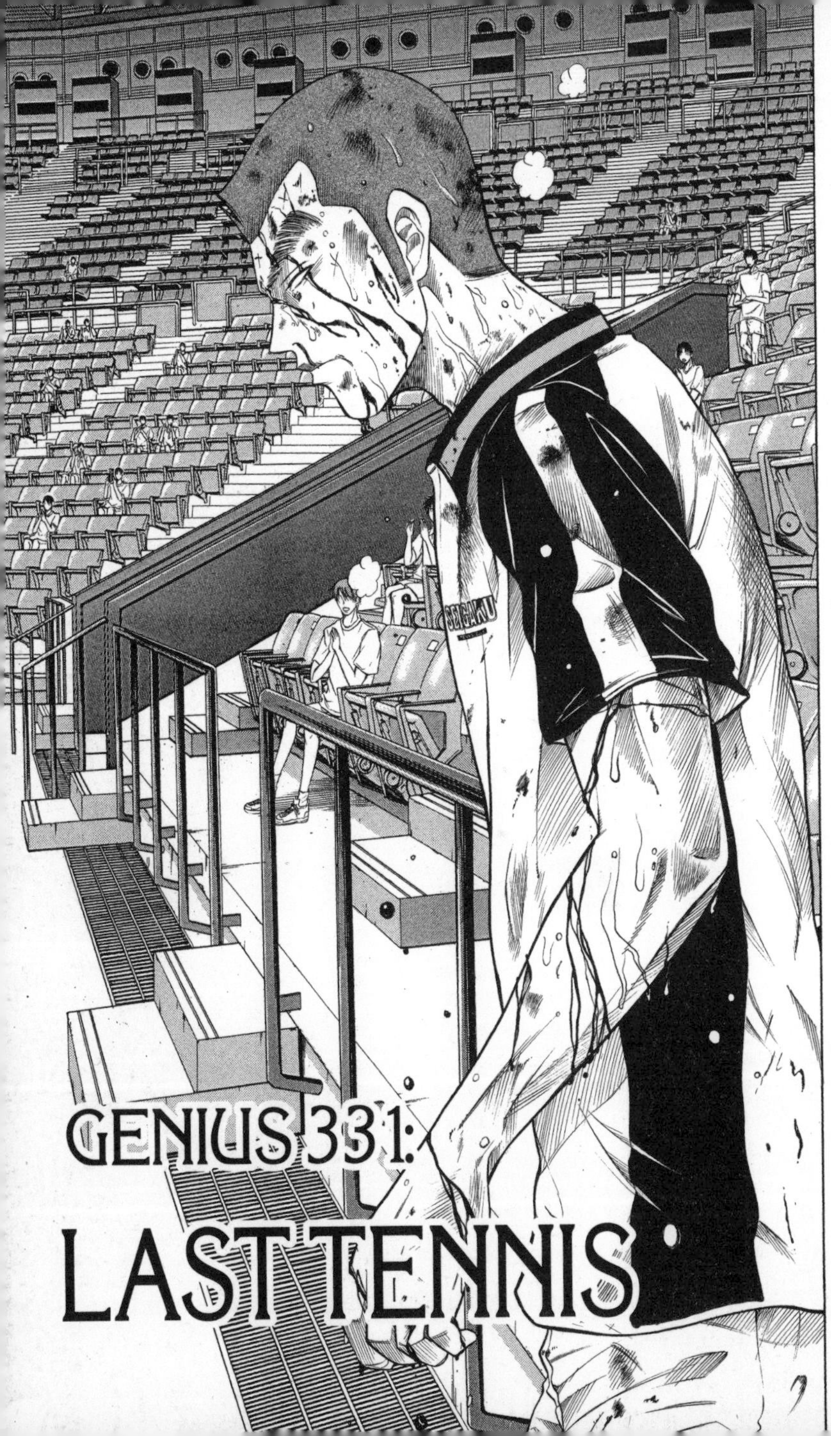
GENIUS 331:
LAST TENNIS

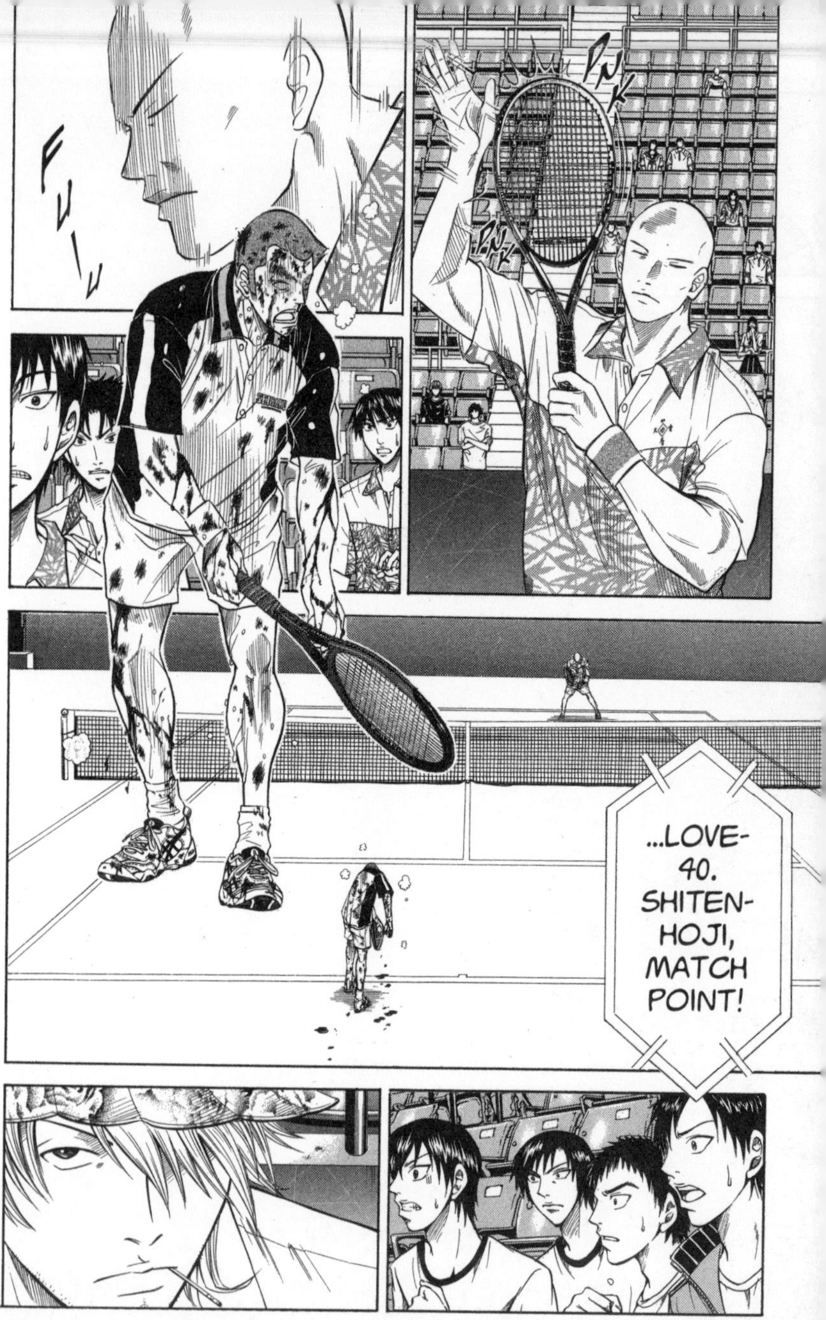
PNK
FU-U
...LOVE-40. SHITEN-HOJI, MATCH POINT!

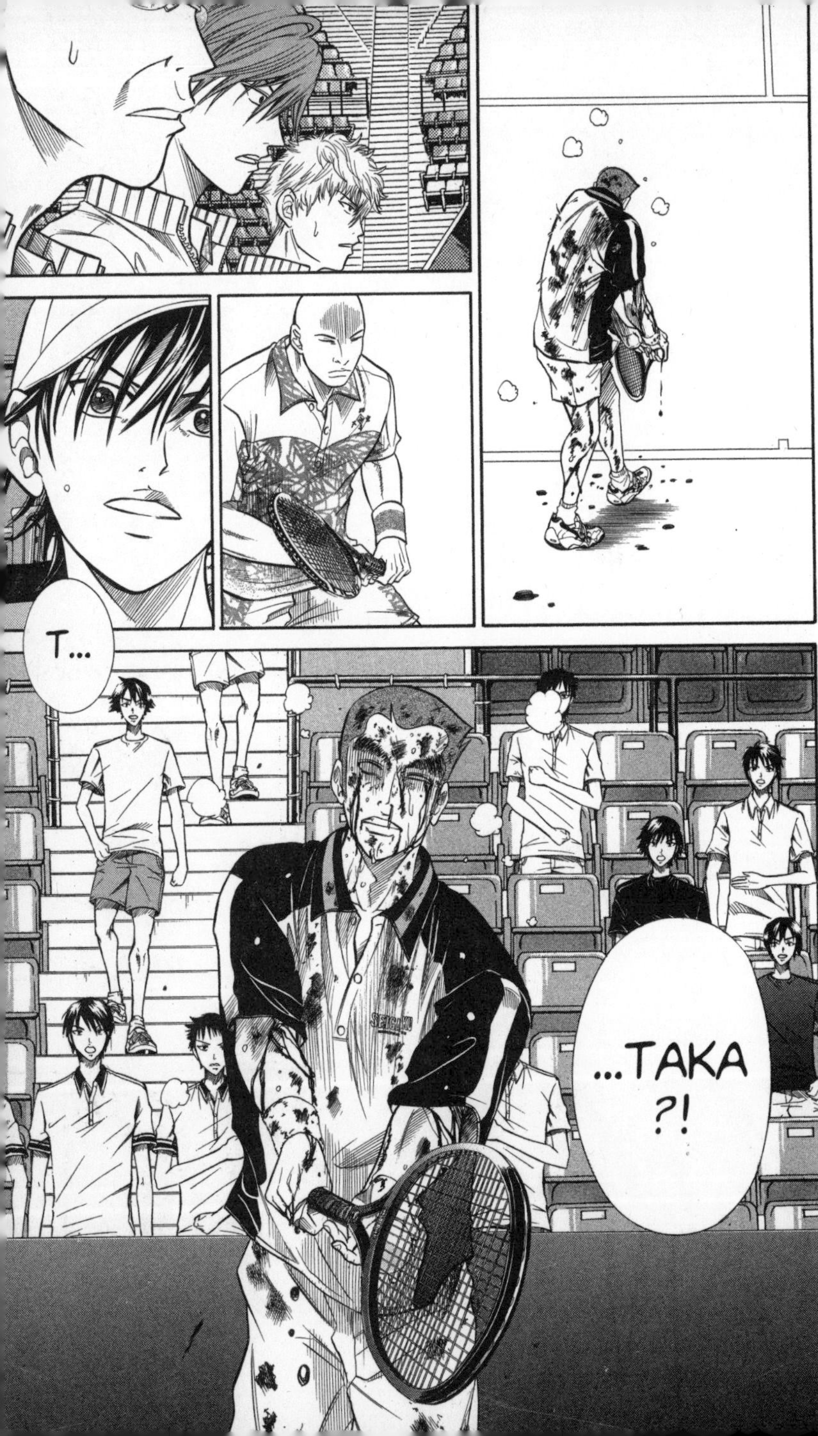
T...
...TAKA ?!

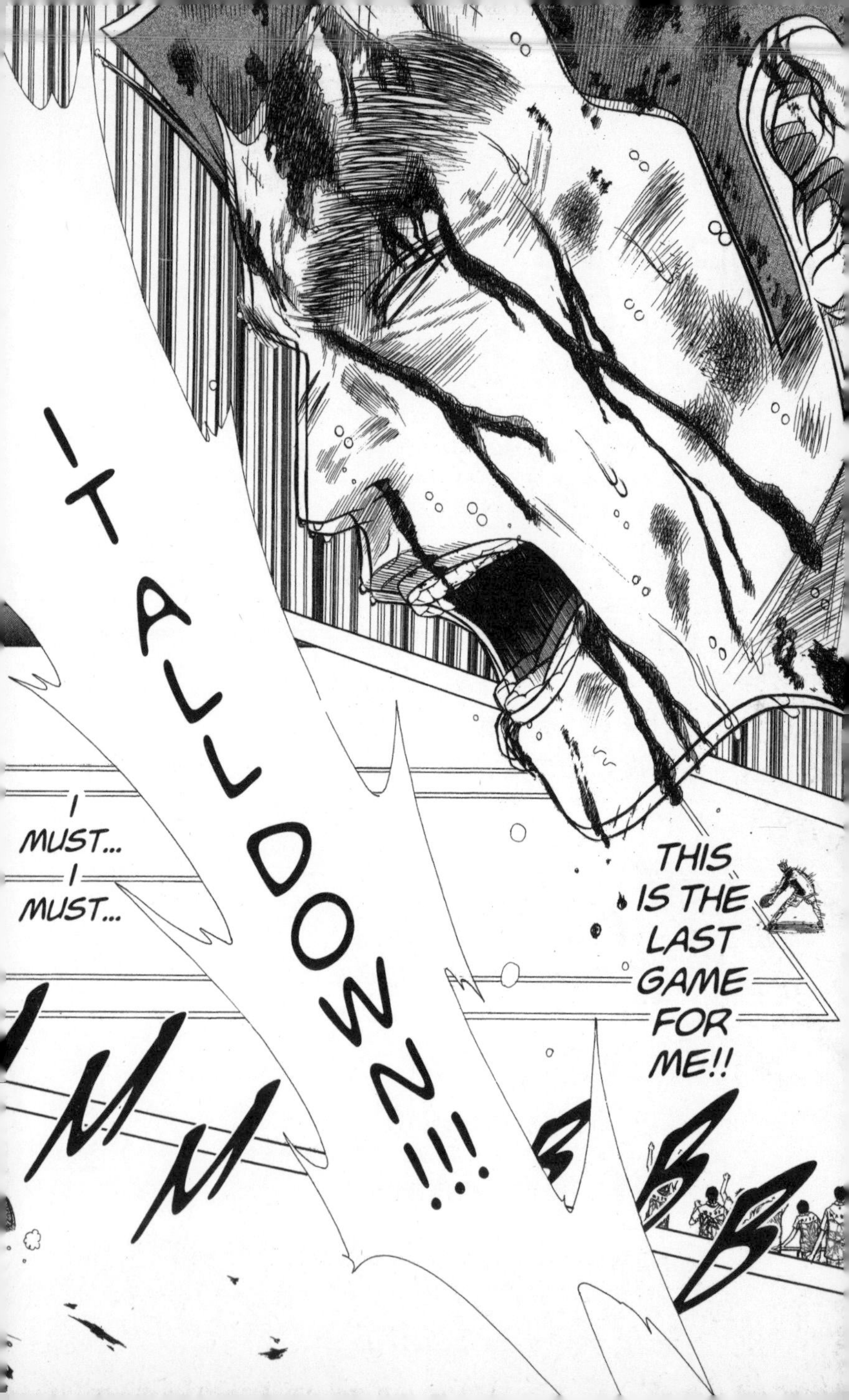
THIS IS THE LAST GAME FOR ME!!
IT ALL DOWN!!
I MUST... I MUST...

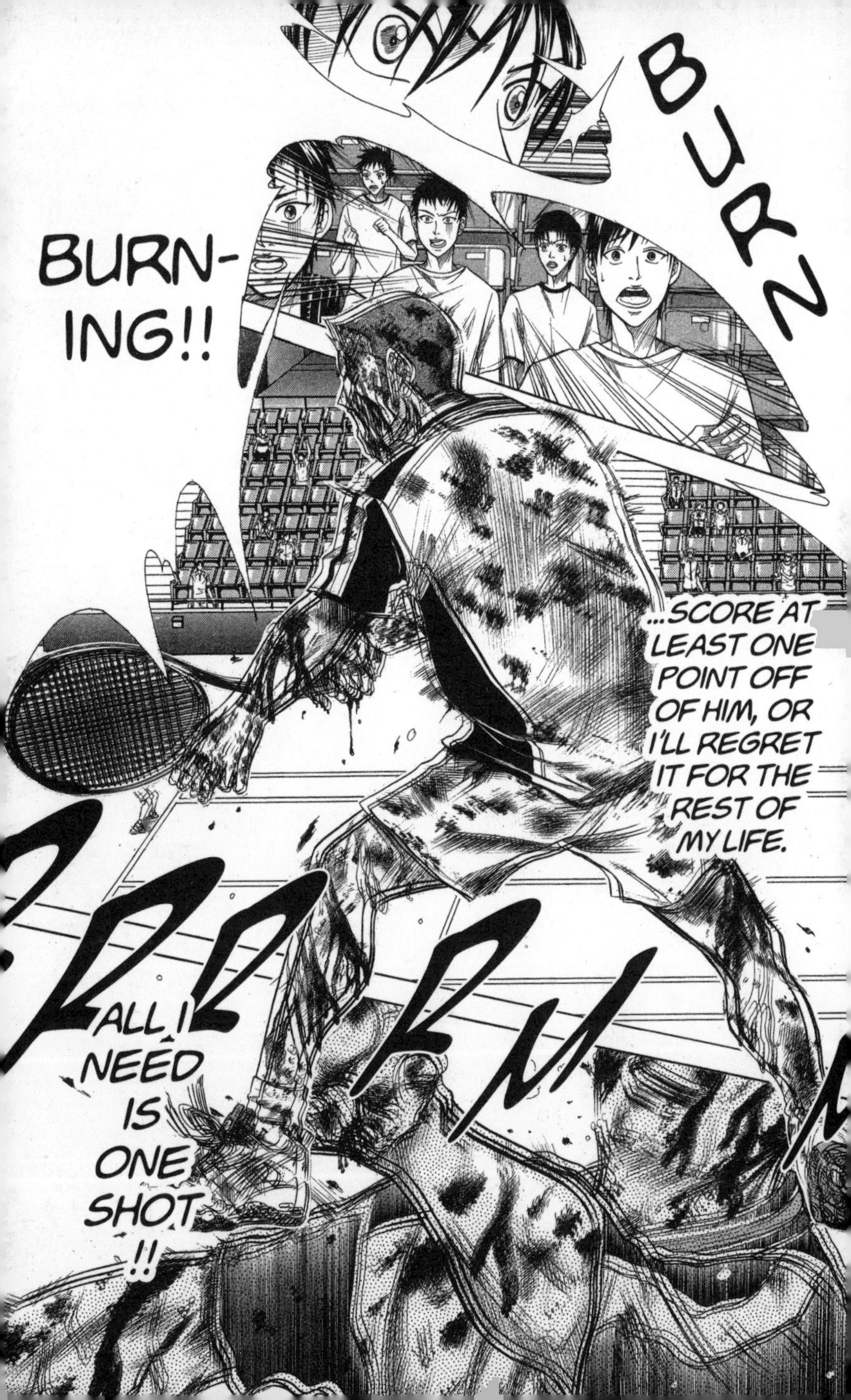
BURN
BURN-ING!!
...SCORE AT LEAST ONE POINT OFF OF HIM, OR I'LL REGRET IT FOR THE REST OF MY LIFE.
ALL I NEED IS ONE SHOT!!

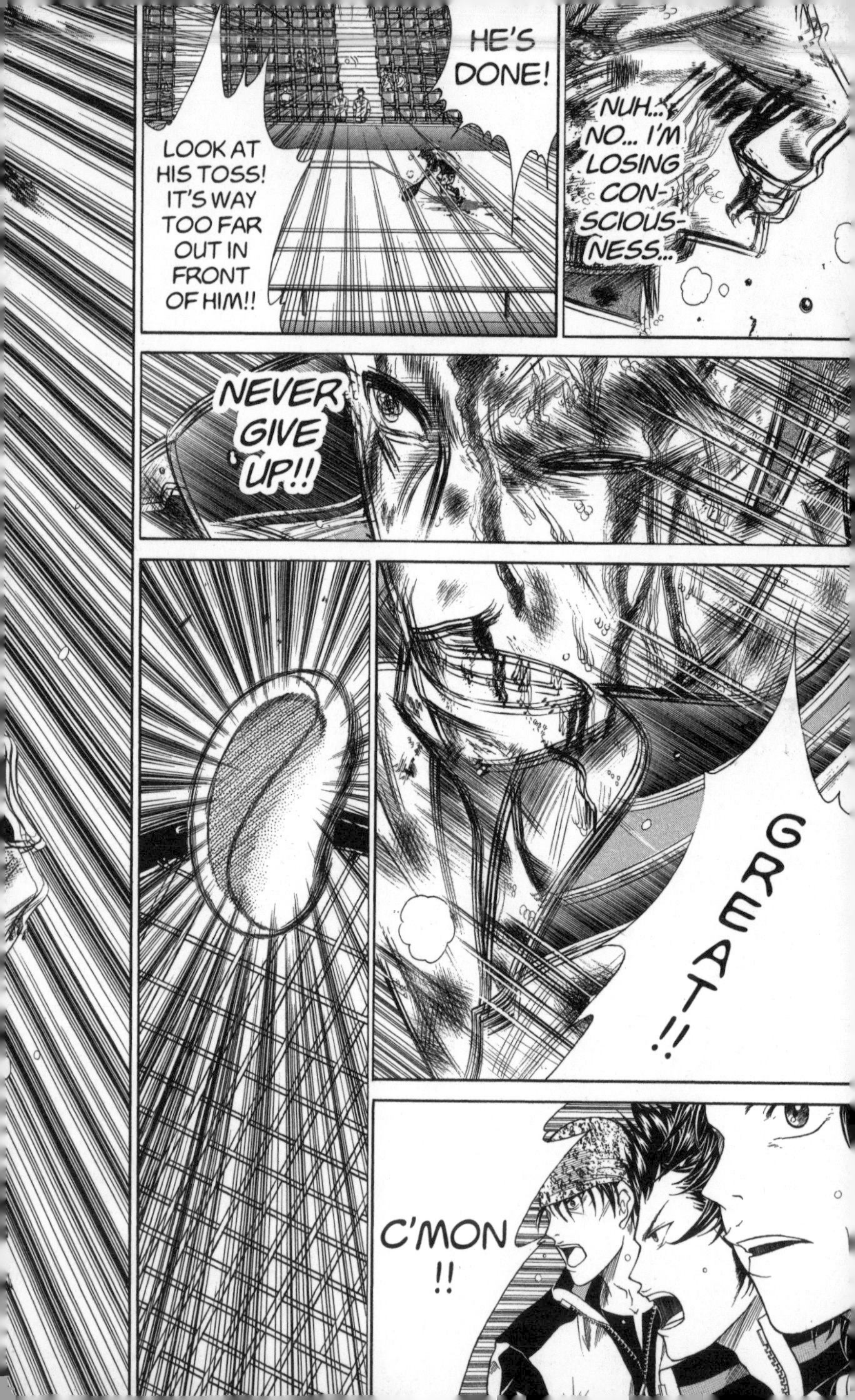
NUH... NO... I'M LOSING CON-SCIOUS-NESS...
HE'S DONE!
LOOK AT HIS TOSS! IT'S WAY TOO FAR OUT IN FRONT OF HIM!!
NEVER GIVE UP!!
GREAT!!
C'MON!!

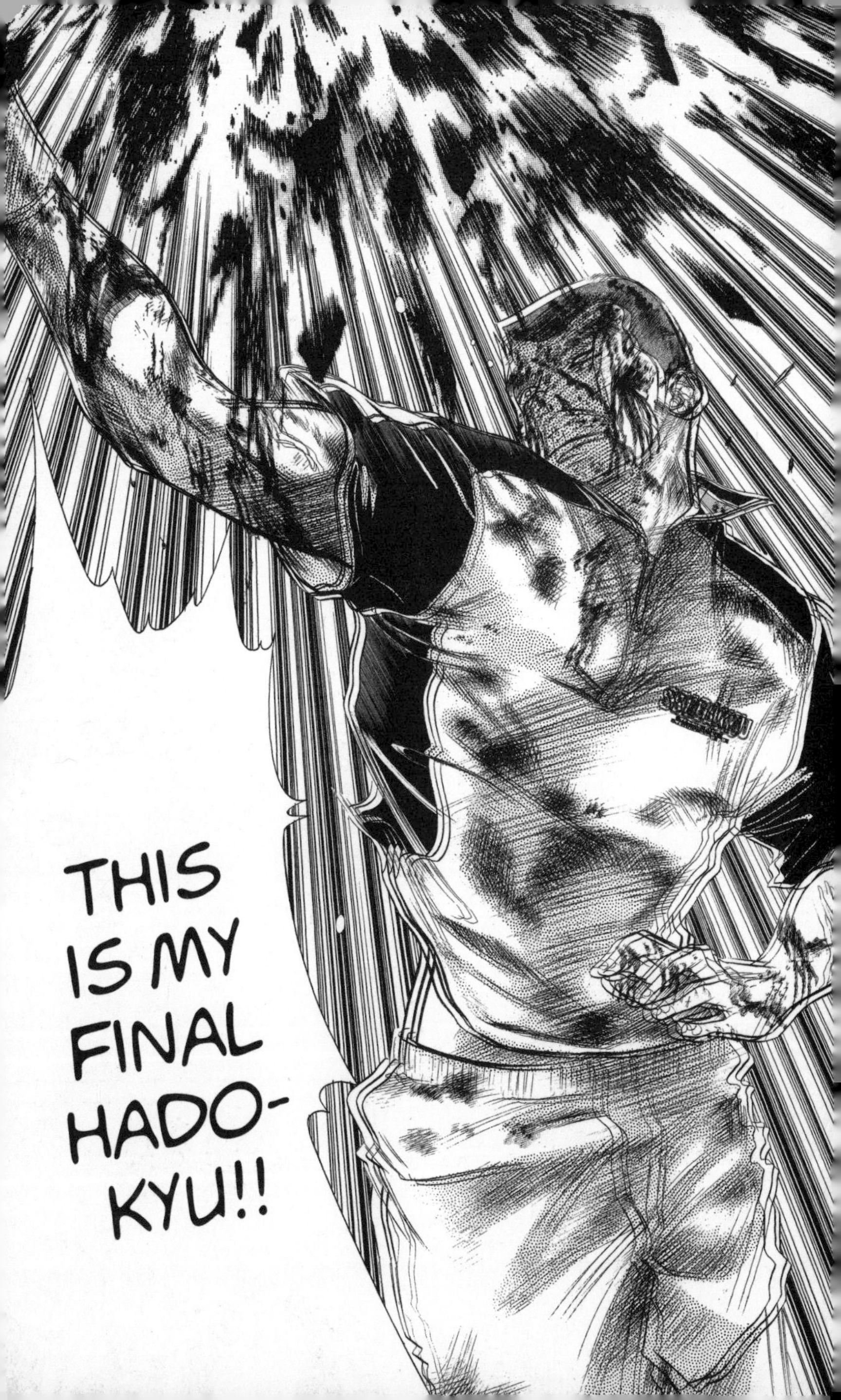
THIS IS MY FINAL HADO-KYU!!

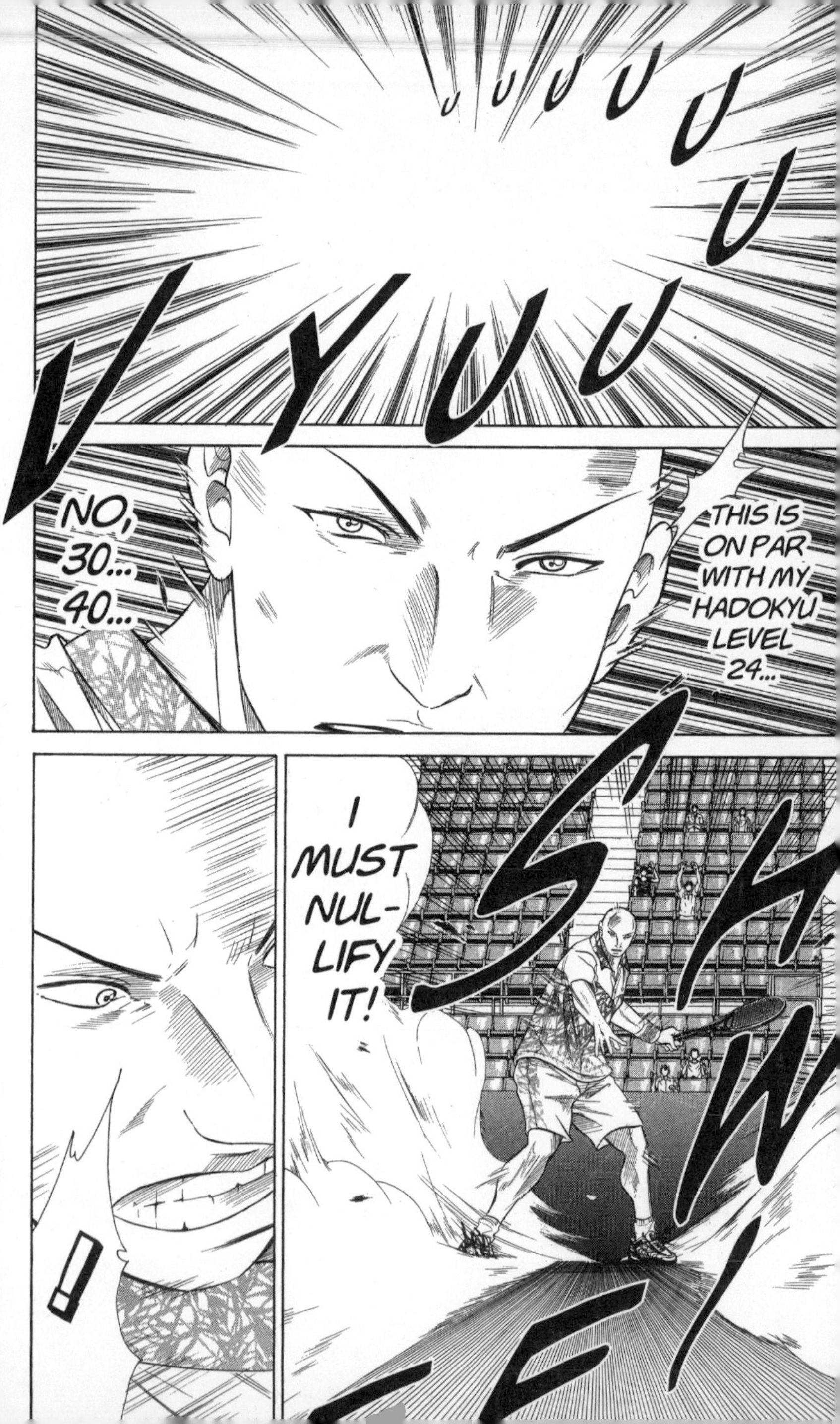
VYUUUUUUUUUU
THIS IS ON PAR WITH MY HADOKYU LEVEL 24...
NO, 30... 40...
SHWEEI
I MUST NUL-LIFY IT!
!

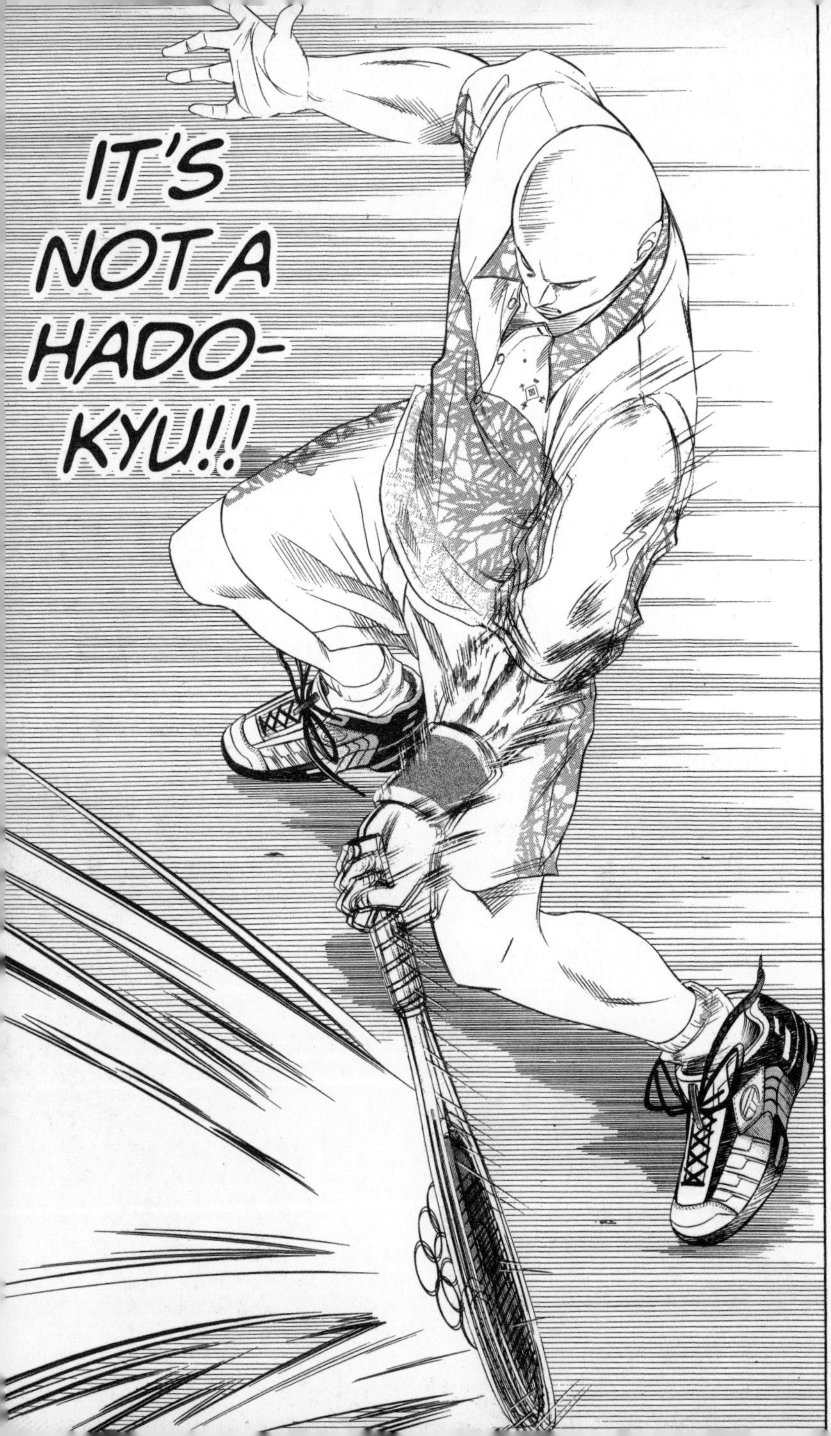
IT'S NOT A HADO-KYU!!

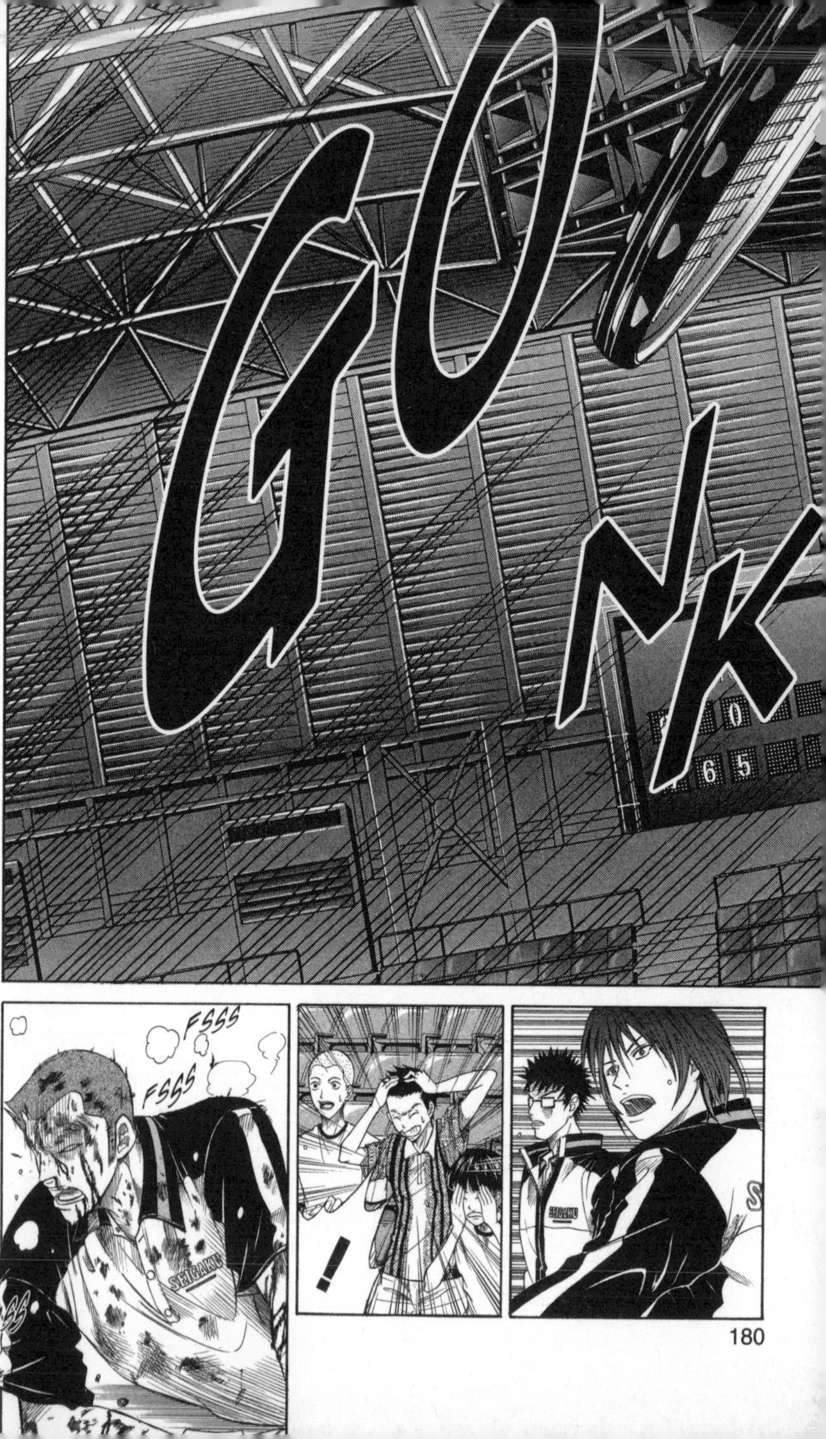
GONK
!
FSSS
FSSS
FSSS
SEIGAKU

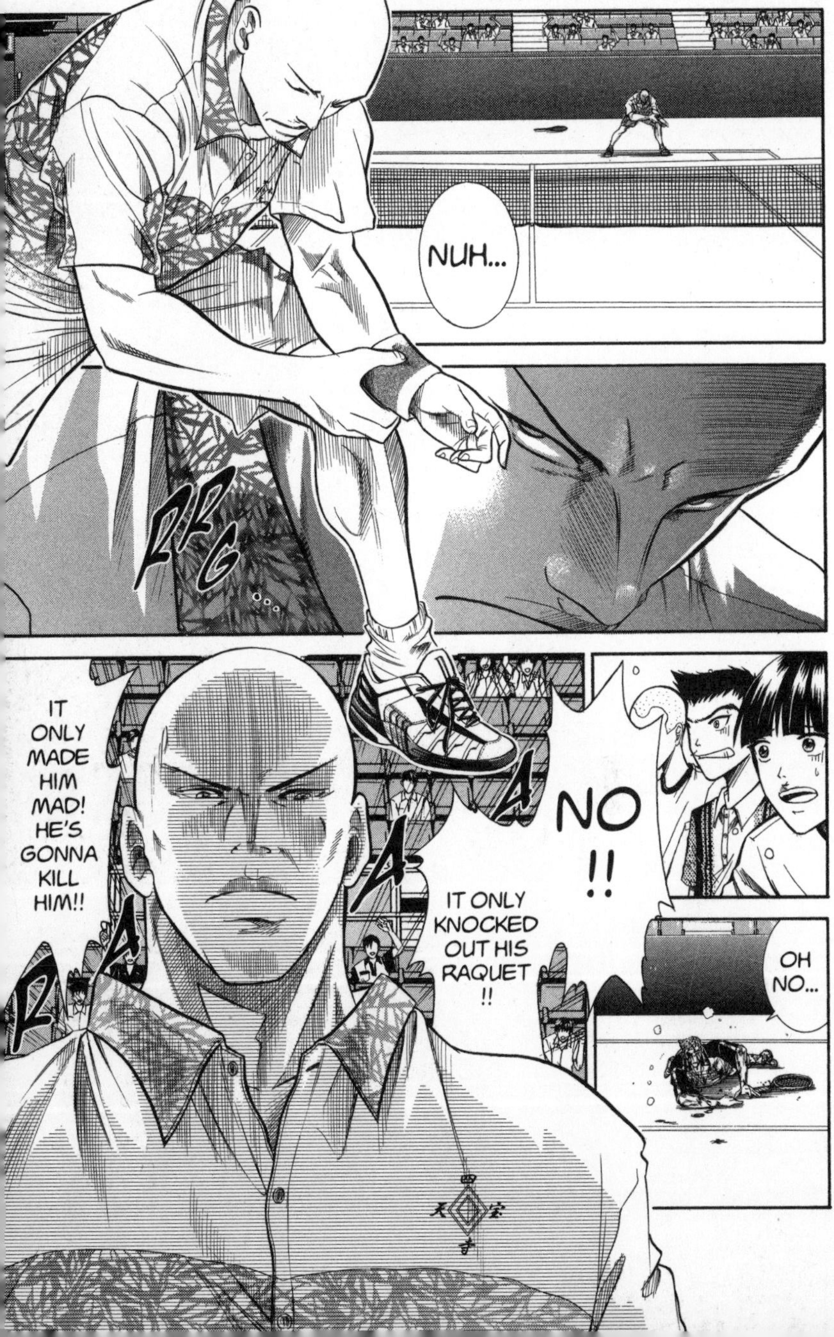
NUH...
NO!!
OH NO...
IT ONLY KNOCKED OUT HIS RAQUET!!
IT ONLY MADE HIM MAD! HE'S GONNA KILL HIM!!

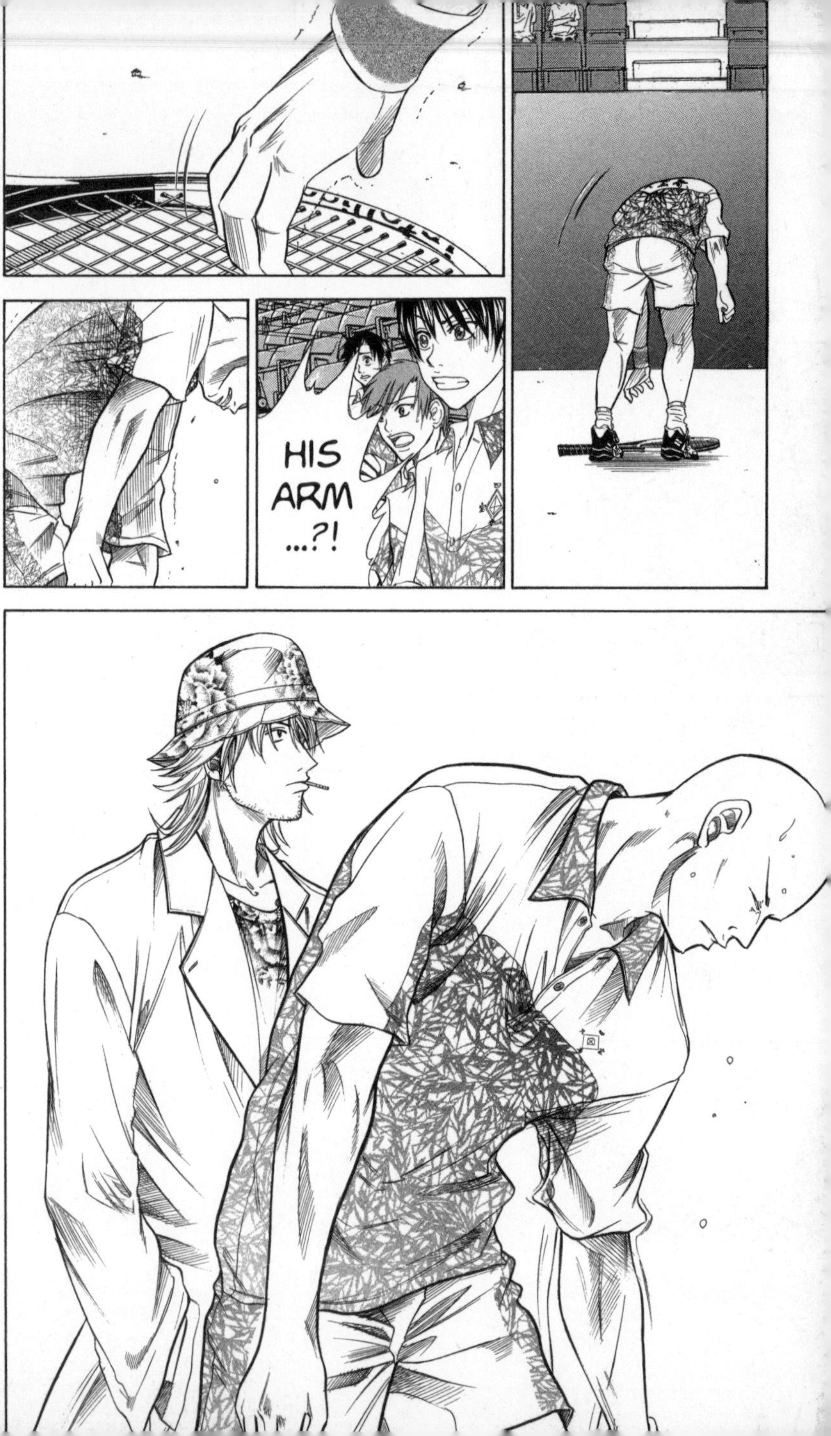
HIS ARM ...?!

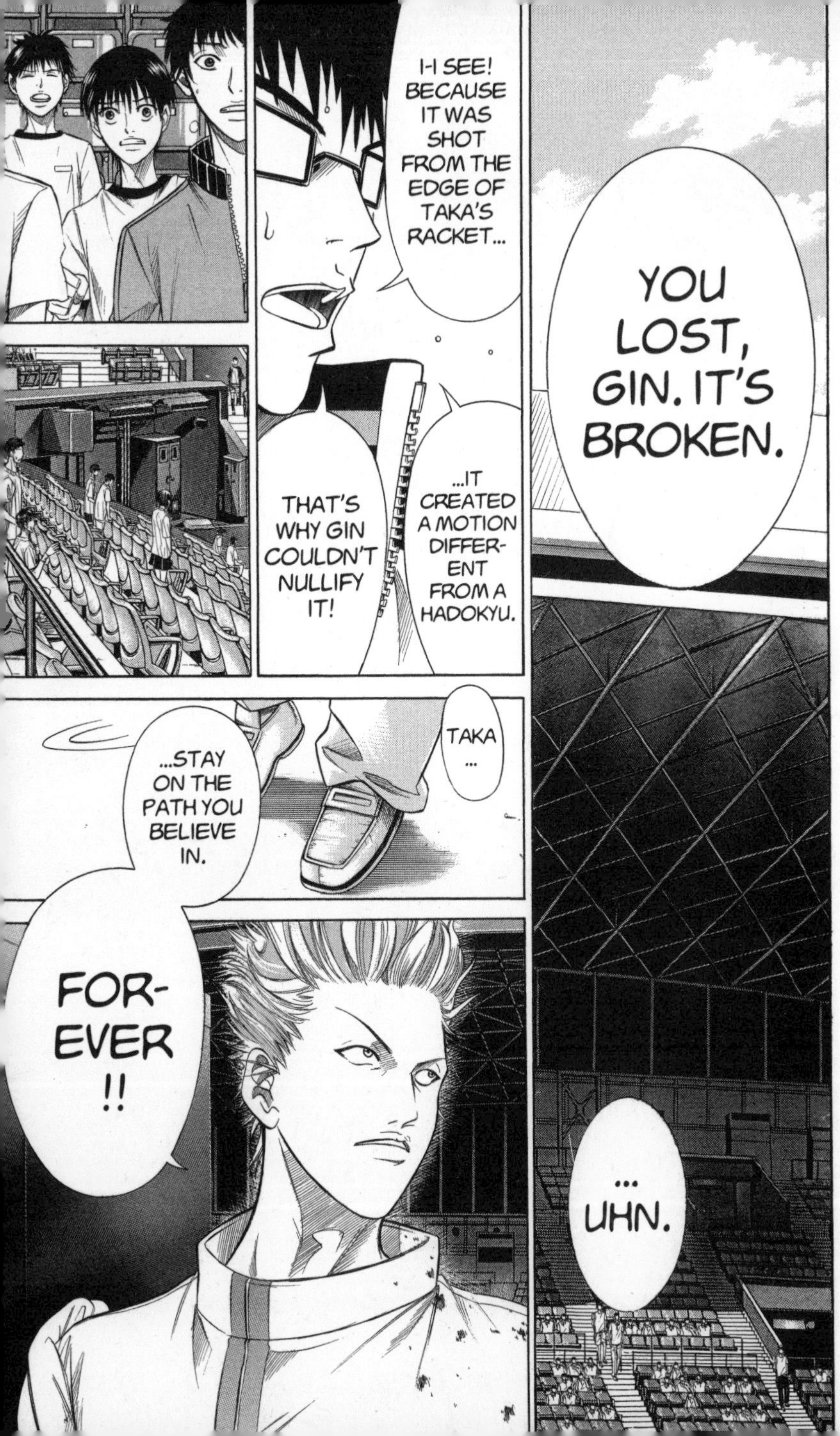
YOU LOST, GIN. IT'S BROKEN.
... UHN.
I-I SEE! BECAUSE IT WAS SHOT FROM THE EDGE OF TAKA'S RACKET...
...IT CREATED A MOTION DIFFER-ENT FROM A HADOKYU.
THAT'S WHY GIN COULDN'T NULLIFY IT!
TAKA ...
...STAY ON THE PATH YOU BELIEVE IN.
FOR-EVER !!

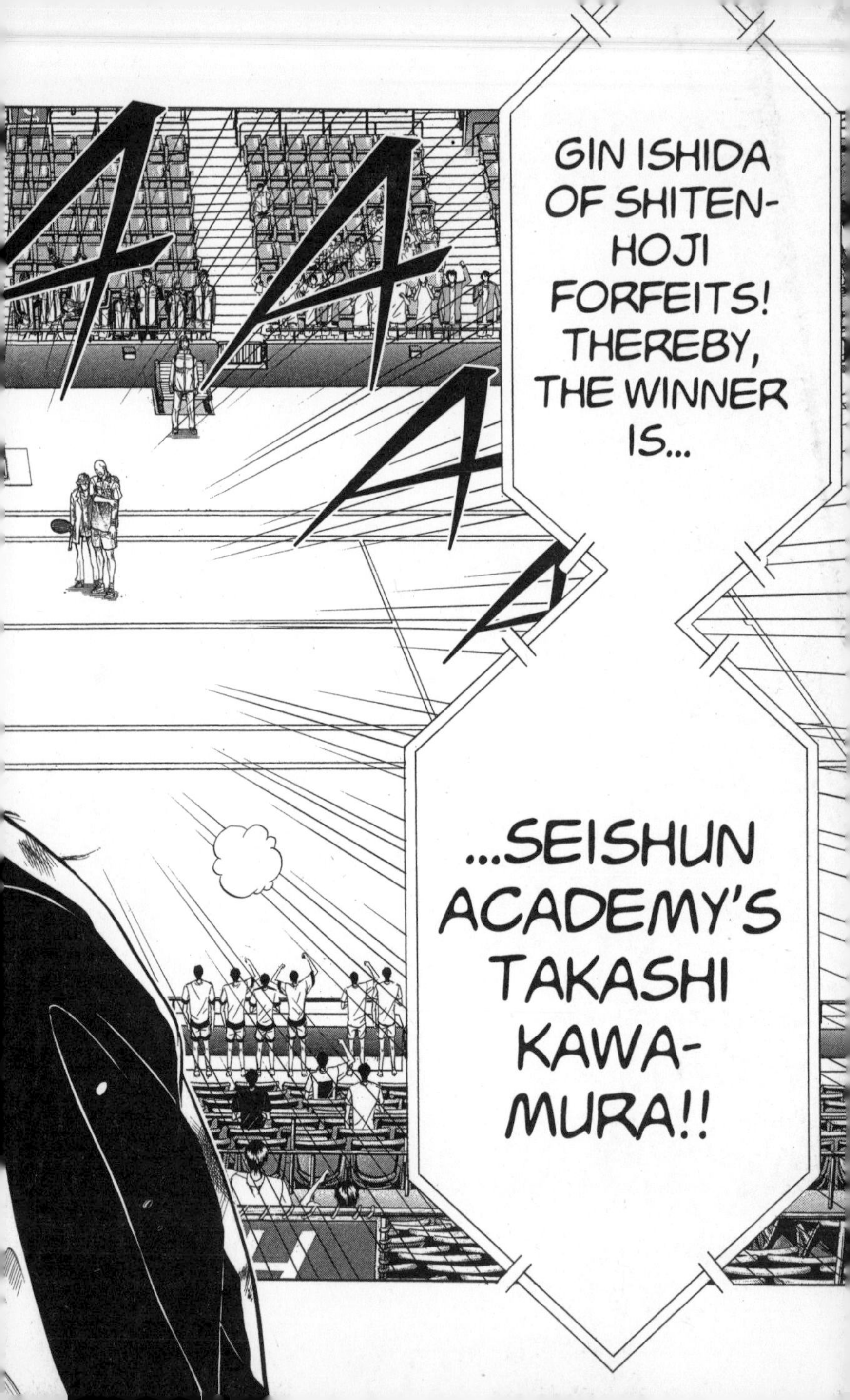
GIN ISHIDA OF SHITEN-HOJI FORFEITS! THEREBY, THE WINNER IS...
...SEISHUN ACADEMY'S TAKASHI KAWA-MURA!!

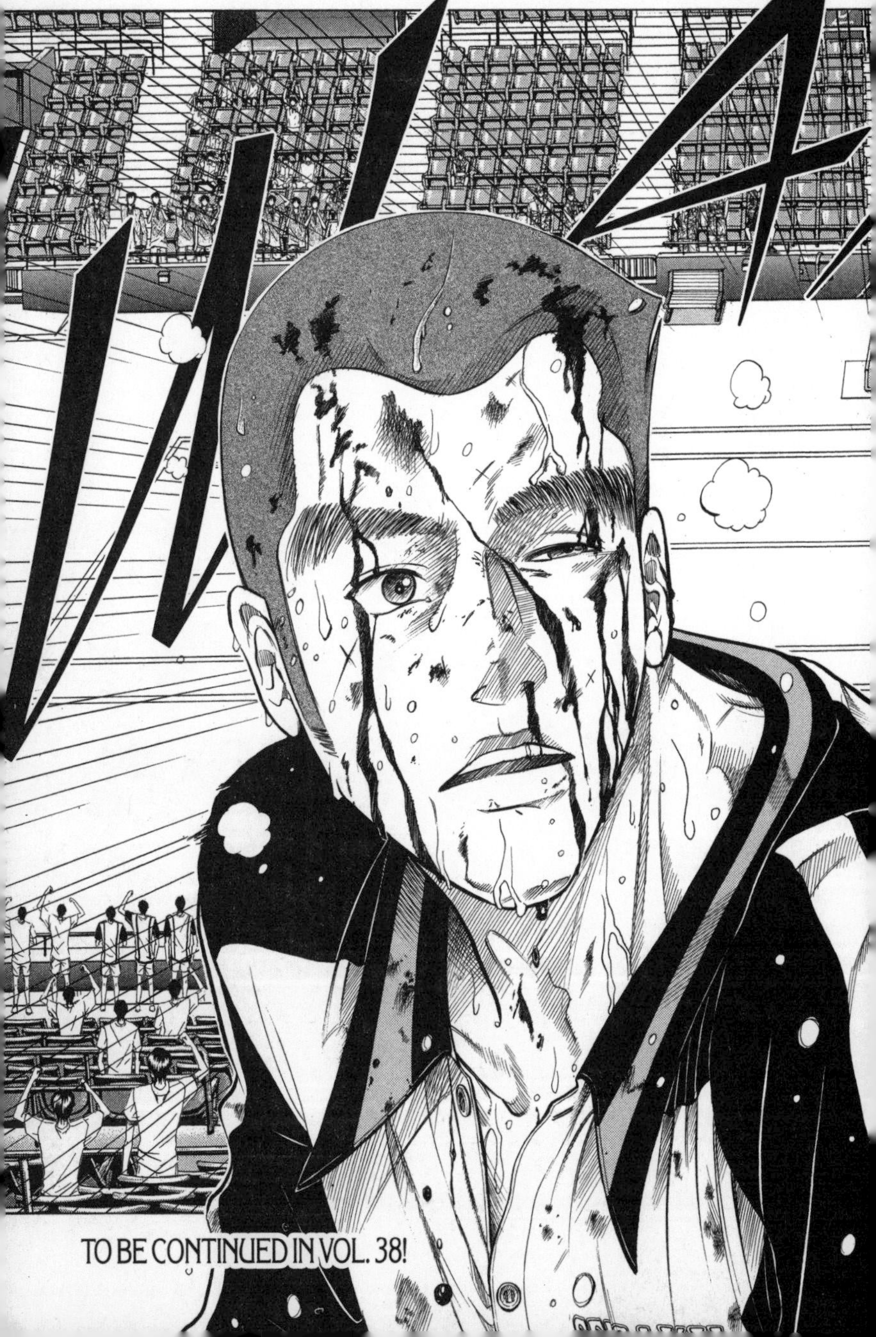
TO BE CONTINUED IN VOL. 38!

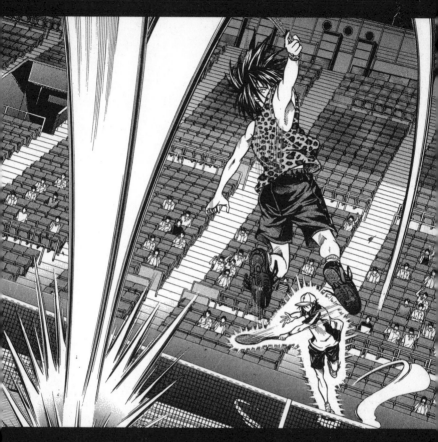

Clash! Ryoma and Kintaro's
One-Point Match

Seishun's semifinal round against Shitenhoji continues with No. 1 Doubles, and now it's captain vs. captain as Kunimitsu and Senri square off for a fight. They're backed up by their partners Sadaharu and Hikaru... or are they?! Later, Ryoma steps onto the clay against Shitenhoji's seventh-grade prodigy Kintaro, and this time neither of them are holding anything back.

Available July 2010!

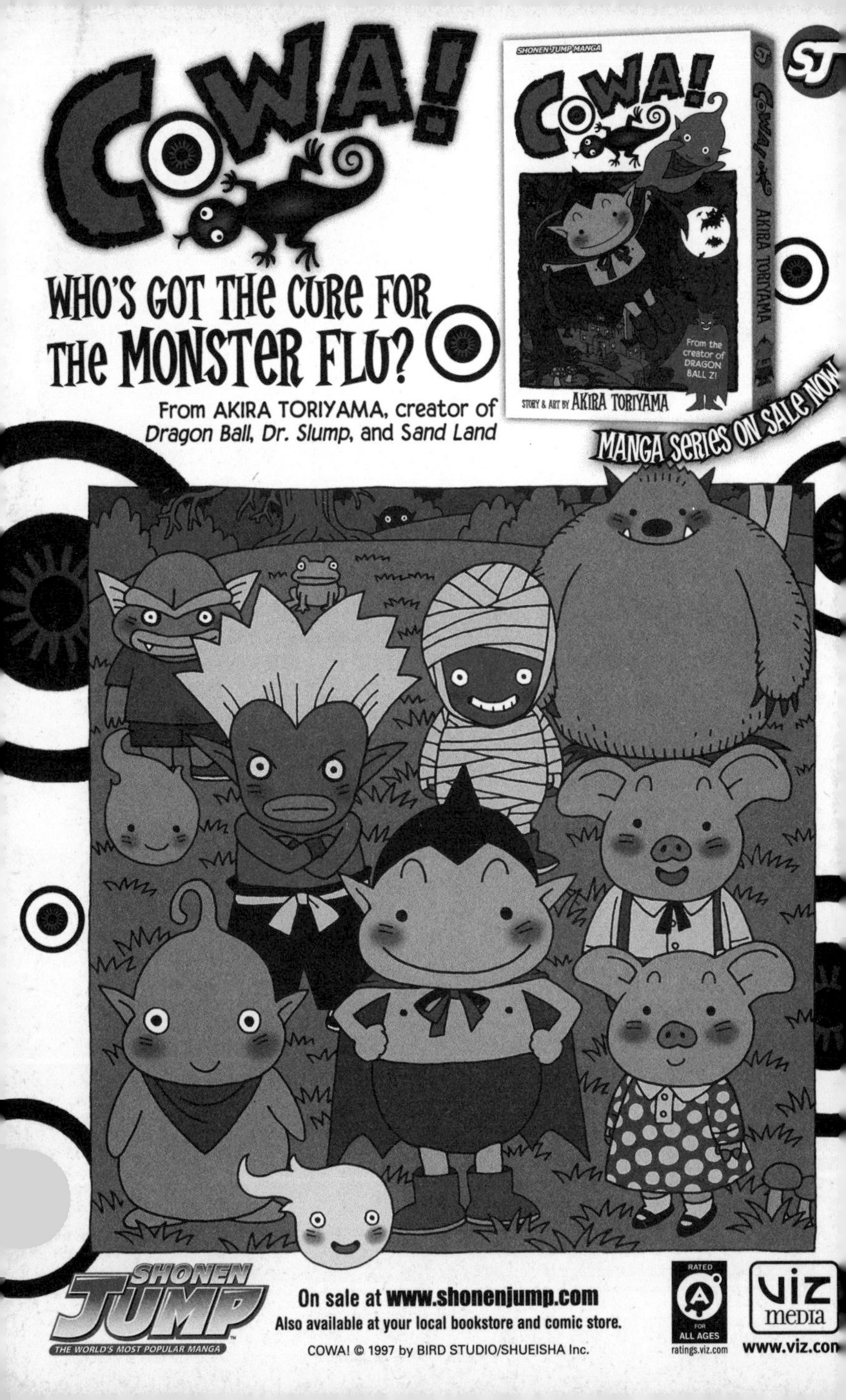
COWA!
WHO'S GOT THE CURE FOR THE MONSTER FLU?
From AKIRA TORIYAMA, creator of Dragon Ball, Dr. Slump, and Sand Land
SHONEN JUMP MANGA
COWA!
From the creator of DRAGON BALL Z!
STORY & ART BY AKIRA TORIYAMA
AKIRA TORIYAMA
SJ
MANGA SERIES ON SALE NOW
SHONEN JUMP
THE WORLD'S MOST POPULAR MANGA
On sale at www.shonenjump.com
Also available at your local bookstore and comic store.
COWA! © 1997 by BIRD STUDIO/SHUEISHA Inc.
RATED A FOR ALL AGES
ratings.viz.com
VIZ media
www.viz.com

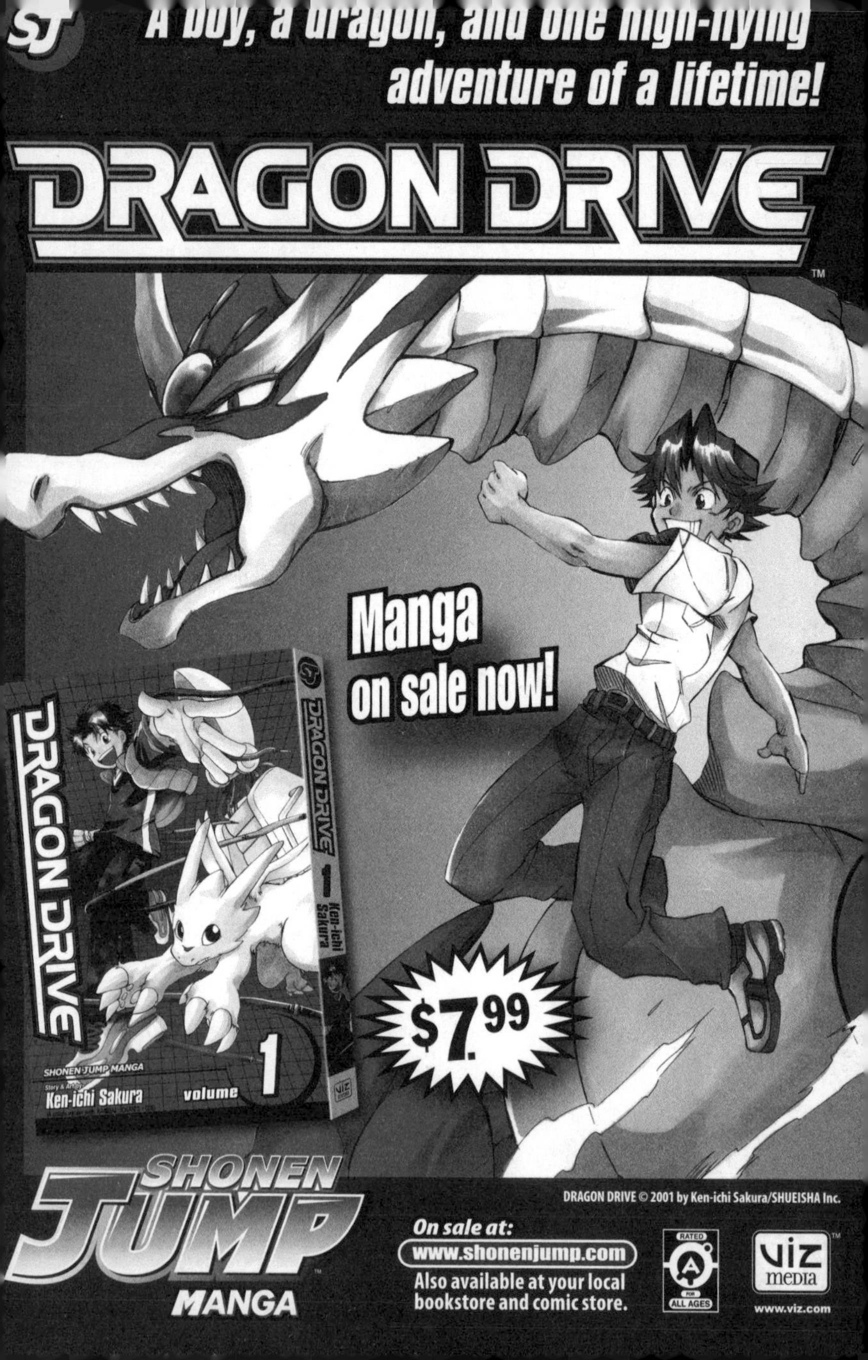

SJ
A boy, a dragon, and one high-flying adventure of a lifetime!
DRAGON DRIVE™
Manga on sale now!
SJ
DRAGON DRIVE
1
Ken-ichi Sakura
SHONEN JUMP MANGA
Story & Art by
Ken-ichi Sakura
volume 1
$7.99
SHONEN JUMP™ MANGA
DRAGON DRIVE © 2001 by Ken-ichi Sakura/SHUEISHA Inc.
On sale at:
www.shonenjump.com
Also available at your local bookstore and comic store.
RATED A FOR ALL AGES
VIZ media™
www.viz.com

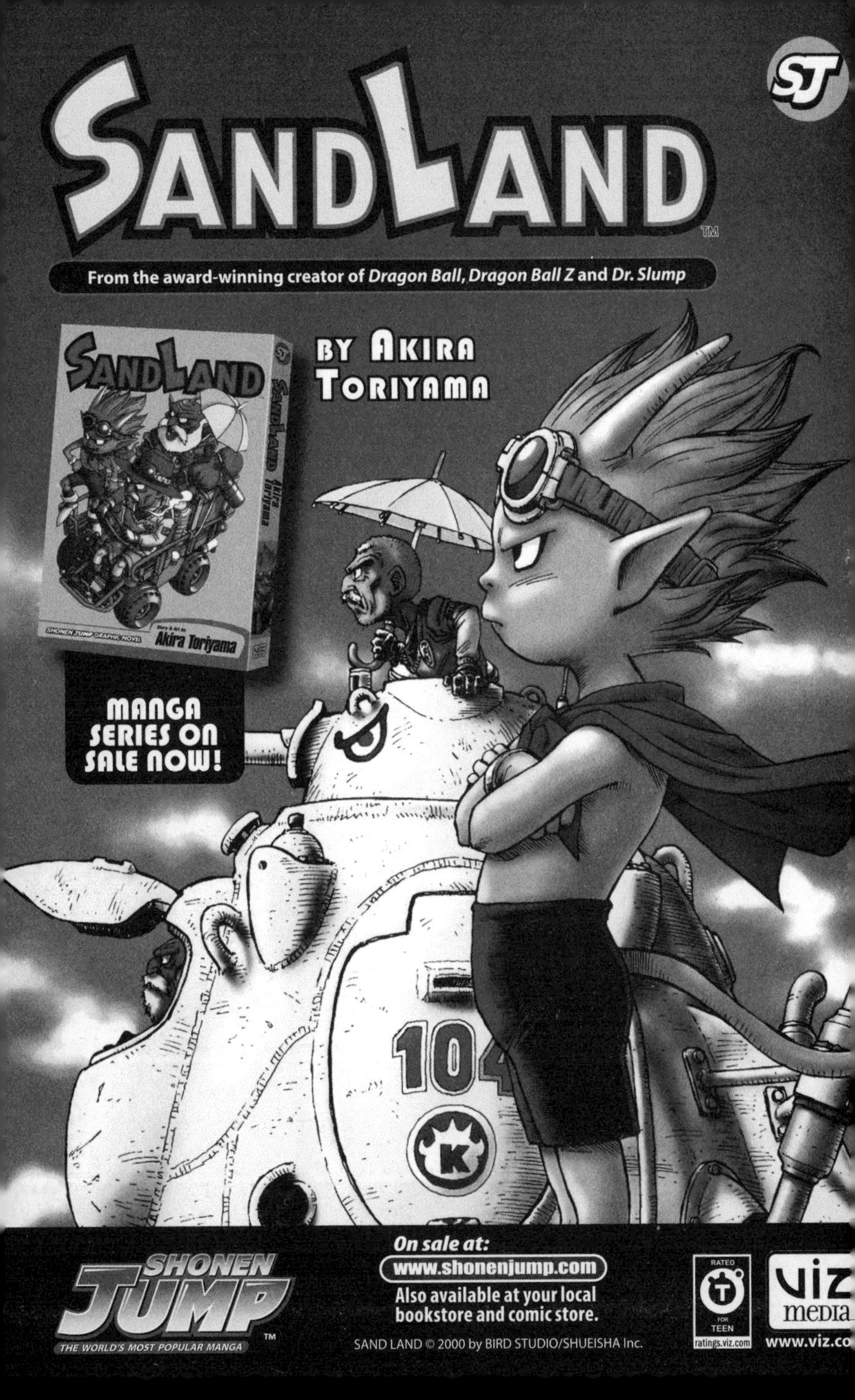
SJ
SANDLAND™
From the award-winning creator of Dragon Ball, Dragon Ball Z and Dr. Slump
BY AKIRA TORIYAMA
SANDLAND
SHONEN JUMP GRAPHIC NOVEL
Akira Toriyama
MANGA SERIES ON SALE NOW!
104
K
SHONEN JUMP™
THE WORLD'S MOST POPULAR MANGA
On sale at:
www.shonenjump.com
Also available at your local bookstore and comic store.
SAND LAND © 2000 by BIRD STUDIO/SHUEISHA Inc.
RATED T FOR TEEN
ratings.viz.com
VIZ media
www.viz.co